NORWAY
Christiana (Oslo)

SWEDEN
Stockholm

O St Petersburg

O Reval (Tallinn)

ENMARK
Copenhagen

Baltic Sea

Russian

Kiel

Potsdam O Berlin

erman Empire
XCronberg

O Warsaw
Poland

Empire

burg

O Carlsbad
O Marienbad

Austria

Vienna O

Bad Ischl O

Budapest O

Austro - Hungarian

Hungary

Empire

RUMANIA

O Bucharest

ITALY

to Austria
1908-9
Bosnia

SERBIA

BULGARIA
O Sofia

*Adriatic
Sea*

Montenegro

Ottoman Empire

O Rome

O Gaeta

O Naples

Corfu

*Aegean
Sea*

GREECE

O Athens

Malta

UNCLE OF EUROPE

By the Same Author

RUSSIA'S DANUBIAN EMPIRE

THE AUSTRIAN ODYSSEY

WHERE THE LION TROD

DOLLFUSS

THE ANSCHLUSS

EAGLE AND UNICORN

THE LAST HABSBURG

BETWEEN TWO FLAGS
(Slatin Pasha)

UNCLE OF EUROPE

Gordon
Brook-Shepherd

COLLINS
St James's Place, London
1975

William Collins Sons & Co Ltd
London . Glasgow . Sydney . Auckland
Toronto . Johannesburg

First published 1975
© Gordon Brook-Shepherd, 1975

ISBN 0 00 211856 4

Set in Monotype Garamond
Made and printed in Great Britain by
William Collins Sons & Co Ltd Glasgow

For my Nicky
A daughter of Europe

CONTENTS

LIST OF ILLUSTRATIONS

The acknowledgements for permission to reproduce these illustrations are made in italics.

FOREWORD

What matters about any King is his reign. What mattered about the reign of King Edward VII was foreign affairs. What mattered about foreign affairs then was Europe. What mattered about his Europe was European society.

Given those admittedly over-simplified propositions, it may well seem remarkable that, so far as I know, no study has been devoted in any language to the role he played in the Europe of his time. This book will, I hope, be a first step towards filling that gap.

King Edward's position as the social leader of that glittering era which bore his name was unchallenged. But life in England and in Europe during the first decade of this century was not only, as it might appear, one long and extravagant garden-party. Critical issues were being debated and decided underneath the glitter, for the half-dozen dynasties and five hundred families who led the social round of that vanished world also presided over its destiny.

It is in this sphere that Edward VII's importance needs to be argued and reassessed. Was he, as most contemporary continental observers believed, one of the shrewdest and most influential statesmen of his time? Or was he, as some of his own countrymen thought, simply a genial *bon vivant*, obsessed by the pursuit of pleasure, and interested only superficially in the art of diplomacy as an elegant cloak to wear over all that restless hedonism inside him?

And, if one inclines even slightly to the continental view, what was his real part in the most critical decision that England had taken for a century in foreign affairs – abandoning her 'splendid isolation' of the Victorian age and teaming up with France and Russia against the rival Great Powers' camp of Germany and Austria-Hungary? This historic realignment, which took place during his reign, drew the political battle-lines which, less than five years after his death, became the military battle-lines of the world war, a war which destroyed the old order he had loved. Was he, in this process, the 'Peace-maker', as most English and French apologists have argued? Or was he the 'Einkreiser', the baleful encircler of Germany who helped to bring on the war, as most German historians have maintained? And, in either capacity, how exactly did this prince of pleasure double with his 'alter ego', the prince of politics?

To try and find the answers, I have gone back beyond the familiar layers of Edwardian memoirs to two groups of primary sources. The first are the diplomatic archives of the time, and especially those of Germany and France, in addition, of course, to those of Britain. The sixty-odd massive volumes of *Die Grosse Politik der Europäischen Kabinette* (1871–1914) contain hundreds of references to the activities of Edward, both as Prince of Wales and as King. Yet these volumes were only beginning to appear when Sir Sydney Lee was writing his monumental official biography of Edward VII in the early twenties, while their very important French counterparts, the *Documents Diplomatiques Français*, had not then appeared at all.

Both series were, of course, fully available (together with all our own *British Documents on Foreign Policy*) by the time Sir Philip Magnus wrote the second official biography of the King nearly forty years later. But that one-volume work, an achievement of compression in itself, was understandably too weighed down under the riches of Royal Archives material to allow any separate exploitation of foreign archives. One study this present book tries to give is the first thorough look at Edward VII as he appeared day by day and month by month to the continental diplomatists and statesmen he was working with.

But formal archives can only at best reconstruct for us the dry bones of the past. For the touch of flesh and blood – and there can be fewer sovereigns where getting that touch is more important than with Edward VII – we have to search elsewhere. Four years ago, therefore, I started out on what might best be described as a royal paper chase through castles, country mansions and villas up and down the continent. My object was to seek out families who once belonged to the King's circle of friends and political allies, with the hope of finding unpublished letters, diaries, or any other contemporary material about him that had survived two world wars and one cold war. Some of these family papers one hoped to find turned out never to have existed. Much more that had been written was lost or destroyed. But there were some lucky, unexpected finds.

The most munificent of these were the private papers of King Edward's great friend – indeed, his one true *ami de coeur* – the Marquis Luis de Soveral. This Portuguese diplomatist was perhaps the only man who knew the secrets of the King's private life as well as sharing to the full in his political confidences.

Soveral, who stayed on as Minister in London after 1901 simply to be with his royal patron, became a European legend in his own right. Before his death in 1922 he had been pressed with handsome offers from both sides of the Atlantic either to write his own memoirs or to publish a book of his own on Edward VII. He had always refused, and it was an exciting experience when, in November of 1973, I became the first outsider to go through the piles of his unsorted manila folders with the present Countess of Soveral.

I must express my warm thanks to her for her help and hospitality, and also to David Muirhead, at that time British Ambassador in Lisbon, who smoothed the path for me. The papers of the famous 'Blue Monkey', as he was affectionately known, certainly lived up to his reputation. They contained some quite new information about the King's secret political activities; scores of personal letters from both King Edward and Queen Alexandra, the existence of which was unknown in London; and a flood of correspondence from and about almost everyone who mattered in the King's world, including his last and greatest love, Alice Keppel.

Sir Ernest Cassel, that extraordinary German-Jewish wizard who rose from being an obscure immigrant bank clerk to becoming a financial giant of the British Empire in less than twenty years, was second only to Soveral in the King's affections and trust. I have also been given access to all of his unpublished papers and letters that bear on King Edward and must thank Earl Mountbatten of Burma and the Senior Trustee of the Broadlands Archives for this valuable facility. I would also like to acknowledge the help of Mrs Mollie Travis, the archivist at Broadlands, and to thank Lord Mountbatten for one or two personal anecdotes of Edward VII that he sent me along with the Cassel papers.

The third of the King's closest friends who particularly interested me was the Austrian diplomatist, Count Albert Mensdorff, a second cousin of King Edward's and Austrian Ambassador in London for most of his reign. Unlike the Soveral and Cassel papers, Mensdorff's private diaries had been available to students for some years at the Haus- Hof- und Staatsarchiv in Vienna (to whom, as a broken and penniless figure who had just managed to survive the Hitler era, he had sold them for a pittance in 1945). But, as far as I know, this uninhibited chronicle of his had never previously been used for all that it can tell us about Edward VII and the social and political scandals of his time.

This trio have provided the bulk of the new material about King Edward. But many helpers in half a dozen countries have supplied useful titbits. In Austria, for example, an old shooting friend of nearly thirty years' standing, Baron Alfons von Pawel-Rammingen, produced pictures and anecdotes about his great-uncle's villa in Biarritz where, in 1906, King Edward helped to promote the betrothal of his niece Ena to King Alfonso XIII of Spain – a match of political as well as romantic interests. My thanks are also due in Austria to two faithful research assistants from many previous books, Dr Karl Zrounek, formerly librarian of the Austrian Parliament, and Frau Annelise Schulz, formerly *Daily Telegraph* correspondent in Vienna.

In France, the present Marquis de Breteuil has produced some interesting extracts from the diary of his grandfather, who was probably the most trusted of all King Edward's French friends. Unfortunately the diary did not continue into the critical days of the Entente Cordiale. The descendants of several other one-time Parisian 'confidants' of the King's, like M. de Courcel (currently Secretary-General of the Quai d'Orsay), have searched, sometimes in vain; but I am nonetheless grateful to them for their trouble. From Biarritz the Duke de Baena (himself an irrepressible survivor from Edwardian days) and M. Casenave have produced many memories of the King's stays at this, his favourite sea-resort.

There were several helpers (who had best remain unnamed) who provided similar services in respect of the most beloved of all the King's continental spas – Marienbad, now, of course, known by its Bohemian name of Mariánské Lázně in the People's Republic of Czechoslovakia. Partly as a result of this, it has been possible to include a separate chapter on King Edward's annual August pilgrimages to Marienbad, a place where pleasure and politics combined more closely than anywhere else on his calendar. Also from the former Habsburg Monarchy, and present Communist realms, Dr István Gál in Hungary has supplied much valuable information about the King's visits to Budapest as Prince of Wales.

There were occasional useful finds in Germany as, for example, when Princess Charlotte of Hohenlohe-Langenburg discovered, in her husband's writing-desk in the family castle a forgotten letter of King Edward's about the Prussian menace. But, in general, I have had to rely on the mass of unexploited material in the *Grosse Politik* and other official archives or memoirs of the day in describing Anglo-German problems and the extraordinary love-hate relationship between Kaiser 'Willy' and his English 'Uncle Bertie'.

In Britain, thanks to the wholesale destruction of the King's papers after his death by his secretary Lord Knollys, relatively little personal documentary material has survived. What there was (apart from the Cassel papers) has mostly appeared in print already in the two official biographies already mentioned, both of which, of course, have been constantly consulted for this present work. But there have been one or two lucky dips, even in the English Edwardian bran-tub. I am particularly grateful to Mr Victor Malcolm, for example, for sight of all the King's hitherto unpublished letters to that great love of his middle life, the actress Lily Langtry. On the same romantic theme, Victor Cavendish-Bentinck managed to produce from the photograph album of his Aunt Venetia the only picture I have ever seen of Edward VII and Alice Keppel happily and informally together. (It was also, in all probability, the last private picture ever taken of him: he was dead little more than a fortnight later.)

As abroad, so also in England, my thanks go to those who looked hard in family papers, even if they came up with little new: the present Duke of St Albans, for example, whose forebear, the 10th Duke, was a great social friend of the King's, Brigadier Arthur Fortescue and Sir Edward Goschen, whose grandfather served as his Ambassador to Vienna and Berlin. The gracious permission of Her Majesty the Queen has been given to reproduce the relevant extracts from her great-grandfather's letters, wherever discovered in Europe and to whomever written. The Queen's Librarian, Mr Mackworth-Young, and his staff at the Royal Archives Windsor have again been their uniquely efficient and helpful selves.

The editors of both English editions, Adrian House of William Collins in London, and Tony Godwin of Harcourt Brace Javanovic in New York, produced many valuable ideas (fortunately mostly the same) for expanding some sections of the work and rearranging others. My grateful thanks are also due to Monica Hutchinson, who coped expertly, though under considerable time pressure, with most of the typing.

A word about the blending of all this material, old and new. The reader will sometimes find that, as we follow King Edward around Europe, the apparently trivial appears cheek by jowl with the obviously important. And he will always find that high society and its scandals seems inseparable from high politics and its intrigues. This, for better or for worse, was how the whole Edwardian globe revolved, but it is a juxtaposition which applies particularly to Edward VII himself.

To both his private and his public worlds, the King brought the same gifts of friendship, and the same sense of loyalty, the same love of people and the same talent for handling them. He was not only the last of England's monarchs to exercise any strong personal influence on foreign affairs, a ruler who used dynastic diplomacy to place him in the front rank of the European statesmen of his day. He was also, and pre-eminently, a man who loved life, and he carried this geniality and zest even into politics.

It is this dual aspect of the character and technique of Edward VII that has made this book so enjoyable for me to research. I hope it may also make it enjoyable for others to read.

Inevitably, for me and for many of my countrymen, there is a whiff of nostalgia about all this as well. England under the Stuarts was gay though not yet great. England under Queen Victoria became great, yet was no longer gay. The England of Edward VII was both great and gay. One wonders, writing these lines, when we shall see either quality again.

'Hugh's', Hambleden, GORDON BROOK-SHEPHERD
September 1974

PART I

1841-1901

1841-1901

A EUROPEAN CRADLE

He began as a child of Europe; or rather, of German Europe. Indeed, unless one went back for centuries, that 'wonderfully large and strong' infant son, with his 'dark blue eyes, finely formed but somewhat large nose, and pretty little mouth',[1] who was born to Queen Victoria on 9 November 1841, had scarcely a drop of native island blood in his veins. For a prince who was to become the most English of English kings since the Tudors, it was a strange start to life.

The Hanoverian King George III of England and his equally German wife, Charlotte of Mecklenburg-Strelitz, were the infant's great-grandparents. His grandfather was Edward Duke of Kent, one of the seven dim and dissolute sons of that marriage, and therefore every ounce as German as his title was English. That same grandfather, when he was at last bribed by the court to break with Madame de St Laurent – his mistress for twenty-seven years – and make a suitable marriage, had chosen, in 1818, another German princess, this time of the house of Saxe-Coburg-Saalfeld. She was herself the widow of the Prince of Leiningen, while the Duke of Kent's other brothers had also married German princesses – a Brunswick, a Saxe-Meiningen, a Hesse-Cassel, and so on. Finally, the Duke of Kent's only daughter Victoria who, in 1837, had succeeded to the throne of England, had completed this Teutonic picture by linking that throne with yet another German house by her marriage in 1840 to Prince Albert of Saxe-Coburg-Gotha.

Parents, grandparents, all the great-uncles with all the great-aunts and, behind them, the Hanoverians, stretching back with England's crown on their heads to the eighteenth century – it seemed to be nothing but German princedoms, many of them mediatized and some of them, like Prince Albert's, no bigger than an English county. Now it was the general fate, in the nineteenth century, of tiresome little problem states like Rumania or Bulgaria to be ruled by such imported (and imposed) foreign stock. But Queen Victoria's England was not some Balkan dumping-ground for unemployed German princelings whom Napoleon (to be followed by Bismarck) had swept off their thrones. It was the heart and centre of the greatest Empire the world had yet seen, an Empire so vast and so varied that only a quintessential

Englishness, distilled in and exported from the homeland, could sustain it with an elixir of patriotic strength.

Though this need was only dimly felt in the nation at large when Queen Victoria's first son was born, the dilemma of identity which hovered over the crown of England was already sharp. It was expressed in the two names with which the ten-weeks-old infant was baptized in St George's Chapel, Windsor, on 25 January 1842: Albert Edward. It came out even more in the discussion as to which name should come first. Lord Melbourne, the Queen's very English Prime Minister, was only echoing the sentiments of many of his kind when he wrote to Queen Victoria questioning the priority that she and her husband were determined to give to Albert. While acknowledging that this was 'also an old Anglo-Saxon name', derived, perhaps, from Ethelred, it had long fallen out of use, whereas Edward was such 'a good English appellation' and would be popular in the country because of 'ancient recollections'.

A clearer hint that the nation's interests in 1842 would no longer be served by flying these Germanic banners at court could not have been written. Nor, as regards the writer, could any other Englishman have been found with greater influence over the young Queen. Nonetheless, his advice was ignored. 'Albert Edward' it remained, at the font, and as long as Queen Victoria lived. As if to emphasize the point, only two of the sponsors she selected for his baptism, one great-aunt and one great-uncle, were 'English' (that is, Hanoverian). Of the other four, three were Saxe-Coburgs and one was Prussian, no less a person indeed than the recently crowned King Frederick William IV himself. Traditional England was represented at this first ceremony for its crown prince mainly by the phalanx of officiating Anglican bishops, headed by the Archbishop of Canterbury, and by the old Duke of Wellington who, at the Queen's wish, carried the great Sword of State in and out of the chapel.

If the Teutonic atmosphere had hung heavily enough over the infant's baptism, it became at times quite suffocating during young Albert Edward's early upbringing. To be sure, the prince's governess, who had charge of him till he was seven, was English (Lady Lyttelton). So were the two tutors (Henry Birch, followed in 1852 by Frederick Gibbs) who took him through his ten years after the nursery, up to the age of seventeen. Yet both governess and tutors were but the firmly-held instruments of an educational regime that had been drawn up by Germans, with German thoroughness, German pedantry and, most important of all, with a German spirit behind it.

One of the co-architects of this programme was old Baron Stockmar, a fussy little Coburg doctor turned courtier who had spent the whole of his bachelor life throne-making, match-making and child-raising for his tiny royal house. To Bismarck, contemptuously surveying a continent whose royal pastures seemed to be scattered with Coburg seeds, this house was merely 'the stud-farm of Europe'. For Stockmar, these seeds had a mystic power. Indeed, if carefully planted, transplanted, nurtured and grafted, they were, in his eyes, capable of rejuvenating the most decayed or blighted of dynastic trees. Needless to say, he was the self-appointed gardener of the entire process. As early as 1831, he had helped to establish one Coburg, Prince Leopold, on the throne of the new kingdom of Belgium. Even this triumph paled before the successful role he had played in making that same Leopold's nephew the husband of the Queen of England. From 1840 onwards, with a permanent suite of rooms allotted to him in Buckingham Palace, the Baron's last and greatest ambition was to impregnate the English monarchy as thoroughly with the Coburg spirit as it was impregnated already with Coburg blood. In that way his little homeland, a comical irrelevance in physical size and weight, could leave its mark in all the corners of the earth.

This meant above all else that Queen Victoria's heir had to be trained as a Coburg or, at least, on sound Coburg lines. It was an aim with which the boy's father, Prince Albert, wholeheartedly agreed. He was the other co-architect of the rigorous educational programme devised for the child; and Albert's devotion to his own German family tree – so tiny at its roots, yet so wide in its branches – was shown by the way he still clung to it from his much loftier perch across the Channel. Indeed, even after he had been designated Prince Consort (not without opposition and loud mutterings of protest from the English Establishment), he swore to remain *ein treuer, fester Coburger*, faithful to his own Lilliputian house.

He himself could never succeed to the throne of England. Nor could he hope to control his adopted country's destinies from behind the scenes during his lifetime. His wife's Ministers would see to that; so would his wife's loyalties. Probably the only passion that Queen Victoria felt more strongly than her love for the handsome husband she had married was her loyalty to the constitutional crown she wore. But what the Prince Consort could hope for was to sway England by proxy after their deaths, by making another *treuer fester Coburger* out of their son. Like Stockmar, he was a fanatic with a mission. The luckless human object placed under this burning-glass for the next twenty years was Albert Edward, or 'Bertie' as he was soon called for short.

The reasons why this mission failed – at least in the sense its sponsors desired – were largely the same reasons why the Prince Consort himself failed in English society. It was an ironic business. Prince Albert had so many of the characteristics that the Victorian Englishman traditionally cherished as his own. He was diligent, thrifty, upright, honourable, and virtuous in both his private and his family life. He was even in tune with the economic credo of the age, interested in material progress and technology, very keen on making money and very good at saving it. (When his Windsor farm cattle won prizes at agricultural shows, he would pocket the coins on the spot, as though he were short of the train fare home.)

This very perfection as husband, citizen and businessman was, of course, one cause of his unpopularity. He lacked that essential concomitant of the Victorian age – hypocrisy, and the private indulgence in a few saving vices, if it was only cards or alcohol. Outwardly, he was just like the stiff frock-coat which was the symbol of that age. But his trouble was that he was just the same inside as well, without any of the concealed soft lining which alone made the garment comfortable to wear. Not many people in English society admired him for that. Even fewer liked him for it.

The second thing that jarred about Prince Albert was that he was a dedicated intellectual. The English have rarely felt at their ease with intellectuals in any branch of political life. To have one perched on the arm of the throne was particularly disturbing. Yet it was an academic at heart that Albert had become in Germany (after an incongruously lusty youth at Coburg) and an academic he remained. The happiest days of his life had been the eighteen months spent as a student at Bonn University where, despite that debilitating Rhine valley climate, he often started on his books at 5 a.m. And perhaps the most significant object he took with him to England after his marriage was the reading lamp, complete with green silk shade, which had lit his path through such a maze of student learning. He brought with him the spirit of the academic as well as its symbol. Throughout his life, he remained dogmatic rather than pragmatic. Everything had to be culled from books, then mapped out on paper, and the plan adhered to. There was no room for instinct, and little feel for compromise. Anything further removed from the Englishman's 'Wait and see' would be hard to imagine.

There were countless other things that grated. His sense of humour, for example (and there are few more fundamental distinctions between nations), was of that heavily explicit Germanic variety which is incapable of turning against itself. There was in him little wit and less fun. Nor could he ever come to terms with the Englishman's idea of sport.

He regarded cricket as a ludicrous game, but he did so for the most ponderous of reasons: that so few of the twenty-two players could take exercise simultaneously. Shooting, too, he could only see as a functional sport, whose proper object was to provide the maximum quantity of game. Accordingly, both at Osborne and at Balmoral, he organized continental-style deer drives (instead of individual stalking) that produced hetacombs of carcasses, and also protest cries of 'Massacre' in the press. Even when he did consent to stalk the beasts on foot in Scotland, he had trenches dug so that he could approach their feeding-grounds unobserved. The ghillies snorted at this unsporting 'German trick', this lamentable example of 'furrin' ways'. One can hear all Britain snorting with them.

Foreign was just how the Prince Consort struck the English; and the more he toiled for his vision of Coburg-England, the more foreign he became. Even his worthiest labour for the nation, the organizing of London's Great International Exhibition of 1851, drew less than the gratitude it deserved from the people at large. As for the great English aristocrats, they, for the most part, regarded him as a *parvenu* as well as an intruder. The Duke of Beaufort, for example, felt it quite beneath his dignity to attach his son as Lord-in-Waiting to Prince Albert's frumpish court. Poor Albert; he did not even possess that one quality which every Englishman expects from every continental – charm.

The purpose of dwelling on the character of Prince Albert (and above all on his essential and incurable foreignness) is, of course, to point to the total contrast with his own son. Whether 'Bertie' grew up to be such a different creature because he was simply made that way, or whether he fled up the opposite path in life as a direct reaction against his father's guidance, advice and example, we shall never know. It was probably a mixture of both. Whatever the explanation, the contrast amounts almost to caricature.

The father devoured books and was bad with people. The son disliked books and was superb with people. The father worked by the rule; the son by instinct. The father was so overwhelmed by the duties of life that he found neither the time nor the appetite to enjoy it. As for the son, ironically enough, we have to turn here to his father's native language to put the contrast in a single word: 'Bertie' was *lebensbejahend*, which means that he said a loud yes to life, all his life. The horses, the gaming-tables, the tireless zest for travel and new faces; the taste for vintage wine, matured cigars, for gay company at gargantuan meals of gourmet quality; above all, the worship of beautiful women that was to produce several tender friendships as well as a stream of casual affairs and a string of regular mistresses – this, and much more besides, in the son's behaviour was not merely repugnant to the father, it was incomprehensible. Baron Stockmar strove to chase the licentious Hanoverian out of Bertie's blood and replace it with the prim Coburg strain. What England ended up with in the young prince – luckily for him as well as for her – was neither. In his way of life and, later, in his way of ruling, he became instead more like a throw-back to the Tudors.

The agonizing tussle that went on before the paths of father and grown-up son were prematurely parted can be imagined. There are few infants who do not project some image of their manhood, even in the nursery, and Bertie was no exception. When he was only four years old, the elderly Lady Lyttelton was complaining to his mother that he was 'uncommonly averse to learning', and would hamper her lessons not merely by paying no attention but by crawling out of sight under the table, by upsetting a pile of those hated books, or by any other bit of sabotage that occurred to his rebellious little mind. Baron Stockmar (who was certainly shown this nursery bulletin) would not have been reassured when the royal governess added that her young charge was developing instead a taste for 'violent exercise and enjoyment of life'.[2]

It was the same tale, but in even more dramatic form, when he passed through the hands of his tutors. The more violently he rejected his academic medicine, the more his insensitive father increased the dose until, under Gibbs, he was doing six hours a day at his textbooks, six days a week. The fact that his elder sister Victoria ('Vicky', the Queen's first-born) and his next younger brother Alfred were both model pupils by comparison did not make things any easier. Bertie groaned, screamed and stamped his way through the royal schoolroom so that, by the time he was 15 even Stockmar was moved to suggest that they ought perhaps to let up for a bit. Otherwise, he warned, the Prince of Wales might either get a brain storm or be put off studying for the rest of his life. The first calamity never happened. But by now it was too late for Stockmar, or anyone else, to prevent the second. They should all have heeded Lord Melbourne's wise advice, given when the Prince was still an infant, not to overdo the educational regime, nor to expect too much from it.

Bertie's home life, though affectionate, regular and safe, did not provide much sorely-needed light relief from this relentless tutorial grind. Occasionally, the routine at Windsor would be varied when small groups of Bertie's old nursery playmates were brought in from nearby Eton College for brief afternoon calls. They were carefully selected according to the high character as well as the high rank of their parents so that no moral germs were likely to escape their young mouths in conversation and contaminate this embattled and dis-infected Prince. Even boyish fun was killed stone dead. Bertie's father never left the room during these visitations from the outside world, and the presence of the Prince Consort was enough to squash the spirits of the gayest youth.

Prince Albert did have his son instructed in those indispensable royal arts of shooting and riding. As soon as Bertie entered his teens, he was allowed to go out with the guns on the pheasant shoots at Windsor Park, and take his place in the grouse butts or 'deer-drives' up in Scotland. But the gulf between father and son yawned even wider at play than at work. To the Prince Consort, as we have seen, shooting was a functional business, whose twin aims were to provide the maximum of exercise for the body and the maximum of game for the larder. For his son it was just one of the pleasures of life. These outings nurtured the boy's enduring love of dogs and horses as well as his unaffected, undemanding love of nature. But they were all too few and fleeting, and, once back within the walls of Windsor or Balmoral in the evenings, the fresh air would be shut out again, in every sense, as, before dinner, Prince Albert would declaim long passages from Hallam's *Constitutional History* to his captive family audience.

Every now and then, that regal imp in Bertie that was soon to take all Europe by the tail would burst forth. One story has it that, while prowling around remote corners of the Castle where he certainly had no business, he saw through an open bedroom door the bridal dress of a housemaid, laid out for her wedding. On an impulse, the young Prince popped into the room and smeared the white garment with some red ink he found at hand. The psychologists might have found much food for thought in that bizarre episode. As it was, Bertie landed up before his father, who gave him a sound beating for his prank. What had probably annoyed the Prince Consort above all else was the waste of good ink.

All in all, it was a grey childhood for one born to the purple. Signifi-cantly, the only brilliant flashes in it, which must have dazzled his frustrated spirit like comets bursting in from another universe, came from abroad. These episodes shaped the man as well as the boy, and the King as well as the Prince. Edward's passion for foreign travel and, later, for foreign affairs, can only be understood in their light. The first, and in some ways the most important such experience, was the week he spent in Paris in August 1855 with his parents and his sister Vicky, the Princess Royal.

He owed it to an unexpected twist of high politics. The England he had grown up in was, if not actively hostile to France, at least diffident towards the historic enemy across the water. The old Duke of Wellington had only been dead for three years, and his annual Waterloo commemoration dinners at Apsley House had symbolized the conservative, distrustful temper of the nation. As for Queen Victoria, her own instinctive dislike of France had been redoubled when, on 2 December 1851, Napoleon Bonaparte's nephew had seized power, proclaimed the Second French Empire, and appointed himself as Napoleon III to rule it. For a while, shudders of apprehension ran down England's spine, in case this brilliant adventurer should try to succeed where even his uncle had failed, in subduing England. Indeed, in August of 1853, the young Prince of Wales had gone with his mother to Spithead to attend a naval review designed as a demonstration of British strength to warn France's new ruler off any adventures. Yet, only two years later, the Queen of England and her heir were being fêted in Paris. The reason for the transformation was Napoleon III's astute offer to fight alongside England against Russia in the Crimean War. The process had been speeded along, at the personal level, by the highly successful preparatory visit which Napoleon and his radiant new bride Eugénie had paid to London in April of 1855. Queen Victoria had been captivated by the grace and charm of both of them. From that moment on, there was no more talk of imperial *parvenus* residing at Versailles.

The trip to Paris that same summer, which lasted from 20 to 27 August, was intended to cement the new alliance. The political cement, like the alliance itself, soon crumbled away into fragments that were not to be moulded together again for almost half a century. But what did form on the spot, and last for good, was Bertie's life-long love-affair with 'la belle France'. Little could the boy have guessed, though it fitted well enough into the long sweep of history, that, fifty years later, he would come to Paris himself as sovereign and cement a firmer and more fateful Anglo-French partnership into place.

What must have overwhelmed this future architect of the *Entente* as a mere child in 1855 was the sudden contact he made, not simply with another city and another country, but with a totally new way of looking at life, and of living it. Here, in Paris, was a court that managed to be splendid without being stuffy, and a throne occupied by someone who actually seemed to enjoy this earnest business of ruling. Who was right, the crusty Baron Stockmar or this gay imperial couple? There was no doubt in Bertie's mind. He had been on their side long before he had met them.

Above all, there was the romantic strangeness of almost every episode of that magic week, the physical and atmospheric contrast with everything he had known at home. That splendid contemporary painting by Hippolyte Bellangé which depicts the stag hunt given by Napoleon III for his guests in the Forest of St Germain on the sixth day of their visit, puts on canvas what the young Prince of Wales was to carry always in his memory. On the lawns in front of a golden-yellow château, a pack of stag-hounds gather around a bevy of huntsmen who are almost as numerous as the dogs. They are dressed, not in those heavy grey tweeds which match the mists of Scotland, but in rich brown coats trimmed and belted with gold, with matching tricorne hats perched sideways on their heads, and, on their feet, shiny black boots which stretch right up to the knees. Each man carries a gleaming brass hunting horn, whose tube forms a circle big enough to be slung round the body. At the moment captured by the artist, they are sounding a massed fanfare to signal the start of the hunt to the leaping dogs, whose yelps of excitement can almost be heard. Mounted officers of the imperial guard ride on the lawn among the crowd of guests, who seem to consist largely of lovely ladies in silks and parasols.

All is movement and colour, except for the English royal family who stand, with Napoleon III, at the foot of the steps surveying the scene. The Prince Consort, with a dark frock coat and a black silk hat, looks rather like an undertaker at a circus. Next to his father, a Scotch bonnet on his head, stands the small figure of the Prince of Wales. The look of wonderment on his face is understandable. Nothing he had yet seen in his fourteen and a half years had ever been as different as this from the chilly bleakness that so often went with Balmoral and those German-style deer-drives there, methodically organized by his father.

Everything about that week had been for him just as new and just as dazzling. The court ball at Versailles, for example, when he had won many compliments for his dancing; or the solemn moment when his mother had taken him, in Highland costume, to pay homage in the Invalides at the tomb of England's most formidable enemy. As though the great Napoleon himself had snorted at the sight, a clap of thunder sounded from the skies as, only forty years after Waterloo, the young English prince went down on his knees at the Queen of England's bidding. The erotic vibrations of Paris and of the ladies of the imperial court must also have gone straight to the heart of this very physical but very frustrated teenaged boy who was just reaching puberty. It is characteristic of all the English accounts of this 1855 visit that this particular aspect, which probably made the deepest mark of all on young Edward's imagination, is not even mentioned. It was appropriately left to a Frenchman, writing more than a century after the event, to put his finger on the boy's racing pulse:

'In the Tuileries he breathed for the first time that *odore di femmina* whose trail he was to follow for the rest of his life. The scented, alluring women not only kissed him (was he not a child?) but also curtsied to him, and as they bent forward, their décolletage revealed delights that were veiled at Windsor.'[3]

Clearly, this was not a city, and this was not a court, where a growing boy would have to let off steam for long with ink-pots. When the beautiful Empress Eugénie later sent him a locket with a curl of her own hair inside (entwined, admittedly, with wisps from the head of her husband and infant son) it must have seemed like a permanent invitation to Paris as well as a memento. Bertie was not long in accepting.

Finally, there was the glorious feeling that he had been a success, perhaps *the* success of the entire visit. Of course his famous mother, plumpish and plainish though she was now becoming, had exuded a regal confidence that even her beautiful hostess could not yet match. Connoisseurs noted, for example, that whereas the Empress Eugénie, on taking her seat at a reception, would first give a fleeting glance behind her, to make sure all was in place, the Queen of England just sat herself straight down. She *knew* the chair would be there. But the stolid Prince Consort, who was on very foreign soil in every sense of the word, made little impression; neither did that paragon of the Windsor nursery and schoolroom, Princess Vicky. Little Bertie, in his Highland dress, was the only real personal hit with the Parisians. After watching them all leave from the Gare de Strasbourg on 27 August, the Countess d'Armaille wrote in her diary that whereas Prince Albert 'followed [the Queen] bashfully, very bald for his age and looking very tired . . . his little boy, on the contrary, kept looking all around him, as though anxious to lose nothing of these last moments in Paris'.[4]

This, presumably, was the day that young Bertie had pleaded with the Empress to arrange for him to stay behind in Paris for a few more days, assuring her that he wouldn't really be missed in England because 'there are six more of us at home'. There was more in that unsuccessful plea than the usual attempt of any schoolboy to prolong an outing.

Whether it was because Bertie had behaved in such an exemplary fashion during that week in Paris, or whether it was because travels inside England were somehow more complicated to arrange (a walking tour, incognito, of the West Country in the autumn of 1856 had to be abandoned at Honiton after his identity had leaked out and loyal demonstrations erupted at every village), the young Prince was soon allowed longer escapes abroad. On 26 July 1857, for example, he was dispatched with four carefully selected boy companions* and a small suite to Königswinter, on the opposite bank of the Rhine to his father's beloved Bonn. How Prince Albert regarded this expedition was indicated by the fact that he had attached to the party the Reverend Charles Tarver, who was his son's Latin tutor and personal chaplain. But young Prince Edward was much more disposed to enjoy life off the Windsor Castle leash than to cultivate his soul and the classics. Indeed, there was (for his guardians) an appalling moment the very first evening at Königswinter when young Bertie, having imbibed a little too freely of that treacherously light-tasting Rhenish wine, publicly kissed a pretty girl who had caught his eye. Had the Prince Consort heard about the incident he would probably have ordered the whole party back to England the next day. As it was, it seems to have leaked out at home only to the Gladstone family, causing England's Chancellor of the Exchequer and future Prime Minister to expostulate to his wife about 'this squalid little debauch'.

Whether Prince Edward embraced any more Rhine maidens is not known. The other reports that reached home of the month he spent there would all, however, have satisfied his father. The Prince Consort would have been particularly pleased to learn that, on 16 August, his son was the guest of honour at a dinner given by the 84-year-old Prince Metternich at his castle of Johannisberg. Here the young Prince of Wales was offered, by this venerable conscience of the old European order, a mixture of magnificent Metternich hock and sparkling Metternich reminiscences. Though Bertie was, by now, getting accustomed to knowing famous people, the great Metternich quite overwhelmed him with his talk and his presence; or perhaps he was simply bemused to see this incorporation of half a century of European history sitting there at the head of the table and talking to him. When he recorded the meeting in his diary, Bertie could only compare his host with that one other living legend he had met, the Duke of Wellington. For his part, Metternich loftily remarked of his young royal guest that he had seemed 'embarrassed and very sad'.

The evening at Johannisberg was the social and intellectual highlight of the Prince's month in the Rhineland. From there he and his party travelled to Switzerland, where they did some sedate walking tours along the foothills of Mont Blanc and over the Grosse Scheidegg

---

* Charles Wood, later Lord Halifax; George Cadogan, later the Earl of Cadogan; Frederick Stanley, later the Earl of Derby; and William Gladstone, eldest son of the great Liberal statesman.

pass. After Metternich, even the Alps must have seemed less awe-inspiring than expected. The party eventually landed again at Dover on 27 October 1857. Bertie had been abroad for nearly four months. It was the longest period so far spent in his life away from both his parents and Baron Stockmar's straitjacket.

His next lengthy continental tour, a trip to Italy and the Mediterranean during the first six months of 1859, was on grander and more elaborate lines. The Prince of Wales was now in his eighteenth year. As though he were a province or a prison rather than a person, he had acquired an official governor, Colonel Robert Bruce of the Elgin family, instead of a tutor, and an equerry, Captain Charles Grey, instead of a mere travelling companion. Both set out for Rome with him on 10 January 1859, and Mr Tarver, his Latin teacher, was also in the party again, this time, indeed, with his wife. But if the Reverend Tarver was hopeful that, once in the Eternal City itself, the study of the classics would at last sweep all before them, he was to be sadly disappointed.

Bertie ploughed doggedly, but without enthusiasm, through his morning timetable of studies, which began before breakfast. In the afternoons a team of *savants* piloted him round the ruins of ancient Rome (some of them, like the Forum, still not opened up); around its churches, great and small; and in and out of the museums and picture galleries. This cultural bombardment seems to have made few dents. The Prince Consort, who had, of course, planned the entire programme with the aid of English *ciceroni* from Ruskin downwards, was depressed by the letters his son wrote. The hapless father still clung to the hope that all these learned guides imparting so much erudition would lead Bertie to the philosopher's stone and turn him suddenly into an intellectual or, at least, a man of letters. Instead, the young Prince reacted, as he was to do throughout his life, by preferring the concrete to the abstract, and the study of people above all else. If he lingered in a Roman art gallery, it was more likely to be in front of a portrait of a lovely woman than of a classical landscape. The thing that most intrigued him about the city's Protestant cemetery was not so much the tombs of Keats and Shelley but the fact that his own equerry, Captain Grey, who was walking round beside him, had unexpectedly discovered an ancestor's grave.

Still, the long stay in Rome (he did not leave until the end of April) had many distractions. He saw the spring carnival and rode up and down the Corso pelting the crowd with flowers and confetti, and being pelted back. He went twice a week to the opera, and found Verdi and Bellini particularly enjoyable. It was also in Rome that he took his first steps on that public stage of Europe which he was eventually to dominate. He was received by Pope Pius IX who, to Colonel Bruce's horror, got on so easily with the young Prince that he even touched on the thorny question of the Roman Catholic hierarchy in England. Three weeks later, to keep the protocol balance between the spiritual and the temporal powers, the Prince received a decoration from King Victor Emmanuel, then only the ruler of Sardinia but soon to rule over a unified Italy. The young Prince, who had conversed with the pontiff in French, now proposed a toast to Victor Emmanuel in the same language. His European profile was beginning to emerge; and another part of it was sketched in by a short stay at Lisbon on the way home with his young cousin, King Pedro V of Portugal.*

But it was, in fact, the New World that finally gave Bertie the self-confidence he needed to take his appointed place in the Old. After an undistinguished and uneventful spell at Christ Church College, Oxford ('The only use of Oxford is that it is a place for *study*,' his indefatigable father had written to him at the commencement of term), the summer came round again, and with it, the question of what to do with Bertie during the holiday months. Quite apart from the fact that foreign travel seemed, on balance, to do the boy more good than anything else, it was the only way of avoiding him getting sucked into the vortex of the London season. Queen Victoria agreed with her husband that their son was not yet ready to be exposed to the moral dangers of *that*. Even if, in their heart of hearts, they perceived that he wanted nothing more in life than to leap head first into these delectable pitfalls, another long journey would at least postpone the evil day.

But where to? He had more or less 'done' the near continent (the Easter vacation of 1860 had been spent on another visit to his Coburg relatives). Moreover, he was now well into his nineteenth year, and a boy no longer. A great and far-sighted decision was taken. The young Prince was anyway due to visit the great colony of Canada as soon as he was deemed mature enough. It was now arranged that he should go on from there and visit America as well. The Prince of Wales in Washington would be a considerable happening even today. In the year 1860 it was a breathless and epoch-making event. No heir to the throne had ever set foot on the other side of the Atlantic before, let alone visited the American Republic.

The man directly responsible for the idea was President Buchanan, who had served as American Minister in London before he had entered the White House in 1857. He had not had an easy time at the Court of St James and it was with the object of improving Anglo-American

* The King's father was Prince Ferdinand of Saxe-Coburg.

relations that he wrote to Queen Victoria soon after the Canada tour was announced and invited the Prince to spend a few days with him. The idea was none too popular in some conservative quarters in London, and the Prince Consort, for once, deserved full credit for the imaginative way in which he beat down such opposition. Whether or not he was really dreaming of Coburg culture bringing enlightenment to fur-trappers and Red Indians is beside the point. The visit would be beneficial, he maintained, to those broader interests of Empire which every English prince ought to foster. In any case, the British Ambassador in Washington, Lord Lyons, approved of the idea, while President Buchanan had guaranteed a fervent welcome.

America lived up to its President's promise. To some degree, the Prince had his mother to thank for this. Before he left England, Queen Victoria had laid down certain emphatic conditions for the journey. In Canada, he could be received as her heir, and function as her deputy. This enabled him, for example, personally to confer the accolade of knighthood on the two Speakers of the Lower Canadian Parliament at Quebec. The fact that his suite was headed by no less a person than the Duke of Newcastle himself, Secretary of State for the Colonies, lent added emphasis to the official seal on the Canadian tour.

But from the moment, on the afternoon of 20 September 1860, that the royal party crossed the Detroit river and set foot on American soil, the Prince of Wales became, on his mother's orders, Baron Renfrew (his usual incognito) who was visiting the United States 'in the character of a student'. The Queen had even prescribed that, in order to maintain that pose, her son was to put up at hotels throughout his American journey, with the sole exception of his stay at the White House. Thus, without ceasing for one instant to be His Royal Highness in the eager eyes of the American people, the Prince of Wales could become Bertie to himself. Nothing could have suited him, or the occasion, better. He could enter this great land of 'Hail-fellow-well-met' prepared to take a slap on the back as well as a curtsey. The tour which now began was a happy blend of both.

Like so many British colonies which were to turn independent in the century to come, the Americans of the 1860s nourished an ambivalent attitude towards the Crown in their republican bosoms. Fiercely proud of their status as a free state, there was, not very deep down, a nostalgia for the romance and tradition that monarchy had symbolized. The country was humming anyway, for the electoral campaign which was to result in the return of Abraham Lincoln to the White House was in full swing. The unexpected arrival of the Prince of Wales in the midst of all this ferment was the best piece of razzamatazz any American election campaign could have wished for. Wherever the Prince appeared, mere excitement turned to tumult. At Detroit itself, then at Chicago, Cincinnati and Pittsburgh, each of the thrusting new cities seemed to excel the others in the heartiness of welcome. The Prince arrived at St Louis, his farthest point west, in time for the town's autumn fair. These are always great local occasions but, for decades to come, old Louisans were to look back with pride to this fair of 1860, when 100,000 people gathered to see the Prince of Wales. There was a lustiness about his reception, a blend of familiarity and respect in both the crowds and the officials, that Edward had never met with before, and was never to meet again.

Ceremony and protocol were much more to the fore during his few days at the White House, where he arrived from Baltimore on 3 October. Formal dinners, presentations of Ministers and their wives, historic ceremonies (such as the planting of a chestnut tree near Washington's tomb) all symbolized the fact that he was now in the nation's capital, and so caught up again in the red tape and gold braid. But this did not prevent Bertie, when he wrote from the White House to his mother, admiring the pretty face of the President's niece, Harriet Lane, as well as the noble architectural features of the city.

The final stage of his visit, New York, was a return, with a vengeance, to the atmosphere of St Louis. He had never before seen crowds like the 300,000 New Yorkers (his own estimate, in another letter home) who jammed Broadway to cheer themselves hoarse as he drove to the Fifth Avenue Hotel with the city's mayor, Fernando Wood. The luxury of the hotel deeply impressed the Prince, who had not expected such standards anywhere in the New World. By insisting on paying his own bill, the Prince in turn deeply impressed the management, who had not expected such scrupulousness on the part of royalty from the Old World.

The climax of the whole tour, a great ball at the New York Academy of Music on the night of 12 October, was a mixed success. What the *New York Evening Post* described as the 'American nobility' had flocked in their thousands to attend this social event of the century. Indeed, they flocked far too profusely, some two thousand gate-crashers having poured in with the three thousand ticket-holders. As a result, soon after the Prince arrived at 10 p.m., part of the floor collapsed under the excess weight of all this bejewelled big business. He had in fact already shaken hands with the first fifty couples of the 'enormous procession of socialites' lined up for presentation when the terrifying crack rang out and some of those at the rear of the queue disappeared up to their thighs in splintered wood. As most of them fell slap into the rows of theatre seats which the special floor was covering, nobody was seriously hurt, though many a toilette was ruined.

Anglo-Saxon calm prevailed, and an army of carpenters got to work. They hammered away well and truly, but a little too hastily, for when they were about to bow out, like medieval tumblers at a feast, it was noticed that they had nailed up one of their comrades under the replaced boards. After a further delay to release him, dancing finally started soon after midnight, the Prince opening proceedings with Mrs Morgan, wife of the New York Governor. This was the second unfortunate aspect of the evening. The hall was full of young girls just as pretty as Harriet Lane, but Bertie hardly got his arm around a single one of their slender waists. The wives of New York's officials, bankers and industrialists had first claim on him instead. No wonder he wrote home to mother: 'The great ball took place, but it was not successful.'

His own performance in America had, however, been most successful, far beyond his, or anyone else's, expectations. In political terms, it had helped to open up the blocked channels of sympathy between the two nations. In personal terms, it had established the young Prince as an international figure in his own right, and a magnetic one at that. He had, at last, done something that his father could not have done; moreover, it was something that could not have been learned from books. 'He has won all our hearts,' President Buchanan wrote to his mother; and ordinary Americans had indeed sensed what they would have called a vote-winning quality in the youth. 'Come back in four years and run for President,' a man had shouted to him from the crowd.

He never went back and, for that matter, never crossed the Atlantic again. But from now on he always carried with him, during the long years ahead as Prince of Wales, and later as King, a respect for this rich and vigorous nation; a liking for its informal style; and a soft spot for its own brand of 'forward' feminine charm. Perhaps, too, he always carried a sense of gratitude for what it had done for him. That visit as an infant to Paris had shown him a first glimpse of the European stage he longed to tread. The visit as a youth to America had given him the confidence to step out on it. The time for that entrance from the wings was now approaching.

*   *   *

Two other milestones in his personal life had to be passed first. The first, the death of his father in 1861, came the year after the North American tour. Filial grief apart, it has to be viewed in the same context: it added immensely to the son's feeling of self-confidence. This was more than a stern parent who had gone, a parent for whom he could feel natural respect and devotion if barely a spark of real human contact. It was the living personification of the Coburg creed who had disappeared as well. True, the grief-stricken widow promptly resolved to complete her husband's mission and bring the Prince of Wales into manhood, and then on towards kingship, in accordance with the sacred programme. But, with old Baron Stockmar in retirement and removed from the scene as well (he died in 1863), the Coburg philosophy could only now rule at Windsor by proxy, and by petticoat. However formidable Queen Victoria was in that role, she could not be a complete substitute for the trio that had once included both the Prince Consort and his oracular Baron.

Indeed, even the circumstances of Prince Albert's death had seemed to suggest that the struggle to turn Bertie into a prim Coburg was already lost. What the Prince Consort died of on 13 December 1861 was typhoid fever, and nothing but the fatal germ and the bad sanitation that released it were directly to blame for that. But, indirectly, the germ may have been helped on its path by the patient's low spirits and weakened resistance; and what, more than anything else, had brought the Prince Consort to such a low state at that time was the scandal over his son's first known love-affair.

Bertie was serving for ten weeks at the Curragh Camp in Ireland, attached to the Second Battalion, Grenadier Guards, in order to broaden his experience. His young fellow officers doubtless felt they were only carrying out the spirit of that mission when they smuggled the delectable Dublin actress Nellie Clifden into his bed one night. The news got out, probably through a flushed and excited Nellie. An episode that would have been considered both healthy and normal for an English prince of Tudor, Stuart or Hanoverian days was now greeted by the keepers of the Coburg conscience as though the monarchy itself had collapsed. In November, shortly before catching typhoid, Prince Albert had been deeply depressed by a letter from old Stockmar in Coburg which described how, all over the continent, they were now shaking their heads or smiling behind their fans about Miss Clifden's latest and most prestigious conquest. On 25 November, with a streaming cold and the typhoid germ already in him, the Prince Consort had struggled to Cambridge to see his son to discuss with him the lax state of his morals and a remedial tour of education around the Near East. The next time Bertie saw his father was on his death-bed at Windsor three weeks later. The Prince Consort was too far gone even to recognize his erring son, let alone give him any last words of caution or advice. There was, for them both, a cruel but fitting logic about this way of parting.

The second and very different milestone that the young Prince now passed on his road to manhood was, of course, his marriage. The search for a suitable bride for the Prince of Wales had been going on already for some years. There are desultory references to the subject in Queen Victoria's correspondence as early as December 1858, and the newspapers – as usual ahead of the court in such romantic matters – had floated their speculations months before that. The Coburg clan on the Continent (King Leopold of the Belgians in Brussels and the inevitable Baron Stockmar) had put forward some names. From Berlin, Bertie's elder sister, Vicky (who had herself been married in January 1858 to the ill-fated Crown Prince Frederick William of Prussia), added one or two more. Their lists showed that while all Europe was wide open to Edward as Prince of Wales, and later as King, the range available to him as a marriage suitor was a good deal narrower.

To begin with, there was the unbridgeable gulf between religions. England's future Defender of the Faith could not possibly marry a Catholic princess. That ruled out not only all the multitudinous Habsburgs, Braganzas and Bourbons, but also the pick of the current German candidates, Princess Marie of Hohenzollern-Sigmaringen. Politics, too, had to be considered. Her Majesty's Heir-Apparent should, if possible, avoid marrying into a foreign dynasty with which Her Majesty's Government might become diplomatically embroiled. On top of all this came the consideration imposed by Bertie's own roving eye: the bride-to-be had to be uncommonly attractive for there to be any chance of a successful match.

It is extraordinary to note how everyone concerned in the quest fervently endorsed this purely physical aspect of the matter, as though it were a Protestant beauty queen and not just a Princess of Wales they were after. Thus one early (1859) favourite, Princess Elizabeth of Wied, was admitted even by Stockmar to be 'rather dowdy' and was ruled right out by Crown Princess Vicky of Prussia as being 'not . . . at all *distinguée*-looking, certainly the opposite to Bertie's usual taste'. One by one, the Princess of Weimar, Princess Hilda of Dessau, and Princess Marie of the Netherlands were struck off as being either too delicate and not pretty enough or too slow-witted and not pretty enough. Again, the common disqualification was their looks. One outsider, Princess Marie of Altenburg, was black-balled for being 'shockingly dressed' as well.[5]

There was, it seemed, no royal maiden the length and breadth of the Continent who fulfilled all three pre-conditions of faith, diplomacy and pulchritude. Queen Victoria had to settle in the end for a daughter-in-law who measured up to only two. Denmark was a politically awkward country to choose in that there was clearly going to be trouble soon between her and Prussia over the border Duchies of Schleswig and Holstein; and England, through her former Princess Royal, now had the closest of dynastic links with Prussia. On the other hand, Princess Alexandra, eldest daughter of the next heir* to the Danish crown, was both undeniably Protestant and undeniably pretty. It was this second point (the first was anyway taken for granted) which carried the real weight in the controversy over the 17-year-old girl's claims.

The battle that went on throughout 1861 was nonetheless an envenomed one, with some of the continental Coburgs, as well as all of the Prussian camp, lined up against the match. But it was the Keeper of the Queen's Privy Purse, Sir Charles Phipps, who put the essential argument in plain human terms when he observed: 'It is of the first importance that the Prince of Wales's wife should have beauty, agreeable manners, and the power of attracting people to her, and these the Princess Alexandra seems to possess to a remarkable degree.'† Bertie himself appeared to agree with this verdict when he first saw the young lady in question at an elaborately contrived meeting while both were 'sightseeing' in Speier Cathedral in September 1861. A year after that, the couple were formally betrothed. A rumour which floated around in the summer of 1862 that the Russian Czar might have his eye on Princess Alexandra as a bride for his own son had spurred Queen Victoria into clinching the marriage contract.

It was to bring the political complications the Queen had so feared when – only four years later, in 1866 – Prussia duly attacked Denmark to wrest the border Duchies from her, and the court at Windsor was torn between sympathies for the Prince of Wales's Danish bride, on the one hand, and his Prussian brother-in-law on the other. Nor did it end there. For the rest of the nineteenth century and, more important, for the first decade of the twentieth, when Edward was on the throne himself, the anti-Prussian lobby of England found a permanent focusing point around Alexandra. Though she was never a significant figure politically, the intensity and consistency of her feelings acted as a catalyst for many of her English sympathizers. At the most, they disliked, distrusted and perhaps feared the Prussians. Alexandra, whether

---

* Prince Christian of Schleswig-Holstein-Sonderburg-Glücksburg, who duly inherited the throne in November 1863 through his wife, Princess Louise of Hesse-Cassel.

† It was significant that even the opponents of the match used a physical argument against her: a scar on her neck, which was her only blemish, was said by them to have scrofulous origins.

as Princess or Queen, positively hated them. Her husband could not have remained entirely unaffected by this domestic pressure, especially after his own infidelity put him so heavily in his wife's private debt.

For the fact soon had to be faced that Princess Alexandra's good looks, which had been placed in the marital scales like a golden counter-weight to all the political dross hidden under her trousseau, were not good enough to keep her husband at home for long. Indeed, for the best part of half a century, she was to become the most courteously but most implacably deceived royal lady of her time. It is a moot point whether any wife could have been found in Christendom to square the circle of her husband's demands, for Bertie had a general passion for new faces and new experiences which compounded his particular passion for the fair sex. Yet one only has to look carefully enough at Alexandra's portraits to see why she could never establish the same sustained physical hold over him that several other women did. Her finely-chiselled, long-boned and long-nosed features were of a classical loveliness that, in not untypical Scandinavian fashion, lacked feminine fire and warmth. She was the true example of what those Prussians she so detested would have called *eine fade Schönheit*, a boring beauty. As Oscar Wilde was to observe later in the century, the company of that type of female perfection can always be bettered by dining opposite a lily stuck in a wine-glass.

Of course, neither the political nor the domestic reefs which lay ahead were seen, or at least heeded, on the wedding day. Nearly all royal weddings serve as vicarious and sublimated romances for the nation at large, and this one was no exception. When the Princess arrived at Gravesend on the *Victoria and Albert* on the morning of 7 March 1863, Bertie looked as though he was getting off to a doubtful start as a bridegroom by arriving late at the quayside. But he more than made amends, both to his fiancée and the ecstatic crowds, by fairly sprinting up the gangway and kissing her heartily in public. After an acquaintance consisting of only two chaperoned meetings, the couple could scarcely be expected as yet to feel love for one another. Yet they looked genuinely happy together, and that was all that either they or England needed for the moment.

They were married on 10 March in St George's Chapel, Windsor, where, barely fifteen months before, the funeral service for Prince Albert had been held. To mark that awful memory, Queen Victoria watched the ceremony from the seclusion of Catherine of Aragon's closet above the aisle, the black of her widow's weeds relieved only by the blue sash of the Garter. She was, by choice, the only sombre member of the congregation. The floor of the chapel below was ablaze with the colour and glitter of the men's uniforms, hung with medals and orders, and the full court dresses of the women hung with jewels (those of the Duchess of Westminster alone were reputed to be worth half a million Victorian pounds). The bride looked appropriately radiant in a many-tiered gown of silver satin trimmed with Honiton lace and garlanded with orange blossoms. The groom looked very far removed from the picture his bride had conjured up a few hours earlier, when she had declared that she would be marrying her Bertie that day even 'if he were a cowboy'.

The young man who stood at her side at the altar was neither quite tall enough nor quite slim enough for the Prince Charming of legend. Moreover, his blue eyes popped rather too much and his wavy brown hair grew rather too little for him to be called really handsome. But even without the general's uniform he now wore, under the resplendent robes of the Garter, his was a manly and royal presence. The strong nose and severe gaze were unmistakeably those of someone born to give orders and not to take them. The large mouth and thick lower lip spelt assurance as well as indulgence, as though he knew that all the physical delights of life were his for the taking, and had, indeed, been mostly taken already. Only a weakish chin, which fell away too swiftly under those prominent lips, rather spoilt this commanding impression; but a full beard was soon to take care of that. Bearded or clean-shaven, however, it was above all an open and frank face, without spite or malice.

His bride's joke about the cowboy had been made to his own sister Vicky, the Crown Princess of Prussia who was, of course, at the wedding. It was her husband, the Crown Prince Frederick, who 'supported' the Prince of Wales at the altar, thus serving as the royal equivalent of best man at a marriage that Potsdam had striven to prevent. But it was his 4-year-old son William who was by far the most significant representative of the House of Hohenzollern present that day, both as regards the future of Europe in general and that of the bridegroom in particular.

Dolled up in Highland dress and tucked away almost out of sight, the future Kaiser of Germany grew increasingly angry, as the wedding ceremony dragged on, that just because this English uncle of his was marrying this Danish lady, everyone was totally ignoring *him*. He was flanked by two more of his English uncles, Prince Arthur, Duke of Connaught, and Prince Leopold, Duke of Albany; and it so happened that these two brothers of the bridegroom were also wearing kilts. The temptation proved too much for the frustrated Willy. After trying, unsuccessfully, to cause a diversion with his Highland dirk, he spent the rest of the service alternately digging his tiny nails and sinking his tiny teeth into these august but vulnerable calves on either side of him.

This might be called the first of a lifetime of anti-English gestures, though this is perhaps too hard on the infant. The incident was nonetheless indicative of much that lay ahead. As that formidable child grew up, he became as jealous of his Uncle Bertie hogging the European limelight as he was jealous of him now, the centre of all eyes and the object of all envy in St George's Chapel. Moreover, both as a man and as a ruler, William was to demonstrate that same fury he was showing as a 4-year-old at being left out of things; and also that same tendency to use any violent impulsive gesture that came to hand to draw attention to himself.

But perhaps the most instructive touch about this little tableau at the Windsor wedding is that both of the infant's English victims seem to have sat quietly through the ceremony as though utterly unperturbed by the child's painful tantrums. To be ignored in this way was worse than to be resisted. And this was precisely what, later in life, Willy was to suspect both his Uncle Bertie and his Uncle Bertie's England of doing. If there was one thing above all else that the future Kaiser and his Wilhelminian Germany could not forgive the English for it was that, do what they might in Berlin, they could never visibly rattle them in London.

PRINCE OF PLEASURE

The Queen lent them her beloved Osborne House, on the Isle of Wight, for a seven-day honeymoon, and then the bridal pair returned to the mainland to start on that most enthralling task of all newly-weds, setting up home for themselves. There were, in fact, two of them to set up. Marlborough House, the handsome mansion in Pall Mall that Christopher Wren had designed for the great English soldier-duke in 1710, was being refurbished as their London residence. Old Sandringham Hall, in the centre of a 7000-acre estate in Norfolk, was undergoing much more drastic reconstruction as their future country seat. The Prince had taken possession of both a year or two before his marriage, so that by the spring of 1863 the alterations were already far advanced. But now both these bachelor establishments had to be adapted once again as family homes, and a woman's taste woven into the changes alongside his own.

If Marlborough House was to become their social showcase, it was Sandringham, the domestic retreat in East Anglia, that captured both their hearts. Throughout the long and chequered married life ahead, this was the place that never failed to bring them a little closer together, and to give them their happiest hours. Apart from its seclusion, its appeal to Alexandra probably lay in the flat and somewhat bleak countryside surrounding it, a landscape not unlike her native Denmark which lay due east across the North Sea. To the Prince of Wales, it offered that life of the merry, hospitable English country squire which would have well suited him had he not been born instead to be a king. One half of him always hankered after this rustic existence and here, in the depths of Norfolk, dressed in comfortable brown tweeds, he could indulge in it: laying out flower-gardens, planting forests, cutting rides and ditches, inspecting his stables, kennels, dairy farms and piggeries, and, late every summer, as the shooting season approached, debating with his keepers how best to flush the partridge up out of the stubble or drive his pheasants a yard or two higher over a line of elms.

There was, indeed, not much more than the plentiful game preserves to show for his investment when, in 1861, the purchase of the estate was completed for the sum of £220,000,* drawn from the capital reserve of the Duchy of Cornwall. The owner, the Hon. Spencer Cowper, came from an old county family but had neglected the property for years past and had rarely lived in the modest shooting-box that stood on it. His reason for selling would doubtless have amused the new royal owner. Cowper had recently married his mistress and though the lady in question, Lady Harriet d'Orsay, was of suitable rank, the ménage as such was rather less suitable for Norfolk's old-fashioned society. Thus the newly-wed Cowpers moved to the Continent and now, in 1863, the newly-wed Prince of Wales prepared to move into the rebuilt house.

It proved to be a long business, much longer than they had bargained for. There were delays over the architect's designs and bigger delays over executing them. Not until the autumn of 1870, seven and a half years after their wedding and after further expenditure of £80,000, was the new Sandringham ready to receive them. It was new in every respect. Mr Cowper's plain but dignified Georgian house had disappeared altogether in the reconstruction, swallowed up by the sprawling mock-Tudor mansion that now stretched out along the lawns like a many-tiered wedding-cake laid on its side. It was a typical product of the massive ornamentation which was the hallmark of mid-Victorian style. If the external façade, with gables and tall chimney stacks pointing in all directions, looked far too fussy for any classical taste, the interior could only be described as suffocating. Each sitting-room had crammed into it more sofas, chairs and stools than any company of guests could seemingly require. Each desk and table was piled with more cameos, bronzes, china dogs, carvings and velvet or silver-framed portraits than any four furniture legs could reasonably be expected to support.

Apart from the Goya tapestries (a gift from Alfonso XII of Spain) which looked down on the dining-table, there was scarcely an item in the whole building which would strike the visitor's eye as unmistakably regal. Indeed, had the visitor wandered in by chance; had he not looked closely enough at some of the faces and signatures on the photographs; had he not perceived that those toy figures of animals were not trinkets from a parish bazaar but Fabergé creations sent by the Tsar of all the Russians, he might well have thought he had strayed into the showpiece mansion of some Midlands industrialist rather than into the country seat of a future king. In the clothes they wore, both the Prince of Wales and his bride imposed their very personal and

---

* Modern equivalents are difficult to give; but if the sums mentioned throughout this chapter are multiplied by about twenty, a rough idea of present-day values emerges.

basically simple tastes upon the world of fashion around them. It seems strange that they should submit to all the stifling mannerisms of the day when furnishing their own home.

Yet a true home it was, and a true home was what it felt like, the moment one crossed the hearth. On this point all who visited Sandringham – whether a relative for a long stay, a guest for a weekend shoot, or a mere caller for Sunday tea – were agreed. And one of the main reasons for this was a sense of almost childish fun which pervaded every corner of the cluttered house. The Prince was something of a prankster all his life and Princess Alexandra's gaiety had not yet been overshadowed by domestic rifts, uncertain health and Danish melancholy. Nor were the high jinks confined just to the billiard-room, smoking-room and skittle alley (the last being the Prince's own idea) which formed a natural recreation annex to the building. The ballroom was turned, in wet weather, into an arena for tricycle races, and the grand staircase was often converted, with the aid of a large silver tray, into a carpeted toboggan run. In the main hall, a large stuffed baboon stood guard, his paws holding up a salver for visitors' cards. He was the epitome of the Sandringham spirit in these early married days.

For the next thirty years, until, that is, the beginning of the twentieth century, Sandringham and Marlborough House were the twin fulcrums of English social life as well as the twin homes of Prince Edward and his wife. The tremendous impact that the couple had on society was due, not merely to their own rank and zest for entertaining, but to the fact that, with them, the monarchy had re-emerged into society like a sun breaking again through a heavy bank of cloud. The cloud in this case was the veil of seclusion which Queen Victoria had drawn over her life in an exaggerated (and, for the throne, dangerous) gesture of mourning after the Prince Consort's death. For years to come, England and her Empire were still to be ruled by an almost invisible plump little sovereign in widow's weeds. But now, in the newly-wed Prince, the nation at large could see not only the Heir-Apparent but also, once more, royalty itself apparent.

He proceeded to cast his net far wider than his mother would ever have done herself; far wider, indeed, than she ever approved of him doing. If there is one word that sums up these decades of princely hospitality in Pall Mall and Norfolk, it is variety. There were, of course, plenty of landed noblemen in the Prince's *coterie* – conventional shooting companions like Lord Suffield of Gunton Hall, or the Earl of Leicester of Holkham; and also rather less conventional ones, like 'Harty-Tarty' or Lord Hartington, and his handsome mistress, the

German-born Duchess of Manchester.* (Hartington was, incidentally, one of the very few members of Prince Edward's inner circle who could dress as shabbily and as sloppily as he chose in public and remain both unrebuked and unrepentant.)

But where the Prince of Wales broke entirely new social ground was that he brought in, together with these scions of feudal England, the leaders of contemporary industrial England. Riches, as well as blue blood, became a passport into society. There was only one condition, as far as the royal host was concerned. The newcomer to the circle had to possess some wit as well as much wealth. Prince Edward would have been reluctant to dine with King Croesus himself had that fabled monarch been a dull fellow. Fortunately, most of the Victorian plutocrats to whom the Prince now opened his doors – whether it was the first wave of Jewish bankers or the later wave of South African diamond millionaires – had a flair for living as well as a talent for making fortunes.

The Prince rounded off his English circle with a third group of friends who were often neither high-born nor rich. These were what we would now call the meritocracy of the kingdom – the working officials of the court; the administrators of England and the Empire; and a whole swarm of others who had risen to the top of the professions or the arts. Normally, these people existed only to serve the Crown in their various capacities. The Prince of Wales now made the best of them its personal friends as well. They would have been called *Beamtenadel*, or the nobility of officialdom, by his German relatives. That somewhat supercilious word conveys precisely how continental courts felt such persons should still be treated. By including them, and the new world of finance and industry, into the royal circle, the Prince of Wales may well have helped a little towards saving England from the fate that was to befall so many of those other courts.

On an afternoon in December 1873, Bishop Magee of Peterborough arrived to stay at Sandringham, invited for the sake of his sparkling Irish wit as much as for his episcopal gaiters. His description of being welcomed in the entrance hall, clothes still crumpled from a long journey, shows what this social jumble of the Prince's looked like in the flesh.

'I find the company pleasant and civil,' Magee wrote, 'but we are a curious mixture. Two Jews, Sir Anthony de Rothschild and his daughter; an ex-Jew, Disraeli; a Roman Catholic, Colonel Higgins; an Italian duchess who is an Englishwoman, brought up a Roman

---

* The famous 'Double-Duchess', so named because after her first husband's death she eventually married her lover, who became the 8th Duke of Devonshire.

Catholic and now turning Protestant; a set of young Lords and a bishop . . . We are all to lunch together in a few minutes . . .'¹

* * *

In London, this liberal outlook of the heir to the throne was perhaps best shown by his activities as a clubman. One of his favourites, significantly, was the young Cosmopolitan Club just off Berkeley Square. This had been founded with the aim of bringing together men of any rank, profession or nationality who had done something really worth while in their lives and who could talk really well about it. The Prince was also a member of most of the more famous clubs, yet his relationship with these strongholds of the old social order was not always a happy one. He quarrelled with the Travellers', for example, because they black-balled a very rich but very self-made man he had put up for membership. And he had a fierce argument with the committee of White's, who rejected his plea to allow smoking in the morning-room. As a result of this argument, the Prince of Wales not only resigned but founded a club of his own, the Marlborough, almost opposite his town house, where he and his friends would be free to do as they chose.

Though they did not entirely succeed in this ambition (their habit of playing shirt-sleeved bowls in the backyard, for example, had to be abandoned after all the neighbours in Pall Mall complained of the nocturnal racket), the Marlborough did become one of the most free-and-easy establishments in clubland. What is more to the point, its first list of four hundred members, each of whom could only be elected with the Prince's approval, gives us the most reliable register ever compiled of his personal friends. Again, what leaps to the eye is the breadth of his contacts and the mixture of his tastes. Boyhood friends like Lord Carrington were, naturally, included, as were fond figures from his undergraduate days, like the 10th Duke of St Albans. But so were men from his own household like Colonel Kingscote and Francis Knollys; English diplomats like Sir Charles Wyke, the Minister at Copenhagen; foreign diplomats like Count Maffei of the Italian Embassy in London; Rothschilds *en masse*, to represent the world of finance; adventurers and explorers like Colonel Valentine Baker and Captain Burnaby; and men like Harry Chaplin to represent the racing world. It was the clubland equivalent of Bishop Magee's tea-party at Sandringham; and, unlike that tea-party, it went on merrily throughout Prince Edward's life.*

* The club flourished until the outbreak of the World War in 1914 and struggled on until after the Second World War, finally closing its doors in 1952.

Mention of Harry Chaplin's name brings us to another important aspect of the Prince of Wales as the leader of English society, his role as a sportsman. He never achieved outstanding skill himself at any game. But the mere fact that he indulged in so many of them meant that he represented the Crown to the nation in a way that his mother never could, and never would. Moreover, sport itself being a natural mixer of classes, this in turn helped to bring the nation a little closer to that otherwise remote crown. As regards the upper layers of society, shooting was a good example of this.

To judge by accounts given by the descendants of sportsmen who often shot next to Prince Edward, he was an uneven performer, and distinctly average when compared with Lord de Grey, Harry Stonor and other great English marksmen of his day. He was, however, engagingly unperturbed by all this. It never occurred to him to boost his tally by allowing the beaters to pile up in front of his stand or grouse-butt heaps of birds that he had not, in fact, shot (almost a standard practice with continental royalty). Nor did he ever choose anything but the most expert company available – men who could knock down fifty pheasant clean in the head with fifty successive cartridges – however much they showed up his own performance. Nor did he mind where he shot, as long as the sport was good and the atmosphere congenial. He was as happy at Hall Barn, Beaconsfield, the estate of the newspaper proprietor Sir Edward Lawson, as at any of the great feudal houses of the realm. His fondness for yachting, and his catholic tastes at Cowes, produced a similar social leavening of the noble with the rich. The equivalent of Lawson afloat was the grocer millionaire Sir Thomas Lipton who, favoured by a bountiful wind from the Prince, literally sailed into high society on the deck of his yachts.

But it was horse-racing rather than yacht-racing which brought the Prince of Wales closest to the nation at large, as well as to its titled and moneyed classes. Not many people in the kingdom could own a race-horse (indeed, the Prince did not start up his own string until 1877); but tens of thousands could attend the race-meetings held up and down the country all the year, while tens of thousands more could bet on the results. The Prince had wretched luck with his horses for the first ten years and enjoyed only mixed fortunes for nearly ten years after that. But a double triumph came in 1896, when Persimmon carried his colours (purple, gold braid, scarlet sleeves and a black velvet cap with gold fringe) to victory in both the Derby and the St Leger. The whole country went wild with excitement. So did the Empire which, from the hill-stations of the Himalayas to the desert outposts of the Sudan, had shared by telegraph in the good news (and, to a modest degree, in the profit). Next to escaping assassination or surviving a serious illness – both of which the Prince of Wales also managed in his time – there is nothing that makes the English monarchy so popular with its subjects as a royal win at the races.

None of this, however, made the heir to the throne any more popular with his mother. Indeed, the discovery that horse-racing was becoming the Prince's favourite outdoor pastime horrified her almost as much as the news that baccarat had replaced dancing as his favourite indoor recreation. To Queen Victoria, still faithful to the stern precepts of her beloved Albert, gambling men and racing men stood in the very ante-chamber of the Devil, only a step or two away from that trap-door which led straight down to eternal fire. No good, surely, could come of her own son keeping such company.

To a limited extent, the Queen proved right, for the 'fast set' of Marlborough House produced at least two acute embarrassments for Prince Edward and the Crown. The first came as early as 1870, when the Prince had to appear briefly as a witness (though not, merciful heavens, as a co-respondent) in the divorce suit filed by Sir Charles Mordaunt against his flighty 21-year-old wife. The second came twenty years later when the future King of England again had to appear in the witness-box, this time for days on end over a libel action arising from a card-cheating scandal at Tranby Croft, a house he had stayed at for the Doncaster races. Horses and gambling games: what a background for the public cross-examination of the heir to the throne! On this occasion, the nation appeared to agree with the Queen's verdict. It was somewhat illogical, in view of the delight that same nation always took in the Prince's triumphs on the turf. But illogical or not, the feeling was there. *The Times* urged the Prince of Wales to sign a solemn pledge never again to play cards for money. Queen Victoria wrote despairingly to her daughter Vicky in Berlin: 'The Monarchy almost is in danger if he is lowered and despised.'[2]

Did the Queen ever realize that, to some degree, she was herself to blame for all this? Prince Edward was a hedonist down to the soles of his royal feet and no leash could have been fashioned strong enough to hold him back entirely from the pursuit of pleasure. Nonetheless, had he been given, earlier in his long existence as Prince of Wales, enough work of the type that really interested him, it is arguable that the pursuit would have been less headlong or, at the very least, less continuous. And, in this connection, it was no use simply piling on his head honorary Presidencies (such as that of the Society of Arts) or Colonelcies (such as that of the 10th Hussars or the Rifle Brigade). It soon became clear that the only affairs of state which fascinated the Prince were foreign affairs, and in this field it was a slow uphill battle to win either recognition or influence with the Queen.

It was not until 1886, for example, that he was given regular access to secret Foreign Office documents (through the handing over of the same golden key that his father, as Prince Consort, had once used to open the special dispatch boxes). Even this precious concession was not made by his mother but by his personal friend and fellow-member of the Turf Club, Lord Rosebery, who happened to be serving a five-month spell as Foreign Secretary at the time. The Queen, though she did not revoke the privilege, was angry that it had been granted behind her back, and did nothing to extend it further. It was an unhappy and inescapable vicious circle. The larger the Prince of Wales loomed in his mother's eyes as an irresponsible playboy, the less work she entrusted to him; and the less he was given to do, the harder he went on playing.

The result can be seen by his calendar for that year of the Tranby Croft scandal.[3] The published social engagements alone (and many more were, of course, unpublished) show that, out of the 365 days, 36 were spent shooting and 53 at race-meetings. Forty of his evenings in London were passed at the opera, or at theatres and dining clubs (these last being entirely private outings). A week was spent at Cowes in August; and three weeks soon after that at the German Spa of Homburg. In the autumn, another three weeks were passed in the Scottish Highlands at Balmoral and, naturally enough, there were repeated trips throughout the year to his own home at Sandringham. Various sundries (attendance at a cricket match, a Horse Show and a Smoking Concert; several visits to picture galleries; and appearances at five weddings) round off the register. Of the sixty-odd lunches and dinners recorded, more than forty were with his family or his personal friends, and usually the latter. Even excluding normal holidays such as Christmas and Easter, there are still more than sixty days left quite unaccounted for, and these, presumably, were devoted entirely to further private pursuits. Only one day of the year shows an official nil return. On 13 May he is listed as ill in bed with influenza.

* * *

To lead this hectic round of pleasures cost an immense amount of money, and money was something of which the Prince was always short. For the first twenty-seven years of his married life, his regular official income never exceeded £115,000 a year, and this sum was only raised by Parliament to £150,000 in 1890 after a long struggle. Yet this was below even the basic annual rent-roll income of most of the leading landowners of the country whose riches, in turn, failed to match the fortunes of the industrial and financial magnates. There were occasional windfalls, like the capital sum of £60,000 granted with the increased income in 1890 and, much more satisfying, the large cash rewards in prizes and breeding fees which his stable began to earn at about that same period. But despite these infusions, the Prince of Wales was nearly always in debt and, especially when abroad, he suffered the double ignominy of being pressed by creditors on the one hand and pestered by money-lenders on the other. On several occasions the Queen, who was quietly accumulating a considerable fortune of her own, helped him out. At other times, the Rothschilds – English, Austrian or French – would come discreetly to the rescue. But this was no way to go on. Some regular and reliable financial safety net was needed. His very first engagement recorded in that diary for 1891 signified, to those in the know, that the Prince had found one. The entry read: 'January 1 – Left Sandringham to shoot with Baron Hirsch at Wrotham Hall, Norfolk.'

Freiherr Maurice von Hirsch auf Gereuth[4] (to give him the full baronial title he had acquired on 2 April 1869) was, of course, anything but an East Anglian squire. He was, in fact, one of the most ruthlessly successful *entrepreneurs*, and totally tragic figures, which the Continent had thrown up that century. His story is remarkable, not only for its own sake but for the way it illustrates one of the most admirable aspects of Prince Edward's character: his unshakable loyalty to his friends and helpers, no matter what it cost him in patience or even embarrassment.

Hirsch, the son of a Jewish banker to the Bavarian court, had made the greatest of his several fortunes out of financing Turkish railways and, by the 1880s, the immense scale of his wealth (which even surpassed that of the Rothschilds) was matched only by the scale of his social ambitions. He became the most lavish spender to be found anywhere in the Habsburg Monarchy; but his problem was that there was hardly one person among the entire 'first society' of that Monarchy who could be persuaded to help him spend his money, let alone offer him their friendship. He was Jewish and he was a *nouveau riche*. That was quite enough to rule him out in the eyes of the fossilized aristocracy of Franz Josef's day. The fact that Hirsch had bought himself a barony to add to his father's plain 'Herr von' only compounded his offence. This was where the future King Edward came in. When the two men first met (in Paris in April 1890), Hirsch undertook to keep the Prince not only afloat but buoyant in financial waters. In return, he was hoping to be launched on to those glittering social waters that he so pined after. If not a formal bargain, it was a tacit understanding, and his royal patron fulfilled his part beyond Hirsch's wildest expectations.

The baron not only found himself invited, by the Prince and through the Prince, to all the most brilliant functions of that London season of 1890; (Hirsch, never the man to do things by halves, had rented a Piccadilly mansion and a Suffolk shoot, as well as that Norfolk country house). His protector even carried the flag back to Vienna for him by trying to establish him socially there in person. On 6 October 1890, when passing through the Austrian capital with a party of shooting friends, the Prince scandalized the Austrian court by coupling Baron Hirsch with the King of Greece as his two guests of honour at a lunch given in the Grand Hotel. Both as Prince of Wales and, later, as King, Edward would constantly 'astound the *bourgeoisie*'. But this was a case of *épater les archeducs*, and one suspects that he thoroughly enjoyed it.

Hirsch, for his part, promptly repaid the compliment by whisking the English party off in a special train to his Hungarian estate at St Johann. Here, an average of ten guns shot no less than a thousand brace of partridge apiece on each of ten successive days, a phenomenal total of some twenty thousand birds. With rueful delight, the Prince of Wales commented: 'This . . . will quite spoil me for any shooting at home.'

For the next six years until his death, Hirsch continued to bask in the Prince's favour* at London seasons, and to pay handsomely for the privilege. Yet his money did not entirely dissolve into mounds of caviare and fountains of champagne. In 1890, at the Prince's instigation, he had purchased a thoroughbred yearling filly, 'La Flèche'. Two years later she carried his colours to victory in three classics – the Thousand Guineas, the Oaks, and the St Leger – and the Cambridgeshire. Thus Baron Hirsch achieved lasting fame, on the English turf at least.

All the outside influence in the world, however, could not make any real impression on his behalf in Vienna where, for example, the doors of the Austrian Jockey Club still remained closed to him, despite these notable racing successes. It was when he realized this that, during the last two or three years of his life, he became a positive nuisance to the Prince, constantly pestering his English patron for fresh favours and introductions in a final attempt to batter down the imperial walls of the Hofburg Palace. Those walls stayed up, however, and Hirsch only battered his head and threw his money at them in vain. He died, a

* Though never in Queen Victoria's, who deeply offended her son by refusing to accept his Bavarian banker friend. On this subject, at least, she was one with the Austrian Archdukes.

sour and bitter man, on 21 April 1896. Whether even the Prince of Wales's forbearance would have lasted had Hirsch lived much longer is questionable. But there is no question that he kept faith with this sad little Midas to the end.

*   *   *

It is easy to portray Prince Edward becoming, despite the occasional public scandal and the perpetual money problem, the unchallenged lion of society. It is harder to give an accurate picture of the Prince of Wales as the family man at home. The image is distorted by most of the contemporary accounts given by courtiers which, though first-hand, are over-discreet at best and plain sycophantic at worst. And the whole domestic scene is anyway overshadowed by his notorious infidelity with a multiple and unbroken skein of mistresses. Not unnaturally, therefore, people have always been more interested in what he was up to when he left his home than what he did while still inside it.

He was, however, a genuinely home-loving man, as so many incurable polygamists are, and he relished his own pipe and slippers at his own fireside as much (or perhaps one should say almost as much) as all those extra-marital boudoirs. If we consider him first as a parent, he was certainly as devoted and conscientious towards his children as his own father had been, yet without any of the Prince Consort's heavy and humourless approach. The five children to survive out of the six* his wife bore him had come rapidly and, as regards the interests of the dynasty, in the right order and mixture. First came two sons, Albert Victor Christian Edward (Prince 'Eddie', later created the Duke of Clarence), who arrived prematurely on 8 January 1864. He was followed on 3 June 1865 by George Frederick Ernest Albert (the Albert seemed inescapable), who was eventually to ascend the throne as King George V. There was a year's pause and then, at yearly intervals, and all born at Marlborough House, came three daughters: Princess Louise, on 20 February 1867; Princess Victoria, on 6 July 1868; and Princess Maud, on 26 November 1869.

They grew up at Sandringham where they became a part of the informal and, at times, almost zany atmosphere of the house. Remembering the horrors of his own childhood, their father saw to it that they had as many toys as books and, as regards the latter, that they concentrated on modern subjects rather than the classics. They roamed the house, as well as the grounds, almost at will, to the astonishment and occasional discomfort of the guests. With the servants and estate

---

* Their last, Alexander John, was born at Sandringham on 6 April 1871 but died the next day.

workers (ordered by their father to address them simply as 'Prince Eddie' or 'Princess Maud' instead of the formal 'Your Royal Highness'), they were on easy, affectionate terms. It was a happy start to life, and a thoroughly suitable one, had the owner of Sandringham been merely a Norfolk squire. Opinions were, however, divided as to whether this was the best way to bring up the children of the next King of England. Their grandmother, Queen Victoria, had severe doubts. 'Ill-bred, ill-trained . . . wild as hawks,' was her verdict on Eddie and George, when aged 8 and 7 respectively. 'Rampaging little girls' was how the three little princesses had been described a year earlier.[5]

What must have troubled both parents was not how those hawks and rampaging little girls behaved in the nursery or the donkey-cart, but how they turned out as young men and women. One cannot escape the feeling that, for the Prince of Wales in particular, his children grew up to be something of a disappointment to him. As regards the girls, it was a simple matter of their looks. All fathers want pretty daughters, and Prince Edward, who was a willing slave to feminine beauty all his life, must have ached for one. What would he not have given to have sired a young woman so ravishing that, when she took his arm on the lawns of Goodwood or Ascot, she would have outshone even his own latest conquest. Instead, his wife had presented him with three daughters to none of whom he would have given a first, let alone a second glance had they passed him in the street. Even in the formally posed and carefully retouched court photographs of the day, the oldest girl, Princess Louise, appears positively plain, with a long, lemon-shaped face and listless eyes. The next one, Victoria, had the same rather unfortunate features and, though the gaze was more lively, it also had something spiteful about it. Only the youngest, Princess Maud, had even the rudiments of her mother's good looks and vivacity. Not surprisingly, she was by far her father's favourite child.

The fate of these three girls was in proportion to their looks and, considering that they were princesses of the greatest Empire on earth, it could not be considered brilliant. Princess Victoria never married at all, and became something of an embittered spinster as a result. The best that the tongue-tied Princess Louise could manage in the way of a husband was the Scottish Earl of Fife, who had to be given a dukedom to make the match look more acceptable. The only one to marry royalty was Princess Maud who, on 22 July 1896, became the bride of her cousin Charles, second son of the then Crown Prince Frederick of Denmark. By an accident of Scandinavian politics twenty years later, Prince Charles became King of a Norway that had dissolved its old union with Sweden, and Princess Maud thus ended up as a Queen. But at the time of the wedding her husband, who was an impecunious naval officer, was not considered much of a catch. And, in any case, her father's dream would have been for all his daughters to have married kings.

Their mother may have borne some slice of blame for the fact that this dream never materialized. Princess Alexandra made hardly any effort to get her daughters married, preferring to keep them cosily around her at home and imagining (naïvely as well as selfishly) that this was what they wanted. But the basic reason was one that the father must have found hardest to face and to bear: they simply were not attractive enough or remarkable enough to do any better than they did.

The two boys, even when taken together, were not much of a compensation. Prince Eddie, in fact, was a calamity for any parent to have to contemplate. Physically, he was almost as unattractive as the two elder sisters. Mentally, he was the dimmest of all the children, so dim and lethargic that his tutor, the Reverend Dalton, had to write him off as incapable of being educated. Morally, he was as dissolute as any of those Hanoverian great-great-uncles. Worse perhaps, for later generations were to indulge in the horrifying speculation that Jack the Ripper, that notorious, never-discovered murderer of London prostitutes in the 1880s, might have been none other than the Duke of Clarence. The mere fact that this fancy could even be floated demonstrates the unwholesome power of the legend he left behind him. It was perhaps a blessing for his parents, and certainly a blessing for the English crown, when this elder son of the Heir-Apparent died at Sandringham of influenza on 14 January 1892 at the age of 28.

That left Prince George, who now took over not only his elder brother's position of second in line of succession but also his betrothed, Princess May of Teck. 'Georgy', as he was known, was the best-looking of all the children; indeed, in an unassuming way, he was quite handsome. Moreover, he was cheerful and conscientious and, especially when compared with that unfortunate brother of his, a paragon of virtue. Perhaps it was this last quality which prevented him from ever being his father's idea of the perfect son. If Eddie had had too much unbridled vice, even for the highly permissive tastes of the Prince of Wales, Georgy was a little too good. As for the boy, he lived in awe and trepidation of this whirlwind of a father. While he was young there was only one place where he felt his equal and that was on the shooting-field (where he was, in fact, by far his superior). Though the two men came closer later on, Prince George as a youth became an extreme example of a mother's boy. Princess Alexandra lavished affection on all her children, but the almost unhealthy devotion she developed for this sole surviving son of hers threatened, at times, to destroy him as an independent personality. Service in the navy made a man out of him, though not in the eyes of his 'darling Motherdear', as he used to call her. Even when he was 25 years old and in command of a warship, she would write sending him 'a great big kiss for your lovely little face'.[6] The truth is that she never wanted him to grow up, just as she never really grew up herself.

With Georgy, as with all her children, Princess Alexandra could easily prolong the romantic idyll of those early married days. But it had soon come to an end with their father. There was, indeed, no stopping the clocks for the restless squire of Sandringham (where, incidentally, he always kept them half an hour fast). Quite when the Prince of Wales launched out on the first of his many extra-marital affairs is not known, but it was certainly very early on in his married life. Already in November 1866, when he was visiting St Petersburg to attend the wedding of his wife's sister Dagmar to the Tsarevich Alexander, there were stories that he was doing more than simply flirt with the beauties of the Russian capital. More lurid tales trickled back from Paris which he visited, again by himself, the following year. By the summer of 1868 (when Princess Victoria was born) his love-affairs at home in England had grown too numerous to hush up. Apart from what were described, in general, as 'his troop of fine ladies', the first of the many actresses in his life was now named in person: Hortense Schneider. From then on, he darted up a continuous trail of forbidden silks and satins, the conquests ranging in age from débutantes picked straight out of presentation balls to mature married matrons of society, and spanning in rank the entire social scale.

By any formal code of behaviour, his conduct can only be condemned. Yet there are three points that can fairly be made, if not in defence, then at least in mitigation. The first concerns opportunity, which is as large a factor as ethics in the morals of most men. Having once invited infidelity, the Prince of Wales was overwhelmed by it. As soon as his susceptibilities became known, most of the ambitious beauties of the day set their sights on him, either for themselves or for their daughters (or, in some cases, for both). Snobbery is a powerful aphrodisiac and many a lady in society (to say nothing of those outside it) considered it preferable to be loved by the heir to the throne than to be snubbed by him. Prince Edward needed to be only an ordinary mortal sinner to have started down the philanderer's path. But, given the way that path was smoothed, swept and strewn with roses for him, he would have needed to have been something of a saint to turn back.

The second point concerns his relations with his much-tried wife. Even after all her six children had been born, she remained, in her outward appearance, much the same attractive woman who had stood by his side in Windsor chapel. If there was, by now, a hint of neurotic tautness in that long, dark face, she had kept her slim figure and a waist that was the joy of her dressmaker and the envy of other women.

But she was no longer as mobile nor as gay as that bride of 1863. A bout of rheumatic fever in 1866 had left her with a stiff knee which hampered her in everything from skating on Sandringham ponds to dancing in London ballrooms. Moreover, also partly as a result of that illness, she was becoming more and more hard of hearing, and thus drifting steadily towards that walled-in world of the deaf which shut her off from much of the boisterous and wide-open world of her husband's social round. And so, as well as the waning of his physical desire for her came a fading of ordinary human contacts. He always met this with great kindness and forbearance, the same qualities he brought to bear over her appalling unpunctuality. (A minor defect among ordinary mortals, this was a very serious matter for royalty.)

For her part (and it was a much more difficult one) she responded by treating his amorous escapades as though they were the pranks of some uncontrollable schoolboy. Indeed, she once described him as 'my naughty little man'. There is much more tenderness than bitterness in that phrase and it shows the devotion he could inspire as well as the love she could give. The warm human qualities of both partners thus kept a marriage afloat that otherwise would have grounded fast, with a crunch for all Europe to hear.

That same human warmth – and here we come to the final point – lights up the Prince's own love-affairs, or at least the serious ones. Whenever a woman became his mistress over a number of years, she became also his friend. She not only lived with him as such but also parted from him as such. For the most part, these were the liaisons that even his wife was prepared to acknowledge because she realized that an element of true companionship was embedded in all the passion. A good illustration of all this, and a particularly radiant one, was the Prince's long attachment to the famous Lily Langtry.

Mrs Edward Langtry, a penniless unknown from the Channel Islands,* arrived in London early in 1877 and soon had all female tongues wagging and all male heads turning. What turned the heads was a classical profile on top of a marble-white neck and shoulders,

---

* Her nickname of the 'Jersey Lily' derived half from her birthplace and half from a painting by Millais, which depicted her looking like the beautiful white flower she held in her hands.

giving the impression that some Greek goddess had landed in the capital. What wagged the tongues was the zestful way in which the newcomer promptly used these charms to embark on a spectacular career as a courtesan and an actress. If there was a betting certainty in London that spring, it was that the paths of Mrs Langtry and the Prince of Wales would soon cross and join. This duly happened at a supper-party on 27 May, with the anticipated result. Lily Langtry became the Prince's mistress, and though each eventually shared his or her favours with others, the relationship lasted for nearly thirteen years. She also became his first official mistress, that is, openly recognized as such and openly invited as such (even by a sensibly tolerant Princess Alexandra to Marlborough House itself).

Not unnaturally, in view of Lily Langtry's stunning good looks, cheerfully lax morals and lack of any social background, she has always been regarded as the purely physical passion of Prince Edward's middle life. With someone who was 'not quite a lady' the heir to the throne could surely share only his bed and little else. Yet the letters he wrote to her over the years, both during and after their liaison, show that even here, affection, friendship and loyalty developed on the Prince's side alongside the physical bond.

An endearing feature of these hitherto unpublished letters is that so far from exercising his normal prerogative of sending them through the mail franked only with the royal cypher, they all have halfpenny stamps stuck on them (ending up with those bearing his own head), as though the writer were an ordinary member of the public slipping something in the pillar-box on the corner.

Their contents are just as unaffected. When the two of them are parted, he seems to think of her most fondly when he himself is at his happiest – dispatching a brace of pheasant to her, for example, at the end of a good day's shooting, or in his cabin on the *Britannia* or the *Osborne* at Cowes, especially when the weather has been as splendid as the racing. There is usually little more than ordinary regatta news to give her – the names of new socialites with yachts there; who gives the most brilliant parties, and so on. But in listing the 'belles' of the Cowes season whom he is constantly meeting, he is at pains to assure her that, rather to his own surprise, he is not flirting with any of them.

By the summer of 1885, his 'fair Lily's' success as an actress was increasing not only the frequency but also the length of their separations, as she departed for more and more tours, first in England and then abroad. But he takes this all philosophically. Indeed, even in the first flush of their romance, he seems quite prepared to put her career before his own pleasure.

The Prince of Wales and Princess Alexandra with their first child later Duke of Clarence.

Above: Edward and his family. *L. to r.* the Duke of Clarence, Princess Maud, Princess Alexandra, Princess Louise and the Prince of Wales, *seated* Prince George and Princess Victoria.

Above: The Veleta – at an informal house party in Scotland.

Below: The Royal house party at Ascot, 1896.

'Cher Luis' – The Marquis de Soveral fences and strikes attitudes for Princess Alexandra's camera.

A letter written on 5 September of that year while on a visit to the Swedish royal family at Stockholm, is all about this, and her own family news:

'. . . I am glad to hear you are in harness again and most sincerely wish you all possible success in yr tour though I fear you have hard work before you. I am very glad to have the list of Towns in which you play. I hope also that yr Brother will obtain the Margate Recordership wh would be a great thing for him . . .

'Since the 2nd I am the King's guest. I told him I had heard from you and he particularly begged to be remembered to you and wish you success in your Profession . . .'[7]

This same concern for her acting career and for her own and her family's welfare is echoed in most of the letters of the period. On 25 November 1885, writing after 'a heavy day's shooting' at Downham Market (and apologizing for his unsteady hand), he tells her that, in his view, the Irish Press was 'so unkind' in its notices of her Dublin performances. He also enquires whether her sister-in-law had 'inherited anything by Ld Ranelagh's death' (and, a fortnight later, writes again to say how sorry he is that she hasn't).

The following month, January of 1886, shows him absorbed in her new London stage productions as though he were her manager. It also shows him in his characteristic role of helping his friends, male or female, to the utmost.

Thus, on 19 January:

'. . . I shall (D.V.) be able to go to your performance on Thursday week and I count upon *you* to reserve the box for me.

'I should much have liked to see the Dress Rehearsal as I might have given you perhaps a few hints. Will it be on Monday, Tuesday or Wednesday next week? I am anxious to know on account of my evng engagements – or is it in the day-time?'

A week later, he writes to assure her excitedly that he hopes to be in his box 'sharp at 8' on the opening night and that he has meanwhile been busy filling the theatre with the right people for her:

'I am so glad that so many friends of ours have taken Boxes. I begged Fife today to take a Box, wh he said he would.'

Then, almost shyly, he suggests a day and time for their next meeting. Everything must have gone off well for after the first performance he writes to her late on the evening of 26 January from the Marlborough Club:

'Just 2 lines to tell you again what a success I thought your piece was. You have certainly acted better tonight than I have ever seen you and I feel sure that in a week's time you will act *still* better . . .'

He seems always ready to help her friends and relatives, of either sex. An undated letter written in the summer of 1886 promises her, for example, the 'Ascot Enclosure Ticket for Mr S.' which she had asked him for. The season was evidently getting into full swing, for he adds, with an almost audible sigh: 'When shall I ever see you again? You are so busy! and so am I!'

That winter, Lily Langtry left on another of her long American tours. The Prince took the separation philosophically ('Perhaps you are right to "make hay while the sun shines" '); but, for the first time in the correspondence, one feels that the ocean is not the only thing that divides them. The famous actress had evidently been quoting newspaper gossip to him about a certain 'Mrs P.', and she earns a sharp rebuke for it in a letter dated 11 December 1886.

The Prince was quite convinced that all the allegations about the indiscreet behaviour of the lady in question, who was clearly well known to him, were both unjust and unfounded. He was equally emphatic about the general unreliability of press reports when they purported to reveal what was going on in society.

On 3 February of the following year he sends her more reprimands about newspaper stories and warns her (though whether this was connected with the Press is not clear) that the tales she had heard about Lady Brooke were quite untrue. Clearly, he was determined to defend other women s reputations as well as Lily's.

The irony about that last rebuke is that it was none other than Daisy Brooke (later Countess of Warwick) who, in five years' time, was destined to replace Mrs Langtry and become the second of the Prince's official mistresses. Her spell lasted from 1891 to 1898, when their ways most amicably parted – hers to embrace radical Socialism and his to embrace the last and greatest love of his life. But the point to note is that throughout the nineties, when the Jersey Lily had become a faded and overblown rose, one and then two romances behind in the Prince's forward march, he continued to correspond fondly with her and to show the same concern for her welfare.

There was, for example, the matter of her daughter Jeanne, whose photograph the Prince had specially asked for when he was writing her those stern letters to America. By 1899, Jeanne was grown up and Lily was clearly determined that the girl would not have to use the same side door into society that she had used herself. In March of that year she wrote to the Prince of Wales, who was wintering in Cannes, about it. First he sent her a holding reply saying he was pondering the matter. But the master of protocol soon had the answer. He thought it could be solved by one of Lily's relatives being formally launched into court society and then bringing Jeanne in after her. 'There seems to me nothing simpler than Mrs H. L. being presented at a Drawing-Room and in her turn presenting her cousin, Miss J. L.' The only question was, which illustrious hostess would oblige?

A second letter to Lily, written from Cannes on 25 March 1899, shows how happily he had solved that problem too for her:

'Many thanks for your kind letter. I am so glad that Lady de Grey* has been so nice and sympathetic about Jeanne. I met her twice at dinner before leaving England and begged her to go and see you, so as to give you advice about yr girl going out into society – and am so glad she did so. All you tell me seems very satisfactory and the presentation by Mrs H. Langtry at the Drawing-Room, "C'est le premier pas qui coute!" . . .

Hoping to see you soon after my return home.'

That this kindly letter also proved almost most effective is shown by a note which his son, Prince George, wrote to Lily Langtry on 1 July of the same year. He encloses with it the photograph of himself which he had promised to send and asks, in return, not only for her own photograph but also 'for one of your daughter, whose acquaintance I was so pleased to make the other day at Newmarket'. And he ends by hoping that 'the stuff I gave you for your hay fever will do it good'.

The Jersey Lily's daughter had been well and truly launched into society, thanks to 'A. E.'s' efforts. And the Jersey Lily herself appears to have ended up almost as one of the royal family circle.

* * *

Mrs George Keppel was, of course, that last and greatest love which eclipsed Lily Langtry, Daisy Brooke and all other women in Edward's life – both as Prince of Wales and, later, as King. Indeed, the story of her reign over him goes properly with that of his reign over England, which it completely spanned. Yet she needs introducing here, if only because it was just before the turn of the century that she first entered his life.

The exact point is, not surprisingly, a little blurred. According to one account, he dined with her for the first time when Prince of Wales on 27 February 1898, after which social encounter 'an understanding . . .

* Gladys, Countess de Grey, later Marchioness of Ripon.

arose almost overnight'. In another version the Prince first clapped eyes on her when inspecting the Norfolk Yeomanry (in which her husband was an officer) later the same year, and finally snatched her away from all other competitors on the lawns of Sandown Park Races a few weeks after that.

It is not hard to visualize what had attracted him. She was, at this time, 29 years of age, old enough and intelligent enough to be a companion as well as a mistress. Physically, she had the advantage of being, like him, on the short side, yet with a beauty that was particularly striking because it fell out of the normal pattern. Mrs Keppel's face and figure had more about them of the sensuous Latin woman than of the fair and slender English rose, yet she was as much a native as that flower itself. Moreover, she had the immense advantages of being, unlike Daisy Brooke, the soul of discretion and, unlike Lily Langtry, very much a lady.

Alice Frederica Keppel was the youngest daughter of a sailor, Admiral Sir William Edmonstone, who came from a long line of Scottish baronets and who had died ten years before her first meeting with the future King. In 1891, three years after her father's death, she had married the Hon. George Keppel. He was handsome and well-born (his father was the 7th Earl of Albemarle) even if, being a third son, he was not rich by any standards, and positively hard up by the standards of the Edwardian big spenders.

If, on top of all these qualities of birth, character and appearance, one had to name the things about Alice Keppel that captivated the Prince of Wales the most, these would probably be her natural gaiety and her tremendous zest for life. An unfamiliar story told about her when she was an old woman illustrates this better than most of the familiar anecdotes told about her in her prime. She lived on until just after the Second World War, a white-haired vision of vanished Edwardian elegance which had survived into the post-Hitler era. On one of her last birthdays, when she was approaching 80, she was asked how she regarded the prospect. With the laugh that had captivated an heir to the throne nearly fifty years before, she replied: 'Oh, eighty is such a *dull* age! Now ninety, on the other hand, is rather chic. So I shall start counting from ninety.'

It was this spirit of saying 'yes' to life, and living every moment of it, that she had shared with her royal lover. He himself was 57 when he first met her, a portly man with a closely cropped grey beard and a head from which much of the natural covering had receded. But if he was already gorged by life's pleasures, he was not yet satiated by them. And now, he had found the woman who was to help him make the evening of his life in every way the most radiant and rewarding time of all.

* * *

Finally, the man who, outside the Prince's immediate family, came, together with Alice Keppel, to stand closer to his affections and his confidence than anyone in the kingdom. This was the Portuguese nobleman, diplomatist, courtier and ladies' man *par excellence*, the Marquis Luis Augusto Pinto de Soveral, known to two generations of Europeans as the 'Blue Monkey'. This genial figure, with his curled black moustache, black imperial beard, heavy black eyebrows – all set off against the white flower in his buttonhole and the white kid gloves in his hand – had about him an aspect which was dandified but (with the swarthy, almost simian virility which had given him that nickname) also manly. He was a remarkable figure in his own right as well as for the unique position he was eventually to hold with the British crown. For if his royal friend became Europe's uncle, Soveral became its darling. Of all the stars that twinkled in the Edwardian firmament, his twinkled the brightest.

This was remarkable in that, though of an old Portuguese family, he was not born one of the grandees of Iberia. His father was, in fact, a Visconde or Viscount, and Luis was only to be created a Marquis by the King of Portugal in 1900, as a reward for his personal and political services. Neither did he possess any huge estates, nor inherit or accumulate any great fortune. Indeed, it is clear that he did not always find it easy to live on the sumptuous private scale required of him. This money problem could have been one reason why he never married, though the bewildering profusion of women who floated in and out of his life is a more likely explanation.

It was the qualities of the man himself, therefore, that were mainly responsible for his phenomenal success. He was a great *raconteur* and conversationalist in an age that prized good conversation and had time for it. His wit became a household word in Edwardian society, yet it was never barbed. Brilliant people are often rude. Discreet people are often dull. Soveral's combination of brilliance and discretion was the first of his many rare qualities. Another was the ability – one that is difficult to analyse but easy to recognize – of being both a man's man and a woman's man. The ladies never begrudged him his masculine club evenings. His men friends never seemed to be jealous (even if they could not help being envious) of his phenomenal success with the ladies. With the exception of a few politically inspired attacks, not a harsh word is recorded against him. Nor was he ever tactless or spiteful or sarcastic about anyone in return. Even the countless husbands he cuckolded seem to have been prepared to forgive him everything for such gentleness.

This combination of qualities immediately appealed to the Prince of Wales when they first met in Berlin. When Soveral was transferred to London in 1884 (where he remained, with one brief interruption, for the next twenty-five years), the two men gradually became inseparable. The 'Blue Monkey', in fact, was the one true *ami de coeur* of the Prince's life. One has the feeling, with all his other men friends, that, however close they stood to him, a thin glass wall still separated them from establishing a completely natural and human relationship. Only Soveral smashed that glass wall, because only Soveral had lived inside the Prince's private world. His other friends knew all about his love-affairs and often helped admirably with some of the arrangements. But Soveral had been part of that life, ever since the days when, as comparatively young bloods in Berlin, they had patronized together those notorious all-night 'love-orgies' arranged by the officers of the Prussian Garde du Corps. Then, and in countless later forays, whether launched from the Hotel Bristol in Paris or from the drawing-rooms of the great houses of England, it was only Soveral who actually shared some of the adventures as well as all of the secrets. He was the one man with whom the Prince came to feel, in that expressive German phrase, that he could 'go out and steal horses'.

A condition of this relationship was that Soveral, as well as never feeling self-conscious in royal company, should also never be obsequious. This was made very plain early on in their friendship. At a London dinner-party the Prince of Wales once teased Soveral about a Portuguese colonial hero called Serpa Pinto, who was then challenging England's might with a tiny band of soldiers in southern Africa. When the chaffing got too strong, Soveral called out across the table:

'Sir, you may make as many jokes about me as you please, but, I beg of you, leave my country alone!'[8]

That was the end of the teasing. The future King of England raised his glass to his friend and calmed him down with a few words spoken in heavy Berlin dialect that only they could understand. Soveral had made his point once and for all. The respect he felt for monarchy was too deep to degenerate into servility, and it commanded respect in return.

Before Soveral had finished his first long spell in London (as Portuguese Chargé d'Affaires) he was already treated almost as a member of the Prince of Wales's family as well as a special intimate of the

Prince himself. On Christmas Day 1894, for example, the Prince, sending him the season's greetings in a telegram from Sandringham, added: 'Which day may we hope to see you here? Any day that suits you will be convenient.'[9] It was more a question of 'dropping in' than following a royal command.

When, the following year, Soveral was appointed Foreign Minister of Portugal, all his friends were torn between pleasure at his promotion and sorrow at losing him. Writing to Soveral on 13 October 1895, the Prince of Wales first congratulated him on the appointment but then added: 'I deeply regret that it obliges you to leave England where you will indeed be missed by your many friends and admirers amongst whom I wish to be counted.' The Prince's letter ends by hoping that Soveral's post will not be a permanent one, so that he can one day return to the Legation off Portman Square; and in another letter sent the following month from Sandringham to the new Foreign Minister in Lisbon, the Prince of Wales tells him: 'Everyone is asking – when is Soveral coming back?'

Soveral did come back, but not before he had rendered England one invaluable service. In January of 1896, when relations between England and Germany were near breaking-point over the mounting crisis between the English and the Boers in southern Africa, Soveral nipped all ideas of German military intervention in the bud by announcing flatly that not one German soldier would be allowed to land at Portuguese Lorenzo Marques, the only sea-base from which a force from German East Africa could march inland. Soveral's first thought in this was to help his English friends, but he may also have prevented a European conflict in the process.

It was very much as the conquering hero, therefore, as well as the sorely missed friend, that in 1897 Soveral returned to his old London haunts. (One of these had gone out of business while he had been away, as the Prince of Wales had already informed him in a telegram to Lisbon: 'Delighted to hear that you are returning here as Minister to England but alas "Amphytrion"* is closed.') Princess Alexandra seems to have been equally happy to see this special friend of her husband's again. A night or two after he had reappeared in London she sent him the following message through her Lady-in-Waiting, Charlotte Knollys:

'The Princess hopes if you have nothing better to do that you will look into her Box at the Opera this evening. Welcome back again, Sir Luis!'

* A favourite London evening haunt of the Prince's.

That gay message was the forerunner of something else. Soveral, now gracing once again a London he was not to leave for the rest of his career (and for most of the rest of his life), became, over the next few years, the great *confidant* of the future Queen of England as well as the *alter ego* of its future King. And when, finally, he also won the friendship of Alice Keppel, the great mistress of that future King, the most extraordinary and exalted quartet to be found anywhere in Edwardian Europe was complete.

PRINCE OF EUROPE

The long restless wait on the steps of the throne had a European, as well as an English, dimension. In that pursuit of pleasure which the Prince of Wales had substituted for royal power, his eyes and his footsteps turned naturally towards the Continent. Above all, they turned towards France where, as a 13-year-old boy, he had captured French society and been even more captivated by it. On both sides, first impressions were only confirmed as time went on.

Indeed, it is hard to see how, without France, Prince Edward could have survived all those decades in the Windsor ante-chamber; or, at least, have survived them, as he did, quite without bitterness. During the second half of the nineteenth century, France in general (and Paris in particular) formed a matchless arena for his struggle against boredom and frustration. To continue for a moment the saga of his love-affairs, it was here that he found some of the loveliest and most accessible women of the Continent waiting to fall into his arms. What is more, he found also a climate of calculated tolerance in sexual matters. This was best expressed by French society's acceptance of the *maîtresse* as a figure in her own right, a philosophy he himself had copied in England with the elevation of Lily Langtry to that position.

Ironically, it was France which also provided one of the very few examples we know of a society woman flatly refusing to share her bed with him, though the refusal was conveyed in a charmingly French way. The story was eventually told by the 101-year-old Marquise d'Harcourt to Prince Edward's own niece, Princess Marie Louise, who recorded it, without mentioning the lady's name, in her own memoirs.[1] It appears that, while on one of his many visits to Paris, the Prince of Wales was, as usual, the guest of honour at a great ball. As usual, he made advances to the prettiest girl to catch his eye and who, like himself, had been invited to stay overnight at the house. Again according to pattern, the girl murmured her flattered acceptance, suggesting that she should identify her bedroom for him by placing a rose outside the door.

The rest of the episode was far from usual. When all was quiet in the early hours, the Prince duly prowled the upstairs corridors and duly found the promised token. But when, after a quiet tap on the door, he was bidden to enter, he found no sign of his noble lady in the room. Instead, it was one of the kitchenmaids who rose up from the pillow to greet him. We are not told whether she proved a good substitute, at least in her looks, and whether the Prince stayed or fled.

Whatever else it was that this prince of pleasure sought, Paris always seemed to provide the answers – if not the only answers available, then certainly the most congenial and convenient. The *gourmet* (and the *gourmand*) in him found the best food and wine in the world, combined with those elaborate menus of which Alexandre Dumas's *Dictionnaire de la Cuisine* gives us a contemporary index. The lover of 'daring' plays, roguish but not lewd, found offerings enough in the repertoire of the Théâtre Français. The man who was only really fond of music that he could hum was well suited by the capital of Jacques Offenbach. (It was also, of course, the home of other composers who were greater musicians if lesser entertainers; but no matter.) The Prince, who had become, despite his portly frame, the arbiter of elegance, felt at home in the city of elegance.

Nor did he have to forego too many of the joys of English life to savour all this. Longchamps and Auteuil were the only other race-courses in Europe whose autumn meetings compared in all-round brilliance with the Ascots and the Goodwoods he presided over every summer in England. And if the pheasant shooting provided at home by hosts such as Lord Suffield at Gunton Hall or the Duke of Devonshire at Chatsworth was superb, a weekend's sport with the Duc d'Aumale at Chantilly or the Duc de Bisaccia at Esclimont was not to be sneezed at. Apart from London clubs, the Cowes yachting and the Scottish moors, France provided most of what he enjoyed in the English social round while sparing him everything he disliked about it. And, if he were missing home comforts, then Lily Langtry or, later, Alice Keppel could usually be coaxed over from England and installed at the Hotel Vendôme. This was only a few yards from the old Hotel Bristol, where the Prince, in his travelling guise of 'Baron Renfrew', would be staying with just one *aide*.

There was something else too, the attraction, what one can only call the intellectual flavour of French life. There is rather a mystery about this, for the Prince of Wales was no intellectual and (thanks to the counter-productive efforts of Prince Albert and Baron Stockmar) he was not even widely read. Yet all his life he enjoyed the brilliance of Parisian conversation almost as much as he enjoyed the sensuality of Parisian life. Perhaps the Oscar Wildes of Paris were discreetly kept at a distance from him, or told to control their verbal fireworks when they did join his table. Perhaps his own love of wit, allied to his position, his almost faultless French, and his incomparable fund of European gossip, enabled him, when taken altogether, to hold his own in the most scintillating company.

Above and beyond all this, however, was the fact that, whereas in Victorian London clever talk centred largely around men's clubs, in Proustian Paris it centred largely around women's *salons*. The Prince could enter into the spirit of any entertainment arranged for him by the Princesse de Sagan, the Comtesse de Pourtalès, or the Baronne Alphonse de Rothschild (three of his regular Paris hostesses) if only because they were women and, in the case of the first two, beautiful. Whatever the reasons, the empathy which grew up over the years between the Prince of Wales and France was a total one, enveloping his body, mind and spirit. It was to have as strong an influence on his political thinking as, in the opposite sense, did all that gradually accumulated distaste for the Prussia of his German relatives, with its puritanical, military pipe-clay capital.

The fortunate thing, as regards France, was that, apart from one or two passing phases, his personal passion for the country could run smoothly on, parallel with his political convictions, for more than forty years. The country to which he was most devoted and where he felt most at home happened to be the mortal enemy of Prussia, the country he came most to dislike and where, despite all the blood links, he felt least at ease. The equation had a lethal balance about it.

It came into play for the first time as early as 1866, when the Prince of Wales was only 24 years old. This was the summer of a fratricidal war between Austria and Prussia, the two great German-speaking powers of the Continent, for the mastery of central Europe. On 6 June, ten days before the war had even broken out, he told the French Ambassador in London, the Prince de la Tour d'Auvergne, that although his sister and brother-in-law were 'Prussian', he was praying for an Austrian victory. Moreover, the best way to contain Prussian militarism was for France and England to join hands in an alliance.[2] When the Prince spoke those words, the 5th Marquess of Lansdowne, who, as Foreign Secretary early in the following century, was to regard himself as being almost the English inventor of the Entente, was a political unknown barely out of his teens.

Only one cloud troubled this early Francophile enthusiasm of Prince Edward's. It eventually rolled on, but it was very dark while it lasted. This was the shadow of French Republicanism. When, in 1870, the French liquidated the Third Empire of Louis Napoleon and installed a President in the Elysée Palace, they set their most ardent English admirer a real poser. His devotion to the beautiful Empress Eugénie could never be dimmed, and when, in September 1870, she fled to England ahead of her husband, the Prince of Wales, without consulting either his mother or the Cabinet, impulsively offered her a house to live in.* The Queen and her advisers found his action distinctly inconvenient, for England, bowing to the inevitable, was already preparing to recognize the new Republic.

That decision was all very well for a government which had a head but not a heart. But it was quite another matter for the Prince of Wales, who was a mixture of head and heart, especially where France was concerned. His head told him that the new regime in Paris had removed one of Europe's monarchies from the scene. Self-proclaimed or not, Louis Napoleon had sat on a royal throne. To topple his crown was to tilt at them all. Had not the radical young mayor of Birmingham, Joseph Chamberlain, just declared in a public speech that he would be neither horrified nor surprised if a Republic were to be set up one day in England? While it is unlikely that such a prospect of being overthrown ever seriously entered Queen Victoria's head, her son, whose inheritance lay in a distant and more uncertain future, may well have felt a pang of fear. Yet, on the other hand, Paris was still Paris, whoever received his mother's ambassadors there, and whoever greeted him in the name of France when he stepped off the boat-train from Calais.

Throughout his life, Edward never quite lost a feeling of condescension towards these Republican rulers of France. In matters of style and protocol, for example, they remained amateurs in his eyes to the end. Indeed, during the first years of the Republic, he could be quite brutal about it. 'I don't want the Princess to be seen with that cook,' he was said to have told a French friend when he and his wife were planning a visit to the Paris races in 1878. The 'cook' was the wife of the then President of the Republic, M. Grévy, and the Prince, with a rare disregard for etiquette, made every effort to avoid their box at the Auteuil racecourse.

But eventually he mellowed. The Republican scare soon died down, at least in England, and the Prince himself was an involuntary factor in this. In November of 1871 he was smitten with typhoid fever after a house-party with the Earl and Countess of Londesborough, whose drains were evidently not up to their hospitality. That same disease which, exactly ten years before, had destroyed the Prince Consort's life, proved the making of his son. By Christmas, when the Prince of Wales was out of danger, a tidal wave of public rejoicing had engulfed the Palace, carrying up the crown to a crest of popular affection it had not

---

* Chiswick House, which belonged to the Duke of Devonshire and had been loaned by him to the Prince

known for decades. The thanksgiving service at St Paul's Cathedral, attended by the recluse Queen herself, was a national hymn to monarchy. Not one radical squeak could be heard. With these sweet strains in his ears, augmented by an appropriate offering from the Poet Laureate, the invalid prince, 'pale as yet, and fever worn' (in Alfred Tennyson's words), departed for a convalescent tour on the Continent. There was no need to fear Republicanism now, and the Prince's tour could happily begin and end in his beloved Paris.

One suspects, in fact, that Bertie would have found something to say for a Paris of the *Communards*, provided the ladies were left their elegance, the wine-cellars their claret, and the city its gaiety. These bourgeois Republicans of 1871 were prepared to do all that, and more. Indeed, under them, a tacit separation of power from privilege soon developed. The politicians ran the country but were not admitted to society. The aristocrats reigned, supreme and unmolested, over their own *beau monde*, and simply ignored the state. It was not long before the Prince's friends reconciled him to this equitable state of affairs. Men of impeccable pedigree, such as the Marquis de Lau, or General Gallifet, persuaded him not only that these Republicans were reasonable people but, more important, that they had come to stay.

Equally telling from the Prince's point of view, they proved, on the whole, to be as fiercely anti-Prussian as any French monarchist. Leon Gambetta, for example, the firebrand who dominated the political scene for the first ten years of the Republic's life, had a favourite motto which might have come straight from Prince Edward's innermost thoughts: *Le Prussianisme, voilà l'ennemi.* Moreover, Gambetta had all the verve which the Prince savoured in any Frenchman. The squat, dishevelled French orator and the plump, immaculately groomed English prince must have made an odd couple. But the attraction of extremes, added to their common political philosophy, drew them ever closer together and they had many an informal meeting on the Prince's visits to Paris from 1879 onwards. The Prince put these occasions to good use. As Gambetta wrote of his royal English friend:

'It is no waste of time to talk with him even over a merry supper at the Café Anglais. He loves France both in a gay and a serious sense, and his dream of the future is an *entente* with us.'[3]

When the Prince wanted to talk seriously with Gambetta, and in a setting more discreet than the Café Anglais, he would ask one or other of his trusted Paris friends to arrange a meeting in their homes. The diary of the Marquis Henri-Charles de Breteuil,* who was probably the

* I am indebted to his grandson, the present Marquis de Breteuil, for these extracts.

closest of all those friends, describes just such a private luncheon-party he organized at forty-eight hours' notice on 12 March 1881 at the Prince's request. There were only five men present apart from the host: the Prince of Wales with two equerries, Lord Dupplice, and Gambetta himself, who had been asked by the Prince to name 'any day and hour' that suited him, and assured that the occasion would be kept quite secret.

Gambetta arrived, as he was bidden, on the stroke of midday, and Breteuil gives a vivid if somewhat disdainful description of his entrance: 'One had to admit that this short, fat man, with his red shining face, his Cyclops eye, his long hair and his heavy, vulgar walk, seemed to spread himself across the elegant floor of our drawing-room like an oil-stain on a piece of silk.'

After a 'bon shake-hand' from the Prince, however, and an excellent meal, Gambetta soon launched out on to a stream of anecdotes and diatribes against his political enemies which followed one another in such brilliant and breathless succession that everyone, as usual, promptly forgot all about his appearance. As regards the European scene, Gambetta's principal complaint was the spinelessness of French foreign policy and the fact that, for the past ten years, France had 'only done what Monsieur Bismarck wanted'. The Prince, needless to say, did not discourage this talk. Indeed, he advised Gambetta of one step that France should take straight away to improve her standing abroad. That was to replace the then Ambassador in London, Monsieur Challemel-Lacour, 'who lived with his cook and was esteemed by no one'. Gambetta (who was at that time President of the National Assembly) promised to make the change 'the very day he formed a government'. The Prince left after three hours of good talk and hospitality, highly satisfied with the event.

A trip that the Prince made to Paris in the spring of 1881, to urge the merits of a new Anglo-French commercial treaty on a dubious French Government, showed that he was ready to serve the cause of that *entente* with more than merry suppers. By this time, the Prince of Wales seems to have grown quite content with the new order of things in France. Indeed, in one respect, they suited him ideally. He was about the only person, and certainly the only distinguished foreigner, who had managed to keep a foothold in every social and political camp in Paris at the same time. In the autumn of 1878 he may have cut the wife of the new French President on a private occasion; yet earlier that year he had formally proposed the health of that President's predecessor, Marshal MacMahon, on a public occasion. This was at the opening of the great Paris Exhibition in May of 1878, and the Prince of Wales had already made a diplomatic event of it by his presence alone. In his capacity as organizer of the British section of the Exhibition, he was the only member of a major European royal house to attend.

The speech with which he followed up his toast showed that it was France, and above all Anglo-French friendship, that he had come to honour in the Republic's name. Speaking partly in English and partly in French, he again floated the banner of this friendship and put his personal monogram on it. The prominent part he had resolved to play in organizing the Exhibition was, he told his audience, 'the best way of showing sympathy for the French people to whom I owe so much'. Yet these formal honours paid to the French Republic did not prevent him from cultivating the regimes it had displaced. That same summer, he visited the town houses and country castles of Royalists and Bonapartists alike. He was also at home with the industrialists and the Jewish bankers of the Republic, as he was with their counterparts in England. He was, in fact, friends with everybody in this Parisian vortex, yet, apart from the ultra-nationalists who still hated the English for burning Joan of Arc, he seems to have had no enemies.

*   *   *

With the two ancient empires of Europe, Tsarist Russia and the eleven-nation Habsburg Monarchy, the Prince's contacts were, by contrast, much more intermittent. Russia, for example, he only visited three times during all his travels as Prince of Wales. On each occasion, family reunions provided the pretext. The first such occasion was that visit of October 1866 (which had produced all the rumours of love-affairs with Russian beauties) to see his sister-in-law married to the future Tsar, Alexander III.

However, it is only fair to say that, whatever the Prince of Wales got up to when he reached St Petersburg, he had set out for the Russian capital with more weighty matters than casual romances on his mind. To begin with, he was impelled by strong curiosity to have a look for himself at this mysterious realm of the Romanovs, which seemed to menace the British Empire at so many points of the globe – through its Black Sea outlet to the Mediterranean, in Persia and, above all, along the enormous Himalayan frontier with India. 'It would interest me beyond anything to see Russia,' he had written to his mother on 14 October 1866, when pleading with the Queen to allow him to go in person to the wedding.

Much more important for the long-term future, he was already turning over in his young mind whether this historic enmity between

71

England and Russia was as immutable as the Queen (and most of her Ministers) believed. Was there *no* way of turning the two great rivals into friends, especially now, when their two courts would be closely linked by marriage? The day before addressing that appeal to his mother, the 24-year-old Prince had written another and much more remarkable letter to the Prime Minister of the day, Lord Palmerston. It included a phrase that might have been taken straight from the Prince's private political programme for France.

'I should be only too happy to be the means in any way of promoting the *entente cordiale* between Russia and our own country . . . I am a very good traveller so that I should not at all mind the length of the journey . . .'4

In fact, beyond the flirtations at endless St Petersburg balls, a brief visit to Moscow, a military review and a wolf-hunt (in addition, of course, to the wedding itself, held in the Winter Palace on 9 November), nothing of note happened during the Prince's stay. But that had been no fault of his, and he pursued this personal campaign for an Anglo-Russian *rapprochement* whenever family gatherings gave him the chance.

The next opportunity came on 13 March 1881. It was sombre as well as sudden – the assassination of Alexander II, blown to pieces in broad daylight on the streets of his capital. This time, the Prince of Wales did not so much plead as insist that both he and Princess Alexandra should represent the Queen at the murdered ruler's funeral and at the inauguration of Alexander III as his successor. The new Tsar of all the Russias was now, after all, the brother-in-law of the Prince of Wales, and it was a situation from which the Prince was determined to make the maximum capital. But how to go about it? A St Petersburg in mourning, with all its palaces heavily guarded against further anarchist bombs, was no setting for delicate diplomatic feelers, even if the British Government had been prepared to sanction them. It could, however, be the setting for personal gestures.

The Prince's suggestion was that instead of simply expressing England's desire for closer relations with the new Tsar, the wish should be symbolized by immediately conferring on him the Garter, which was not only the first order of England but the most coveted decoration in the world. Moreover he, the Prince of Wales, could personally invest his brother-in-law during the visit. The Queen seemed well disposed to the idea but the then Foreign Secretary, Lord Granville, demurred, pointing to all the ceremonial expenses that would arise. Edward, as Prince of Wales or, later, as King, always got irritable when Ministers intervened in the matter of decorations. He always became even more irritable when anybody opposed him doing anything on the grounds of money. Now, with both counts raised against him, he positively steam-rollered the Foreign Secretary into giving formal approval. 'I hope,' the Prince told Lord Granville coolly on the eve of his departure, 'that I may consider the matter as settled, and I will announce it to the Emperor on my arrival that the Queen intends conferring the Garter.'

Announce it he did, and bestow it he did, on 28 March in what must have been a somewhat bizarre ceremony in the barricaded Winter Palace.

The new Knight of the Garter did not turn out to be the enlightened ruler that Russia so desperately needed. Nor, to the keen disappointment of his English brother-in-law, did he show much disposition for friendliness towards the British Empire. Whenever the two men met over the next few years in Copenhagen, for family reunions at the Danish Court, the Prince of Wales found all his overtures politely ignored, while Russian pressure on Afghanistan, the northern gateway to India, steadily increased. Thus, when Alexander III died, at the early age of 49, on 1 November 1894, the family sorrow felt at Marlborough House must have been tempered with a certain feeling of political relief.

By his death alone, however, the little-mourned Tsar had been of some help. There would be another funeral for the Prince of Wales to attend, followed by the inauguration of another Tsar, this time of Nicholas II. What was more inviting and important, there was to be a wedding as well, for Nicholas was already betrothed to the Prince of Wales's niece, Princess Alix of Hesse. This meant that the dynastic link between London and St Petersburg was now tied in a double loop. The new ruler of Russia was Prince Edward's nephew twice over.

The opportunity was too good to miss; and, on this occasion, the government of the day in England (Lord Rosebery's) positively urged the Prince of Wales to make the most of it. He did all he could, first by standing solemnly at the new Tsar's elbow throughout the four-hour funeral services in Moscow and uncomplainingly kissing the lips of the dead monarch in his coffin, despite the fact that 'the smell was awful'.[5] Finally, the Prince blossomed out into his genial best at the wedding in the private chapel of that now familiar Winter Palace. He also bestowed on the bridegroom an honour in Queen Victoria's name. Perhaps mindful of the paltry return the Garter had produced from the former Tsar, this first official compliment paid to his son was more modest, an Honorary Colonelcy of the Scots Greys. Indeed, the political going was destined to be almost as slow with Nicholas II as it had been with his father. The new ruler, who was an unknown quantity politically, turned out to be a *quantité négligeable*. Whereas the father had been difficult to steer because he was so obdurate, the son proved hard to grasp because, in the Prince of Wales's own words, he was 'as weak as water' and, like water, simply ran through the fingers.

Nonetheless, the Prince of Wales, in making his effort to get the weakling's sympathies, had also stamped his own personality on the great international concourse gathered in St Petersburg. The praise of him in the Russian press was echoed by the enthusiastic welcome he received on his return to London. The Prime Minister, Lord Rosebery, declared that he had 'rendered a signal service', not only to England but also 'to Russia and the peace of the world'.[6] It was the highest public compliment the Prince had enjoyed during his forty-odd years as a roving royal ambassador. Unfortunately, the fruits of this 'signal service' were not to ripen for some years yet in the musty air of the Romanov court.

*   *   *

If the Prince's visits to Russia were rather more politics than pleasure, his journeys to that other great empire, the Habsburg Monarchy, were nearly all pleasure and no politics. Indeed, Austria-Hungary gradually became for him a social playground second only to France in his affections, and with the one advantage, that it never became a Republic. He had first passed through Vienna and made the acquaintance of the Emperor Franz Josef in February of 1862, the year before his marriage. Ten years later, he had returned for a week's stay, this time with Princess Alexandra. Though the visit was supposed to be purely private, the young couple were given a sobering dose of Habsburg court protocol when they were obliged to spend an entire day paying formal calls on each of the twenty-seven Archdukes who happened to be in the capital at the time.

But the first chance the Prince of Wales had to explore the Austrian empire properly (and *en garçon*, which with him was another word for the same thing) came the following spring when he went, as President of the British section, to attend the opening of the Vienna World Exhibition of 1873. His brother, Prince Arthur of Connaught, accompanied him. Ten days were spent on functions and festivities in the capital and then the princes escaped for the informal part of the journey, a trip down the Danube to the Hungary they had heard so much about. They embarked at Vienna early on Sunday, 11 May on a steamer specially rechristened the *Ariadne* after the Prince of Wales's own cruising yacht. With him in his suite were Francis Knollys, his Private Secretary; two equerries, Colonel Arthur Ellis and Colonel Charles Teesdale; Lord Suffield, his friend, shooting companion and fellow-member of the Marlborough Club; and Lord Dudley, with his lovely raven-haired wife Georgina.[7]

It was a merry party from the moment they weighed anchor. They put in twice along the Danube (at Komárom and Visegrád) for sight-seeing trips and did not reach Budapest until eight that evening, much later than expected. Despite that, some 20,000 people were waiting to cheer him ashore, and another vast crowd applauded as he went on to dine at the National Casino, Hungary's most fashionable club, founded and run along pseudo-English lines. He was back in his apartments at the Hotel Hungaria by half past ten which, by the standards of Budapest night-life, was barely tea-time. The Hungarian press put this down to the Prince's deference to the feelings of Queen Victoria, a thousand miles away. She would have disapproved, they pointed out, 'if her son had enjoyed worldly pleasure on the Lord's Dall'. There is no race on earth less naïve than the Magyars, so one may well wonder whether those journalists had their tongues partly in their cheeks. If there was one thing the Prince of Wales was always prepared to work a seven-day week at, it was 'worldly pleasure'.

Certainly, everyone could see him hard at it for the next few days and nights. There was, for example, a combined gipsy fête and rowing regatta (the one very Hungarian, and the other very English) on the Archduke Josef's Margaret Island on the Danube, then a private property; and more gipsy music after the opera late that same night, when both the English princes had their first attempt at the Czárdás, the Hungarian national dance. The *grande finale* to the visit was a ball in the Hotel Europa (later, alas, to become a police headquarters) at which everyone, including the Prince of Wales, danced until five in the morning.

Budapest had lived up to his expectations and he had turned out to be just as the city had expected and hoped: an English prince, with all of the Englishman's dignity and none of his stuffiness. On leaving, he was paid a fulsome compliment reminiscent of that suggestion made to him in New York thirteen years before, that he ought to return to America and run for President:

> 'Your Royal Highness should stay on here. You would be returned to Parliament at our next elections by any constituency in the country.'

He promised to return, and he did. There was a brief forty-eight-hour visit in 1881, but it was not until September of 1885 that he was able to come back for a proper stay. This time, he had a new and fascinating travelling companion, Crown Prince Rudolph, the ill-fated heir to the Habsburg throne. The two men had become friends after Archduke Rudolph's visit to London in February 1878 and, despite the nineteen years' difference in their age, there was much they had in common. Both were the sons of sovereigns who looked as though they would go on ruling for ever. Both shared a well-justified reputation for fast living, though whereas the Prince of Wales stopped at over-indulgence, the Archduke had moved on to unbridled excess. There was even an indirect family link. Rudolph had married Princess Stephanie, a daughter of King Leopold of the Belgians, himself a member of the Coburg clan.

This third visit, like the others, was studded with the usual brilliant evening entertainments at Budapest. But now, for the first time, the Prince also went deep into the Hungarian countryside and sampled the quality of the Hungarian shooting. The picturesque *pusta*, with its enormous reserves of game, made a strong impression on him, and little wonder. On 28 September, for example, there was a shoot as the guest of Count Festetics at Udvarhely, once a hunting-ground of medieval Hungarian kings. The estate covered no less than forty thousand acres, with stags roaming the plain not as single animals, as they usually appeared in the Prince's home forests of Balmoral, but in great herds of completely wild beasts. Forty of them were shot in all that day (the Prince accounting for seven), as well as 421 brace of partridge. Not surprisingly, from now on, he looked at Hungary as a sportsman's paradise as well as the gayest country of central Europe.

Three years later (after an unpleasant incident in Vienna we shall come to later) the Prince of Wales was back in Hungary again. This time, the Austrian Emperor Franz Josef himself played host, in addition to the Archduke Rudolph, and it is through the Emperor that we are given a rare and rather surprising glimpse of the Prince of Wales as a horseman. By 1888, he had neither the figure nor the wind to ride for long without effort. But the effort simply had to be made on 13 September of that year because, among a host of other royal guests, he was attending the military manœuvres at Belovár, and that meant an arduous day on horseback for all of them. The Prince, adorned in Hungarian uniform for the occasion, was clearly determined not to let England down in this international company. At some cost, he succeeded nobly, as this letter, written by the Emperor three days later to his devoted actress friend, Katherina Schratt, shows:

'We were often long hours in the saddle. I tried my best to shake the Prince of Wales off with sustained spells at the trot or the gallop but I couldn't manage it; the plump fellow kept up the whole time and lasted out incredibly. But he did get pretty stiff, and as he had split his red Hussar trousers and had nothing on underneath, it was all rather unpleasant for him.'[8]

Some idea of the riding standards that Albert Edward had been up against is given by a conversation which took place after the closing manœuvre. General Hennenberg, commanding the Hungarian cavalry, was introduced by the Emperor to the Prince of Wales. The Prince congratulated him on the magnificent horsemanship of his hussars. 'Hussars?' the General replied. 'But, Your Highness, they are only our Honveds!'*

Fortunately, those army manœuvres turned out to be the only exacting feature of the whole tour. The Prince, who was thoroughly enjoying himself, now had nothing but a novel holiday to look forward to. As his *maître de plaisirs*, Archduke Rudolph, wrote to Princess Stephanie just before they broke camp at Belovár:

'At last I can write to you again; I haven't had a minute for the last few days. The Prince of Wales arrived on the tenth and I was given the job of entertaining him. He is going to Rumania and will come to us at Görgény for the shooting. He is in excellent spirits and wants to see everything and take part in everything that is going on. The old boy is as indefatigable as ever ("*Unermüdlich bleibt er immer, der Alte*").'[9]

The visit to the Rumanian royal couple† at their summer palace of Sinaia in the Carpathians and the shoot with Archduke Rudolph in nearby Transylvania were, perhaps, the most vivid memories of all the Prince's Danubian travels. The ancient fortress town of Görgény-Szentimre (to give it its full name) had baleful associations for any British royal visitor: the original fortifications had been built by that ardent seventeenth-century champion of Protestantism, Prince George Rakóczi, with whom Oliver Cromwell had corresponded as a kindred spirit. But the mansion under the ruins of Rakóczi's fortress had nothing to do with war or politics. The hills around Görgény were famous for their bear-hunts and when the Hungarian Government heard that their Crown Prince had a liking for the sport, they presented him with the castle and the shooting rights for miles around.

* Newly-formed Hungarian Army contingents, made up of ordinary recruits.
† King Carol I and his wife, the German-born Princess of Wied.

The bears of Görgény did not live up to their reputation between 8 and 11 October 1888. Though the royal hunters* moved higher and higher up the surrounding forests of Kasva and Adorjan in search of prey, the bears, driven from the low ground by the dry heat, went higher still. Only three of them were sighted the whole time and they all managed to slip through the enormous ring of beaters and escape. Yet, despite his disappointment (for the Prince of Wales had never hunted bear), life in Transylvania offered compensation enough. Everything from the early morning rides up into the mountains (beginning with four-in-hand horse carriages and then transferring, as the going got rougher, to pony-carts) to the peasant dances by torch-light which ended the long day back in the castle courtyard, had about it that special Magyar magic which is both ethereal and earthy. Even the weather, which had ruined the hunting, gave a helping hand here. It was so warm that the pear trees in the park of Görgény had blossomed that autumn for a second time.

On 12 October the Prince of Wales returned via Budapest to Vienna and then spent another week in Austria in the Crown Prince's company. On 18 October, after a stay of five weeks in central Europe, the Prince of Wales boarded the Orient Express at Vienna for Paris and home. Archduke Rudolph was at the station to see him off and, as the train drew away, the two men called out a cheerful *Au revoir*. In fact, they were never to see each other again. Three weeks later, the 17-year-old Baroness Marie Vetsera came into Prince Rudolph's already tormented life. Less than three months later, on 31 January 1889, he ended that life, and hers with it, with two bullets fired in the bedroom of his shooting lodge at Mayerling, in the Vienna woods. The Austrian Empire had lost a tragic heir; the world had gained a romantic legend.

The Prince of Wales, who had lost a friend, was astounded as well as shocked by the news. Though he had known all about the Crown Prince's violent moods, his unhappy marriage and his political frustrations, nothing had foreshadowed an end as dark as this. The shock was to be aggravated by Queen Victoria's attitude. The Queen seems to have regarded Crown Prince Rudolph as some archducal Beelzebub. She had opposed her son's attendance at Rudolph's wedding to Princess Stephanie in May of 1881, and had flatly turned down his earlier request to get the Order of the Garter for his Austrian friend. And now, his mother refused even to let him go to Vienna for the Archduke's funeral. The Queen was quite adamant. Evidently she felt that the fewer

---

* The Austrian Archdukes Frederick and Otto and the Portuguese Duke of Branganza were also in the party.

official contacts her Bertie had with *that* man, even if he were now in his coffin, the better it would be.

All these decisions of hers, taken together with the purely social nature of her son's visits to Austria-Hungary, were an accurate reflection of relations between England and the Habsburg Monarchy during the second half of the nineteenth century. These were amicable without ever becoming close. There were many inter-marriages between the aristocracies of the two countries, and the upper classes of the Austrian Empire (particularly the Hungarians) were almost anglo-maniac in their tastes and habits. But there were few political links and even fewer dynastic contacts. Indeed, had it not been for Prince Edward's pleasure-trips and personal friendships, there would have been as good as none at all. Just because there were no direct ties of blood or marriage between the two courts (and therefore no need to exchange periodic letters about betrothals, name-days and baptisms), Queen Victoria had been happy to regard the Habsburgs as though they ruled by the Grace of God on some waterless planet of outer space.* Her successive Foreign Ministers, because of the routine business of diplomacy, realized that Vienna was, in fact, much nearer than that. But, so long as Austria kept the Balkans quiet, they, in turn, were happy to leave Austria to herself.

*   *   *

It was a very different matter, both for Prince Edward and for England, with the fourth great continental power, the Germany which Austria had first unsuccessfully fought in 1866 and then finally allied herself with twelve years later. Germany, in fact, came to represent the crucial political challenge to England as Queen Victoria's reign moved on. It also produced the crucial personal challenge for her son.

The political problem was posed by the rise of Prussia from a Hohenzollern kingdom to a great continental empire – and all within the bewildering space of six years. Three short but savagely convincing military campaigns were all that her 'Iron Chancellor', Otto Bismarck, had needed to achieve the transformation. First, in 1864, had come his attack to the north against little Denmark, to settle the quarrel over the border provinces of Schleswig-Holstein. The unequal struggle was finished in a few weeks, but they were weeks of horrible family strain between Sandringham and Windsor. Princess Alexandra, whose home country was being invaded and humiliated, was violently anti-Prussian.

---

* During the whole of the fifty-three years in which she and the Emperor Franz Josef occupied their thrones in parallel, the two sovereigns met but once – and then only for a few minutes of obscure conversation at the railway station of Innsbruck.

Queen Victoria, whose 'Vicky' was, after all, married to the heir to the Prussian throne, could not bring herself to condemn Berlin at heart. The Prince of Wales, at first torn between the two, was soon pulled rapidly to his wife's side, as much by his own convictions as by her pleading.

Bismarck's second blow was struck two years later to the south, against Austria-Hungary, the only power that could challenge Prussia for supremacy in the German-speaking world. Once again, thanks to the awesome efficiency of the Prussian war machine and the brilliant use of railways to bring it swiftly into action, the issue was decided in a matter of weeks. The Prince of Wales had no close relatives involved on the losing side in this case; but the alarm and repugnance that he already felt towards Bismarck's Prussia is shown in a hitherto un-published letter which he wrote on 5 August 1866 to his cousin, Prince Hermann of Hohenlohe-Langenburg.* It was penned only a month after the Prussian victory over the Austrians at Königgrätz, and though the purpose of the letter is purely private – to agree to be godfather to Prince Hermann's newly born daughter Feodora – the Prince of Wales soon switches into politics:

'This dreadful war has brought much pain and anxiety to us all. I simply cannot understand how the fine Austrian army has had to suffer such setbacks. The Prussians, of course, conducted their cam-paign well, but what a pretty reputation they have left everywhere behind them, plundering and destroying at every turn! . . .

'Let us hope we will soon have peace, though I don't doubt it will be a shameful peace that the Prussians will enforce . . .'

And then (with a few spelling mistakes, even in this German tongue he wrote so fluently) Bertie goes on to tell his cousin of the exhausting summer season that has just ended and of the healing peace of the Highlands that now awaits him.

Finally, four years after Königgrätz, Bismarck struck his third blow, this time westwards, against the traditional enemy, France. This developed into a longer and tougher struggle than the first two; but the triumph, when it came, brought a laurel wreath larger in propor-tion. In 1871, at the ceremony of victory in Versailles, Bismarck declared his Prussian King to be a German Emperor, with an empire made up of all the principalities and minor kingdoms which had

---

* Indeed, it was, until 1972, an unknown letter. It was discovered then in the drawer of a writing-desk at Langenburg by Princess Charlotte of Hohenlohe-Langenburg, who was kindly searching through the family archives on my behalf for any material relating to King Edward.

fought on the losing side ever since 1864. The country which Queen Victoria had once called her 'dear little Germany' was now no longer dear nor little. At the heart of Europe, astride the crossroads of the Continent, there crouched a military power the frightening like of which had not been seen since the *Grande Armée* of Napoleon's day.

Nor was there only a military threat from this brand-new empire of which the English Princess Royal would one day be Empress. The elemental physical vigour of Bismarckian Germany had an economic aspect which also caused disquiet. Though this energy sustained the Prussian military machine, it was both separate from it, and broader than it. It found expression, for example, in the leap in German population; in the expansion, violent yet sustained, of industrial output; and in the worldwide thrust of foreign trade. Prussian adrenalin was being pumped through the veins of the whole German race, turning those chocolate soldiers of the old operetta principalities into real soldiers, and making the Bavarian just as business-minded as the Rhinelander.

Two things flowed from this transformation. The first was a cult of the monumental, symbolized in the massively ornate architecture of the new Berlin. The second was the spirit which inspired that cult, the messianic worship of power. This inevitably took on military forms because the uniform of the Prussian Junker, though it had no place on the factory floors where this new Germany was being born, was still the sacred vestment of the state. The sheer speed of the economic upheaval had left social and political change floundering so far behind that no responsible middle class could emerge in time to control the strength which that very class was creating. So the power of the new Germany fell into the hands of the dying but still dominant ruling caste of the old. And they, the Junkers, used it the only way they knew how.

The ancient dynasties of Europe reacted to the arrival of this thrusting newcomer as age so often reacts to the challenge of youth. The Austrian monarch, Franz Josef (an emperor if there ever was one), was, for example, thunderstruck when he was told that a new German Empire had been proclaimed. He turned pale and, for several minutes, could not bring himself to speak, which was perhaps just as well. Hostility was combined with, and partly inspired by, a dread that this newcomer was bringing with him the eclipse of the existing order because he, and he alone, was riding the wave of the future. This feeling of resentful unease was fully shared by England, with whom the new Germany promptly clashed as a commercial and industrial rival.

Throughout the half-century ahead that Bismarck's creation was to last, the Germans always remained something of *parvenus* in the imperial league. And they soon made matters worse by assuming, with indecent haste, all the habits and pretensions of the older members. An empire needed an imperial capital, so Berlin was converted within two decades into a brassy imitation of one. An empire needed overseas colonies, for prestige as well as trade, so, in the '80s and '90s, overseas colonies were snatched up wherever, in remote jungles and deserts like the Congo in western Africa or Tanganyika on its eastern coasts, areas were still left unclaimed by the other European powers. Finally, as a direct consequence of this, came the most dangerous status symbol of all, the acquisition of an imperial navy.

Germany's first two emperors were of the modest variety and did nothing to aggravate their uneasy fellow-monarchs. William I, the conservative old king on whom Bismarck bestowed the title on 18 January 1871 in the Palace of Versailles, neither sought nor wanted the honour anyway. His son, Frederick, who succeeded his 90-year-old father on 7 March 1888, had the stamp of a very different and more progressive monarch about him. Yet he too shared his father's lack of bombast, and both he and his wife, the Prince of Wales's sister Vicky, were appalled by the signs of it which were appearing in their own son William, that petulant infant of the Windsor wedding.

Then, on 13 June 1888, the fateful blow came, both for Vicky in Berlin and for her brother Bertie in England, as well as for their two countries. The Emperor Frederick, mortally ill with throat cancer long before he ascended the throne, finally succumbed to the disease, and Prince William became the new ruler of Bismarck's Germany at the age of only 29. His uncle was at the Ascot races when he heard the news. He promptly abandoned the meeting to hurry to Berlin. From that day on, no one in Europe – and least of all the Prince of Wales – was ever going to feel totally relaxed again.

One must, from the start, try and be fair to the new German Emperor, as his Uncle Bertie always struggled to be. The conventional explanation for William's theatrical arrogance, both as a man and a ruler, is that, from infancy, his left arm, crippled after his mother's difficult labour and breech birth, never grew beyond a twisted stump. For the rest of his lifetime, and ever since his death, the Kaiser's withered arm was to be toted around by contemporaries and historians alike as some voodoo symbol, unlocking all the extravagant workings of his mind. It is, of course, natural that his affliction should have produced a permanent tendency towards 'over-compensation', especially in such a vain spirit as his. But it also needs to be said, some fifty years after the Kaiser's death, that, had he been born with two arms as straight as ramrods and as strong as oak trees, he might well have turned out much the same.

It was not just that he was much cleverer, as well as much more neurotic, than either his father or his grandfather. His inheritance was different as well. The German Empire of 1888 was in the full thrust of all that vaulting economic vigour and political ambition that Bismarck had given it. Dominant already on the Continent, Germany was by now also fairly screaming for her 'place in the sun' outside Europe, and for the prestige to match her power. William II would have needed to be a man of quite exceptional restraint to have ignored these daemonic forces thrusting up beneath his throne, and to have resisted all the temptations they conjured up. As we know, he never tried; but he should not be judged more harshly than that.

At the personal level, William's accession had brought about a sudden and drastic change in the relative positions of the English uncle and the German nephew. Though nearly twenty years older, and already unchallenged as the leader of European society, the Prince of Wales remained only an Heir-Apparent, with all the signs of a long wait still ahead. But, however brash and however young, the nephew was now an 'All-Highest', the third Emperor of the third Empire in Europe. In any confrontation, all that the older man could do, until a crown was his to wear, was to fall back on tact and patience, knowing that his inheritance, when it came, would be far more glorious than his nephew's and that his influence, if he played his cards right, far more widespread. But as regards precedence and protocol, he knew that he was eclipsed from now on until the day his mother died; and protocol, as he also knew, can be a savage thing.

The first impact upon the Prince of Wales of his nephew's imperial glory was both quick to come and painful to bear. In the autumn of 1888, less than four months after William's accession, came the incident of the great Vienna snub. The new Kaiser had barely been crowned when, putting all the conventional restraints of mourning aside, he invited himself on inaugural visits to the Russian and Austrian courts. When Queen Victoria remonstrated with him over this unseemly haste, he had blandly replied that in view of the dangers confronting the institution of monarchy all over the globe: 'We emperors must stick together.'[10] But if the brand-new Kaiser was prepared to include his grandmother, as Empress of India, in the imperial circle of Europe, he was determined to keep Uncle Bertie, a mere Prince of Wales, out.

Only seven years before, when that same uncle had given a ball at Marlborough House in honour of Kalakaua, the King of the Sandwich Islands, the native potentate had been given the honour of dancing the opening quadrille with Princess Alexandra. His was the only crowned head present, and that, for host, was that. But the indignation felt by his other guests, all of whom were European, many of whom were also royal, can be imagined. Among those affronted in July 1881 by these extravagant English ideas of precedence were Kaiser William's own parents, the then Crown Prince and Princess of Germany. Whether in 1888 the new German Emperor still remembered that Marlborough House ball or not, it was the same relentless weapon of protocol that he now turned against his uncle.

The Prince of Wales was visiting Vienna before beginning that pleasurable holiday in Hungary and Rumania which has already been described. He had twice written to the Kaiser to try and establish the dates his nephew had fixed for his own state visit to Vienna so that they might all meet up. He had been puzzled to receive no reply, but not unduly disconcerted. It was, therefore, a contented and unsuspecting Prince of Wales who, after arriving at breakfast-time in Vienna on 10 September 1888, tried on his gorgeous new uniform as an Honorary Colonel of the 12th Hungarian Hussars. With its gold-frogged tunic and red breeches, it flattered even his portly figure. So attired, he awaited his first talk with the Austrian Emperor.

Then came the bombshell, delivered as gently as possible by Franz Josef himself. After producing a programme (automatically accepted by his English guest) which involved the Prince of Wales leaving Vienna on 3 October, the Emperor casually added that the German Kaiser would arrive in the Austrian capital on that same day. If the Prince had thought at first that this was a flexible schedule which could be easily rearranged, he was disabused of any such idea the following day. The British Ambassador at Vienna, Sir Augustus Paget, turned up at the Grand Hotel the next morning with 'a most disagreeable communication'. The Austrian Foreign Minister, Count Kalnocky, had been embarrassed but emphatic when tackled on the subject. It was the Kaiser William's wish that he should hold the stage alone while in Vienna. As he was now a crowned head paying an official visit, his host could do nothing but comply. This King of the Sandwich Islands was not only getting the opening dance. He was having the whole ball to himself.

The incident touched off a furious family row between Potsdam and Windsor, with the Queen unequivocally on her son's side. The Kaiser denied, rather implausibly, having wanted to avoid the Prince of Wales in the first place.[11] But he added the revealing complaint that his uncle still treated him as a nephew, and not as the German Emperor. This, Queen Victoria exploded in a letter to her Prime Minister, Lord

Salisbury, was 'perfect madness' and 'too vulgar and too absurd, as well as untrue, almost to be believed'.[12]

The carping and haggling did not die out until the summer of 1889, and what was significant for the future about this faintly ludicrous episode was the real damage it did to Anglo-German relations. Though the dent was eventually smoothed out, it had been real, it had been deep, and it was remembered. It was the Kaiser's behaviour at Vienna which had convinced Lord Salisbury, for example, that the German Emperor was 'not quite all there'. That was a verdict that carried its weight behind the scenes throughout the long years Lord Salisbury was in power.* Even Queen Victoria, in a letter to him at the height of the quarrel, had sensed that this was much more than a family affair:

'As regards the political relations of the two Governments,' she wrote, 'the Queen quite agrees that that [sic] should not be affected (if possible) by these miserable family quarrels; but the Queen much *fears* that, with such a hot-headed conceited and wrong-headed young man, devoid of all feeling, this may, at *any* moment, become *impossible*.'[13]

Edward was to echo those sentiments heartily enough after he had succeeded to the throne. In the meantime, however, there was nothing much that he could do but swallow his pride (or at least a portion of it) to save appearances all round. His nephew was yearning to visit England in his new glory as Emperor and, as Uncle Bertie's hurt feelings were threatening the trip, the Kaiser consented at least not to hurt them further. Replying on 23 June 1889 to a tactful letter from Queen Victoria, he told his grandmother, rather equivocally, that he heartily agreed with her in regarding 'the Vienna affair as concluded'. No apology, but an agreement to pretend they could forget. It was not much, but just enough to enable the Kaiser's visit to be fixed for the beginning of August.

The Queen did her utmost to make that visit a success. As an advance sop to her grandson's vanity, she told him that, while in England, he would be given the dignity of Honorary Admiral of the Royal Navy and, as such, would attend a naval review in his honour at Spithead. There is something touching, as well as psychologically significant, about the genuine delight which this news gave the Kaiser. 'Fancy wearing the same uniform as St Vincent or Nelson,' he exclaimed, 'it is enough to make me quite giddy.'

* The 3rd Marquess of Salisbury served as Queen Victoria's Conservative Prime Minister (with only one three-year interval) continuously from 1885 until the end of the reign. For most of the period, he was also his own Foreign Minister.

Giddy or not, the new Admiral of the Fleet did show both a detailed knowledge of and an increasing passion for naval affairs during his five-day stay in England, most of which was spent in or around Cowes and the Isle of Wight. His Uncle Bertie was all affability; the toasts were cordial; the naval review was its usual magnificent self; and the old Queen at Osborne House nearby heaved a sigh of relief that the family seemed reconciled. But those with eyes to see (and the Prince of Wales was one) saw that summer the first disturbing outlines of a dark picture of the future. To begin with, the new English Admiral arrived with a miniature fleet of his own. Even though the great years of German naval expansion still lay nearly a decade ahead, an escort of twelve men-of-war was not exactly modest for a land power like Prussian Germany in 1889. Moreover, the Kaiser showed on this visit that he was already not above offering suggestions as to how the Royal Navy might be improved by adopting technical innovations introduced in Germany. If this worried the English admirals, who could understand the scientific jargon, it both worried and irritated Uncle Bertie, who could not. All in all, it was a reconciliation with rasping undertones.

There was one particularly unfortunate outcome of that visit. The Kaiser became keenly interested in the Cowes Regatta and the Prince of Wales, who was Commodore of the Royal Yacht Squadron, duly had his nephew elected as a member. As far as his own pleasure in yachting was concerned, he had as good as elected his own executioner. During the next few years it was on the blue waters of Cowes, more than anything else, where relations between uncle and nephew sank from being merely bad to becoming truly appalling.

The *Hohenzollern,* in which the Kaiser always arrived, was not only the largest and most powerful royal vessel afloat. With its sleek, high-raked lines, it looked more like a warship than a pleasure yacht. No greater nor more eloquent contrast could be imagined between this lean monster and the sprawling *Victoria and Albert,* which seemed to conjure up a vision of panama hats and parasols on deck, and English breakfasts under English silver dish-covers below. The same German determination to outshine and impress was applied to the actual regatta. The Kaiser had had a racing yacht, the *Meteor I,* specially redesigned to beat his uncle's *Britannia,* which it promptly did. Moreover, beating the *Britannia* took precedence for the Kaiser over everything else in the social programme. The German diplomat Hermann von Eckhardstein, in the first volume of his revealing if sometimes misleading memoirs as Attaché in London, describes how, in 1893, both yachts were becalmed in a race round the Isle of Wight. The Kaiser flatly rejected his uncle's proposal to call it a day so that they could both land in time for dinner with the old Queen. 'The race must be fought to a finish, no matter when we get back to Cowes,' the master of *Meteor I* signalled back. As a result, they both arrived at Osborne an hour and a half late, to a very frosty reception.[14]

The climax, on all accounts, came at the regatta of August 1895. It was twenty-five years after Prussia's crushing victory over France in 1870, and the exact anniversaries of two of the decisive engagements of that war, at the Alsatian towns of Wörth and Weissenburg, fell plumb in the middle of Cowes week, on 4 and 6 August respectively. What should the Kaiser do but include his two new cruisers, named after those battles, in his naval escort for that year? To add insult to injury, he gave a jingoistic address to the sailors of the *Wörth* as she lay at anchor in the waters of the Solent. The English and German press, always itching to get at each other's throats, roared their mutual abuse for months over the incident.

The Kaiser was sufficiently enraged himself as to declare, once back in Berlin, that he was 'finished with England'. He was still far from that. Though, to his uncle's immense relief, the Kaiser never turned up again in person, he arranged that his presence there should still be felt. Before leaving Cowes, he had commissioned a new yacht from the English designer of his uncle's boat. The product, *Meteor II*, took to the Solent in its imperial owner's absence in August 1896 and decisively out-sailed the *Britannia*. Had the Prince of Wales been like his nephew, he would have promptly built yet a bigger and better boat. Instead, he quietly withdrew *Britannia* from all future races.

Even that gesture of renunciation did not quite close the calamitous saga of Cowes. After four years of calm, there was another squall in 1899. *Meteor II*, still without the All-Highest on board, won the Queen's Cup race yet again. The Prince of Wales, who had risen to toast his nephew's victory at the annual banquet of the Royal Yacht Squadron, went on to express polite regret that the German Emperor could not have been present to witness his yacht's victory in person. The Prince was deliberately extending a political olive branch to Berlin. As he told Baron Eckhardstein after the banquet, he had sought to demonstrate in public that Anglo-German relations were moving back to a healthier state, 'whatever I may think about my nephew in private'.[15]

The nephew lost no time in living up to those private opinions. The very next morning, the august members of the club were horrified to read a long telegram in English from the German Emperor pinned up on their notice-board. After accusing the regatta racing committee of all manner of misdemeanours and blunders, it declared: 'Your handicaps are simply appalling.'

The Kaiser had attacked the English at their most sensitive spot, their tradition of fair play. The affront had been quite open, and it had come right on the heels of his uncle's gesture of reconciliation. That uncle was reduced to despair when he read the offending message. 'What on earth does the Emperor want?' he sighed. 'The best proof that our handicaps are fair is the fact that he and his *Meteor* have won the Queen's Cup after all!'

It would be too much to claim that the cause of Anglo-German friendship was sunk on the waters of the Solent. Yet what these days we would call a 'Cowes syndrome' was beginning to affect the political judgement both of the Prince of Wales and of the Queen's Ministers. If the German Emperor, apparently all-powerful since his dismissal of Bismarck in 1890, would flout and abuse the rules of a regatta just out of personal spleen, what guarantee was there that he would keep to any political bargain, when vital national interests were at stake? A sovereign he might be; but was he a gentleman? Was he, indeed, as Lord Salisbury had wondered ten years before, quite right in the head? These were the invisible question-marks hanging over any dealings with Germany during the last years of Queen Victoria's reign.

They were critical years, for there was soon something far graver to argue about than the handicaps of the Royal Yacht Club. On 11 October 1899, two months after that final tiff at Cowes, the long-smouldering war in South Africa broke out, with the mighty British Empire ranged against the small but very tough Boer Republic of President Kruger. The conflict had a pendulum effect on both the personal relations between the Prince of Wales and his imperial nephew and on the political relations between England and Germany. At first, they seemed to move closer together. Then, abruptly, they swung farther than ever apart.

The initial *rapprochement* owed much to the alarming discovery made by England on the outbreak of hostilities that she stood alone in Europe – without even a continental sympathizer, let alone a continental ally. Clearly, that 'splendid isolation' that had characterized the late Victorian era could be called splendid no longer. The Queen's Ministers were in several minds as to what they should do about it and where they should look; but the pro-German faction, led by the Colonial Secretary, Joseph Chamberlain, seemed to be gaining ground.

Indeed, for a brief moment in these last weeks of the century it looked as though the Kaiser himself might make good some of the havoc he had caused in Anglo-German relations. After an acrimonious personal dispute with the Prince of Wales over the composition of the imperial suite had been settled,* the German Emperor arrived on 19 November 1899 for a five-day visit to his long-suffering grandmother. It was nearly four and a half years since he had last set foot in England and there was much ground to be made up. Yet the fact that he was accompanied not only by the Empress Augusta and two of their children but also by his Foreign Minister and future Chancellor, Count von Bülow, suggested that political as well as family breaches might now be filled in. Ironically, in view of later developments, the mere fact that he had come so soon after the outbreak of the Boer War was regarded as a hopeful sign of solidarity. Was this, then, the alliance England needed?

One way or another, it would have to be a clear-cut choice for, by now, all the major continental powers were ranged in two opposing camps. Running north to south down Europe was the Triple Alliance, completed in 1882, of the so-called Central Powers – Germany, Austria-Hungary, and Italy. Enveloping this compact group were the 'wing-powers' of Europe, France and Russia, who had concluded their defence treaty as recently as 1894. French rivalry with Germany and, to a lesser degree, Austrian rivalry with Russia in the Balkans were the basic antagonisms that underlay these alliances. France, through her massive loans to her new Russian ally, was the leader of her camp. On all counts – military, political and economic – Germany dominated her grouping. It was thus between France and Germany that England, eventually, would have to choose.

The Emperor's advisers had also been mulling over the alliance problem and had decided to hasten very slowly. Time, they considered, was on Germany's side. England's colonial quarrels with both France and Russia seemed so irreparable that, with every year that passed, John Bull would surely become more and more prepared for a total commitment on Berlin's terms. The problem in November 1899, as they saw it, was to check the Kaiser's impetuousness before he even set out for London, in case he were seized by one of those sudden bouts of Anglomania at Windsor and tempted to reveal Germany's hand too soon.

Accordingly, the most influential of those advisers, Baron Holstein of the German Foreign Office, had drawn up a special *aide-mémoire* to act as a bridle on his imperial master. It was richly trimmed, as befitted

* The Prince of Wales violently objected to the inclusion of Admiral von Senden und Bibran, who had made himself objectionable at Cowes and whom the Prince suspected of malicious trouble-making. The final compromise was that, though the Admiral came to Windsor, he produced on arrival what amounted to a written apology for his past behaviour.

the wearer. 'Beyond any question,' it began, 'Your Majesty is more gifted than any of your relations, male or female.' However, Holstein continued, these gifts did not bring the rewards they deserved because the Emperor always treated his English relatives 'so openly and honourably' that they knew his plans and thus were able wickedly to frustrate him. But now had come the opportunity to change things:

> 'The English journey offers Your Majesty the opportunity of righting this topsy-turvy situation . . . All that Your Majesty need do . . . is to avoid all political conversations.'[16]

Holstein's line of polite reserve was followed at Windsor not only by the Kaiser but by Bülow in his own talks with Mr Chamberlain and with Queen Victoria herself. It was a perfectly reasonable policy to adopt. Germany had spoiled so much in the past by an excess of zeal. Time *did* appear to be on her side. The English fruit *did* seem to be still ripening on the tree. There was also the genuine difficulty of assessing Chamberlain's strength. Could he really carry the Cabinet against his own Prime Minister, Lord Salisbury, and colleagues like Balfour and Lord Lansdowne* – all of whom were either cool or hostile to the idea of a German alignment? In similar circumstances, England, the past master of 'Wait and see', would have followed a similar line.

As a result, little of substance developed during the Kaiser's stay. But both at Windsor and at Sandringham, where, after an absence of nearly twenty years, he went afterwards for a few days' shooting with his uncle, the display of dynastic cordiality was, for once, unmarred by any untoward incidents or outbursts. The Kaiser departed in a momentary glow of all-round goodwill. So much so indeed that, as soon as he had set sail for home in the *Hohenzollern*, Joseph Chamberlain decided that the time was ripe for him to make his big move. In a speech at Leicester on 29 November, the day of the Emperor's departure, he returned to his old theme of the underlying ties of blood and common interest that bound the Anglo-Saxons and the Teutons together. 'No far-seeing English statesman could be content,' he said, 'with England's permanent isolation on the continent of Europe.' Then he came right out with it: 'The natural alliance is between ourselves and the great German Empire.'

It was one of the most dramatic and unqualified public utterances on English foreign policy to be heard for many a year, and it seemed to herald a new era. But in Berlin, the policy of caution prevailed. Less

---

* Then Minister of War, and soon to take over the office of Foreign Secretary from Lord Salisbury.

than a fortnight later, Chamberlain's public offer of an alliance was given what everyone in England interpreted as an equally public rebuff. On 11 December 1899 the same Bülow who had just heard the English ask at Windsor for closer and friendlier ties stood up in the Reichstag to give what would now be called a state-of-the-nation message. His theme was the envy which Germany's growing strength had aroused abroad and the need for Germany to press on and increase that strength still further, no matter what the world felt:

'Without strong forces on land and sea, there is no other way for a nation like ours – soon to be sixty millions strong, living in the centre of Europe but also stretching out its economic feelers in all directions – there is no other way so far discovered to fight the battle for existence in this world. In the coming century, the German nation will either be the hammer or the anvil.'

Of peace and goodwill, either with England or with anyone else, there was not a mention.

The speaker of those words was a somewhat smug and slippery individual. Yet Bernhard von Bülow was no blinkered Junker who only left his Pomeranian estates for a regimental dinner at Potsdam. He was an intelligent, widely travelled and highly cultured aristocrat, with an apt quotation drawn from a choice of two dead languages and several living ones forever on his lips. Moreover, he was the son of a diplomat and had had long years of diplomatic training himself, serving five years as Minister to Rumania and four more as Ambassador to Rome before taking over the German Foreign Office in 1897. For a man of that enlightened background to produce an outburst of that sort at this delicate moment in his country's fortunes showed what mesmerism the daemonic spirit of the new Germany could exert. Everyone who rose to power in it wanted to play Bismarck, but without that great man's iron will and, most important of all, without his restraint. In this way, strength produced only bluster, and bluster created both the appetite and the need for more strength.

Bülow's lurid picture of the world as some Wagnerian blacksmith's forge, with Germany causing all the sparks to fly, was uncomfortable enough as a vision of the new century. But the immediate effect of that speech (which no British Minister would ever forget and which Chamberlain, for one, would never forgive) was to expose Anglo-German relations once again to the full force of the South African crisis. On grounds of racial solidarity alone, German public opinion had always been solidly behind the Boers in their struggle against the

English settlers. In his notorious 'Kruger Telegram',* the Kaiser had yielded to this feeling once already, long before full-scale fighting had broken out. Now, with the war raging, he divided his time between lecturing his English uncle on how to win it and scheming how Germany could profit by it.

A good example of the former came just before Christmas of 1899, after British troops had suffered a series of grave defeats at Boer hands. When the news of this so-called 'Black Week' reached Berlin, the Kaiser used it as a text for a New Year sermon to his uncle.

His letter to the Prince of Wales dated 21 December[17] harped on England's heavy losses and ended with an even more irritating postscript. This consisted of 'Random Thoughts' by the Emperor and his military advisers on the course of the campaign and the lessons which England might draw from it.

Undeterred by the icy politeness with which this first batch of unsolicited advice was received, the Kaiser sent his uncle another instalment six weeks later. On this occasion, not content with lecturing the English, he used their most sacred idiom against them. Why was England *so* distressed about these defeats? Surely, her famous sporting traditions had taught her how to take a beating? After all, the German Emperor went on, when Australia had beaten England in the 'great cricket match' of 1898, the island kingdom had taken it calmly enough.

This, even if well meant, as it might have been, really was too much. It would have been better had the half-English Kaiser known nothing of such matters than to get them so subtly yet so totally wrong. Indeed, in a tart reply dated 8 February 1900, to his imperial nephew, the Prince of Wales implied just that:

> 'The British Empire,' he wrote, 'is now fighting for its very existence . . . We must therefore use every effort in our power to prove victorious in the end.'

The most graphic example of the Kaiser's international mischief-making over the Boer conflict was, fortunately for him, never fully known about at the time. The Tsarist archives published long afterwards show that during the very week when he was commiserating with his English uncle and his English grandmother over the bloodshed and setbacks in South Africa, the German Emperor was suggesting to the Russians that the time might now be ripe for a joint action to

---

* On 2 January 1896, Kruger's forces had overwhelmed and captured a force of 600 English irregular troops which had crossed into the Transvaal with the object of overthrowing the Boer Republic. The next day, the Kaiser dispatched a telegram of congratulations to President Kruger over maintaining his independence from 'outside attacks'.

'paralyse the power of England and deal it a mortal blow'. On New Year's Day of 1900 he assured the Russian Ambassador in Berlin, Count Osten-Sacken, that if his august master, the Tsar, should now feel tempted to move his armies against India he, the Kaiser, 'would guarantee that none should stir in Europe'.[18] France, too, he attempted to inveigle into the 'plot'.

This episode has come to be regarded by historians as the classic example of the Kaiser's congenital duplicity, and bad faith. Had the full facts leaked out in 1900 that, certainly, is how the English would have seen it, and it would have 'out-krugered' the Kruger Telegram in its impact. Yet what it revealed was something rather different from, and more dangerous than, calculated double-dealing. It gave a glimpse of that fantasy world in which the Kaiser lived, a world of flashing half-lights where the striking of heroic poses and the weaving of astounding conspiracies became addictive without ever becoming quite real, even to him.

There was one more of these histrionic gestures of his to come during Queen Victoria's reign. On 18 June 1900 Baron von Ketteler, the German Minister to China, was assassinated in broad daylight on the streets of Peking. The crime, which was grave enough in itself, also highlighted the problem of providing extra protection for the whole of the international community in a Chinese capital paralysed by the xenophobic Boxer rebellion. The situation was altogether too much for the Kaiser to resist. He became Atlas in a spiked helmet – prophet, crusader, saviour and warlord all in one. It was not just the Chinese he would teach a lesson. Europe, too, would learn who her new master was. It was in this vein that, on 3 July 1900, he declared, *à propos* of the China crisis, that 'no great decision would be made in the world in future without the German Kaiser'. Even this was an improvement on the blood-curdling harangue he had delivered six days before on the quayside at Bremerhaven, when addressing German troops embarking for the Far East:

'There will be no quarter, no prisoners will be taken! As, a thousand years ago, the Huns under Attila gained for themselves a name that still stands for terror in tradition and fable, so may you imprint the name of a German for a thousand years on China, and so deeply that never again shall a Chinese dare so much as look askance at a German.'

The full text leaked out, despite all the attempts of a horrified Bülow at censorship. He himself described the speech as 'probably the most harmful that William II ever made'.[19] Even that underestimated the disastrous way those words were to go echoing round the world for years to come. To the Prince of Wales, and indeed to most Englishmen, it was not simply the bombast that was so distasteful. Even worse was the chilling alien note of it all. No other European ruler could have brought himself to speak thus, and no other European people would have swallowed such talk without outbursts of ridicule or protest. This man and this nation who together sought to dominate the Continent had somehow become strangers in its midst.

Nor did the Kaiser help matters when it came to organizing the international army to rescue the Europeans of Peking. He affronted the other powers by taking for granted their approval of a German officer, Count Waldersee, as Commander of the force. He then fired the eager imagination of his own people by publicly fêting Waldersee and creating him Field-Marshal especially for the expedition. As so often, melodrama ended in farce. Waldersee's army did not reach China until 27 September 1900. Six weeks before that, however, Peking had been entered by other allied forces and the European missions were already safe. The Kaiser's soldiers thus never even got the opportunity to rival Attila's Huns in China. But in Europe, the label was to stick to them nonetheless.

Though the most alarming of all her imperial grandson's escapades, that turned out to be the last one Queen Victoria would ever have to endure. At half past six on the evening of 22 January 1901, after a reign of sixty-three years, seven months and two days, the old matriarch died at last. For Prince Albert Edward, the long wait for the crown of England was over.

*   *   *

Even the old Queen's death-bed did not bring uncle and nephew together for long. At first, the Kaiser's English relatives were rather touched (and his own court rather offended) by his behaviour. He boarded the train for England the very day, 18 January, that he was brought the news that his grandmother's condition had become serious, even though this had meant abandoning Berlin's celebrations to mark the two-hundredth anniversary of the Hohenzollern dynasty.

But grandson Willy's behaviour in and around the death-chamber at Osborne House soon became too much to bear, as histrionics supplanted even that very genuine devotion he was known to feel for the Queen.

He had, for example, argued his way to the bedside for the final vigil. In fact, his one good arm was helping to support his grandmother when she drew her last breath. As soon as death was pronounced, her

German grandson tried to take over all the funeral arrangements as though it were his own mother who had died at Potsdam. It was he who insisted on measuring the dead Queen for her coffin (she had forbidden undertakers to appear). Indeed, when the moment came, he would have placed her body in that coffin himself had his Uncle Edward, who by now had really had enough, not intervened. This most intimate act of family piety belonged, he told his nephew firmly, to the dead woman's sons. The Kaiser was put out, but not for long. He returned soon afterwards, bearing a huge Union Jack which he proceeded to hang up above the coffin (and which he eventually carried back with him to Berlin).

But there had been more in that gesture of rebuke than the new head of the family putting an over-zealous mourner in his place. At the advanced age of 59 years and two months (which was still more than four years less than his mother's enormous reign), the uncle was now a fellow-monarch as well. Moreover, it was soon made plain that the new sovereign was not going to waste one minute of this great inheritance that had come to him so late in life, nor renounce one particle of the prestige it had brought with it.

The Kaiser was next to him when they took the dead Queen's coffin – placed on a pall of white satin and edged with a heavy fringe of gold – down to the pier-side for the short sea journey from the Isle of Wight to the mainland. Both men were dressed identically in the uniform of a British Admiral of the Fleet as they followed the coffin on to the *Victoria and Albert* at the head of the funeral cortège. All around them, in the waters of the Solent, columns of British and foreign warships nearly ten miles long were anchored in salutation, each with its colours at half-mast.

It was a hushed moment. But then, as they stepped on to the deck, the Kaiser saw his uncle come alive in a flash as he noticed that the standard on the royal yacht above his head was also at half-mast. A message was sent instantly to the captain, demanding an explanation.

The puzzled answer came back: 'The Queen is dead, sir.' Replied Victoria's son and heir: 'But the King of England lives!' His own standard was promptly hoisted to the top of the mast-head. It was not to be lowered again, in the literal or the metaphorical sense, for the next ten years.

PART II

1901-1903

4

KING OF ENGLAND

Within twenty-four hours of his mother's death, King Edward was showing a new tilt for the crown of England, as well as a new technique for wearing it. Both were displayed in the speech he made to the Privy Council at St James's Palace in London on 23 January, after swearing his oaths of accession to the Archbishop of Canterbury. The words were addressed to his subjects, but all Europe was affected by their message.

The fresh slant that he was to give the monarchy was expressed in the simple sentence: 'I have resolved to be known by the name of Edward, which has been borne by six of my ancestors.' It sounded a reasonable, uncomplicated decision. Yet it was enough to have caused Queen Victoria to stir on her funeral bier and to have made his father, the Prince Consort, leap right out of his mausoleum at Frogmore.

It had always been the firm intention of both parents that their son should be crowned Albert Edward, and that he should reign as King Albert, in memory of his father. The son had done nothing in their lifetimes to disabuse them of the idea. Now, after much private reflection during the last months of his mother's life, he had shattered that hope with a few words. His reasons were a mixture of common sense and sentiment.

Though the new King went on to speak of his 'ever-lamented and wise father' and to suggest it were better that the name of Albert the Good should be allowed to stand alone, this reference was made more out of tact than humility. The one who would stand alone in history, as she had done for most of her life, was the old Queen. Her position as the revered matriarch of Protestant Europe had been based, of course, on her various German connections; but though the connections themselves were still there after 1901, her family prestige as the central figure in all this heraldic tapestry was quite irreplaceable. In any case, the new monarch wanted to push those Germanic qualities, which had almost stifled the court throughout Victoria's long reign, a little farther into the background. He wanted to be plain King of England, and to carry an almost aggressively English name, even if, more than any other of Queen Victoria's children, he was to speak to the end of his days with a strong German burr.*

Moreover, for all his cosmopolitan ties and his German blood, Edward VII now seemed drawn back to the island stance of his Tudor forebears. Though he had toured large slices of the British Empire as Prince of Wales, he was never to set foot once in it as King. (One must exclude visits to places like Gibraltar and Malta which were merely convenient staging-posts on his Mediterranean journeys.) The plain truth was that the Empire overseas, like domestic politics at home, simply did not interest him, to any sustained or compelling degree. Europe was both his personal love and his political passion. He rightly sensed that, to use a modern phrase, this was also where the 'real action' would be in his time, and that, despite all the alarms and excursions of Great Power clashes and rivalries in the swamps of Africa or along the ridges of the Himalayas, it was across the Channel and in the heart of the old continent that the supreme challenge to England lay.

The other new note which the King struck in the first hours of his reign, his change of technique, was just as unexpected. He delivered his speech of accession, which lasted eight minutes, without a single word written down on paper. Nor had he even memorized it from writing. He had simply thought out what he wanted to say on the train up from Portsmouth that morning and had then stood up and said it, without flaw or hesitation. The assembled Privy Councillors were flabbergasted when, upon asking him for the text for general publication, they were told by the King that no text existed. He had assumed, he blandly informed them, that somebody was taking his words down as he spoke. At this, they had to put their heads and their memories together and reconstruct it.

Nobody could remember anything quite like this. The speech had indeed ushered in a totally new concept of kingship. Here was complete self-confidence in a monarch, yet coupled not with pompousness but with simplicity and informality. Here was the power of the impromptu spoken word as against the laboriously prepared document. Here, above all, was the implicit belief in direct human contact and in dealing from the heart as well as the head. For England, all this was to be felt primarily in a new atmosphere at court and in society. Europe was to feel it in a different field. That accession speech foreshadowed a new and very effective style of royal diplomacy.

* * *

King Edward was not, of course, the only ruler on the scene with a

---

* When the Royal Titles Bill was passed by Parliament, Edward VII was formally described as: 'King of Great Britain and Northern Ireland and of the British Dominions beyond the

political style of his own. The German Emperor, who stayed on in England throughout the Queen's funeral ceremonies, now took the chance to pursue his equally characteristic but very different technique. London gossip had it that he had lingered on as a debt-collector and was busy raking back all the private loans that the House of Hohenzollern had extended to the new King during those long, extravagant locust years he had spent as Prince of Wales. Nor was this merely the tittle-tattle of the tap-rooms. The French Ambassador, Paul Cambon, one of the wisest and best-informed men in London, reported to his government[1] that, during King Edward's 'stormy and somewhat protracted youth', the Prince had, on one occasion, not dared to approach his mother to pay off his debts for him yet again. Instead, through the aid of Baron Hirsch, he had got the money through his sister Vicky before the premature death of her husband Frederick and while she was still German Empress. Hirsch had put up the cash, variously estimated at between 15 and 25 million French francs, but the Empress had guaranteed the transaction. According to Cambon, the Emperor William was now intent on settling his mother's claims in the intervals between attending his grandmother's funeral rites.

Whatever the truth of this, the Kaiser was also after something much more important than money. For if King Edward took the opportunity of his accession to lay stress on his Englishness, the Kaiser seized on the same occasion to do the reverse, namely to tighten their Germanic blood ties still further, and to make political capital out of those ties. As the French Embassy in London reported during the funeral week:[2]

'In going to Osborne to catch his grandmother's last breath, William II fulfilled a family duty; in prolonging his stay, he is carrying out a political act and indeed an act of the highest politics. He seeks to implant himself on the spirit of the English people and conquer it . . . He is the nephew here but he wants to turn himself into the uncle . . . The Press is ecstatic in his praises; he is the lion of the funeral ceremonies.'

Had the French diplomats but known it, the Kaiser was rather spoiling things, at least in the eyes of his English relatives, by being too much of the lion. But, at first, he did seem to be making a little progress on the political front. After the funeral, for example, King Edward was heard to express his hope that the family ties between him and the German imperial house 'would now spread to relations between the two great nations'. The two men were declared (at least

seas.' His friend, Lord Rosebery, had suggested 'King of all the Britains' to bring out the imperial concept. But the idea was soon dropped, though it did survive in the 'BRITT : OMN : REX' on the coinage of the realm.

from the German side) to be 'of one mind'. Their discussions even ranged so far as to examine certain signs in the air of a rapprochement between Russia and America. Such a strange new coalition, it was agreed, 'could be a great danger for the whole of Europe'.[3]

Though this last speculation was some seventy years ahead of its time in January of 1901, the Anglo-German 'rapprochement' was highly topical, and its prospects looked on the whole brighter the longer this dutiful and affable German Emperor stayed. Then, speaking at a farewell luncheon the King gave for him at Marlborough House on 5 February, the very last day of his protracted stay, he nearly ruined it all by going too far.

In an emotional peroration that dragged in Shakespeare, Schiller, Luther and Goethe, as well as Providence and the inevitable 'two Teutonic nations', he declared:

'We ought to form an Anglo-German alliance, you to watch over the seas while we would safeguard the land. With such an alliance, not a mouse would stir in Europe . . .'

This was just the sort of sweeping bombast that King Edward, his Ministers and the bulk of his subjects disliked and distrusted. Moreover, in political terms, it implied moving too far too fast. After generations of isolation, England was certainly not going to plunge head first across the Channel, but rather to put one toe in the water to see what it felt like. Pragmatism would anyway remain the English style, whatever course she took. This was something the emotional Kaiser, always prone to the dramatic poses of the *beau sabreur*, never would and never could understand.

He now returned home (as his mortally sick mother had been begging him to do for the past week), quite oblivious to the possibility that he might have overdone things in London. Moreover, he disembarked still under the spell of his English visit; so much that, when Bülow travelled to Homburg to meet him, he found the Kaiser not only sporting a tie-pin with Queen Victoria's initial on it, but constantly wearing civilian clothes, in the English fashion. He even stayed in this garb when his officers from the local regiment at Frankfurt came to dine with him. This was a strange and, for them, a somewhat disturbing fad of their 'Supreme War Lord'. Indeed, there were mutterings that he was overdoing his 'Anglomania'.

Of course, the fad did not last long. Nor did his mood of confident affability towards the English. He had not been back in Germany for many weeks before a report reached Berlin from London that the French were having some success there by spreading rumours that the

German Emperor was secretly siding with the Tsar against England. The Kaiser seized his pen and wrote on the telegram:

'Hell and Damnation! Fancy suspecting me of that! I can't make the British out. Such lack of character is positively awful! These people are really beyond redemption!'

For some months to come, however, family illness and family bereavement continued to bring uncle and nephew together. The Kaiser, for all his doubts and his mistakes, was thus still able to pursue what one might call his funeral diplomacy of 1901.

In February it was King Edward's turn to come to a German sick-bed. The Dowager-Empress Vicky, English mother of the Kaiser, and the King's favourite sister, was slowly dying of cancer, that same disease that had struck her own husband down after his pitifully brief reign of a hundred days. She was at Friedrichshof, the castle near Cronberg in the Taunus mountains which, as a young bride, she had fashioned on the lines of Flete, the Devonshire home of the Mildmays, to remind her always of England and English country life. The Kaiser, who, the month before, had ignored his mother's illness in order to stay on in London for political talks with his uncle, was now eager to make use of that illness to continue those talks in Germany. It was arranged that the two sovereigns should travel in their separate trains to Frankfurt, where they would meet up and go on to Cronberg together.

For King Edward this was a novel experience: his first journey abroad, the first of so many, as a reigning monarch. He soon realized that, from now on, travel was going to be quite a different matter from those carefree trips to the Continent as a princely young blade or a middle-aged *bon vivant*. He had often managed, in those days, to preserve his incognito as 'Baron Renfrew'; and it was sometimes just as well he did.

There was no hope of that now. Though he left Marlborough House as though he were still Prince of Wales – taking with him as his suite only his doctor, Sir Francis Laking, and his secretary, Frederick Ponsonby – he found the London crowds lining the streets all the way to the station to wave goodbye to their ruler. There were also inescapable badges of kingship at Sheerness where, on 23 February, he boarded the *Victoria and Albert* to cross to Flushing. Though, on his own instructions, no ceremony or guard of honour saluted his embarkation, two British cruisers and a coastguard vessel put out to sea to escort the yacht to the other side. That meant one warship for each member of the suite.

The exasperations began as soon as the new King landed

on the Continent. Ponsonby's own description can hardly be bettered:

'When we were alongside the jetty at Flushing, we heard a large number of people apparently singing hymns. I thought this a very proper way of spending Sunday evening, but what I could not understand was why they sang the same hymn over and over again *ad nauseam*. I asked Sir Henry Howard, His Majesty's Minister at The Hague, who came on board as soon as we arrived, and he explained that it was the Boer National Anthem, and that the mass of people who were singing had originally intended to sing it on the jetty but that, owing to his representations, the authorities had kept them outside.' As Ponsonby drily added: 'I got to know this hymn very well.'[4]

The train journey up the Rhine to Frankfurt proved even more trying than the reception at Flushing. The Germans, like the Dutch (who, after all, could be forgiven for being fanatically pro-Boer) also shouted anti-English slogans at several of the stations *en route*. Nor did the King much relish the one effort that was made to show some pro-British feeling. At Düsseldorf, the headmistress of the local girls' school had lined all her pupils up on the platform, and then, in a piercing voice, had led them in a rendering of 'God Save the King' as the royal train approached. Two things doomed the good woman's venture. The first was that it was now two o'clock in the morning and the King, like everyone else on the train, was aroused from his sleep by the sudden din. But the main snag was that the King's train was anyway not scheduled to stop at Düsseldorf. It therefore steamed steadily past the rows of screeching schoolgirls and on into the night, with its irritated passengers trying to regain their slumber.

Altogether, this was not a happy way for King Edward to see Germany for the first time as King. The German Chancellor Bülow sorrowfully commented later:

'Politically, the King's journey had an unfavourable effect on his future attitude to Germany. Indeed, his entire judgement of German conditions was influenced by it. Contrary to the theoretical Germans, who like to derive their judgements from books, or from the depths of some ethical conviction, the English base their judgement directly on what they observe themselves . . .'[5]

Both in and out of office, the Kaiser's Chancellor was much too prone to philosophizing. But though that verdict leans too heavily on the effect of one train journey up the Rhine, it does bring out the cardinal point about England's negative attitude towards Wilhelminian

Germany, namely that this was a subjective reaction. Most of the English leaders of the day simply did not feel at ease with this Teutonic nation with whom they were supposed to be 'united both by interest and racial sentiment'. It was altogether too restless, brash, emotional and unpredictable. England's sovereign epitomized this unease; and by epitomizing, furthered it.

There was more irritation awaiting him now, in his imperial nephew's welcome when they met and dutifully embraced at Frankfurt station the next morning. In Germany, as in England, the King had pleaded that no formality whatsoever should be attached to his visit, which was that of a brother visiting a mortally sick sister. Accordingly, the King and his two companions got off their train dressed in plain civilian clothes. Yet there to greet them was a cluster of German military uniforms as bright as a flower-bed on the station platform, with, at the centre, the brightest bloom of all, the Kaiser, attired in the ceremonial garb of a Prussian General. (His passion for 'English' civilian clothes was now evidently over.)

He must also have annoyed his uncle more than a little by his behaviour during the next twenty-four hours. It was glorious winter weather, and the great pine forests around Friedrichshof, with, behind them, the peaks of the Taunus mountains, were sparkling under snow and sun. So invigorating was it that the stricken Empress, who had already been much cheered by her brother's arrival, ventured into the fresh air for the first time in weeks. Smothered by shawls and rugs, she appeared in a Bath-chair and was wheeled in the sun along the sheltered paths of the castle parks, talking to three of her married daughters* and to the King.

If the family reunion and the brilliant weather helped to revive the dying woman a little, they seem to have put steel springs into the boots of her ebullient son. On that first day, he drove the King from Cronberg station to Friedrichshof in his own sleigh, drawn by a pair of prancing Hungarian greys, of which he was immensely proud. Then, having dropped his uncle, he sleighed off at top speed through the forests to Homburg, where he was staying. He reckoned to do the trip in twenty-five minutes compared with the normal time of one hour.

He was back again at Friedrichshof two hours later for a luncheon (without, of course, the invalid, who stayed upstairs in her rooms); and King Edward, much as he disliked it, felt constrained to put on Prussian uniform himself for the occasion. In the afternoon, he also felt obliged to sleigh over to Homburg, to pay a return call on his

---

* Princess Victoria of Schaumburg-Lippe, the Duchess of Sparta, and Princess Frederick Charles of Hesse.

nephew. But then the Kaiser, not content with all that, wanted to come back to Friedrichshof yet again for dinner. That was really too much. The King pleaded tiredness – doubtless quite genuinely in view of that Düsseldorf headmistress – and went quietly to bed in this castle that was anyway almost a house of death.

King and Kaiser stayed on for most of that week. There were, unavoidably, other meals together, and these managed to produce at least one amusing situation. This was on the third day at Friedrichshof when the King, who was superstitious over such matters, discovered to his horror that they had been sitting thirteen at dinner. It was doubly awkward, as the castle at that moment needed all the luck it could get. Then the King had an inspiration. He cheered up his embarrassed secretary by assuring him it was 'all right after all': Princess Frederick Charles of Hesse, who had been at table with them all the time, was expecting a baby. For the most part, however, the atmosphere was either gloomy or tense, or both. Ponsonby, who had never before seen uncle and nephew so much together, wrote of these winter days at Friedrichshof: 'One always felt there was electricity in the air when the Emperor and King Edward talked.'

The King left his sister's bedside realizing that she had a year at the most to live. Accordingly, both he and the Kaiser made their summer plans so as to be near her. King Edward booked his usual suite of rooms at Ritter's Park Hotel at Homburg in order to take the waters there for three weeks from mid-August. The Kaiser arranged to be either at Homburg or Wilhelmshöhe from 10 August to 24 August, so that the two sovereigns would each be conveniently placed to re-visit the dying Dowager-Empress together.

The rapid march of her illness outpaced this timetable. On 4 August, after a series of misleading statements from Berlin claiming that the Empress's condition was 'quite satisfactory' (this despite the steady stream of dark-clad relatives who, for days past, had been converging on Cronberg from all over Germany like a flock of princely crows), it was suddenly announced that her long-standing malady was spreading and that 'the strength of the illustrious patient is fading fast'. Her son was already returning from a cruise in Norwegian waters on the *Hohenzollern* and he now steamed as fast as the yacht's boilers would allow back to Kiel. He arrived at Friedrichshof in time to be with her when she died in agony on 5 August.

When the first alarming bulletin had been issued the previous day, King Edward was also afloat, on the *Britannia* in the Solent for Cowes Week. He was preparing to leave for Cronberg with Queen Alexandra when the news came that his sister was already dead, and in fact they did not arrive in Germany until four days after that, to attend the various funeral ceremonies. This gave the Kaiser the chance unctuously to reproach his uncle for a certain lack of feeling.

There were some macabre touches, and even more macabre rumours, about the burial of this very English Princess Royal in German soil. Her death, like her life, symbolized the tug-of-war between her native country and her adopted one. There were stories at Cronberg (later denied from Berlin) that she was being buried, at her request, in an inner wooden coffin made of English oak, around which an outer casing of ornamental zinc made in Germany would be placed. This arrangement would in fact have told her life story very aptly.

Bülow had an even more dramatic tale. The Kaiser, he claimed, told him the morning after the Empress's death that she had wanted her naked corpse to be wrapped in a Union Jack and sent home to England to be buried there. The Kaiser had decided to ignore his mother's wishes which, he felt, 'might offend the sensibilities of the German people and the dignity of our country'. The Chancellor had entirely agreed.[6]

As it was, poor Vicky was buried on 13 August under leaden skies and to the jingle of Prussian spurs at Potsdam, that barracks town full of infantry drill grounds and cavalry riding schools, with streets laid out in squares and even its trees trimmed as though for a parade, which was the cradle of German military might. As if to ram the point home, the streets were lined, as they had been at Homburg, where the first part of the ceremony had been held, with thousands of German troops. But at least one pair of Prussian spurs belonged to the dead woman's dear brother. King Edward and the Kaiser marched at the head of the procession to the Friedenskirche each wearing the blue uniform of the Prussian Dragoon Guards. There was a bitter-sweet reason for this. Old Queen Victoria had been the Regiment's Colonel-in-Chief.

The King left the next day for his cure at Homburg, as originally planned. Queen Alexandra accompanied him there but stayed at the spa for only thirty-six hours – a nominal gesture to protocol – before leaving him alone with his friends and travelling herself up to Copenhagen, to spend the next three weeks with her own family. This was quite typical of the married life (routine would be a better word) that the King had been leading for many years before his accession.

At Homburg, the King was again made to realize that, whatever delights the crown had brought with it, privacy was not one of them. He had paid several visits to the spa as Prince of Wales and, as such, had been able to mingle fairly freely and casually with the other

visitors, who anyway contained a good sprinkling of European nobility.
But when he showed himself the first morning as King of England,
it was a different story. From the moment he appeared outside the Park
Hotel at 7.30 a.m. to walk to the mineral springs, he was surrounded by
a ring of jostling spectators, who could recognize him from his
portraits displayed in every shop window. He was absolutely furious.
For years he had enjoyed the best of both worlds, living both grandly
and informally. Was this really all over and done with? His suite made
tactful representations to the spa directors and they in turn put tactful
pressure on the public. After a few days, the crowds did behave a little
better. However, a much more exasperating event took place during
the second week of the King's stay. This was a visit to his imperial
nephew at Wilhelmshöhe on 23 August for what were intended to be
serious political talks.

That long day started off in the most trying fashion – a four-hour
journey by train, with the King uncomfortably corseted in his uniform
as a Prussian Colonel-in-Chief. The next thing to try the King's nerves
was the reception that awaited him on arrival. Though the meeting
was supposed to be without any pomp and ceremony, in view of
court mourning for the Empress, the Kaiser had again been unable to
resist that perpetual itch of his for military display. In fact, he had
ordered no fewer than 15,000 German troops into the town for the
occasion. The streets were jammed with soldiers, and when the visitors
arrived at the castle they realized with a sinking feeling that this
entire mass of troops was now going to march past the two sovereigns
in parade. (It must have been a sinking feeling in every sense for they
had breakfasted only on eggs at 8 a.m. in Homburg and were now
famished. Not until after two o'clock, when the last salute was taken,
could they all go into the castle for lunch.)

Nor did the political talks which were held after lunch provide much
relief. The Kaiser was passionately interested in every aspect of world
affairs and was also extremely well informed about them. The trouble
on this occasion was that he was better informed on a purely English
matter than his English guest. He mentioned the 'trouble at Malta'
and said he had been interested to hear that the British Government
were even thinking of giving the island colony its independence. King
Edward, who had not heard a word about the whole matter, was
made to look extremely foolish. His temper was not improved, and
there were ructions at home afterwards.*

* In strict theory, the Colonial Secretary was not obliged, as was the Foreign Secretary, to
consult the King directly before taking any important step; and this was the reason Mr
Chamberlain later gave.

But the King himself was largely to blame for the confusion which now descended over the Anglo-German discussions themselves. Elaborate preparations had been made both in London and Berlin in case this Wilhelmshöhe meeting (which had been arranged in principle during the winter) could serve to lay any foundations for some formal understanding or agreement between the two sides. In Berlin, they had been debating again the whole problem of an Anglo-German alliance, how it might affect relations with other powers (and especially with Russia), and what stance the Kaiser should best adopt. For his part, King Edward had been armed by his Foreign Secretary, Lord Lansdowne, with a special guidance memorandum on the subjects that might crop up between the two sovereigns. It dealt, and dealt in some detail, with such matters as the indemnities which the Western governments were seeking in China after the ravages of the Boxer Revolt; the claims of German shareholders in the South Africa Railway Company; joint policy in Morocco; and relations with the ruler of Kuwait, a sheikdom which the Germans might want to use as the terminus of their projected trans-Caspian railway.

Though none of this was above the King's head, a lot of it was too much for his patience and too little for his dignity. It was not the monarch's business to debate with a fellow monarch, for example, whether £130 per shareholder was enough to buy out the German railway holdings in South Africa; this was what Ministers and civil servants were trained for and paid for. But if the concept of Lansdowne's memorandum was itself somewhat naïve, what the King did with it was more inept still. On 11 August at Homburg, where he had a family meeting with the Kaiser after the funeral, he had fished the memorandum out of his pocket and handed it over to his nephew – simply, one suspects, to get rid of the wretched thing. An astonished German Foreign Office had spent the next ten days preparing a point-by-point comment, which was then sent to the King, who passed it on to his Berlin Embassy. (Sir Frank Lascelles, King Edward's very pro-German Ambassador to Berlin, was summoned to Wilhelmshöhe for the meeting.)

No great harm had been done; perhaps even a little good. Lansdowne's paper had revealed no great secrets of British policy and, together with the German reply, had helped to clear minds on both sides. But Lansdowne, who was already a little resentful over the direct personal influence that the new monarch was clearly seeking over his country's foreign policy, was angry and horrified.[7] It was the sort of blunder which might have cost a First Secretary his career. The King of England was no junior diplomat, but a ruler who had more experience of Europe's great men and matters than any Minister or official in his realm. But if he needed a sharp reminder that the minutiae of paperwork and of detailed negotiation were neither his proper business nor his natural bent, this was it. Throughout his reign, he hardly ever pocketed a diplomatic memorandum again. From now on, it was to be all like that Accession Speech: intuitive, unrehearsed and informal.

It was past ten o'clock that night, after another four-hour train journey, that the King thankfully got back to the Park Hotel at Homburg. Nothing was, in fact, achieved by this long and trying day at Wilhelmshöhe. Not only were no foundations for any Anglo-German agreement laid, as people like Lascelles had fondly hoped. In the months that followed, the King's Ministers decided that, though friendly relations with Germany were both necessary and desirable, a formal alliance with her was neither of those things. The feelers that were stretched out, this time from the German side, were thus politely left dangling.

This was not, as the Germans supposed, solely due to Lord Salisbury's hostile influence. The entire Cabinet had mulled over the obvious political objections to alienating France, Russia and even the United States by tacking England on to the Berlin-Vienna axis.[8] But the great difficulty was the same one which had prevailed ever since Mr Chamberlain had floated his vision of the great Teutonic partnership two years before. England was just not psychologically ready to move straight from her generations of cautious detachment from all continental entanglements to a position of total and formal commitment to either one of the rival camps. Dedicated bachelors often fall suddenly in love and marry. With nations, the leap is much rarer.

It was on 19 December 1901 that Count Metternich, the new German Ambassador in London,* was officially informed of the British Government's decision to suspend the talks. King Edward certainly agreed wholeheartedly with this decision, though it is impossible to say whether Crown or Cabinet was pressing the harder for it. What is clear is that, despite the formal end to the negotiations, the Kaiser himself would not give up hope. This year of death-bed diplomacy ended with a long New Year's greeting message which he wrote to his uncle on 30 December and in which all the emotional and political Anglo-German strands of the last twelve months were woven together again. To begin with, there were the family links. The King had found at Windsor Castle a Highland suit that had once belonged to the Kaiser's ill-fated father, the Emperor Frederick III, and he had sent it to Berlin as a Christmas present for his nephew. The Kaiser was

---

* His predecessor, Count Hatzfield, had died on 22 November.

clearly touched and delighted. The letter to his 'Dearest Uncle', written in English,[9] begins with a flood of family memories that the gift had brought back:

'The last time I wore Highland dress at Balmoral was in 1878 in September, when I visited dear Grandmamma and was able to go out deer-stalking on Lochnagar. Dear Grandpapa's gigantic old "Jäger" was still in waiting on Grandmamma and looked after my rifles, while a very nice old but fine [*sic*] Head-Keeper, with a good Highland name and a splendid face, stalked with me . . .'

Then, after a reference to the two family funerals they had attended together during the past year, and particularly to Queen Victoria's, came the sentence:

'What a magnificent realm she has left you, and what a fine position in the world!'

Whether or not there was a sigh of unconscious envy behind those words, they served to introduce another ringing appeal for partnership between England and Germany. It was, as ever, a bit too ringing. The Kaiser wrote of the two countries:

'They are of the same blood and they have the same creed and they belong to the great Teutonic race which Heaven has entrusted with the culture [*sic*] of the world.'

Finally he told his uncle that he need not worry about any critical voices raised in Germany:

'I am the sole arbiter and master of German foreign policy and the Government and country *must* follow me even if I have to face the musik [*sic*]. May your Government never forget this . . .'

This was, of course, precisely what neither the King nor his Government ever could forget. Poor Kaiser William; he tried so hard. But because he saw everything about England either larger than life or upside down, he so often achieved the exact opposite of what he intended. That letter, which was meant to strengthen the ties between Berlin and London, must have made the King doubly relieved that his Cabinet had just decided to trim them.

*   *   *

The fact that England had now turned down the German option had opened up other horizons. One was in the Far East. The breakdown in the negotiations between England and Germany of 1901 had been, first and foremost, a turning-point in European affairs. Yet it also had an Asiatic aspect, for both the English and the German sides had envisaged bringing Japan into the agreement as a third party who would help them both to keep the Russians in check.

This European divorce now produced an Asiatic child. The English and Japanese were, after all, the two powers who had the strongest mutual interest in blocking Russia's expansionist aims in central and north-eastern Asia respectively. They had come into serious contact with one another and had seen what each had to offer. Moreover, they were the two 'odd men out', for each country then stood politically isolated in its own continent.

When the idea of bringing Japan into England's calculations had first been mooted, King Edward had sounded none too keen. There may have been, in this attitude, a sense of reluctance to join hands with a yellow race, a reaction which would certainly have been felt, and much more strongly, by the Kaiser. But what probably lay at the root of the King's own hesitation was the plain fact that Japan was just about as far removed as one could get from being a European power. Europe was his world and his stage and he would have had the same initial twinges of doubt if his government had suggested instead that America should suddenly be introduced on to that stage.

However, these doubts were soon overcome, for even if the union looked a strange one, its advantages were too obvious to be missed. When the English-educated Marquis Ito, a former Prime Minister of Japan, announced his intention of visiting London at the end of 1901 the King took the lead in urging the government to organize the most elaborate welcome possible for him. The fact that Ito was suspected by the Foreign Office of being secretly pro-Russian made it all the more important, in the King's eyes, to make a fuss of him.

The itinerary that the Japanese statesman had mapped out for himself made it all too clear that England was now dealing with another culture, as well as another continent. The Marquis, coming from St Petersburg and Berlin, announced his arrival in London on, of all days of the year, Christmas Eve. As the King and Queen, following the German practice established by Queen Victoria, always made that evening the centre-piece of their family celebration, there could be no question of receiving him then. But as soon as Boxing Day came, King Edward wrote to Lord Lansdowne:

'Though he arrives at a most inconvenient time . . . I think every possible civility should be shown him on account of the great importance of our being on the best possible terms with Japan. I am therefore anxious to receive him in uniform tomorrow, with you being present . . .'[10]

This duly took place, as did the rest of the programme the King had suggested for Marquis Ito, which included a weekend at Bowood with Lord Lansdowne and a luncheon given by the Marquess of Salisbury at Hatfield House. The day before the Japanese visitor left for Paris, the King conferred on him, as a final sweetener, the G.C.B. By December of 1901, there was probably nothing that even such an influential Japanese figure as Ito could have done to block the proposed pact, since a draft of the agreement had already received the imperial consent in Tokyo. But King Edward was taking no chances and, in any case, England now had to look on this rising sun of Asia with very different eyes in the future.

The Anglo-Japanese alliance that was formally signed in London on 30 January 1902 was essentially aimed, by both countries, against Russia. It was not a direct and automatically binding military alliance, since the only circumstances in which English and Japanese soldiers would actually fight side by side were the rather improbable ones of a general war between the great powers fought out in Asia.* All that really concerned both partners was the eventuality, which looked increasingly likely, of Russia and Japan settling their Far Eastern quarrels by the sword. If this happened, England promised to remain strictly neutral. This pledge was all Japan wanted. Apart from its moral value, it would help to localize any clash, and would also bar British coaling stations all over the world to the Russian fleet. The Japanese had calculated – all too accurately, as a complacent Russia was soon to learn to her cost – that it was at sea that they would smash their Russian challenger beyond hope of recovery.

King Edward did not, for one moment, lose sight of the European context to which everything was related. The day after the Japanese alliance was concluded, it was he who suggested to Lansdowne that there should be 'no loss of time' in informing the German Government officially of its signing. He knew that his imperial nephew had nothing against such a treaty. He also knew that the Kaiser liked to be the first man in Europe to be told about anything new and important. Again, Lord Lansdowne took his sovereign's advice. A delighted message of congratulations which the Kaiser sent back to London was their reward.

---

* Thus, if Japan had to go to war with more than one foreign power specifically to safeguard her hold in Korea, England pledged her military support. Conversely, if England had to fight two or more powers (Russia and Germany?) to defend her interests in China, Japan would come to her side.

The other opening created by the rejection of an Anglo-German pact lay much closer at home and much closer to the King's own heart – the chance to realize his dream of a lifetime by linking England with France. Whereas Edward VII had only operated from the wings over the treaty with Japan, he was to step out into the centre of the stage once the French act opened. But before he could start to plan that triumph, he had a year of mixed personal fortunes ahead.

*   *   *

Few sovereigns can have looked forward more eagerly to their coronation than King Edward. He had, after all, been waiting for it long enough, and as a greying middle-aged Heir-Apparent in the '80s and '90s, he must have sometimes asked himself whether it would ever take place at all. Even when the turn of the century came, his mother still looked as tough and indestructible as asbestos. It was just possible that he would die before her, killed off by over-indulgence, boredom and sheer frustration.

As it was, he would be well over 60 by 26 June 1902, which had been fixed as coronation day. As one French observer was to point out, he would be ascending to the throne at a time when, according to the statistics, 75 per cent of monarchs could expect to be descending to their tombs. (The same writer[11] went on, rather unkindly, to add that if kings had to be passed fit by medical commissions before being crowned, Edward VII would have been declared 'ineligible for service'.)

But in this monarch's case, it was not merely the interminable process of ripening that had made the fruits of office look so delectable. For all his informality, King Edward loved the solemn ceremonial of kingship for its own sake and for what it symbolized. Moreover, long before he succeeded to the throne, he was already acknowledged as the greatest expert in Europe on matters of precedence and protocol. At the pageant of his own coronation he would be the master of ceremonies as well as the central actor. Finally, there was the thought that this glittering event would draw all the world, and especially all the European old order which was still the heart and muscle of that world, to his own capital. He would be related to many of the royal envoys sent to attend the ceremony. Related or not, there would scarcely be one among them he would not know. He would be in his element in every sense of the word.

The preparations quickened in pace during the first months of the New Year. By the end of May, the Ministries of Whitehall, the clubs of Pall Mall, all the great buildings in the City and all the illustrious private houses of Mayfair and Belgravia were vying with each other with special decorative designs, executed in flowers and electric bulbs (or, in the case of the Mansion House, in gas-burners, with five thousand prismatic globes mounted in crystal shades and bronze flambeaux).

The Earl Marshal duly issued his authorized 'Order of Procession', and the *London Gazette* gave details of routes and police regulations for the great day in order, as the spacious phrase went on, 'to secure the commodious access and return of carriages conveying persons to and from Westminster Abbey'. The names of the foreign warships attending the great naval review at Spithead were announced, as were those of the foreign guests who were to occupy some of those coveted seats in the Abbey. In the early morning of 27 May, the first route rehearsal was held. There was a feeling of pleasurable excitement in the air.

At the very end of the month, on 31 May, this feeling was heightened when both King and country received the finest coronation gift either could have wished for. After weeks of negotiations, which had see-sawed as anxiously as the fighting before them, peace terms were agreed in Pretoria. The Boer War, which had cost England so much in blood and treasure, and even more in prestige and pride, was over at long last. Even now, the issue was by no means spent as a source of friction between England and Germany, and particularly between King and Kaiser. But the war itself, which had reduced England to her nadir of popularity, and esteem all over the Continent, was ended. The King could now be crowned as the ruler of a nation at peace.

King Edward himself was in the best of spirits and went briskly about his normal social round, which continued alongside all the extra demands of coronation year. The levées continued at St James's Palace, as did the court receptions at Buckingham Palace. He attended the spring race meetings at Kempton and Newmarket and, on 5 June, paid his second visit to Epsom in three days to see Ard Patrick (owned by the wealthy but distinctly non-patrician Mr J. Gubbins) win the Coronation Derby in pouring rain.

It was this weather that was partly responsible for the impending disaster. Even by the robust standards of an English summer, it was exceptionally wet and freezing. Nor did there seem any early prospect that it would warm up or dry out. For the main Ascot meeting, which was being heralded as the most brilliant of all Royal Ascots, the ladies were being cautioned to take warning from the 'slight chill' that the King had caught and told to 'forgo a trifle of the charming daintiness of fashionable footwear in favour of something rather more pro-tective'. The King was already seen to be suffering from that chill on

14 June when, with Queen Alexandra, he went down to Aldershot to attend a military review. The heavens went on pouring while 30,000 drenched troops wheeled and marched on a quagmire of a parade-ground, bordered with the thousands of dripping black umbrellas of the spectators. There was some concern when it was announced that, due to his cold, the King could not attend the actual parade and that the Queen would take the salute instead. It was Queen Alexandra who also had to deputize for him when Royal Ascot opened a few days later. Throughout that meeting he stayed away, 'resting quietly at Windsor'.

Still, neither the court nor the public dreamt that anything serious was wrong; and they were not helped by the King himself. On 23 June, when returning to London from Windsor, he refused to listen to his doctor's advice to make the journey quietly by car and travelled instead in full style by train to Paddington, and thence with a cavalry escort to the Palace. It was the insistence on keeping to his coronation plans that finally led to them being torn up. Later that day, his condition became worse and his doctors now told him that he would certainly die unless operated on immediately.[13] The King, who only a few days before had informed those same harassed men that he would turn up at Westminster Abbey on 26 June even if it meant him dropping dead while being crowned, was forced to yield before this verdict. The next morning, a shocked and astounded world was told that King Edward VII was seriously ill and that the coronation had been indefinitely postponed. It was now a case of 'God Save the King' in deadly earnest.

Happily, the operation – for acute appendicitis – was a complete success, and the patient's stamina was such that, by 5 July, he was officially declared to be 'out of danger'. The Kaiser joined in the genuine and general rejoicing. He was at a regatta dinner at Travemünde near Lübeck when the good news reached him that same evening, and he promptly interrupted the proceedings to call for three cheers from the whole company. This made some amends for an unfortunate incident which had happened a few days before and where the Kaiser, for once, was more sinned against than sinning. At the end of June, a German torpedo-boat had been sunk in an accident, killing the commander (who showed great bravery and bore a distinguished German name) together with several of his men. Though King Edward had only left the operating table a few days before, he found time and energy to send a message of sympathy to his nephew. He sent it in English, which was not unreasonable in the circumstances, and was anyway the language in which the two men nearly always corresponded. There were, however, some chauvinists in Berlin who *did* find it unreasonable. The *Berliner Neueste Nachrichten*, for example, asked complainingly why the King of England had not written this personal message in German, and criticized the Kaiser for not sending his reply in that language. (It must be added that some anti-German sections of the British press were capable of similar pettiness.)

But the German press had nothing to do with an extraordinary anti-English and anti-Edward outburst which the Kaiser gave vent to the following month. Indeed, the whole significance of it was that the German Emperor thought his words would remain secret. And so, but for a pure chance, they would have done.

In July 1902, an American-owned yacht which was cruising in Norwegian waters happened to put in at a harbour where the *Hohenzollern*, with the Kaiser on board, was lying. The Emperor, true to his nature, which was both curious and gregarious, paid them a visit. The passengers were all presented by name and the Kaiser was soon launched on his favourite topic, world politics. Before he had gone very far, England came in for some violent criticism, which the Kaiser presumably thought would go down well with these men from the New World. There was not a real English statesman left, he declared. Old Lord Salisbury was not a man but 'just a protoplasm'. Not content with that broadside, the Kaiser then launched into a personal attack against King Edward's whole character and permissive mode of life. If he behaved like his 'Uncle Bertie', he assured the astounded Americans, then 'the German people would soon get rid of me'.

The trouble was that one of those American yachtsmen was, quite unbeknown to the Kaiser, not an American at all, but an Englishman named Humphreys Owen, who had once served as an Honorary Attaché in the British Diplomatic Service. He promptly reported the whole incident to the Foreign Office,[14] adding that, when the American party was entertained afterwards on the *Hohenzollern*, the Kaiser gave them a repeat performance.

It is not clear whether King Edward was ever told about this. As he was still convalescent, it is unlikely. At any rate, the Foreign Office memorandum on the subject, which turns up in a docket for the year 1908, has no mark at all in the marginal space entitled 'How disposed of', and the bottom space for 'Action completed' is equally blank. But though the King would certainly have been annoyed had he read it, he would not have been astounded. Uncle Bertie's 'high life' – complete with mistresses, racehorses, gambling, perpetual over-spending and over-eating – was always a source of horrified fascination for the nephew, whose own mode of living was so different and so dull. He could never comprehend how England, the severe England of his beloved 'Grandmamma', could allow their King to get away with it all. (Neither, for that matter, could a lot of people in England, particularly poor Queen Alexandra.)

*   *   *

All went well when the coronation was duly held, on 9 August. Indeed, even the weather was now kind, and the only person who nearly collapsed was the aged Archbishop of Canterbury, Dr Temple, whom the King had to help to his feet at the end. But the postponed event was in a minor key. There was a shortened service; fewer and less illustrious foreign guests; far fewer troops on parade; and much less decoration than in June, both public and private. (The King, in a characteristically practical gesture, had himself expressed the wish that nobody 'should go to double expense' on his behalf.) That great assemblage of European royalty, with himself at its centre, to which King Edward had so looked forward, had not materialized. For that, London would have to await the crowning of his own son nine years later, when Europe's old order paraded all together for the last time.

If there had been no foreign monarchs present at King Edward's coronation, one did arrive in England immediately afterwards and managed to enrage the King almost enough to cause him a relapse. The potentate was the Shah of Persia and the argument was over an English decoration.

There was much in the situation that, especially to a later age, would appear trivial and shot through with preposterous vanity. Preposterous it may have been. But trivial, in 1902, it certainly was not. Throughout the Victorian and Edwardian eras, British honours and decorations were far and away the most coveted in the world. No one realized this, and with greater relish, more than King Edward VII himself. Moreover, he and his Ministers manipulated them as glittering little instruments of British foreign policy. Many were to be the time when the path to a treaty or a concession was successfully paved by a shower of English ribbons, stars and medals on foreign nobility and officialdom. Even when no direct political object was in view, they remained cheap and reliable purchasers of goodwill. But King Edward always insisted that he should supervise the purchasing, and this fact had been either ignored or forgotten by Sir Arthur Hardinge, the British Minister in Teheran. After many frustrating weeks trying to persuade the Shah to pay a visit to England, the envoy had finally promised him the Garter if he came. That did the trick, and the Shah set out solely to collect the coveted item.

Lord Lansdowne had raised the matter with the King at Windsor in June, when the monarch was sickening for his illness, and the royal temper was therefore not at its best. There had been precedents for this most Christian as well as most exalted order being awarded to non-Christian sovereigns. Queen Victoria had given it, for example, to two Sultans of Turkey and even to the Shah's own father, Nasir-ad-Din. (It had not brought him much luck; he had been assassinated in 1896.) So the question was: would the King, for equally good political reasons, make another exception now for another aspiring infidel? The King said no, both on that occasion and again after he had fully recovered from his illness. This was the awkward situation when the Shah, accompanied by an enormous suite, arrived in London on 18 August and went down to Portsmouth two days later to lunch with the King on the *Victoria and Albert*.

Lansdowne and the Foreign Office were in a pretty pickle but they resolved that if the Garter was the only thing that would attach the Shah to England (and help detach him from Russia) then the Garter he would get. Lansdowne accordingly produced a document, which he himself had prepared, stating that the Lord Chamberlain's office was to revise the rules of the Order to enable a special version of it to be awarded to non-Christian recipients, after suitable modifications to its design. The noble Marquess, who was lacking neither in imagination nor in courage, sprung this compromise without warning over the lunch table; he asked King Edward to read the document over, and claimed afterwards that the King had nodded his assent. But it seemed that King Edward had either been waggling his head in astonishment or because he could think of no better reaction. The Shah, meanwhile, was deeply offended because of the delay and departed in a sulk together with his large suite, who were forbidden to receive any English decorations at all.

Lord Lansdowne, now a desperate man, took desperate measures. He ordered Garrards, the Court jewellers, to fashion a non-Christian version of the Garter insignia by leaving out the Cross of St George. This was to be done within three days, so that the Shah could get his precious order before departing for home. The Foreign Secretary then penned a letter to King Edward on his yacht, explaining what he had done and why, and enclosing coloured drawings of the special design. This was the envelope that the King opened on the morning of 24 August in Pembroke Dock, where the *Victoria and Albert* then lay. The yacht's boiler might have burst, such was the explosion which came. The King took Lord Lansdowne's letter with its enclosures and hurled them through his cabin porthole into the sea. Fortunately, the package landed instead in a pinnace-boat tied up right underneath the cabin and was retrieved from there by a stoker.

It did not prove so easy to retrieve the tense three-cornered situation between the Shah, the King and the Foreign Secretary. The Persian ruler, still garterless, left England breathing fire and brimstone at King Edward and his Ministers. He had been made angry enough by the forty-eight hours spent in London before travelling down to Portsmouth to see the King. Everyone of consequence who could be absent from the capital was up in Scotland, preoccupied with grouse, and those who had been commanded to remain for the Shah's benefit seem to have had difficulty in concealing their sulkiness. The receptions given for him at Marlborough House had therefore been wooden to a degree, and entertaining him elsewhere had also been a problem. He did not like opera and had insufficient English to enjoy the theatre, so he was trundled off to ballet performances at the Alhambra and fireworks displays in damp weather at Crystal Palace.[15] And now this humiliation on the royal yacht. Had the Russians been sufficiently well informed and quick off the mark to offer him a new treaty, he would probably have signed it on the spot.

In London, this comic opera episode now turned into a grave political crisis. Lansdowne said he would resign unless the Shah got the Garter he had promised him. The new Conservative Prime Minister, Arthur Balfour, who had succeeded the ailing Lord Salisbury, decided, after long deliberation, to back up his Foreign Secretary. For weeks it looked as though the government of England might trip and tumble over a strip of bejewelled elastic.

Finally, on 3 November, swayed by an eloquent plea from Balfour about the difficult and dangerous game England had to play in Persia against the much stronger Russian hand, the King gave way. The Shah got his Garter in its traditional Christian form. A fierce reprimand had to be dispatched, on the King's orders, to Sir Arthur Hardinge in Teheran; but Downing Street could breathe again. Anything further removed than this whole episode from the politics of the present day could scarcely be imagined. But that is precisely its relevance in a reconstruction of Edwardian Europe.

* * *

The other problem to preoccupy King Edward that autumn was his German nephew's private visit to England or, rather, a political rumpus which threatened to cancel it altogether. The occasion was a tour of Europe which the three leading Boer generals (Botha, the Commander-in-Chief; Christian de Wet and Jacobus Delarey) had set

KING OF ENGLAND

Edward while still Prince of Wales.

Alice, The Hon. Mrs. George Keppel.

Above: A contrast in royal styles – an informal meeting with the Kaiser at Friedrichshof.

Below: The Shah of Persia on board the King's yacht at Cowes during his stormy visit in 1902.

out on after the Pretoria peace terms had been signed. That they should be officially received in England was reasonable enough, as they were distinguished ex-enemies coming to London with the express object of negotiating some retrospective improvements in the terms. But once the British Government had politely but firmly refused any concessions (which it duly did when they arrived in England in August), it was another matter altogether when the gallant trio set off to continue their propaganda efforts on the Continent. After his own experience only the year before on the quayside at Flushing, the King could neither be surprised nor offended at the tumultuous reception which the Dutch people gave to the generals during the last ten days of August. When, however, they reached Berlin and asked to be received by the Kaiser, the King and his Ministers sat up sharply and took notice.

The Kaiser began by announcing that he would receive the Boer Commanders, though his advisers warned him against it, pointing to the grave complications it would produce in London. Just how grave these might be was shown in a letter which King Edward wrote on 2 October to his ambassador in Berlin. It was short and to the point.

'The King sees it announced in the papers that the Emperor proposes to receive the Boer Generals. He thinks the Emperor ought to know that his doing so shortly before his visit to England will be very unpopular in the country.

'The King wishes no further comment.'[16]

That was, of course, a thinly veiled warning that if the Kaiser saw the generals there would be no point in him setting out to see his uncle at all. Some anxious days of see-sawing followed. The Emperor, who was again caught in a cross-current between Ministerial warnings and the waves of pro-Boer public feeling in Berlin, at first gave way and cancelled the audience. Then he had second thoughts and suggested seeing the generals after all, though he would have them presented by the Ambassador, Sir Frank Lascelles, thus emphasizing that he did accept that they were British subjects. Finally, after more objections from London and more misgivings in the Wilhelmstrasse, the Kaiser agreed to drop the idea altogether, and the trio left Berlin without their audience.

The way was now clear for uncle and nephew to meet in England. The dates had been fixed to cover the period of King Edward's sixty-first birthday on 9 November, but the matter which had not been fixed was, what sort of meeting should it be? As England had put into very cold storage all discussions for an alliance with Berlin, King Edward was determined to make the visit as much of an informal family affair as possible. The Kaiser was to come up to Sandringham for a few days' shooting with his uncle straight from a military inspection at Shorncliffe. The King was not going to stir outside the Sandringham estate during the visit. There were going to be no banquets at Windsor Castle and no political discussions in London. Even at Sandringham, the King wanted things played down as much as possible. Would the Emperor please not bring *too* large a suite, he wrote to the Berlin Embassy, and would the Kaiser himself *please* wear civilian clothes?

King Edward took personal charge of the entire programme for his nephew's visit. Well aware that the Kaiser would want to meet English Ministers, even though there could be no question of formal negotiations, the King asked the key members of his government up to Sandringham in relays. The German guests were due on the 8th, which was a Saturday. The Prime Minister, Mr Balfour, accompanied by Mr Chamberlain and Mr Brodrick (the Ministers for the Colonies and for War), were therefore invited for the weekend. These three Ministers were to leave on the Monday, when the next group (including Lord and Lady Lansdowne) would arrive for the five days of shooting which was the declared purpose of the invitation.

Tout se bornera à un grand massacre de faisans was, indeed, what Lansdowne had told the French Ambassador in London, Paul Cambon, before leaving to join the Sandringham party.[17] That very shrewd French diplomatist had, in any case, not believed that far-reaching political talks would take place at Sandringham after the guns were put away each tea-time. But he must nonetheless have been glad of the Foreign Secretary's assurances, which he reported to Paris. Both in London and in Berlin, the rumours had started flying about as soon as the procession of Cabinet Ministers to Sandringham was made known. The English newspapers even reported that the Kaiser would be negotiating a regular Anglo-German treaty in the coverts of Norfolk, and one of them pointedly warned King Edward to be on his guard against 'subordinating the political interest of England to family affection'.

At 6 p.m. on 8 November the Kaiser and his retinue arrived by train at Sandringham, where they stayed a whole week. On the Sunday (when, of course, there was no shooting) he and the King and both their suites attended morning service in the village church. The Bishop of Ripon, who preached the sermon, struck a political note of his own when he spoke of 'the two great peoples before our minds today – born of a common stock, possessing common characteristics, a hereditary rectitude and a strong sense of personal responsibility'. If the Kaiser was hoping now that the Bishop's sermon was to be the keynote for his Sandringham stay, he was to be disappointed. He later described to his Chancellor, Count Bülow, the bitterness that Chamberlain in particular had shown at Sandringham towards the German Government because his alliance initiative of 1899 had come to nothing.[18] Though not bitter, all the other English Ministers with whom the Kaiser talked that week were found to be maddeningly cool or, at best, non-committal.

As is so often the case where one sees uncle and nephew together, one can only admire the tenacity with which each pursued his very different course in his very different fashion. The Kaiser plugged steadily on with his political overtures. At one point, he even spent some time trying to persuade the Prime Minister, Mr Balfour, of the need for Germany to build herself a large fleet.[19] King Edward, for his part, went to the most elaborate lengths to make his nephew's stay as enjoyable as possible, and to keep politics at arm's length in the process.

Lansdowne's *grand massacre de faisans* duly took place on the Wednesday at a splendid shoot in the home coverts around Dersingham Woods, which were fairly bursting with birds. (The Prince of Wales was rarely seen to miss that day – a foretaste of the future monarch George V, who was to be ranked among the six best shots in his kingdom.) But it was not only pheasants. On the Monday morning, the Kaiser and the Prince of Wales went out by themselves to the Wolverton Marshes and had what was described as 'capital sport' with the ducks. On Tuesday, and again on the Thursday, the King joined in for partridge shoots, which must have been colourful as well as lively affairs. To put up the birds, no fewer than 100 Sandringham beaters were mustered, each man wearing his blue smock (known locally as a 'dopper') and his traditional low-crowned felt hat with a bright scarlet band around it. According to a retired keeper on the Sandringham estate who still remembers that week, the Kaiser shot well, mounting a light gun with his one good arm, and the only *contretemps* came when members of his military entourage opened up at hares with revolvers pulled from their holsters. King Edward instantly put a stop to that.

Nor was the entertainment only outdoors. For the Friday evening, the last night of the visit, the King sprang a pleasant surprise by summoning the finest English actors of the day to Sandringham to present a special programme of theatricals. They included the great Sir Henry Irving and his troupe, who performed Conan Doyle's *A Study of Waterloo*, an apt reminder of Anglo-Prussian comradeship. Sir Henry bought the privilege at some cost. At 11 p.m. the previous night, the curtain had fallen on a play he was giving at Belfast. He then left immediately with his players for Liverpool and Norfolk, having travelled an estimated 18½ hours non-stop before arriving at Sandringham just in time to prepare for his command performance. Then, as soon as the royal hand-claps had died away, he hurried 18½ hours back across the breadth of the United Kingdom so that the Belfast tour could proceed uninterrupted on the Saturday night. If he had not been knighted already, he would surely have earned the accolade for that one feat of dedication to his king and to his profession.

Though outwardly all went well during the visit, the Kaiser managed to rub the King up the wrong way even when he was not talking politics. He was a perpetual irritation to English eyes on the shooting field, for example. With his high leather boots, his khaki green cape (as often as not topped off with a stiff dark hat or cap), he always seemed to be in uniform, a perpetual reminder of that militarism that the King was not too fond of even on the parade-ground, let alone here.

And then there was that infuriating habit his nephew had of knowing everything better. At the beginning of the visit, for example, the King had shown him his latest motor car, of which he was very proud. But when the Kaiser suddenly enquired whether it was run on petrol or any other fuel, the King had to confess (as he had probably never even seen under the bonnet) that he simply had no idea. The Kaiser thereupon started extolling the special merits of potato spirit for the internal combustion engine, merits which, needless to say, had already been recognized in Germany. Moreover, later that week, he confronted his astonished uncle with a miniature laboratory of glass bottles and chemical samples. He had had them sent over at top speed from Germany so that he could enlighten the King as to how a motor car should really be propelled. This, on top of the eternal politics, was really too much for a week of family shooting.

The Kaiser, whose skin was a strange mixture of the very thick and the very thin, left Sandringham (to stay for a few days with the very pro-German Lord Lonsdale – the famous 'Yellow Earl' – at Lowther Castle) realizing that the visit had not quite gone as he had wished. But it never even crossed his mind that part of the blame might be his. Indeed, he wrote to Count Bülow that though he was 'personally ... quite satisfied', his hosts clearly had made a distinction in his favour between the German Emperor and the German Government, 'the latter of which they would like to send to the devil'.[20]

What his hosts really thought about him was indicated by the remark King Edward was overheard to make as, on 20 November, the

Kaiser embarked on the *Hohenzollern* again at Queensferry.[21] 'Thank God he's gone!' sighed the uncle with heartfelt relief as his imperial nephew headed away for the horizon, and home.

* * *

Whatever the strain had been on this occasion, and however many trials with the Kaiser were still to come, King Edward could now face up to them as a fellow-sovereign. No longer would he have to rely solely on the force of his own personality and on the prestige he had accumulated during more than forty years of travels as Prince of Wales to play his part on the European stage. Henceforth, as ruler over the greatest empire the world had yet seen, he stood as of right at the centre of that stage. Protocol, instead of being a problem whenever he crossed the Channel, had become a weapon. It was only made sharper on the Continent by the fact that he never laid claim to the title and dignity of Emperor which were his. Though not an idle day lay ahead, as King of England he could usually dictate his own pace, and relax. Like everything else in his life, he was to turn this power to pleasurable account.

5

THE KING'S MEN

Edward VII was to reign over England, and preside over Europe, in exactly the same way that he had always dominated society – through an enormously varied circle of acquaintances, at the centre of which stood a small group of constant friends and helpers. Indeed, if he had a genius, as opposed to a mere talent, for anything, it was for people. Much more than learning or the arts; more even than sport, amusements and good living, it was people who always stood at the heart of those overlapping private and public worlds of his. Throughout his life, he was the personification of Alexander Pope's saying that the 'proper study of mankind is man', a dictum of which he would have certainly approved, even if he may not have been able to quote.

When he came to the throne he probably possessed a wider range of contacts among that European 'establishment' which ruled the old Continent than any man of his time. He also had no equal in the way he used that unique personal network in the pursuit of his country's interests, as well as his own pleasure. Always, he preferred to meet someone instead of hearing about him; to talk to someone instead of writing to him; and to discuss any topic of the day in the flesh with the people actually involved rather than study it second-hand from the reports of others. He was the supreme believer in the value of the personal touch and the supreme exponent in applying it. Had he been born fifty years later, and born a commoner, he would surely have been a king of public relations instead of a king of diplomacy.

It is natural enough for a sovereign to operate through a chosen few – be they courtiers or Ministers – in his own kingdom. What was unusual, in King Edward's case, was how he extended this principle outside his realm and applied it to men who were not his subjects. In Paris, for example, his influence as King was exerted indirectly through that same band of social friends we have seen in his company for decades as Prince of Wales. To them he added one politician who, so long as he was in office, could apply direct pressure on events. This was Théophile Delcassé, a one-time journalist and life-long French patriot of the most impassioned stamp who was already Foreign

Minister of France when the King came to the throne.* Like Gambetta, that friend of Edward's during his earlier Parisian days, Delcassé turned his fervour not against England, the ancient foe in the west, but against Prussia, the newer enemy from the east. The political marriage of minds with King Edward was instantaneous.

Delcassé's opposite number in St Petersburg, the Tsarist Foreign Minister Isvolsky, was a similar case, though here the hand of Edward VII was much more noticeable. Delcassé had made his own career, triumphs and setbacks included. But Isvolsky was regarded throughout Europe as King Edward's protégé.

Alexander Petrovitch Isvolsky was a lowly born Kalmuck, from the Mongol tribes of Russia, who needed King Edward's friendship all the more because he had no lack of enemies on his way to the top. One widespread contemporary verdict on him was that he was 'a self-centred pompous *petit-maître*'.[1] Another, by one who both knew and liked him well, was that he was 'first and foremost a snob'.[2] The two views taken together certainly help to explain the man's enormous drive and raging ambition, which took him from his very modest origins to one of the key political posts of Europe.

The first rung up that social and political ladder Isvolsky was determined to climb was marriage to a well-born wife. This quest was complicated by the fact that his face was almost as plain as his birth was humble. Years after, when he was famous, this led one beautiful Russian woman who had refused him repeatedly in his youth to make the delightful remark: 'Not a day passes without my regretting not having married him; but there is never a night when I don't congratulate myself over it.' Isvolsky duly found the right bride, however, an attractive Russian lady of part-German extraction called Countess Töll. With her giving powerful help at his side, he gradually rose in the diplomatic service: Russian Minister in Belgrade, in Munich, in Tokyo, and finally in Copenhagen. Though the Danish court might seem at first sight a step down after the key post in Japan, it was, in the Romanov's tables, a promotion. Copenhagen, because it was a 'family capital', was usually the stepping-stone to one of the few embassies Russia maintained in Europe.† That it eventually led to something even better for Isvolsky was partly due to the happy chance that, in April of 1904, he met up in the Danish capital with the King of England.

---

* Delcassé held the post from 1898 to 1905, a seven-year unbroken spell which was a record for the Third Republic.
† In those days, only the great powers of Europe (and the United States) maintained embassies with one another. Everywhere else they, and all other states, were represented by Ministers at Legations.

King Edward was there with his wife, paying a spring visit to his father-in-law, King Christian. As that monarch was nearly 90 years old; as the food at Amalienborg Palace was heavy and unimaginative; and as the social life there was, by London's standards, almost nil (dinner was served each evening at 6.30 p.m. and the most daring card game played afterwards was Loo, without stakes), Edward VII's journey could be regarded as a pilgrimage of penance to his long-suffering Queen. One can imagine the King's delight, therefore, when, on 14 April, he met that clever talker Isvolsky at a luncheon in the British Legation. It was reciprocated, and with interest, by the Russian diplomat. The men seem to have understood each other from the first and, in a forty-five-minute talk alone after the meal, the King developed his familiar theme of the need for Anglo-Russian understanding. When they parted, the King took the significant step, in a letter to his nephew, Nicholas II, of praising Isvolsky to the skies, and expressing his confidence that the envoy was destined for much higher things in the Tsar's service. That broad hint must have helped. At any rate, it was while Isvolsky was still in Copenhagen that he heard the Tsar was planning a great re-shuffle of diplomatic posts.

Isvolsky had an extremely intelligent German valet whom he now packed off to St Petersburg to spy out the land for him. If the valet should discover that his master was destined to become Ambassador to Berlin (the post Isvolsky was hoping for) he was to telegraph to Copenhagen the one word *Sauerkraut*. If it was to be Rome (pleasant though less important) the signal was to be *Macaroni*. But when the telegram arrived, it consisted of the totally unexpected and unscheduled word *Caviare*. The valet had learned that Isvolsky was to be the next Foreign Minister of Russia and his imagination had easily risen to the challenge. As for King Edward, for the rest of his reign he now had his man at the helm in St Petersburg.*

The King never managed to capture a devout admirer like Isvolsky at the centre of politics in that other ancient imperial capital, Vienna. But then, in some ways, he had an Austrian Minister of his own permanently at hand in London, in the person of the Ambassador, Count Mensdorff. Certainly, there were times when Mensdorff's masters in Vienna regarded him as being as much King Edward's spokesman as their own. The main reason for this would have delighted those long-departed figures of the Windsor stage, Baron Stockmar and Prince

* Isvolsky remained Foreign Minister until 1910 when he was replaced by Sazonov and went to serve, for seven years, as Ambassador to Paris. His *folie de grandeur* can be gauged by the exclamation he made there on the outbreak of hostilities in 1914: 'This is my war! This is my war!'

Albert: Mensdorff and King Edward were second cousins,* and so, as a member of the old Coburg clan, the Austrian envoy was almost given special treatment by the Palace. These family favours often caused envy or resentment; more than once, a grand visitor to court grumbled that a mere Count was being given precedence simply because he happened to be distantly related to the English royal family, as though that were *all* that mattered in this world. But the Count concerned – who was a charming, idle, vain, gossipy and somewhat insipid fellow – was permanently flattered and permanently grateful. His illustrious second cousin hung on to him throughout his reign. Only once did the King contemplate letting his Austrian spokesman go, and that, significantly, was when there seemed a faint chance that he might be made Foreign Minister back in Vienna. The chance passed, and Mensdorff stayed in London.

One link was missing in King Edward's continental chain of *confidants*. He had no one in Berlin. Despite all those Coburg links; despite the fact that his own sister had been, successively, a Hohenzollern Crown Princess, Empress, and Dowager-Empress; despite the plethora of Anglo-German families, there seems to have been not a single courtier, Minister, general, admiral or civil servant in his nephew's capital whom he could trust to share his secrets and effectively plead his cause. Whether this was simply a unique and inexplicable failure of King Edward's genius for communication; whether he did not try hard enough; or whether, in the atmosphere of the Kaiser's Berlin, no German Anglophile could have survived for long is a matter for conjecture. But the fact remains that (apart from the professional efforts there of his own diplomats, who were a mixed lot, enjoying mixed success), the case of England and her King went largely by default. This was a serious gap, and it was only widened by the Kaiser's choice of German Ambassador to London for most of King Edward's reign. Count Paul Metternich gives the impression, in his dispatches, of being an honest diplomat. But he was altogether too gloomy and taciturn a fellow for Edwardian society.

With his own two Foreign Ministers, Lord Lansdowne, who held office until 1905, and Sir Edward Grey, (his successor until the end of the reign and beyond), the King was on correct rather than intimate terms. This was particularly true of Henry Charles Keith Petty-Fitzmaurice, who had become the 5th Marquess of Lansdowne at the age of 21, and had inherited with the title some of the largest estates in the

---

* The grandmother of Albert Mensdorff-Pouilly-Dietrichstein (to give him his full name) was Princess Sophie of Saxe-Coburg-Saalfeld. She was the sister of King Edward's paternal grandfather, Duke Ernest of Saxe-Coburg-Gotha.

realm. His style of life was very much to the King's liking, with its lavish suppers and balls given at Lansdowne House in Berkeley Square, London, and weekend shooting-parties at Bowood, his principal country seat. But where the two men collided – not because they were on opposite courses but because they were too close together – was over France. Lord Lansdowne's maternal grandmother, a Countess de Flahault, had been French. He himself spoke perfect French and, once he turned to diplomacy at the turn of the century, shared the King's ambition of bringing France and England together as allies. As this was an ideal the King had been openly pursuing for nearly forty years, he was, not unnaturally, anxious to go on leading at the head of the field. It was equally reasonable, however, for his Foreign Secretary to want that position for himself. A certain amount of jostling resulted, and it was no less vigorous for being very gentlemanly.

If Lansdowne was the prototype of the feudal grandee, Grey, a much more sympathetic figure, was a typical product of that solid English squirearchy which – together with an army of indigent and ambitious Scots – ran the British Empire in the nineteenth century. There was never a clash of personalities between him and the King, for Grey was unselfish and self-effacing almost to a fault. He was quite happy to sit in his first-floor corner room in the Foreign Office and study Europe (which he never visited officially) from the placid perspectives of St James's Park outside, leaving all the travelling and reporting to his ambassadors, and to his sovereign. Yet, though monarch and Minister established a scrupulous relationship during the five years they were to work together, one feels it was professional rather than personal. King Edward's flamboyant life was certainly not to Sir Edward Grey's modest taste. Nor could the King ever quite fathom this Foreign Secretary of his who, at heart, loved the grass banks of a trout stream more than all the leather-topped desks in Whitehall.

Instead, Edward VII came to operate more and more in foreign affairs through a miniature 'cabinet' of his own. This consisted of a trio of *ad hoc* advisers, all of whom we shall see more of later: for diplomacy, Charles Hardinge, a rising Foreign Office star; for naval affairs, the rumbustious Admiral 'Jackie' Fisher, who adored the ladies and detested the Germans; and, on military matters, the quietly influential Lord Esher. The link between them and the Crown (and, for that matter, between the Cabinet and the Crown) was Francis Knollys, who had first been appointed Private Secretary in 1870 to the young Prince of Wales and who went on to serve him in that capacity throughout his reign. A more dedicated courtier never lived,* yet one feels that he never quite managed to slip happily alongside his sovereign into the twentieth century. For years he wrote out all the royal correspondence himself, standing at a tall desk and composing long-hand letters for hours on end. Only when the growing burden of work threatened almost to crush him did he reluctantly consent to use new-fangled aids like shorthand writers and typists. A Victorian rather than an Edwardian, he nonetheless had one quality useful to a monarch in any age: he spoke his mind frankly in the Palace but kept his mouth firmly shut to the world outside. He pushed this discretion almost to a fault. Eventually, he was to close even his own master's mouth for him by making a wholesale holocaust of the royal papers at King Edward's death.

*   *   *

In the purely private circle of the King's, we must begin with money, and the enigmatic figure of Sir Ernest Cassel, who succeeded Baron Hirsch as the royal banker and financial guide. Cassel was another of those remarkable English Jews who moved in the King's inner group of friends; but, unlike most of them, he had not only started life as a foreigner but had started life with nothing. He came from an un-distinguished background in Cologne, and had had no formal schooling at all after he was 14 years of age. Yet such were his personality and formidable talents that, when only 22, he was earning £5000 Victorian pounds a year as London manager of the international banking house of Bischoffsheim, which he had joined but a year or two before as a confidential clerk.† By the time he became a naturalized British subject in 1878, Cassel was a rich man. By the time he took over from Hirsch, he was a multi-millionaire, operating throughout North and South America and in the Middle and Far East as well, of course, as all over Europe. He was a man of totally different depth and calibre from his flashy predecessor. Hirsch had been merely a gifted operator in international finance. Cassel was the foremost statesman of that world.

His new task was to use those gifts and that position to increase King Edward's statutory income (something over £500,000 a year) to whatever that pleasure-loving monarch needed to keep his private life going, as well as his palaces. To claim, as critics did, that Sir

---

* His own father, General Sir William Knollys, had served the Prince of Wales before him as Treasurer and Comptroller of the Household.

† Characteristically, he had got the post, which had been advertised, by sending an application to London consisting of one short sentence. It stood out a mile among the hundreds of long and flowery letters the bank received from all over Europe.

Ernest actually gave the King money is misleading. What he does seem to have done is to have managed the royal investments in such a way that while all the profits naturally went to the King, any major losses would be absorbed, at least temporarily, by his adviser. King Edward's 'speculations' were thus as safe as tossing a double-headed sovereign.

There is, in the King's voluminous correspondence with Cassel, absolutely nothing which suggests that the monarch either connived at any 'rigging' of the market or even made profit out of privileged knowledge, as thousands of his subjects were certainly doing. Throughout the spring of 1902, for example, King Edward knew, from confidential dispatches, that England was moving slowly but surely towards peace with the Boers in South Africa. Yet it was not until after that peace was publicly concluded that he thought of it in investment terms, with a suggestion to Cassel on 1 June 1902 that it might now be an appropriate moment to make a substantial purchase of Consols.[3]

Business was not always conducted as formally as this. In October of the following year, Cassel was instructed to hand the King the proceeds of a successful investment in notes at Newmarket when the two men met there for the autumn race-meeting.[4]

Why at a racecourse, why in notes, and whether the 'investment' was on a horse or the Stock Market we are not told.

Any impression given by all this that the King's relations with Cassel were not only close but somewhat breezy would be a misleading one. Cassel also stood out from the pattern of the King's other intimates (Jewish or non-Jewish) in that he was something of an introvert. He was the opposite of a 'clubbable man', as all the others were. Moreover, though he lived on the grand scale that his fortune and his ambitions demanded, one feels that he remained austere deep down inside. He wore all the luxury as he would have done a frock-coat – because it was required of him in his new position. His great London house as well as his main country estate at Moulton Paddocks (where the King was a frequent visitor) provided the usual mixture of an excellent cuisine and first-class shooting and hunting. But the life of the Jockey Club and the Marlborough Club (to both of which, thanks largely to the King, he was elected) always seemed to bore him, in contrast to the late Baron Hirsch.

Where Cassel was at one with Hirsch was in the relentless pursuit of royal honours. To his K.C.V.O. of 1899, the King added, as the years went by, the G.C.M.G., the G.C.V.O. and, in 1909, the G.C.B. Any suggestion that these decorations were all spontaneous acts of recognition by the sovereign is disposed of by the story of how the last one came to be conferred. When, in 1908, the Foreign Secretary, Sir

Edward Grey, asked Cassel to make an immediate loan of £500,000 to help the Bank of Morocco out of its difficulties, the financier, without batting an eye-lid, coolly demanded the Grand Cross of the Order of the Bath in return. Hardinge, Grey and everyone else at the Foreign Office were scandalized and even King Edward was taken aback. But, in the end, the half-million pound sash was handed over.

Cassel was not a peacock and one suspects that he wanted this array of honours* only partly on his own behalf, to efface in himself the image and the memory of that obscure German clerk who had come from Cologne to London fifty years before to seek not only fame and fortune but a new identity as well. He was doubtless seeking also to preserve his 'top-drawer' English label for his children, and so project it safely into the future. Here the King's aid was vital, and Cassel was at great pains to link his august patron not only with himself but with his family. It was for Cassel a great public triumph, for example, when King Edward attended the wedding of Maud, his only daughter, to Mr Wilfred Ashley. That marriage put his progeny on the rungs of the top social ladder. But when the daughter of that marriage, Edwina, married in her turn Lord Louis Mountbatten, the Cassels shot right up to the highest rung of that ladder. Their blood had blended with the very royalty that had first acknowledged it.

If Cassel's pursuit of honours (in itself a standard practice throughout Edwardian Europe) caused the King only minor embarrassment, Cassel's pursuit of still more wealth, carried out in the King's own diplomatic wake, evoked much greater criticism at the time. That superb prig (and superb diplomatist) Horace Rumbold was, for example, horrified at Cassel's activities on a visit the financier paid to Cairo in 1902, when Rumbold was serving there under the great Lord Cromer. Cassel, Rumbold alleged in a letter to his father, was actually intriguing to have Cromer removed or reduced in authority so that he, Cassel, could take over Egypt's finances. Moreover, young Rumbold claimed, the financier 'has got H.M. to back him by holding out promises of a share in the spoils'. There is indirect evidence for the first claim, though none at all for the second. But the whole anecdote does show how the Cassel connection, whatever help it brought King Edward materially, could harm him sometimes in other respects.

On the other hand, Cassel always stood ready to carry out not merely grandiose royal commands which brought him public acclaim, such as

---

* King Edward had also, in 1902, made Cassel a Privy Councillor, a step which raised many eyebrows at the time and was to provoke a lawsuit in 1915, on the grounds that Cassel, having been born outside British dominions and not of British parents, was ineligible. Cassel won.

founding hospitals, but also small private requests that were quite unrewarding. An example of this – and further evidence of the King's loyalty to old friends, even when down on their luck – crops up unexpectedly in Sir Ernest's papers, sandwiched between correspondence with the King about horse-racing and high finance.

It is a multi-page letter in a tempestuously rolling feminine hand (indeed, the writing rolls all round the notepaper's edges) from a Mrs Emma Bourke at No. 104 Eaton Square, and begins with the words 'Mon Roi!' What follows that arresting opening is a piercing cry for 'Mon Roi's' help. The good lady's husband, aged 72, is about to go bankrupt. The only saviour left for her to turn to is this sovereign to whom she evidently once stood close:

> 'I scarcely know how to tell you but *feel* you will, for the sake of your friendship – your long friendship – for me give us Your sympathy . . . We have gone through *great* troubles and in the recent unprecedented panic in the City and frightful fall in all Stocks, my husband's firm has almost failed . . .
>
> 'Our whole future depends now on whether we can count on influential people helping and one – oh! mon Roi – you whose slightest expressed wish would carry such weight, won't you, for the sake of a friend in *great distress*, use your influence . . .
>
> 'Forgive the utter egoism of my letter, mon Roi, but it is only because of my *very* sore straits I resolved to write and tell Your Majesty of our terrible trouble. I fear my pretty house – servants and carriage – *all* must go . . . It's a cruel calamity . . .'[5]

The King immediately forwarded her letter to Cassel, with a personal note to the great financier suggesting that: 'It would be more than kind of you if you could be induced to give them a helping hand in their present very serious distress.' We may be sure that Sir Ernest was so induced, and that his helping hand duly saved the good lady's servants and carriage for her. Nothing more, at any rate, is heard of her troubles.

* * *

Apart from prominent Jews, the only other people who, as a group could always rely on a genial welcome from King Edward were the cosmopolitan Americans in Europe (he never met any other variety). This was partly in gratitude for that unforgettable visit he had paid to their country as a young Prince in 1860, more than forty years before his accession. Partly, also, it was because the youth, virility and the wealth of this New World and its prominent citizens always fascinated him (and, in the case of someone like that young débutante Miss

Chamberlayne, dubbed 'Miss Chamber-Pots' by the Queen, her stunning good looks). Some, like Lady Granard and the Duchess of Marlborough, were wealthy American women who had married into the upper layers of English society. Occasionally it was the other way round, as when Venetia Cavendish-Bentinck, a great favourite of the King's, married the wealthy Arthur James, who was of part-American descent. (Mr James does not appear to have possessed the wit of his wife; but he was a keen racing man and racehorse owner, so at least the turf formed a congenial common ground between him and the monarch.)

Quite a few of the King's American friends – and here, as so often in his life, the political and the personal became intertwined – were diplomats. The successive ambassadors to his own court of St James, Mr Hay and Mr Whitelaw Reid, both fell into this category. The King grew particularly attached to the latter, who came to London in 1905 and soon made his mark, socially as well as professionally, from his palatial residence at Dorchester House, where the King was a frequent guest. Indeed, the success Mr Reid had made at this coveted post seems to have inspired envy and intrigue with President Taft in Washington on the part of other wealthy candidates for the job.* The King came down like a gentle ton of bricks on the conspirators. A letter which he instructed his Private Secretary, Francis Knollys, to write to Sir Edward Grey at the Foreign Office tells the story:

'My dear Grey:
The King has desired me to write to you on the following matter. Mr Whitelaw Reid is anxious to stop on here as Ambassador, at all events for the present, and the King is equally anxious he should remain, for he says Mr Reid is the pleasantest and most sympathetic American Ambassador he has known. Mr Taft however has been told that the King does not like him and that H.M. does not approve of his entertainments in London as he thinks them ostentatious. All this is a pure invention and the reverse of the truth . . .'

At first it looked as though, despite this, Mr Reid, who had had a four-year tenure at the Embassy, would be displaced by some other party backer who felt he had paid his President more than enough for a major Embassy. But King Edward's personal testimonial and appeal finally carried the day. In December of that year, Mr Reid was told that he could consider his assignment in London as 'indefinite'. The King wrote instantly to congratulate him and to express his personal joy

* Then as now, the London Embassy was usually filled not by a career diplomat but by a political nominee of the President's.

'that one whom I have learned to know as a friend will not now leave my country'.[6]

What wealthy American visitors sought in their quest for the King of England's favour was obvious enough: an escape from that relentless democracy imposed on them by their Declaration of Independence, a divine sanction for some inequality in their republican society which they, by their own hereditary fortunes, had anyway made unequal. Monarchy was the only institution which could provide that bene-diction. Europe was the place for monarchs. Edward was Europe's monarch *par excellence*.

The established giants of this new society – men like Carnegie and Pierpont Morgan – were, in fact, entertained by King Edward at Windsor. But the thousands of lesser American figures who flitted through Edwardian Europe in this resplendent decade were very happy to take home much more modest souvenirs than that. An invitation to the royal yacht at Cowes, to the royal box at Ascot,* or even to tea – whether on the lawns of Buckingham Palace or on the veranda of the golf club at Marienbad – any of these, accompanied, if possible, by a photograph, were sure of their pride of place for ever on the grand piano of a Boston mansion or the dressing-table of a Newport holiday home. The uncle of Europe was also godfather to the Eastern seaboard.

As Jules Cambon wrote in a witty dispatch from Washington to M. Delcassé early on in the reign:

'The truth is that the ruling Republican party is the party of wealth and therefore the most susceptible to the seductions of English society, and M. Hay, who is completely bowled over [*honnêtement infatué*] by the contacts he has made in London, is more affected by this than anyone.

'England realizes this vulnerability and exploits it with subtlety. In my presence recently, an American was rendering thanks to the wise providence of the authors of the Constitution who had abolished all titles of nobility. Had it been otherwise, he assured me, King Edward could have reconquered his country with a few barons' coronets.'[7]

Though King Edward had not the remotest thought of reoccupying the American colonies by any means, there was nonetheless a political

---

* They had to be careful, however, even on fairly relaxed social occasions like these, not to let their natural informality go too far. Before Edward came to the throne one American-born Englishwoman rashly asked him at a race-meeting: 'And how's your mother?' 'Madam, My Mother is your Sovereign,' was the icy retort, and it was a long time before the Prince of Wales spoke to that particular lady again.

undertone to his ostentatious welcome for American financiers and diplomatists. It was his imperial German nephew (always quicker than he was to think of politics in global terms) who had first courted America for the sake of its enormous weight, if ever thrown on the evenly balanced European scales. Wherever the Kaiser made a thrust, his uncle was swift to parry. King Edward's growing interest in the White House, which reached its climax in his personal correspondence with Theodore Roosevelt, must be seen in this context.

This remarkable American President was, in fact, about the only pure pen-friend in the King's political life, that is, the only statesman with whom he corresponded frequently but was never destined to meet in person. It was King Edward who started the exchange. The pretext was Roosevelt's re-election in 1904; the underlying reason was renewed German diplomatic activity in Washington. Realizing that he was treading on new and delicate ground with this unprecedented approach, King Edward laboured over his own draft letter with the earnestness of a schoolboy writing his examination essay. Unfortunately, like all such essays, this too had to be submitted to the examiners, in the person of Lord Lansdowne and his Foreign Office advisers. With unusual passivity (doubtless because America was hardly one of his specialities) the King allowed them to drain his letter of most of its spontaneous human warmth.

Thus the King's opening:

'Dear Mr Roosevelt:

Lord Lansdowne tells me that it is not in accordance with precedent that I should send you formal official congratulations on your second inauguration. At the same time I cannot refrain from sending a personal Godspeed to the elected chief of the republican branch of the English-speaking people . . .' was turned into the following stretch of impersonal Whitehallese:

'Dear Mr President:

Although I have never had the pleasure of knowing you personally, I am anxious to avail myself of the opportunity which your inauguration as President affords, in order to offer you an assurance of my sincere goodwill . . . on this notable occasion . . .'[8]

Furthermore, Lansdowne talked the King out of sending the President one of the two personal gifts which he had selected with such great care. The first, which was sent, was a valuable item from the royal collection of miniatures, a portrait of John Hampden, the Englishman who had taken part in the American rebellion which had preceded independence. This, the King reasoned, would tickle Roosevelt's fancy as much as the choice had appealed to him. The second gift King Edward had selected, but which never crossed the Atlantic, was a copy of his mother's *Journal of My Life in the Highlands*, with a request for something from the President's library in exchange.

Finally, the King's reference to a visit by Roosevelt to England ('Were it possible, you should see what a reception would be given to the President of the U.S. by the King of Great Britain and Ireland and by his people . . .') was cut out altogether in the redrafted version. One cannot help wishing that the King had been as imperious with Lord Lansdowne over his letters to the President of the United States as, two years earlier, he had been over all his messages to the President of France.

The delighted surprise with which even the expurgated letter was received by Roosevelt showed how right the King had been to go for the personal and informal approach. A correspondence sprang up between the two men (the President always beginning 'My dear King Edward' and ending 'Believe me, very sincerely yours') which continued, on and off, for the next three years. There was much talk of common interests and common causes between 'the two Anglo-Saxon nations', and even discussion of common policies, such as a joint British-American stand at the Hague Disarmament Conference. From 1908 onwards they continued to keep in touch through personal intermediaries and, when 1910 dawned, Roosevelt, who was planning his European tour, was counting on meeting his royal pen-friend at last. As it turned out, he arrived in London only to walk behind his coffin.

*   *   *

If his Jewish and American friends stand out as the two categories of people King Edward particularly liked, it is even easier to identify the two individuals who, alongside Cassel, stood closest to him throughout his reign. They were the man and the woman who had entered his life towards the end of his time as Prince of Wales: Luis Soveral and Alice Keppel. Now that Edward was King, each name soon became a by-word of Edwardian Europe. They each left more legend behind them than hard fact, but Soveral's papers tell us a little more about Alice's romantic story as well as a lot more about his own.

For Mrs Keppel, in particular, the accession brought greater problems as well as greater privileges. It was one thing to have an Heir-Apparent for a lover but something quite different when that lover became the ruler of the British Empire. To begin with, even to move in the appropriate style at the King's side cost a great deal more money, and money was something that neither Edward VII nor the Hon. George Keppel had to spare. Indeed, in an attempt to put extra cash into the Keppel family coffers after Alice had become the mistress of a king, her husband was obliged to go 'into trade'. Sir Thomas Lipton, the grocer millionaire and yachting friend of King Edward's, found a job for him in his 'Buyers' Association' at No. 70–74 Wigmore Street. This, to judge from the firm's stationery on which George Keppel once wrote a business letter to Soveral, sold everything direct to the customer, from groceries, bedding and tobacco, to cartridges and coal. It also advertised 'Motor Cars Bought, Sold or Exchanged', and it was about this that Keppel, prompted by his Alice, wrote to the Portuguese Minister:

'Dear Soveral,
    My wife tells me you contemplate buying a small motor car for use in London. May we offer our services in the matter . . . ?'[9]

And he goes on to offer a 'great bargain', a small 12 h.p. Sidley, 'only used for 4–5 months and in perfect condition'. New, it had cost £440; Soveral could have it for £300, and he hoped that the prospective client 'won't mind my writing'.

For an earl's son to be a salesman in Edwardian England was bad enough. For the salesman to be the husband of the King's official mistress was an added humiliation. Though George Keppel seems to have taken the whole situation philosophically, there were many in society who condemned him for being so much the *mari complaisant*. As one distinguished survivor from that Edwardian age, who shall be anonymous, commented: 'Had Keppel been put up for membership at some London clubs, the black balls would have come rolling out like caviare.'

Alice Keppel's second problem after 1901 was that of any outsider suddenly brought into the very centre of political power and knowledge – how to hold her tongue, or else how to use it wisely. As it turned out, England was lucky that the monarch had chosen her to share his private life and his private thoughts. She proved such a model of common-sense and discretion that, eventually, not only the King but the King's advisers would come to her for advice or help. This is shown by a remarkable tribute paid to her by Charles Hardinge just after the King's death. In a private memorandum written shortly before he went to India to take up his duties as Viceroy, King Edward's former diplomatic adviser, now ennobled as Lord Hardinge of Penshurst, wrote:

'. . . Everyone knew of the friendship that existed between King Edward and Mrs George Keppel, which was intelligible in view of the lady's good looks, vivacity and cleverness . . .

'I would like here to pay tribute to her wonderful discretion, and to the excellent influence which she always exercised upon the King. She never utilized her knowledge to her own advantage, or to that of her friends; and I never heard her repeat an unkind word of anybody. There were one or two occasions when the King was in disagreement with the Foreign Office and I was able, through her, to advise the King with a view to the policy of Government being accepted. She was very loyal to the King, and patriotic at the same time.

'It would have been difficult to find any other lady who would have filled the part of friend to King Edward with the same loyalty and discretion.'[10]

But Alice Keppel's third problem, once her Edward was King, was harder to solve than lack of money, as well as being more difficult to live with than political confidences. It was protocol, with its constant pin-pricks which could so easily be used by her enemies to drive home deliberate snubs. Even without malice, the liaison produced embarrassments enough, in both the private and the political fields. When and where should the King's mistress be invited? Throughout King Edward's reign, this was a major torment for the great political and social hostesses of the day. In view of her rank, her tact, and the evidently genuine nature of her love for the King, Queen Alexandra soon accepted Alice Keppel, with or without her husband, at Sandringham. This, one must add, was more than one or two great houses of England did: the Marquess of Salisbury, for example, firmly closed the doors of Hatfield House to her. Though most other leaders of society were on her side, some dithered. An undated letter from Constance, Duchess of Westminster, to Soveral reflects what must have been a familiar dilemma:

'Soveral, will you be very nice and give me your advice? The King and Queen are coming to Eaton Dec. 13th to 17th for three days' shooting. Now, shall I ask Mrs G. K. or not? I want the King to be happy but I don't want to annoy the Queen, so please tell me what would be best.

'Will you please come and stay at Eaton too? I know you don't shoot,* but you will be such a help to me with the Queen.'[11]

---

* This is a little puzzling. Soveral's papers show that he must have done some shooting, for they include invoices from London's leading gunmakers, Purdeys.

Unfortunately, we do not know what advice Soveral gave, and whether Alice Keppel spent those five days at Eaton or not.

The Duchess of Westminster's worries were purely social. For the problems that Alice could cause in the official world we must turn to the private papers of that other friend of King Edward's, Count Albert Mensdorff, the Ambassador of Austria-Hungary. *La Favorita*, as he always referred to Mrs Keppel, constantly crops up in Mensdorff's diary, and usually with the pen and ink equivalent of a sniff or a frown. Thus we find the entry for 5 March 1907, describing a large official dinner he had given at his Belgrave Square Embassy, two nights before, for the King and Queen:

'As this was the last evening before the King's departure, he desired that the Prince and Princess of Wales should be present too, and so, in addition to their Majesties I had the successor to the throne and his wife "to look after".* Thirty people at three tables for 10 . . .'[12]

Then comes his list of guests which, apart from royalty, included the Prime Minister of the day, Mr Balfour, the Foreign Secretary, Sir Edward Grey, and two other Cabinet Ministers; two dukes; Lord and Lady Londonderry; Alfred Rothschild and, of course, the ubiquitous Soveral.

Given this company, one can understand the sigh of relief with which Mensdorff concludes:

'Thank God Mrs Keppel had already left (London) so that I could safely express polite regards to her and didn't need to have her, which is never agreeable when the Queen is present. Had she still been here, I would have been obliged to have her, as otherwise he would have been in a bad mood.'

That same summer, in an entry made at Egypt House, Cowes, Mensdorff writes of his week's doings:

'One day their Majesties, accompanied by all the Admirals, on board the *Dreadnought* to watch target practice and submarine manœuvres. Very interesting. Sailed twice with the King on the *Britannia*. One dinner on board the *Victoria and Albert* . . . The King, naturally, is always coming over to see us, as *Favorita* is staying here . . .'

In December of the same year, Alice appears in Mensdorff's diary as the dinner companion of another monarch. He was no less a person indeed than the German Emperor, whom she appears to have charmed, despite his well-known abhorrence of all Uncle Bertie's mistresses.

* In English in the original German text.

Moreover, as neither her husband nor King Edward himself was present, it seems clear that Mrs George Keppel, on this occasion, was engaged in a little diplomatic reconnaissance on her royal lover's behalf. The Kaiser, prolonging an official visit, was staying privately at Highcliffe Castle in the Isle of Wight. Mensdorff, with a large party of other guests – including, as he sardonically puts it, 'La Favorita Keppel with her "lady-in-waiting", Lady Sarah Wilson' – had come down from London to spend a few days at a nearby house, Crichel Down.

The Kaiser came over to shoot, and stayed for dinner. Mensdorff comments, in an entry for 7 December:

> 'It was amusing to see how, at table, in disregard of all rules of precedence, the *Favorita* was seated next to the Kaiser, so she might have the opportunity of talking to him. I would love to know what sort of a report she sent back to Sandringham!'

In January and February of the following year, the *Favorita* pops up in rapid succession in the diaries: at a house-party with Lord and Lady Iveagh at Elveden 'to meet the King', for example; at a dinner given for the King in London by Sir Ernest Cassel the following week; and at Brighton a few weeks later, where the fact that Mrs Keppel had arrived made 'the All-Highest's mood considerably brighter'.

The autumn of that year, when Europe had been plunged by Austria into a Balkan crisis (and the King was consequently 'punishing' Mensdorff by refusing to discuss the affair with him) saw another example of Alice Keppel getting drawn into international affairs, this time with unhappy results, at least for the Austrian envoy. In the last week of October, the King came with a large party to stay at West Dean. Mensdorff, bursting to discuss the critical situation in Europe with someone, started on some of the guests. He records:

> 'H.M. declined to exchange a single word with me about politics. Instead, I discussed the crisis briefly with Reggie (Lord) Lister. *Favorita* also brought it up and I talked a little with her about it. That little, however, was already too much, for when I got back (to London) I found Hardinge rather annoyed that, at West Dean, "you had talked . . . as if you were under the impression that we had prevented at Constantinople that your direct negotiations should succeed".'*

The next day, Mensdorff was taken to task by Sir Edward Grey himself over his remarks to Mrs Keppel, which the good lady must have promptly reported to her monarch.

* This passage Mensdorff wrote in English.

By November of that year, when the King held his usual birthday shooting-party at Sandringham, the guests included not only the Keppels themselves but also so many of Alice's closest friends that Mensdorff, commenting on the list, remarked: 'In other words, quite a lot of *La Favorita*'s entourage.' Considering that, at Sandringham, Queen Alexandra was the hostess at an intimate family party in what came nearest to being her own private home, this is a graphic illustration of how far Alice's position was accepted.

One more extract is worth giving from Mensdorff's chronicle because it shows Mrs Keppel triumphing over her most powerful social enemy, that pillar of the Conservative tradition and of Victorian morality, Lord Salisbury. The Ambassador records that, early in June 1909, after a stay at Poulsdon Lacey, the home of Ronald Grevilles, with the King and Alice Keppel both in the house ('the usual *Favorita* party' is how Mensdorff describes it), the lovers had to part. The King and Queen had accepted an invitation for the following weekend to go to Hatfield, from which Alice was barred. It was possibly no coincidence, however, that she chose to spend that very weekend at Knebworth, the house of Lord Lytton, which was nearby. Coincidence or not, it worked. As Mensdorff, who was also staying at Knebworth, noted: 'All the guests (from Hatfield) came over here for tea – naturally, because *La Favorita* is here!' And a week later comes the entry: 'Some people believe they can discern a cooling-off in the King's feelings for *La Favorita*. I can't say I have noticed it!' The Austrian Ambassador was right.

Useful as it is for these unpublished glimpses of Alice Keppel and the King, the general tone of Mensdorff's diary is quite misleading. Any small, involuntary embarrassments she may have caused King Edward in the English social round* were far outweighed by the political services she could render him and, above all, by the blessings she brought him in their private life together. Of all the mistresses and women friends he had had, she was perhaps the only one who loved him every bit as much for himself as for his crown. We must go back to Soveral's papers for evidence of this real devotion. Here, for example, is a letter of hers from the year 1905. It is undated, but was presumably sent late in December, for she includes New Year greetings to her Portuguese friend:

'I want you to try and get the King to see a proper doctor about his

---

* It is said by one who knew Mrs Keppel well that she always refused to take revenge for any of the deliberate snubs to which she was subjected. The King would often breathe fire and brimstone on her behalf and threaten counter-measures against the offender. But she would always calm him down and persuade him to do nothing.

knee. Perhaps the Queen could make him do so. He writes that it is very painful and stiff and that massage does it no good or rather harm as there is a slight "effusion" on it. This I know ought to be seen at once, for if he gets water on the knee this might mean a stiff knee for life . . . do try what you can with your famous tact and, of course, don't tell anyone *I* wrote to you . . .

> Cher Soveral,
>> From your affectionate old friend,
>> Alice Keppel.'[13]

The truth is that, in Alice Keppel, the King had found not only a woman who, in the evening of his life, would excite him physically as well as relaxing him mentally (a rare enough combination in itself). On top of that he had found, as that letter shows, a mistress who could cherish him as fondly as a wife. No man, not even a monarch, could have asked for more. King Edward certainly didn't. Whether he deserved such love or not is a matter for the moralists. The point to note is that he could inspire it – in Alice Keppel as in others.

* * *

Finally, we must look at Soveral himself, whose great era had come after the King's accession. Indeed, it is from the summer of 1902, when King Edward was suddenly struck down by illness just before his coronation, that the really close relationship between the two men dates. It was noticed at the time that the only person, outside the royal family circle itself, who could walk into Buckingham Palace to visit the patient more or less as he chose was the Portuguese Minister.

For Soveral, unlike for Alice Keppel, the accession brought prestige and influence, untinged by any embarrassments. His position was now unique. Sir Sydney Lee, the classic biographer of Edward VII's, went so far as to claim that, during the reign, 'Soveral filled a place that no foreigner had held in England within living memory'. Certainly from 1902 onwards, the 'Blue Monkey' remained a social and political target that no hostess and no diplomatist in England could afford to ignore.

The women, in particular, he bowled down like ninepins. In an age of stylish philanderers, Soveral stands out as the greatest ladies' man of them all. There is no end, in his papers, to these souvenirs of his distinguished conquests, souvenirs that range from bundles of letters on every sort of crested notepaper to hastily scribbled messages on the back of a banquet menu or a *carnet de bal*, or even plain telegrams that still manage to vibrate. He kept them all. Here are but a few.

From the Princess Henriette de Lieven, a note in French from 116 Champs Elysées, written on a Wednesday, but with no date or year:

'Seductive Minister. I shall be *chez* Laurent at 12 o'clock. After that I will bring you here to show you my apartment and to have a long talk with you.'

From Leonie Leslie (a great beauty of the day), also in French and also undated:

'O monster! What devil got into your head to send me Mensdorff. Do you think that his pale forehead was any substitute for the spider's web I adore so much . . . ?'

From Muriel Wilson, another young beauty of the Edwardian era, and well known to King Edward himself, a note half in French and half in English from 17 Grosvenor Place in London:

'*Si tu ne viens pas au bal vendredi soir, je ne te parle plus jamais, jamais, jamais!*

'Are you too busy to lunch with me tomorrow (Saturday) . . . I am quite alone, but the butler and the parrot are excellent chaperones . . .

'Why did you not speak to me the other evening? You were unkind and I didn't enjoy myself a bit!'

And from a country house-party at Studley Royal, Ripon, there were notes from two desolate ladies Soveral had evidently left behind him the same weekend. One is the Henriette de Lieven of the Champs Elysées apartment, who now implores him to 'think of your poor Princess sometimes'. The other is from Lady Gladys de Grey* herself:

'I am left to my melancholy reflections – when shall I see you again, I wonder?'

Though the ladies are invariably high-born or at least wealthy, the setting is sometimes more modest. Thus a Princess Margaretha writes him this furious little note from 'Willis Restaurant, King Street, St James', after a *rendezvous* that had evidently gone wrong:

'You dear Soveral – I do miss you, sitting here ALL ALONE, and all because those FOOLS at the hotel said I could not lunch with you . . . I am *mad* with rage as you *will* not come tonight and I go to Wales tomorrow. I think life is horrid. Yours in REAL sorrow . . .'

His most intelligent conquest was the wife of an Austrian (or, just

* Family name of the Marquesses of Ripon.

possibly, a German) diplomat he had met at The Hague, when representing Portugal at the 1907 Disarmament Conference there. 'E. von R.', who afterwards pursued him throughout Europe with a stream of beautiful letters in perfect French, was also the most discreet. The method she had suggested to him for arranging a *rendezvous* might have been borrowed directly from the military intelligence services of the day. He was to go into any fashionable store (Whiteleys, for example, if in London) and ask for a catalogue. This he was to post to her with his own secret message written underneath the stamp.

Whether because this was all too much for the harried Soveral, or the lady in question was too little, she is soon complaining:

'No, Soveral, no innocent brochure with its stamp to pull back, but instead total empty-handed failure in all its misery! That is what comes of being a rival of three queens, an emperor and two Kings!'

And then, because she is convinced that a 'misunderstood woman' is simply a euphemism for a compromised one and that to be a 'clinging woman' is a more dreadful thing than either, she suggests he sends her simply a picture postcard with nothing written on it at all, as a sign that he wants no more letters. Only then will she stop 'talking into an empty room'. Whether or not the picture postcard arrived, she goes on writing, with a perceptive passion that would have done justice to a Georges Sand.

If there were any hostesses in England who were not enamoured of Soveral as a man, they were nonetheless desperate to have him as a guest. Next to the King himself (whom, of course, Soveral very often accompanied at country house-parties) the presence of the 'Blue Monkey' was the surest badge of social distinction, as well as the safest guarantee that the weekend itself would be a success. A letter from Lady Somerset, sent from Reigate Priory on 26 March 1910, is typical of scores:

'This is a bombshell of annoyance to hear you cannot come . . . You were my cornerstone. And a lady had arranged to come from the South of France to talk to you while the others were playing bridge . . . Your deeply disappointed friend . . .'

Even the haughty Lord Curzon himself, who had been nothing less than Viceroy of India, approached Soveral with unusual deference later that year. Whether this 'Most Superior Person' of Edwardian England acted out of sheer curiosity or whether, as is quite likely, he was egged on by his wife, he wrote to this Portuguese paragon on 18 September 1910:

'I have never been fortunate enough to persuade you to pay me a visit at Hackwood . . .' A whole week was then named in December, and Soveral was asked whether he could possibly 'spare any part of that time'. If this was not a case of tongue in cheek, then it comes as near as Curzon ever got to bending the knee.

Soveral's popularity with the husbands of all these distinguished and lovely women (a popularity which is evident from the warm correspondence he exchanged with many of his hosts) is a little puzzling in itself. Quite apart from the fact that he must have cuckolded several of them, they nearly all belonged to that condescending breed of Edwardian Englishmen who might so easily have written off a Portuguese lady-killer as a 'smooth dago', or some other such offensive phrase. Yet the extraordinary thing is that men and women alike, and of all nationalities, regarded Soveral himself as the complete Englishman – something he could never have looked in a thousand years.

When, for example, the King's third daughter, Princess Maud, got engaged to Prince Charles of Denmark, Soveral got this letter from that constant admirer of his, the Princess Lieven:

'The Duchess of Devonshire, Lady Salisbury, Georgie Dudley and myself are getting up a subscription to give Princess Maud a diamond tiara, which is what she wants as a present . . . They decided that no foreigners were to be asked to join but we all came to the conclusion that you were such an intimate friend of theirs you could not be considered a foreigner . . .'

Then, as though to explain the need for such an expensive gift, the loquacious Henriette de Lieven continued:

'P. Maud is very much in love but I can't quite see her living on an allowance of £5000 a year in a cottage in Denmark with a lady-in-waiting while he is away at sea. He will never have a penny more than his pay which is 1s. 6d. a day! Please tear up my letter at once!'

Soveral obediently sent off his cheque for £20 and, less obediently, kept the letter.

As has been pointed out already, he was by no means a rich man and, even living as a bachelor rent-free on his Embassy premises, the constant calls for cheques like that one must have been a drain on his relatively modest purse. Fortunately, his English friends also helped him to fill that purse up. One must assume that Sir Ernest Casse helped him with 'investment advice', as he did the King. Alfred Rothschild certainly did. Soveral's papers contain many letters from this other great Jewish financier of Edwardian London, mostly written from his offices at New Court, St Swithin's Lane. In some, he asks for Soveral's opinion on political matters; in others, he asks for Soveral's help in commercial matters. Then come the successful deals he has done on Soveral's behalf: a letter of 8 April 1907, for example, announcing a net profit of £219 19s. 0d. on a transaction for his Portuguese friend.

But it was a woman who was responsible for what must surely have been the easiest Stock Exchange 'killing' Soveral ever made. The following irresistible proposition was made to him in a letter sent on 10 June 1905 from Warwick House, St James, and written (to judge by the handwriting) by the Countess of Warwick herself:

'My dear Friend,

You have done me so much kindness that I should like in a small way to do a tiny thing in gratitude to you. Will you go *this morning* to the Westminster Syndicate 34 Victoria St S.W. and ask for some shares in the Ice Vacuum Company. Sir Vincent Caillard is Chairman and the company is coming out next week, shares £3. I have the chance of recommending one or two *special friends* as a *special favour* to get the shares at £1, and they will get to £20 within a fortnight.

You need only give a cheque for 25% of what you want or even less as they are in no hurry for money (awfully *rich* company).

Mention my name please as it is done as a *special favour* to *me*. (I am getting a lot out of it. I have sent only H. Chaplin, Winston and yourself as my 3 dear friends . . .')

As can be seen, London society had an agreeable habit of putting back for Soveral a lot of what it took out.

That lovelorn lady who had complained of having so many royal rivals to compete with for Soveral's time and attention spoke of 'three queens' being among them. By one of these she certainly meant Soveral's own French-born Queen Amélie of Portugal, who was devoted to him, and in whose arms he was to die in Paris in 1922. Another of this unnamed royal trio (though a 'rival' only in a platonic sense) was Queen Alexandra of England. Soveral kept a stream of affectionate personal letters Alexandra had sent him over the years, as Princess of Wales, as Queen, and finally as Queen Mother, ending up with a shakily written note from her which he received on his deathbed. They are mostly in French and signed fondly, '*Toute à vous, A.*'

How much he had become, for her, a part of the family scene is shown even more sharply in the telegrams that the Queen would fire off on an impulse at suddenly missing him. One says simply: '*Voici le premier jour d'Ascot, et sans vous.*' Another, sent to him at The

Hague on 2 August 1907, is more scolding in tone and shows that the Queen of England herself could be among the hostesses unable to get Soveral when they wanted. It reads:

'*Fachée. Venez du moins le Dimanche. Alexandre.*'

But no one could be *fachée* with Soveral for long. Soon after that telegram, when Soveral was back in London, the Queen demonstrated that she was even prepared to do favours for his beautiful lady companions, if it would make him happy. He had approached her to try and get a Buckingham Palace invitation for one of them. After what appears to have been some delay, Queen Alexandra succeeded, and wrote to him:

'I'm happy to be able to send you after all a ticket for the lovely Miss Wilson! and I hope that you and she will be very pleased.'

Clearly, there was not much that '*Cher Luis*' could ask for and be denied in the royal family; and this is perhaps the most remarkable dimension of this remarkable man. He was not only King Edward's most intimate friend. He was also, separately but simultaneously, the closest friend of both the King's wife *and* of his mistress. He kept the special affection of all three and the special secrets of all three, yet each always knew of this triple relationship. That would have been a notable achievement in any circumstances. But to fulfil such a role when the eternal triangle was a royal one and the romance in question was the talk of Europe, and to fulfil it, moreover, without one recorded blunder in any direction over ten years, was a feat of tact and devotion for which one must seek the superlatives.

Why King Edward, as the married man at the apex of the triangle, had such particular cause to be grateful to Soveral is now clear. It is equally clear, to return again to the international scene, what the significance of this friendship was in political terms.

Unlike Alice Keppel, who only appears occasionally on the wings of the King's diplomatic stage, or Cassel, who usually flitted on and off that stage only when he had a business deal in mind, Soveral was constantly at King Edward's elbow whenever the future shape of Europe was under discussion, or actually at stake. There was only one occasion in the King's reign (and that a tragic one) when Anglo-Portuguese relations as such briefly held the centre of attention. For the rest of the time, Soveral was sought out for advice, not as Portuguese Minister in London, but as the King's unofficial counsellor, and sometimes unofficial spokesman, on European affairs in general.

Given this extraordinary relationship, what then was Soveral's political influence on the King? It can be summed up by saying that, while he did not create King Edward's distaste and fear about Berlin, he underlined it. Soveral was no more 'anti-German' in the subjective sense than Edward VII was (as his German colleague in London, Count Metternich, would grudgingly admit, even if the Kaiser would never believe it). But, like the King, he was a dedicated anti-German politically, fearing, as King Edward did, that the Germany of Kaiser Wilhelm would one day explode with its own seething pressures, and that the sooner all the countries around it could organize their mutual protection from the blast the better. Everything in Soveral's career, beginning with that critical decision in 1896 to keep the Kaiser's troops out of South Africa, followed this same line of watchful suspicion.

Thus in his public life as in his private life, in diplomacy as in dalliance, Soveral was King Edward's *alter ego*. As such, his influence on the King, and through him, on Europe, goes deeper than those yellowing mountains of embossed invitation cards and love-letters would suggest.

PART III

1903

PART III

1993

6

A ROYAL SECRET

The journey which King Edward VII made to Lisbon, Rome and Paris in the spring of 1903 was the most important political expedition undertaken by any British sovereign in modern times. Indeed, one would have to go back to Tudor or even medieval times to find a royal voyage of equal significance. The only historic journey that any of the Stuarts made abroad was for involuntary exile. The Hanoverians rarely budged from their adopted capital. Queen Victoria had made only one official crossing of the Channel before relapsing into nearly half a century of seclusion; and even that one trip, the passage to France in 1855, had been remarkable mostly for its impact on her impressionable young son and heir.

The post-Edwardian scene is equally bare of parallels. About the only subsequent state visit to which a similar importance was attached at the time was the journey which the young Queen Elizabeth II, the great-granddaughter of that traveller of 1903, made to Washington in 1957. That voyage of hers was, indeed, a big step towards mending the painful breach that had opened up between Britain and America over the Suez crisis of the previous year and so towards bringing the two English-speaking nations back to their normal footing of friendship. Yet, though the Queen had doubtless been delighted to make the journey, she had done it at the request of her Prime Minister, whose government had planned and agreed every detail of the visit in advance with the President and government of the United States. The sovereign was thus the willing (and indeed highly successful) instrument of her Ministers' policy.

No greater contrast can be imagined than that with the spring journey of 1903. Not only was this entirely King Edward's idea. He planned and organized every detail of it himself with his own personal agents, all of them working in the deepest secrecy, like the forging of an international conspiracy. His own Ministers of the Crown were not told one word about his initial preparations. Moreover, when the completed plan was conveyed to them, and they expressed their polite doubts and even their opposition, he calmly overrode their objections. Finally, despite the fact that he was setting out on a voyage which was intended to realign the political map of Europe, he declined to take a single one of them with him as advisers. Instead, he plucked an astonished official from his desk at the Foreign Office and turned him into a diplomatic *aide-de-camp* for the journey (and, as it was to turn out, for many another). It was an *ad hoc* royal appointment for an *ad hoc* royal venture.

One of his companions on that voyage primly commented some years later that, in his 1903 progression around Europe, King Edward had 'strained the limits of a constitutional monarch to the utmost'. But if we accept that classic definition,[1] laid down half a century earlier, of the powers of an English monarch – 'the right to be consulted, the right to encourage and the right to warn' – it is clear that King Edward did far more than that. He drove a coach and horses clean through the English constitution, without a moment's hesitation and with a cheery smile on his face. And the only reason that the constitution did not suffer permanent damage was that the hole he had made in it closed up after him. Quite apart from the changing domestic and international climate after his death, none of his successors was to possess either the personal prestige or the sublime self-confidence to attempt such a thing in such a way ever again. What we are considering, therefore, is something which, in the true sense of that much-abused word, is unique in English history. Given all this, it may well seem extraordinary that the story of how King Edward planned this greatest venture of his life has never so far been told.

First, a brief and forgotten prelude to that 1903 journey must be mentioned. The year before, on the afternoon of 6 March 1902, the British Ambassador in Paris, Sir Edmund Monson, was received by the President of the French Republic, M. Loubet. The envoy, who was about to leave for London, had sought the audience on the personal orders of King Edward. The King's instructions show that, already at this early stage in his reign, what he sought was an official visit to Paris. As Sir Edmund reported, directly to the King, and also to his own chief at the Foreign Office, Lord Lansdowne, the French reaction had been favourable. The President, he wrote, 'was evidently much pleased at the possibility of the King's visit to France and of his seeing him in Paris'.[2]

M. Loubet was asked to keep the matter a dead secret for the time being, which he promised to do. However, he did inform his Chief of Police, M. Waldeck-Rousseau, who had always accompanied Queen Victoria on her private visits to Nice, and who would now be responsible for her son's safety on French soil. The Police Commissary had just been badly injured in a street accident to his carriage, and there was a whiff of a vanishing Paris about the President's comment. 'Paris,' M. Loubet sorrowfully told Sir Edmund, 'is being quite spoiled by the steam trams and the electric cars. Even in the Champs Elysées, carriage-driving is often too dangerous as a result.'

As it turned out, M. Waldeck-Rousseau was able to complete his convalescence in peace. The French archives give the rest of the story. A week later, on 12 March, the King told Paul Cambon, the French Ambassador in London (and perhaps the outstanding diplomatist of contemporary Europe) that his visit to France was 'not yet certain'. The following day, King Edward instructed Lord Lansdowne to call it off officially. 'The priority of the coronation and the many preoccupations which were descending upon him at this time had forced him to abandon his idea,' Cambon reported home.[3] The chief of the King's 'many preoccupations', apart from his own coronation, was doubtless his country's negotiations with the Boers. These were to end, only ten weeks later, in the conclusion of the long-awaited Peace Treaty.

Though this 1902 trip remained only an idea on paper, it is nonetheless revealing about both the King's methods and his intentions. When he first launched the Paris plan, he had only been fourteen months on the throne, and much of that time had been devoted to settling in and attending family sick-beds and funerals. By comparison with the normal time-scale of international politics, King Edward had not lost a second in putting his own weight behind a French alignment for his country, once the German option had been disposed of. Moreover, he had done so in a highly personal way. Both the aim and the technique were to be reproduced in much magnified form ten months later.

The great voyage of 1903 crops up for the first time as early as 9 January of that year. On that day, the same Sir Edmund Monson sat down in Paris to write a rather querulous private letter home to his Foreign Secretary. After referring to repeated rumours that the King intended, in the spring, to visit the South of France in his yacht, he mentioned a press report of the day before that the *Victoria and Albert* was actually being made ready for a forthcoming Mediterranean cruise. The Ambassador went on:

'I am always averse from displaying premature curiosity about movements, but the report has naturally excited attention in Paris; and I am likely to be interrogated by Delcassé, and by the President, who has invited me to dine at the Elysée at a not too distant date. I should like, therefore, to know whether anything has been decided as to a Royal visit to the South of France and whether His Majesty is likely to pass through Paris.

'Would you be so kind as to cause me to be supplied with any trustworthy or authoritative information on this subject.'[4]

What Lord Lansdowne wrote back is not known; at least no reply, or copy of one, has been found either in his personal papers or in those of Sir Edmund. But it seems certain that he could have told the worried ambassador nothing either 'authoritative' or 'trustworthy', for the simple reason that he knew nothing himself. Indeed, the first person who seems to have been taken into the full confidence of the King was not his Foreign Secretary but his great friend the Marquis Luis de Soveral, Portuguese Minister in London. It was partly in his capacity as Portuguese envoy and partly in his role of the King's most intimate *confidant* that, on 1 March 1903, Soveral found himself summoned for a private talk at the Palace. When it was over, he drove back to his Legation at 12 Gloucester Place as fast as his carriage could travel and sent the following urgent cypher telegram to his own sovereign in Lisbon, King Carlos II. This message shows us, for the first time, how early King Edward had finalized his plans; how high he was aiming from the very start; and how totally he had kept those in the dark who had either a right or at least a claim to know.

Soveral's telegram begins, in translation from the Portuguese:

'Highly Confidential. H.M. the King summoned me today and told me the following. "My doctors have advised me to take a rest after the arduous work I have been doing recently and so I have decided to make a cruise in British waters. However, political considerations of the highest order oblige me to pay a visit to the King of Italy in Rome and the President of the French Republic in Paris. As the relations between your country and mine are so cordial (our ancient alliance has, indeed, been gaining strength every day), I have decided – if this is agreeable to the King of Portugal – to begin at Lisbon, where I would sail directly." '

Soveral put the remainder of his telegram in reported speech:

'H.M. intends to leave on 30 March and to remain in Lisbon three or four days. The party, which will be very small, will live on board the yacht, unless Your Majesty thinks he should stay at the Necessidades Palace, in which case he would stay with only one A.D.C.

'The royal yacht will be escorted by two cruisers. H.M. the King asked me to maintain the utmost secrecy about this. Here nobody suspects a thing; *not even the Queen herself and not even the King's Private Secretary.** This extreme discretion is necessary in view of the effect which these visits will produce on the powers of the North.'[5] [i.e. Russia and Germany.]

* Author's italics.

What is remarkable about that message – apart, of course, from the lengths King Edward had gone to ensure 'extreme discretion' – is that it is expressed throughout in the plain future tense. Either the King, or Soveral on his behalf, is describing what *will* be done, and not what *would* be done, assuming the invitation to visit Portugal were to be extended in the first place. Both of the two friends in London, the monarch and the envoy, took it placidly for granted that the required invitation would be forthcoming. They were, of course, right.

On 2 March, less than twenty-four hours after that message had reached Lisbon, two urgent personal telegrams[6] from King Carlos arrived for Soveral. The first merely said:

'Name the exact day [of arrival] which is not mentioned. Very pleased with your telegram.'

The second showed that King Carlos not only welcomed the prospect of greeting his English kinsman, but had already resolved to turn the occasion into a full-blown affair of state. He was proposing, he told Soveral, a formal disembarkation ceremony in the Tagus followed by a drive in state coaches into the city, where King Edward and his entire party would be accommodated at the Necessidades Palace. King Carlos also suggested an official banquet at the Ajuda Palace; a gala performance at the San Carlos Opera House; a military review by both monarchs; and, as a diversion, a drive to the lush summer capital of Sintra, with lunch there if desired. All the protocol stops had been pulled out at once.

Two days later, a delighted King Edward told King Carlos via Soveral that he approved the entire programme, with the sole exception of the joint military review.

'He prefers,' Soveral cabled, 'to review his own Regiment* at a parade in their barracks, but not on horseback. As Your Majesty will understand, this is because he does not want to ride horses he doesn't know.'

The truth of the matter was that, even if a docile English charger had been specially shipped out to Portugal for him from the stables of Buckingham Palace, the King would still have been reluctant to climb into its saddle. The days when he had split his riding trousers galloping cheerfully all day at manœuvres alongside the Austrian Emperor had long since ended. A shortening wind and a widening waist had combined to ground him, except for jog-trots on a pony in the Scottish heather.

* That is, the Portuguese Cavalry Regiment of which King Edward was Honorary Colonel.

But if King Edward was gratified by Portuguese hospitality, he was appalled by Portuguese security. Within three days of Soveral's first telegram reaching his King, Lisbon society was fairly buzzing with rumours, which duly leaked out into the Portuguese press. King Edward's horror can be imagined. In another telegram sent to King Carlos on 4 March, Soveral tells how he had been summoned back again that day to Buckingham Palace, where he had found his royal friend 'distressed' at these calamitous leaks. Soveral's cable that same evening to his sovereign is another revealing message. Describing the audience he had just had, he says:

'His Majesty the King has not yet consulted with the Queen *nor with his Ministers.** Moreover, the King of Italy and the President of the French Republic know nothing yet. He does not therefore wish to compromise himself but wants to be in a position where he can abandon his trip should difficulties crop up.'[7]

Accordingly, King Edward had suggested the publication of a disclaimer in the Portuguese press, to the effect that 'it was not yet certain whether the King of England will be cruising outside British waters at all'.

The disclaimer was about as much use as a wine-cork in a breached sea-wall. The rumours flowed on and, in a cable sent to London on 6 March, King Carlos can be heard almost wailing with despair as he informs Soveral that, with all the official preparations in train, it is 'as good as impossible to keep the secret'. Finally, on 14 March 1903, King Carlos was put out of his misery when an official statement was authorized concerning King Edward's forthcoming visit to Portugal. (No other countries were, of course, mentioned.) The announcement contained the rather quaint assertion that the King of England was coming because of his country's ancient alliance with Portugal and 'despite probable sea-sickness due to rough seas at this time of the year'. In the event, this weather forecast was to prove all too accurate.

Four days *after* all this, on 18 March, the Portuguese Foreign Minister Wenceslau de Lima cabled Soveral in London asking if *he* could be told officially of the dates and other details concerning the visit. He knew, he said, nothing apart from what he had read in the newspapers. He sounded huffy about it, as he had every reason to be. But the Foreign Minister of Portugal was by no means the only European diplomat in this plight. It is time to return to France, and to the long-suffering Sir Edmund Monson.

For a full ten days after King Edward had revealed all his plans to

* Author's italics.

Soveral in London, his own Ambassador in Paris still had no inkling of his royal master's intentions. And there was something else, even harder to bear. Sir Edmund had begun to suspect by now that the King was using a private military channel of his own, instead of the official diplomatic one, in order to sound out the ground in France. Yet he could not be certain. It was an infuriating and embarrassing position. In a further private letter to Lord Lansdowne, dated 11 March 1903, Sir Edmund indicated this as plainly as he could:

'Colonel Stuart Wortley,* who is down at Monte Carlo, telegraphed a mysterious message to me yesterday enquiring the dates of M. Loubet's intended departure for Algeria, and of the duration of his stay. His message implied that he had been charged to procure this information for the King. I sent at once to the Elysée and learned that the President will leave Paris on the 12th April and arrive at Algiers on the 15th, returning to Paris about 18 days or three weeks later. I caused Colonel Stuart Wortley to be informed of this; and I hope that, if the King wanted to know at once, His Majesty was not long kept waiting.

'There is no doubt that a visit from the King would cause much pleasure in France, a pleasure in which all classes would share; but I may be mistaken in the origin of Colonel Stuart Wortley's enquiry which, if it related to the King, would probably have been addressed direct to the Ambassador, and not to the Military Attaché . . .'[8]

Sir Edmund's latter ended with the announcement that he too now proposed to leave for a fortnight on the Riviera, 'on his doctor's advice'. Diplomats in Paris traditionally found medical reasons to fit in a winter holiday on the Côte d'Azur. Yet one cannot help feeling that, in this case, the British Ambassador saw little point in remaining at his post if he were to be by-passed in all the preparations for this crowning event of his own career.

Mercifully for him, however, and for many of his colleagues in London, the King had by now let some of his Ministers, including the Foreign Secretary, into his secret. Indeed, Monson's letter of 11 March must have crossed with the 'Very Confidential' message sent to him on the same date from Lord Lansdowne in London. In this,[9] Monson was officially informed that the King was proposing to take a cruise on the Portuguese, Spanish and Italian coasts 'during the earlier part of next month'. He would have been delighted to have met M. Loubet, say at Cannes, but as the royal yacht could not get there before 15 or 16 April (by which time the French President would have only

* British Military Attaché in Paris.

just arrived in Algiers), this particular *rendezvous* was impossible. Lord Lansdowne ended:

'The only alternative would be that the King should meet the President in Paris during the last week of April. But I feel sure His Majesty would prefer the Cannes meeting.* Will you sound the President unofficially and let me know the result?'

At last, Monson had something to get his teeth into, and he lost no time. The next day, 12 March, he reported that President Loubet had 'most heartily' reciprocated the King's desire for a meeting and had suggested Paris in the first days of May as the place and time. He was quite willing to cut short his state visit to Algeria; could King Edward also rearrange his schedule?[10]

In a private letter dated 13 March,[11] the Ambassador went into more detail about his interview. President Loubet, he said, had reacted 'with unmistakable delight' to the forthcoming meeting. Monson went on:

'He said that a visit from the King in the present temper of France would do an amount of good which is probably not realized in England . . . In this capital, His Majesty, while Prince of Wales, had acquired an exceptional personal popularity; and he would find, when he returned here, that this feeling was as warm as ever . . . But this sentiment was not confined to his old friends, but was general among all classes . . .

'He could not lay too much stress on the influence which the King's presence in Paris would have on friendly relations between the two peoples. His Majesty's visit here would be the seal of the rapidly strengthening cordiality and would be universally regarded as such . . .'

The Ambassador added that he personally agreed with every word the President had spoken, including a forecast he had made that Paris would give the King 'a reception . . . of the heartiest description'. Indeed, Monson said, he had long worked and hoped for this very event.†

Though King Edward was now using normal Foreign Office channels, he took care not to leave the matter in Lord Lansdowne's hands, at least so long as the Paris visit itself still had to be finalized.

---

* This, as Lansdowne must have known, was incorrect. The King had been after Paris from the start.
† It is hard to reconcile this with the often repeated statement that Monson himself was dubious about the visit. (See Lee, p. 223; Ponsonby, p. 169, etc.)

On 13 March he wrote out in his own hand the reply that he wished to be conveyed to President Loubet:

'The King quite sees the difficulty in finding a suitable date to meet President Loubet on French soil.

'It was the King's intention of returning to England by the end of April, but in order to meet him he would do so at Paris on 2nd or 3rd May, so as to arrive in England on 4th. This can I hope be managed to suit the President's plans.'[12]

That did the trick, for President Loubet immediately confirmed this new arrangement. Another typical royal touch followed in London. The President's acceptance had to be acknowledged, and Lord Lansdowne was asked by the King to draft a message. But when it reached the King's desk for his approval, the only sentence he left standing was the first:

'The King has heard with much satisfaction that the President will be able to meet him in Paris on May 2.'

At every other point, the King struck out the rather severe and formal language his Foreign Secretary had proposed and substituted something gentler. Thus Lansdowne's: 'His Majesty finds that owing to engagements which he cannot alter he must be in London by May 3 at latest', becomes simply: 'His Majesty thinks that he ought to return to London on May 4' (with an extra day added).[13]

There was an equally significant difference of emphasis between Lord Lansdowne and his sovereign as to how the visit should be treated, now that the King had driven his project through. Paul Cambon, the French envoy in London, says that Lansdowne mentioned the royal voyage to him, including the idea of the Paris meeting, for the first time on 13 March, and had then only done so 'incidentally'.[14] Moreover, when the two men discussed how the event should be staged in Paris, the Foreign Secretary had suggested that it should be 'quite an informal affair'. Cambon was too shrewd to be taken in by that. He knew that his President would want to make a real occasion of it, and he was equally convinced that this was what King Edward desired. He was, of course, perfectly right. When the King was formally asked how he wished to be received in Paris, he blandly replied: 'As officially as possible, and the more honours that are paid, the better.'[15] At this, M. Cambon left for Paris to help ensure that the monarch's wishes were fulfilled.

There were several reasons for Lord Lansdowne's marked coolness towards this solo political foray of the King's. To begin with, his overall relations with the monarch were, at best, correct, rather than cordial. As regards the actual conduct of foreign affairs, there had already arisen between them that embarrassing incident of the 'guidance memorandum' handed over to the Kaiser and their flaming row over the award of the Garter to the Shah of Persia. Moreover, as we have seen, improvement of relations with France was a subject especially close to Lord Lansdowne's heart, both politically and emotionally. He might perhaps have become reconciled to the King indulging in such highly important and highly personal diplomacy had he been invited himself to accompany his sovereign, as would have been normal on a mission of this nature. But even this was not to be.

To his dismay, Lansdowne now learned that the King had resolved to exclude not only him, but all other Cabinet Ministers, from his suite. Instead, it was the most junior of the four Under-Secretaries at the Foreign Office who had been selected to provide such professional expertise as King Edward felt he might need on his progression around Europe. Charles Hardinge had served in none of the three countries about to be visited. His reputation had been made at St Petersburg; and the area he was presently superintending comprised Persia, Afghanistan, Tibet, Morocco and Egypt. With the exception of the last two (which might form useful points of discussion in Paris) none of this was remotely concerned with the trip the King was making. But King Edward had planned the entire journey as a solo venture. In his eyes, this called for an official, rather than a statesman, to be at his elbow. He had taken a liking to Hardinge; and that, therefore, was that. Though all this only took place at the beginning of this century, it smacks more of an oriental potentate of old than a modern British King.

As Hardinge himself was to make clear later,[16] Lansdowne fought the proposed arrangement tooth and nail. Just as Monson in Paris must have been wondering, a few weeks earlier, what he was doing as his King's Ambassador to France, so, in the second half of March 1903, Lord Lansdowne must have sometimes asked himself whether there was much point in him being Foreign Secretary. Hardinge, on the other hand, was as ambitious as he was clever. He rightly sensed that if only he could get aboard the *Victoria and Albert* he would be embarking on an exceptional career as well as a fascinating voyage. But the days passed by and still there was no authorization from his own Foreign Office master. A week before the sailing date, Hardinge was reduced to pouring his heart out to Lady Lansdowne and appealing to her to intercede with her husband. As a result, Lord Lansdowne officially informed him, but 'very unwillingly', that he was to accompany the

King. The ecstatic Under-Secretary could now hurry off to pack.

It seems evident that Lord Lansdowne aired all his doubts and objections before his ministerial colleagues, and the whole question of the King's voyage was presumably discussed in the Cabinet. As the practice of taking official Cabinet minutes was not yet in force in 1903, we have no means of knowing exactly how the Government stood on the matter. The Prime Minister, Mr Balfour, was reported to be dubious. Lord Londonderry, though a personal friend of the King's, was said to be firmly opposed. No Minister is on record as having strongly supported the venture before the King set out (though all, of course, supported it after he returned). The probable consensus was that the King might as well go ahead because it was all his doing anyway and also because, short of creating an international as well as a constitutional crisis, there was nothing anyone could do this late in the day to stop him. What it amounted to was that, with a mixture of secrecy and self-assurance, the King had simply bowled his Cabinet over.*

It is pleasant to note that, while wrestling with his Ministers at home and making all his own official preparations for the journey abroad, King Edward did not neglect the lighter side of the programme ahead. He was quite determined, for example, to see a bullfight while in Portugal. As is shown by the stream of messages which continued to flow throughout March between Soveral and King Carlos, this was no easy matter to arrange. The King of Portugal had already warned, on 8 March, that to put on a bullfight would be difficult because the dates selected by King Edward for his visit fell in Holy Week. That had created protocol problems enough as it was, for a strictly Catholic court and country. On 13 March, however (when he was clinching the crucial Paris meeting), King Edward found time to inform Lisbon that he would still like to see a bullfight 'with all traditional Portuguese ceremony'. The only concession he made was to agree that 'obviously, it could not be on a Sunday'.

A few days later, he was told quite flatly that it was impossible on *any* day during Holy Week; but, despite that, on 24 March, Soveral was asked by his august friend to send yet another cable on the subject to Lisbon. Finally, on 26 March, only four days before the voyage began, King Carlos capitulated. 'Bullfight arranged for Monday afternoon', he informed the King of England who, as ever, was taking his pleasures as seriously as his politics. (It is only fair to note that he also

---

* The Royal Archives can shed no light on the whole of this episode. If any written exchanges between the King and his Ministers took place at the time, they appear to have been destroyed

found time to think about the welfare of his men. Another message which Soveral sent ahead to Lisbon reads: 'It would please King Edward very much if amusements were organized for the crews of ships, such as a drive to Sintra.')[17]

So everything was settled at last. The suite now assembled at Portsmouth to board the royal yacht, which had been polished and repolished for the occasion. Apart from the controversial Hardinge, the all-male party was such a modest and conventional one that the King might have been setting out for a holiday cruise around his own island realm rather than on a long and unprecedented political expedition abroad. He had with him merely his Acting Master of the Household, Sir Stanley Clarke; his doctor, Sir Francis Laking; his Acting Private Secretary, Frederick Ponsonby; his naval Equerry, Captain the Hon. Seymour Fortescue; and, of course, Rear-Admiral the Hon. Hedworth Lambton, whose last voyage this was to be as Commander of the Royal Yacht before rejoining the Channel Squadron for duty. The last two of the party were Chevalier Eduardo de Martino, the King's Marine-Painter-in-Ordinary (and also his *Hofnarr* or court buffoon); and Luis de Soveral, indispensable on this occasion as the Portuguese Minister in London, but indispensable anyway as the King's closest friend.

At 5 p.m. on Monday, 30 March, King Edward himself stepped over the gangway of the *Victoria and Albert*. The royal standard was broken at the main, and the venture had begun. To launch it, the King, as we have seen, had kept in the dark his Private Secretary, his wife and his government. To have ignored any one of those would have been considered irregular with any ordinary sovereign. To have ignored any two might well have been called extraordinary. It is hard to describe a King who had serenely by-passed all three. As he steps on board his yacht, bound for Lisbon, the Mediterranean, Italy and, finally, France, he is best seen perhaps as a gambler who knows the cards, has reckoned the odds, is confident of his own skill and who, above all, is following a compulsive hunch. Only the next five weeks would tell whether he, or his head-shaking Ministers left behind in London, had been right.

7

A ROYAL TRIUMPH

The last message which King Carlos sent to the royal party before they set sail was delivered on board the *Victoria and Albert* on 30 March. It read: 'King's weather here. Hope you have a pleasant voyage.'[1] It was far from 'King's weather' at Portsmouth. In fact, it was blowing such a hard westerly gale, mixed with hail storms, that the yacht's captain decided not to venture out that night. As something of an anti-climax, they settled down to dine and sleep in harbour.

During the early hours of Tuesday morning, however, the wind dropped sufficiently for the yacht to put out to sea and, at 9 a.m., off she went. Portsmouth gave her a fitting send-off. One hundred men of the Royal Marines were drawn up as a farewell guard of honour on the jetty. Royal salutes sounded from Nelson's *Victory* and the battleship *Hero* as, through lanes of warships dressed overall, the *Victoria and Albert* steamed out to the roadsteads off Spithead. There she was joined by the cruisers *Minerva* and *Venus*, her escort for the journey.

The sea was still rough but, despite that, the yacht was barely out of harbour when the King ordered all the members of his suite to parade in full dress uniform for inspection. Ponsonby records:[2] 'It was somewhat painful staggering about the deck in full uniform, but it seemed to amuse the King to see us. Our clothes were all criticized without exception.' Next, King Edward sorted out a prickly problem of protocol, on which subject, of course, he was both judge and jury. The Chevalier Martino had discovered that he was ranked lowest in the suite. This placing, he well knew, would determine not merely where he sat and slept on the *Victoria and Albert*, but also at every palace and embassy they were due to visit on the voyage. An Italian marine painter had, of course, no claim at all to be on a mission of this sort; his inclusion had been another of the King's genial and somewhat Byzantine touches. But people who are not sure where they belong are usually most insistent about belonging, and Martino was no exception. He had the temerity to complain about being put at the foot of the list. Instead of standing on their own dignity, the English members of the suite leapt to his aid. Admiral Lambton, Captain Fortescue, and Frederick Ponsonby all volunteered to take Martino's place. King Edward, so far from being irritated by the situation, seemed to revel in it. Martino's cheek probably amused him, and the attitude of his own staff was highly gratifying. After pondering awhile, he decreed that, to preserve good feeling all round, the Italian painter should just take precedence over the Acting Private Secretary. This grave matter settled, the expedition proceeded.

In Lisbon, meanwhile, they were beset with ceremonial problems of a much weightier kind. The delay in the *Victoria and Albert*'s start threatened to throw out of gear all those festivities which had been hard enough to fit in with the constraints of Holy Week. It was decided that if the royal yacht could make it to her anchorage in the Tagus before 5 p.m. on 2 April, King Edward and his party would land at once, and the scheduled programme could begin that same evening. If, however, she dropped anchor after 5 p.m., the official welcome would have to be held over until the following morning and everything else put back accordingly. It was a nightmarish prospect for any Master of Ceremonies, but the *Victoria and Albert*, by squeezing every ounce of steam out of her boilers, managed to prevent it. Soon after noon on 2 April she was spotted with her cruisers by the lookout on Cape Roca, which is the westernmost point of Europe, as well as of Portugal. Three Portuguese cruisers joined her as she came round the promontory into the outer estuary of the Tagus, and the six ships then steamed together to their appointed positions in the Inner Harbour, where they anchored an hour or so before the 5 p.m. deadline.

It must have seemed to those on board the *Victoria and Albert* that they had dropped anchor in the Middle Ages.* King Carlos came across the water to greet them in his centuries-old *Berantim Real* or Portuguese State Barge, a magnificent green and gold vessel with the Braganza dragon as its figurehead, and propelled by eighty oarsmen, each dressed in bright red from head to foot. After the presentation ceremonies (which the British suite rather messed up by being scattered all over the royal yacht when the summons came), the two kings were taken ashore, a Canaletto-like procession of lesser vessels rowing respectfully in the wake of the State Barge.

King Edward, who had been dressed as a Colonel of the Third Portuguese Cavalry Regiment out in the harbour, was described, when he landed at the Caes das Colombas, as wearing an Admiral's uniform. If he had indeed done a quick change it was not surprising, for the

---

* Unless otherwise stated, the description of the visit to Portugal which follows is taken from the Soveral Papers; contemporary press accounts; and descriptions in the memoirs of Ponsonby and Hardinge.

Portuguese military uniform, with its short coat and wide breeches, revealed his portly figure at its worst. It is unlikely, however, that anyone would have bothered what he was wearing in the pandemonium of Lisbon's quayside welcome. The Portuguese Army fired a deafening *feu de joie* into the night with its small petards. In the vast Black Horse Square behind, half the entire Portuguese cavalry seemed to be galloping around, their plumes shaking to the sound of drums and bugles. Whenever they could make themselves heard above this martial din, tens of thousands of Portuguese civilians (some of whom had rented windows on the royal route for up to £50) cheered dutifully.

A procession of coaches, the equivalent on wheels of the official barges, then drove the two sovereigns and their parties to the Necessidades Palace. The leading one, drawn by four pairs of Arab horses, had been a present to the King of Portugal from Louis XIV of France, whose reign was evoked by the exquisitely painted door panels in the style of Boucher. Safety as well as splendour rather tailed off with the lesser conveyances. Martino and Ponsonby, for example, who were riding together at the rear, grew nervous lest the floorboards of their creaking coach should give way altogether *en route* and force them to trot along like rickshaw men through the gap. But the long ninety-minute drive through Lisbon went off without a hitch, apart from the collapse and death of one of the horses. At the magnificently musty Palace they found that the good Soveral had conjured up everything he could think of to provide the English comforts of home. Bathrooms had been specially installed for the guests; whisky and soda was brought to their bedrooms at night; the ritual cups of tea followed early in the morning. No pains were being spared in the name of hospitality and the ancient alliance.

The first full day of the visit, being Friday of Holy Week, was spent quietly in the country. The two sovereigns drove out to Sintra, the old summer capital of the Braganzas, which lies on the hills behind Lisbon in a landscape of windmills and white villas. They lunched at the Pena Castle, that somewhat nightmarish conglomerate of turrets, which is perched on the highest rocky peak above the town. King Edward doubtless found, as most visitors do, that the lovely view from the castle's terrace right across to the Atlantic more than compensated for its suffocating architecture. Afterwards, they visited a famous estate that had once belonged to an English Member of Parliament, Sir Frederick Cook, and which bore the name of his Portuguese title, Monserrate.

The afternoon trip was done in a yellow automobile, for the Portuguese Royal Family shared all King Edward's *avant-garde* enthusiasm for the motor car. Indeed, some of them were too enthusiastic about it, as two members of the English suite discovered to their cost, when they were taken for a drive round the outskirts of Lisbon by the Duke of Oporto, King Carlos's brother. The Duke's speciality was forcing any car that ventured to follow him into the ditch. This he accomplished by jamming on his brakes at full speed when he reached a side-turning, up which he would then drive himself to escape the carnage. Another trick of his was to drive headlong at a group of pedestrians, scatter them in all directions, and stop just before any of them landed up on the bonnet. This did little good either to the car or its passengers. It did even less for the image of a dynasty already menaced by republicanism.

If the Friday had been an easy day for King Edward, Saturday, 4 April, into which so much of the programme had necessarily been crammed, was extremely strenuous. Indeed, Ponsonby describes it as 'one of the most tiring I have ever spent in my life'. It was also much the most important day of the visit from the political point of view. It began quietly with Soveral taking the King for an informal drive around the streets of Lisbon (with none of the Duke of Oporto's *bravura*). Then, at midday, came a large reception in the Hall of the Geographical Society, where both monarchs were to make their first formal speeches. For the Portuguese, this building, with its memories of the great navigators and the vast power and riches they had once won for their tiny homeland, was a national shrine, more than any palace or even any cathedral. There was now a great sense of excitement as the two sovereigns walked towards the dais, across a carpet strewn with roses and with more roses raining down from the galleries above, which were crowded mainly with the ladies of Lisbon society.

King Edward's speech, drafted by Hardinge and read out in French, rose to the occasion. There was a skilful coupling of England and Portugal as two great powers of sea-faring commerce who had together 'shed a gleam of light and hope upon the darkness of the Middle Ages' and who had then become 'the herald of progress and civilization in every land and sea where our navigators and travellers, with their characteristic boldness and energy, have penetrated and planted their national flags'. This was greeted with applause. But when the King went on to say that 'the integrity and preservation of [Portugal's colonies] is one of my dearest aims and objects', he nearly brought the venerable roof down. The bursts of cheering that broke out from every corner of the packed hall made it impossible for him to continue for several minutes.

In 1890, only thirteen years before those words were spoken, England and Portugal had themselves been at loggerheads over their colonial rivalries, principally in southern Africa. But it was more than the memory of that tension which had now been buried. More recently (and much nearer to home, in North and West Africa and the Atlantic) Germany had appeared as a new challenger to Portugal's waning imperial strength, a challenger potentially more dangerous than either France or Spain. With his words, King Edward had personally reaffirmed* England's obligations to her oldest ally and had thrown a Royal Navy escort around the whole Portuguese Empire. This was what, in 1903, Lisbon was longing to hear and Berlin was dreading. As a comment from the German capital put it three weeks later, King Edward, by taking Portugal and its colonies 'under his protection', had aimed a blow primarily at German aspirations in Africa.³

Saturday afternoon was devoted to a pigeon-shooting match in the gardens of the palace. The competitive slaughter went on for three hours in the boiling sun. King Carlos, who, despite his fatness, was an excellent shot, took part himself, and was most anxious to win the special cup that had been presented to commemorate the event. But when it came to his turn, he missed one of his eighteen birds. An Argentinian gentleman named Senhor Alvear downed all eighteen of his pigeons and had to be proclaimed the winner. King Edward had been an honorary member of this royal Pigeon-Shooting Club since visiting Lisbon as Prince of Wales nearly thirty years before. But he had wisely refused to compete. His marksmanship was well below the prevailing standard and, in any case, he was after more substantial spoils than tame pigeons.

The senior members of Lisbon's diplomatic corps were all on parade and it was on these envoys that the King had set his sights. He was his usual affable self to them all, and especially disarming to the suspicious Germans. In view of the great Paris climax to his travels (which was still an official secret, though no longer a royal one), he was ostentatiously friendly towards the French Minister at Lisbon, M. Rouvier. After the shoot had started, the King got up from his seat, walked over to the French envoy, and, in M. Rouvier's words, apologized for the fact that, when he had arrived, 'he had merely greeted me together with my other colleagues and had not shaken me personally by the hand'. This was one of those meticulous and calculated acts of flattery which were among the hallmarks of King Edward's technique. He knew that it would not just remain a courteous gesture in a hot and noisy palace garden in Lisbon but that it would soon be wing-

---

* The basic obligation was not in question. An Anglo-Portuguese declaration of 14 October 1899 had stated that England would 'defend and protect all conquests or colonies belonging to the Crown of Portugal'. (See BDFP, Vol. 8, Extensive Minute to No. 34.)

ing its way to the French Government in the form of a cypher telegram. He was, as usual in such matters, right. The delighted M. Rouvier reported it all to his Foreign Minister,[4] adding that such deliberate politeness augured well for the forthcoming Paris visit.

Despite the preoccupations of his Lisbon programme, the King seemed to be constantly thinking and planning ahead for those days in the French capital. Several times, Rouvier reported, the King had asked him for the latest news about President Loubet's programme in Algeria, and particularly for the exact date of his arrival at Algiers. This, Soveral confided to the rather puzzled Frenchman, was so that the King could arrange for a squadron of British warships to go and salute the President there. In other words, the King had been planning this particular *coup de théâtre* of his before he left Portuguese soil.

This exhausting Saturday continued with tea, taken with the Queen Mother of Portugal, Maria Pia; and, immediately afterwards, a banquet for one hundred guests, served at the very early hour of 6.30. The reason for this uncongenial timing was a gala performance at the San Carlos Opera House, to which everyone was hurried as soon as the meal had been served. The members of the British suite were probably quite reconciled to a little indigestion if only they could get a chance to rest their legs. Ponsonby describes how Portuguese etiquette had obliged him to stand at the Geographical Society function in the morning, stand throughout the afternoon's pigeon-shooting, and even during the Queen Mother's tea-party. Apart from sitting down at two hurried meals, he had been on his feet all day. Now, to his horror, he realized, on entering the Opera House, that Portuguese protocol required him to remain upright here as well. Three massive gilt chairs were provided for the two monarchs and the Queen Mother. The rest of the audience were expected to stand to attention throughout the entire performance.

After about an hour and a half, he could endure it no longer. Together with Admiral Lambton, he managed to slip out unnoticed from the rear of the royal box during a round of applause. The pair of them went in search of something on which to rest their aching limbs. The foyer and the corridors were quite bare, and all they could find to sit on in the building were two chairs, espied through the open door of the ladies' cloakroom. It was a measure of their desperation that they crossed this forbidden threshold, sank down on the two seats, and lit up cigarettes. The relief did not last long. What Ponsonby describes as 'an aristocratic-looking female' appeared at the door, took one look, and beat a horrified retreat. Soon the corridor outside was seething with indignant women, and the two Englishmen, preferring even weariness to a scandal, moved on again. When the long day came to an end, it had been a happy one for King Edward, but distinctly tedious for his suite.

From now on there was more chance for all of them to relax. Sunday, 4 April, was a leisurely day spent with the British colony in Lisbon. The King attended morning service in the simple English church of the Cemeterio dos Ingleses, which was packed with his expatriate subjects. Then, after lunch at the Legation, he opened the new English Club, and received deputations and loyal addresses (including one from Oporto, whose large English colony bitterly regretted that the King could not go north to visit them in person). This day had been a great morale-booster for the 2000 British who lived and worked in Lisbon. For many years their supremacy among the foreign colonies had been unchallenged in all respects. Recently, however, another nationality had come to rival them fairly closely, both in size and commercial importance: the Germans.

Finally, on the Monday, the King had his bullfight, a *tourada* in the national style, staged at the Campo Piqueno just outside the capital. The arena was packed with 3000 spectators, some of whom had paid the equivalent of £25 to see the spectacle, and the King of England. After a pageant of gilded carriages, caparisoned horses and bull-fighters, mounted and dismounted, the proceedings began. In contrast to the harsher Spanish traditions across the frontier, great care was taken to see that nobody was hurt. The horns of the bulls were padded with rubber balls to protect the picadors and matadors, who returned the compliment by merely outwitting and outmanœuvring the animals, and never attempting to kill them. When everyone had had enough, a herd of tame oxen, with bells hung from their yokes, came clanging into the arena and shuffled the weary bull slowly away. It was a picturesque and bloodless exhibition of skill, and the King must have been rather pleased he had taken so much trouble to see it. It would also have amused him to read in the Portuguese press that the King of England had in fact been most reluctant, as an animal-lover, to attend the spectacle at all, but had finally 'acceded to the wishes of the population' and overcome his repugnance.

The next morning they all reboarded the *Victoria and Albert* and sailed away down the mouth of the Tagus. With his last words on Portuguese soil the King again stressed England's desire 'to see the Colonial Dominions of Portugal preserved'. This had drawn a chorus of hurrahs from his audience. The Portuguese are not a demonstrative people but, as the royal yacht drew out, it seemed that every throat in Lisbon was cheering, and every gun booming, in a farewell salute.

Portugal had not been a difficult target for any King of England to deal with. But King Edward had struck it with such force that the impact was never erased in his lifetime, despite all the efforts the Kaiser was to make. Moreover, neighbouring Spain had taken note of this new and vigorous display of England's interest in what went on south of the Pyrenees. The Spaniards, like the English colony of Oporto, felt very much left out of things because they had not been included in this royal progression. But Madrid's turn was to come – or rather, that of her young King, Alfonso XIII, who was soon to be included most intimately in King Edward's circle.

* * *

On the afternoon of 8 April the *Victoria and Albert* arrived at Gibraltar. Here the King remained, living on the yacht, for five days. He went on shore for dinners and receptions, of course, and was even tempted to do the tourists' trek by hill-pony up to the top of the Rock. This turned out to be a rash expedition. The little Arab mounts, which were safe enough going uphill, looked distinctly unsafe for a man of King Edward's weight and build when it came to tackling the same steep path downhill. The King had to walk, and was extremely stiff as a result.

It was while the King was staying at Gibraltar that the final arrangements for the Paris visit were tidied up. It is important to express it that way for the contemporary English accounts are full of gaps and mistakes. Nothing could be more off the mark, for example, than the version which Hardinge himself gives of these developments, despite the fact that he was on the spot as King Edward's principal diplomatic adviser. He writes, of this sojourn at Gibraltar:

'It was during his stay that the King received the news that President Loubet was to pay an official visit to Algiers and as Anglo-French relations had been very unsatisfactory during the Boer War . . . King Edward decided to make an effort to put Anglo-French relations on a better footing. He had the happy idea of sending four battleships of the Channel Squadron that were lying in the harbour under the command of Admiral Curzon Howe to Algiers to salute the French President on his arrival. M. Loubet was delighted with this unexpected act of courtesy and sent a very friendly telegram to the King, thanking him and expressing the hope that His Majesty would visit Paris on his way home. *It had not been part of the King's programme to visit Paris,** but after receiving this invitation he decided at once to do so and informed the Government of his intention . . .'[5]

* Author's italics.

As we now know, this account is either inaccurate or misleading on every point. The four warships were not just plucked out of Gibraltar's harbour on an impulse. They were there because they had been already brought there for the purpose. As the King himself wrote to the Prince of Wales from Gibraltar on 12 April 1903:

'A. Curzon Howe arrived here yesterday with *Magnificent, Jupiter, Prince George* and *Mars* from Ireland to coal and they leave this afternoon for Algiers, as I am sending them specially to greet President Loubet who is due there on the 15th.'[6]

Before the *Victoria and Albert* had even left Lisbon, a long personal letter was on its way to the King from Sir Edmund Monson giving M. Loubet's detailed proposals for the Paris programme. In this letter,[7] dated 6 April 1903, the King's ambassador reports on a talk he has just had with the French President:

'M. Loubet said that he had, in fact, given up much of the projected tour in Tunisia, and would send M. Delcassé to do part of it while he did the other. He expected to be back in Paris by 9 in the morning of May 1st, and hoped that Your Majesty would not arrive until the early hours of the afternoon in order that the proper preparations might be made.

'Sir Edmund replied that he was certain that Your Majesty would time your arrival in accordance with what was necessary in this respect, and it was your wish that it should be as ceremonious and official as possible.

'To this the President at once replied that he had quite decided to pay Your Majesty the same honours as had [*sic*] been shown to you at Lisbon and Rome; and that he meant to await you at the Station and conduct you to the Embassy.'

The letter went on to sketch out a suggested programme. This included a formal call by the King at the Elysée later on the day of arrival; a banquet in his honour there the following evening, with a provisional list of guests; and a lunch the day after that with M. Delcassé. Finally, despite the fact that French Republican protocol forbade a President ever to dine 'out of his own house', M. Loubet would, in view of this very special occasion, 'stretch a point' if invited by the King to dinner at the Embassy. In other words, while Admiral Howe's ships were still lying at anchor at Gibraltar, the Paris programme had been completed right down to the coloured ribbons.

Though the French capital was looming ever larger in his thoughts as the days passed, King Edward also found time at Gibraltar to look back with gratitude to his stay in Portugal. Apart from the conventional messages of thanks to the Royal Family at Lisbon, he wrote this letter to his great friend there:

Gibraltar, 9 April 1903.

'My dear Soveral,

It would indeed be very ungrateful of me if I did not write a few lines to thank you for all your kindness and attention during my never to be forgotten stay at Lisbon, and the endeavours you made to make my stay a success – which it certainly was, from beginning to end, and in every possible respect.

My only fear is that you may be quite knocked up by all you went through and had to do, as you were at everybody's call. I have no hesitation in saying that the success of the visit is due to you, and I do not know how we should have got on without you, although I am *deeply* grateful to the King . . .

À bientôt, au revoir, and hoping to meet you at Paris on May 1st.
Ever

Yours most sincerely and in true friendship
Edward R.'[8]

What that last sentence meant was that, as a mark of special favour, Soveral was to be included in the King's official suite for the Paris visit, despite the fact that, as Portuguese Minister in London, he had absolutely no status and no business there. The King had originally wanted Soveral to accompany him on the entire voyage. Soveral, however, who seems to have feared that he might become a physical and nervous wreck if he went on from Lisbon without a break, had excused himself for the Mediterranean section of the tour.

After two days of smooth sailing under perfect skies, the pace did, indeed, become hectic again once the King's procession of ships reached Malta. No English sovereign had ever visited the island colony since it was added to the Empire just over a century before. Moreover, Malta had only recently emerged from a period of serious unrest, those troubles which the omniscient Kaiser had been the first to tell his chagrined uncle about in 1901. As though it were marking both the historic nature of the occasion and the restoration of domestic harmony, the island now put on a rapturous reception. Odes and eulogies erupted all over special editions of the local papers.* A typically incoherent one ran:

---

* Most of the details which follow are taken from the Special Number of the *Daily Malta Chronicle* for April 1903, recording the King's visit. This was made available by courtesy of the Director of Information, Malta Government.

'Malta! what can we say for thee
Pearl that art set in the blue!
Telling thy tidings today for thee
Thoughts of thy heart that is true?

England! what can we do for thee
We that are few, that are small?
We may be brave, may be true for thee
Give thee our little, our all.

Edward! what can we bring to thee
Thou that art King of our race?
Glad is the welcome we sing to thee
Fain are our folk for thy face.'

That rather touching pledge in the second verse Malta was to fulfil
to the letter forty years later and two world wars ahead. But the Maltese
demonstrated how 'fain' they were for their sovereign's face the moment
the royal yacht (preceded by the warships *Bacchante, Aboukir, Vindictive,
Diana, Venus* and *Minerva*, and followed by a flotilla of destroyers)
entered Valletta's Grand Harbour on the morning of 16 April. Though
the *Victoria and Albert* had arrived earlier than expected, thousands of
people were already crowding the bastions and the *barraccas* overlook-
ing the harbour to watch and cheer. The King was soon spotted,
seated on the deck of his yacht in the uniform of Admiral of the Fleet,
surveying the scene through his binoculars. It was noted that 'a large
dog' was in close attendance. This, of course, was the King's fearsome
terrier, 'Caesar'. He was not, in fact, particularly large. But his foul
temper, allied to his privileged position, made him a very formidable
animal indeed.

By the time the King disembarked at noon (the moment was signalled
by a salute from every gun of every ship in the harbour and a simultaneous peal of bells from every church tower on the island) the whole of
Valletta was packed solid with people, and all traffic was suspended.
It was well into the Mediterranean spring season, and flowers and
shrubs were worked profusely into the street decorations. The main
Strada Reale, for example, along which the King's carriage now
passed, was ceilinged with ropes of ivy and olive, from which hung
crowns, hearts, harps, anchors, stars and dozens of other devices, all
fashioned in leaf and flower. Italy and Tripoli had supplied tons of
evergreen for the occasion, while the thousands of extra light bulbs
and the scores of extra generators needed to feed them had come from
Berlin – another small indication of Germany's commercial and in-

dustrial thrust. This was, incidentally, the first time that electricity had been used on the island for such grand purposes of display, though the more familiar gas and oil lamps and even the traditional flaming grease-pots on the house-tops were also pressed into service.

The most important function that the King performed during his five days at Malta was to lay the foundation stone for the giant new breakwater which, throwing its two arms out from Fort Ricasoli and Fort St Elmo, would make the Grand Harbour an even larger anchorage than it was, and a good deal safer. This was part of a million-pound development scheme that the Admiralty had been urging on the Government for thirty years, and the solemn ceremony was in keeping with its importance. After the King had declared his stone 'to be truly and well laid, in the name of the Father, Son and Holy Ghost', even the tools he had used were preserved as sacramental objects. The inlaid mortar board, from which he had taken the lime, as well as the silver mason's level and the ebony mallet were all inscribed: 'I was used by Edward VII.'

This ceremony had emphasized the importance of Malta to the Royal Navy and, by inference, the dominance which that navy enjoyed throughout the Mediterranean. The rest of the King's functions were purely local in significance. He was there to be seen, and half-worshipped, by as many Maltese as possible. By the time he left, hardly a man, woman or child on the island had missed the opportunity. The Maltese 'establishment' filed past him on the first afternoon at a special levée held in the Throne Room of the Palace of the Grand Masters. The jostling to get into that queue must have gone on for weeks beforehand. 'We need not say,' as the *Malta Chronicle* unctuously put it, 'that great numbers of the better class of the population of Malta manifested an eager desire to be honoured with the privilege of passing before the King . . . and of receiving a gracious bow of acknowledgement from His Majesty . . .' The paper then printed the names of all the 'great numbers' so favoured. They took up nearly five whole columns of small print, beginning with His Grace the Archbishop and ending with a colonel in the Army Pay Department. In addition, the Government, the nobility, the Chamber of Commerce, the Chamber of advocates and the University all wanted to present their loyal addresses. The unfortunate Hardinge was given only an hour to prepare suitable replies to the lot, and he was still drafting the last when the King started reading out the fourth. Despite that, they all read today as immaculately as though they had been written on the deck of the royal yacht during that leisurely cruise from Gibraltar.

The ordinary folk of Malta had their 'levée' on the Sunday when, at his own suggestion, the King, dressed in civilian clothes, drove for three hours round the island in a carriage and pair. A spectacular night-time Water Carnival in the Grand Harbour rounded off the visit, with models of famous vessels of the previous 6000 years sailing uncertainly round the *Victoria and Albert* in the glare of searchlights and salvos of rockets. The procession began with a reproduction of Noah's Ark which released doves as it went and which also, perhaps as a tribute to the squire of Sandringham, included some red-legged partridge among the creatures on its deck. After Phoenician galleys, Roman triremes, Grenville's *Revenge* and Nelson's *Victory*, the carnival ended with another compliment to the royal presence, a reproduction of the battle-ship *King Edward VII*.

It seems, altogether, to have been a happy and successful stay, and the King wrote cheerfully from Malta to Lady Londonderry on 20 April: 'We have had great doings here of every kind.'[9] Ponsonby is the only one who, for once, strikes a sour note. He found the Maltese organization very slap-dash, no doubt because the Governor, General Mansfield-Clarke, was brand new at his post. Moreover, the chef he had brought with him from Paris 'turned out to be a fraud, so the food was bad'.[10]

If the King's passage across the Mediterranean had any political undertone to it, this lay in the demonstration it gave of England's naval might. Like some genial, water-borne Pied Piper, King Edward had been steadily collecting warships behind him as he went. On 21 April 1903 it was a miniature fleet which left Malta in his wake. Eight battleships, four cruisers, four destroyers and one dispatch vessel now accompanied the *Victoria and Albert* on the next stage of her journey, to Italy. It all made rather a nonsense of the signal sent ahead to Naples. This announced that the King of England would be arriving there 'incognito'.

* * *

After an overnight stop at Syracuse (where the volcano Stromboli erupted in salutation) they anchored at the great south Italian port on 23 April in weather so misty that the Neapolitan coastline looked as grey as the Hebrides. Though the visit here was still described as 'private', not many of the arrangements matched that modest descrip-tion. At the King's request, the Italian fleet had not gone out to meet him. Yet every Italian warship in the harbour, their yellow funnels sticking up through coils of pennants and decorations, let off a salvo of salutation as, towards nine in the morning, the *Victoria and Albert* approached the long mole of San Vincenzo. The Duke of Abruzzi, heading a military mission appointed by King Victor Emmanuel, then came out by launch to convey a formal welcome. It was indeed something of an occasion. King Edward was the first English sovereign to set foot in Naples since Richard Coeur de Lion, on his way to the Crusades.

This was the spring cruising season, and the Queen of Portugal (who had not been in Lisbon in view of Queen Alexandra's absence) was in Naples, with her eldest son. So was the Crown Prince of Germany and his brother, Prince Eitel Friedrich, on board their yacht. All this royalty had to be received and entertained. An evening at the San Carlos Opera House, which had prepared a light musical menu especially for the King's tastes (part of *Aida*, a little ballet, and even less of Wagner's *Meistersinger*) inevitably turned into a gala event. The King, who had earlier seemed moody and out of sorts,* was cheered up by the tremendous ovation he was given as he entered his box. The sight of the many beautiful Neapolitan women in the audience, their ample bosoms heaving with jewellery, must have also had a tonic effect.

Even a private lunch given on the Sunday by Lord Rosebery in his beautiful villa at Posilippo took on a ceremonial aspect. The Neapolitan caterer who had been put in charge of the arrangements decided to stage a banquet fit for a Roman Emperor. No fewer than twenty courses were served, which was far more than at any meal during the entire tour. The party got to their feet, with difficulty, at four o'clock, having been three hours at table.

Considering that the King's visit was supposed to have been unofficial, an oddly feudal note was sounded just before his departure by train for Rome on 27 April. It was announced by the Ministry of Marine Affairs that all Italian sailors who, at that time, were serving sentences in Neapolitan jails would be released in honour of the King of England's presence. This local amnesty was represented in the announcement as having been made 'in response to King Edward's intercession'. It seems highly unlikely that the King was even aware that any Italian sailors were languishing in the prisons of Naples; and, unless some of them had got there in brawls with English sailors on shore leave, it is even less likely that he would have interceded on their behalf. The amnesty was doubtless contrived by the Italian authorities themselves, as yet another goodwill gesture towards their visitor. What is significant is the particular token of esteem chosen.

* He may well have been depressed by dispatches to the yacht bringing very bad news about the campaign in Somaliland, where a British force under Colonel Plunkett had been wiped out to a man, including its commander.

King Edward had been hailed in the Neapolitan press as 'The King of the Sea', a description which his mighty naval escort justified. It was to that King, as well as to the King of England, that the Italians, who had once ruled over this same Mediterranean, had paid their compliment. Echoes of this were to be heard again in the Italian capital.

If, in Naples, there had been ceremonies but no politics, the King's four days in Rome were full of both. The task he had set himself here (as at Lisbon and, soon, at Paris) was to personify, by his own presence, England's new interest in and new commitment to Europe, after her generations of lofty isolation. There was an added complication in the case of Rome, however, for Italy was already politically committed, as the junior member alongside Germany and Austria of the Triple Alliance. The Kaiser, whose country dominated that alliance, clearly felt that his uncle's tour was beginning to chip into his own home ground. The alliance had been renewed earlier in the year and, referring to this event as recently as 19 March, the German Chancellor Bülow had told the Reichstag:

'I think I may say without exaggeration that I hardly know in history an alliance which has been at once so pacific and so strong; so enduring and so elastic.'

As far as the tie with Italy was concerned, it was precisely the elastic that Berlin was worried about (with good reason, as her defection in 1916 was to show). The Germans must have been wondering whether someone might not be planning to give the elastic a gentle tug now. The same idea had occurred to King Edward.

If the visits to Lisbon and Naples had been the first by an English monarch since medieval times, the historians had to go back to the Dark Ages to find the last occasion on which an English King had set foot in Rome. This, apparently, was in 855, when the Saxon King Ethelwulf had spent a year in the Holy City, having sent his infant son Alfred there two years previously, in order to be blessed by the Pope. Restoring a contact that had been broken for more than a thousand years called for a lavish celebration, and the Italian court and government had spared neither pains nor expense. Italy had, of course, only been established as a united kingdom for little more than thirty years and so it was to a great and variegated past that the authorities had looked for inspiration in their decorations.

King Edward, who had been met at the railway station by King Victor Emmanuel III and a host of princes, nobles and notabilities, found himself driving along a Via Nationale flanked with Venetian masts, each surmounted with Roman eagles or gilded lances. But there was a reference to Italy's more recent struggle for unity and independence in the placards of welcome which the Syndic of Rome, Prince Colonna, had pasted up all over the city. Recalling that England had been the friend and protector of the great Garibaldi, leader of the *Risorgimento*, the movement for Italian unification, these posters hailed King Edward as 'the head of that great English nation whose hospitality received our exiles in the time of struggle and danger'.

If an ideal cue were needed, both for the impromptu utterances of the King and the formal addresses drafted by Hardinge, this was it. King Edward seized on the idea the next evening, when he got to his feet at the banquet given in his honour at the Quirinal Palace:

'We both love,' he told his host in an improvised speech, 'liberty and free institutions . . . and have marched together in the paths of civilization and progress . . . It is not long since we fought side by side and, although I am confident that another occasion will not present itself, I am certain that we shall always be united for the cause of liberty and civilization . . .'[11]

That text, as handed to the Press afterwards and so preserved for posterity, had, it is true, been retouched here and there by Ponsonby and Hardinge. The King, for example, had actually spoken of English and Italian soldiers 'often' fighting together, whereas the only example his staff could think of was that contingent of Sardinian troops dispatched to do battle alongside the British and French armies in the Crimean War. But to make such a speech, wholly extempore, which struck precisely the right tone for the audience and the occasion was no mean achievement. It was also quite without precedent at Italian state banquets, where the host and guest of honour had always spoken toasts that were formal and prepared. Indeed, in order to have any record at all to reconstruct, Ponsonby (who fortunately knew shorthand) had been obliged to stand next to the King throughout, resplendent in his scarlet uniform, but with a humble pencil and notebook in his hand. The Italians were baffled and impressed, both by the confidence and fluency of the King of England, and by the secretarial attributes of his equerry.

More formal occasions followed, notably a gigantic military review staged the next day on the Piazza d'Armi. Two complete divisions of infantry, one division of cavalry and all their supporting troops – a total of some 20,000 Italian soldiers – marched, ran, trotted and galloped past King Edward, who had driven to the review by carriage with the Italian Queen. Victor Emmanuel, on the other hand, charged on to the parade-ground with great bravura on a handsome steed. He was accompanied on horseback by his suite, who, for this purpose, included that versatile shorthand writer of the previous evening, Captain Ponsonby. The good Captain, conspicuous in his solitary red coat among all the blue, nearly brought shame on his sovereign and the whole British Army when King Victor Emmanuel and his staff suddenly stopped their galloping horses dead, 'as though they had been shot', and all at the same split second. The Englishman, whom nobody had troubled to warn in advance about this spectacular manœuvre, found himself sitting on the ears of the black Italian charger loaned to him for the parade. He adds modestly: 'Possibly the animal may have been accustomed to riders sitting there, for he never moved, and I slowly slid back into the saddle.'[12]

But the success of the Rome visit was not just due to the performance of the King and his equerries at set-piece events like the Quirinal banquet and the Piazza d'Armi parade. The King was always out to win the quiet trick with the low card, and one such opportunity came on the afternoon of 28 April, when he was driving round the streets of Rome with his host. The purpose of the drive, apart from showing the two sovereigns off to the crowds, was to give King Edward another chance to look at the famous ruins he had not seen since his last Italian tour as Prince of Wales, thirty-one years before. But when they came to the Porte Pia, King Edward had the carriage stopped, and then bared his head. Victor Emmanuel, greatly moved, came to the salute at his side. The Porte Pia was the spot where Italian troops had entered the city on 20 July 1870 as the climax to the campaign that had unified the Italian states into one kingdom. It had also been a King Victor Emmanuel who had entered Rome behind those troops then, the grandfather of the man now sitting next to King Edward. Small wonder that, with his four days in Rome, the King had gained another royal friend for himself as well as scoring another political mark for his country.

Unfortunately, in Italy as almost everywhere else in Europe, this meant that a mark had been scored, directly or indirectly, against Germany. Merely by asserting England's presence again, and symbolizing her new European awareness, King Edward, wherever he went and whether he intended it or not, reduced the prestige of his imperial nephew, the Kaiser. Hitherto, William II had had the European stage almost to himself when it came to imperial progressions. The Tsars of Russia stirred only spasmodically outside their vast, uneasy realms, and rarely on extended tours. For decades, neither Queen Victoria nor the Austrian Emperor Franz Josef travelled abroad at all, except for private holiday trips. With King Edward VII however, another royal standard-bearer entered the field, every bit as foot-loose as the Kaiser, but a great deal more foot-sure. From now on, each took his cue from the other. Indeed, forty-eight hours after King Edward's train pulled out of Rome's railway station, another special train bearing his imperial nephew and a vast German suite was to pull in, as though to make quite sure that the English uncle had done no political damage. An extraordinary game of royal tag had started between these two rulers. It was to last, with all of Europe except France as their joint playground, until the end of Edward VII's life.

Before following the King's train northwards, we must look at the bizarre episode of his visit to the Pope, which was enacted as a separate and self-contained play within the play of the Rome visit. This affair, which stirred up plenty of dust both in public and in private, shows King Edward at his resolute best and his Cabinet at home at their dithering worst. The debate[13] as to whether the ruler of Protestant England should rebuild a bridge left broken for centuries by calling on the Pontiff of the Roman Catholic Church had started back in London in March, as soon as King Edward had told his government about his forthcoming tour. The Prime Minister, Mr Balfour, had counselled against it. Protestant intolerance, though unreasonable, was still strong in England; so why arouse the sleeping dogs of religious strife? The King did not argue the matter further at the time but there seems little doubt that he had not dropped the idea when he set out, and was only waiting for the right moment to revive it. This duly came during those five busy days when the *Victoria and Albert* was lying at Gibraltar after the Lisbon visit.

The Cabinet was still officially opposed to the visit, but among the flurry of messages flying to and fro between London and the royal yacht on the subject, two were received that pointed the other way. The first was a telegram from Balfour reporting on a deputation he had received from British Catholics, headed by the Duke of Norfolk and Lord Edmund Talbot. They had argued very forcibly that for the King to leave Rome without calling on the Pope would be an affront to His Holiness, and therefore an affront to the King's own Catholic subjects at home.* The second was a message from Sir Eric Barrington, Lord Lansdowne's secretary at the Foreign Office, suggesting that, though the Cabinet were still sticking to their official viewpoint, they would not now object if the King paid a purely private call on the Pope. And Barrington added that this, in any case, was what Lord Lansdowne personally hoped would happen.

* Sir Francis Bertie, British Ambassador in Rome, had been making the same points in telegrams sent to London before the tour started.

The King exploded at this point. Long-range nudges and winks, especially when delivered through Foreign Office officials, were simply not good enough for him, on a matter of this importance. He dictated a very peppery telegram back to Mr Balfour, to the effect that the Prime Minister should make up his mind, one way or the other, and say so. Having done that, the King, accompanied by all of his staff except Ponsonby, went ashore for a formal banquet. Alone on the yacht, the hapless Private Secretary found himself with a message to encypher which, in his view, might have provoked the resignation of the Balfour government, had it landed in London in unexpurgated form. Knowing that all the King really wanted out of his Ministers was a clear lead – either a veto, or preferably a free hand – Ponsonby took his courage in his hands and redrafted his master's message.[14] In the form in which the Cabinet received it the next morning, it was a polite request to his government to withdraw their official advice entirely; to assume that the King had never asked for such advice; and to leave it to him to decide everything on his own responsibility.

The immediate result of this message for Ponsonby was a furious row with Hardinge later that evening, and a sleepless night for both of them. It was a very nervous Private Secretary who began decyphering the Prime Minister's reply to the yacht the following day; but he was a very jubilant one at the finish. Mr Balfour, with evident relief, had agreed to step right out of the picture and let the King go ahead as he thought best. There was a historical logic about the position as it had now emerged. It was a King of England who had, personally and publicly, enforced the break with Rome four and a half centuries before. Now another King of England, again acting entirely on his own, was to span the breach.

The only barriers that still had to be removed lay in the Vatican itself. Pope Leo XIII, who had reached the patriarchal age of 93, seems to have looked forward from the start to meeting King Edward, if only out of curiosity. But his powerful Secretary of State, Cardinal Rampolla, was an unyielding figure, still fighting the Reformation and the Thirty Years War. Having failed to block the meeting, he now tried to demonstrate in public that it was the King, and not the Pope, who had suggested it. Largely through the intervention of the Cardinal Merry del Val, a compromise formula was found. On 24 April, the *Giornale d'Italia* was able to announce that 'The Pope understood that King Edward desired to pay him a visit and that it would give His Holiness much pleasure to receive the King'.

But Cardinal Rampolla was not finished yet. When the arrangements for the meeting came to be discussed, he tried to insist that King Edward should also call on him in person, as the Protestant German Kaiser, whose example was constantly being quoted, had done. That argument, of course, was the last one on earth to persuade King Edward to do anything. Rampolla's request was firmly rejected. There was even difficulty as to how the King should travel to the Holy City. At the time, England had no diplomatic representative at the Vatican, while the Vatican was itself still at loggerheads with the Italian Government to which the King was paying his state visit. It would have given offence to the Pope had the King set out from the Quirinal, where he would be lunching on the day fixed. On the other hand, Rampolla's suggestion that he should begin his journey from the English College, which was not nearly as pro-English as its name suggested, was not acceptable to the King. In the end, King Edward started out, in the afternoon of 29 April, from the British Embassy in Rome, riding in the carriage of the Ambassador, Sir Francis Bertie.

Like so many occasions in life that begin badly, the Vatican venture ended by being a complete success. Cardinal Rampolla, who had tried so hard to put sand in the wheels, ostentatiously stayed away – which, had he known it, was the most helpful thing he could have done. Left to themselves, the ascetic Pontiff, with one foot already in the tomb, and his *bon vivant* of a visitor, with both feet zestfully planted on earth, seem to have made immediate human contact. Both men were endowed with courtesy, simplicity, and a common fund of experience that ranged back over decades of European history. It was more than enough to bring them together. There was another thing the two men had in common, springing from these same elements; an instinct for the right word and gesture to match the most delicate occasion. When the King and his party moved through the Vatican State Apartments to the famous Hall of Tapestries, they found, for example, that apart from the armoured figures of the Swiss Guards and the inevitable swarm of scarlet-robed cardinals, the Pope had summoned all the English-speaking Chamberlains he possessed to welcome the English King. They included an American diplomat, a Sussex squire, and a former colonel of the Royal Artillery.

Then came the tricky protocol problem of how the King and his suite should actually greet the Pope. Clear instructions on this had been issued by him in advance. When the great moment arrived and the frail, white-haired Pontiff appeared in his ante-chamber, the royal party all stayed on their feet while the general assembly fell on its knees around them. Moreover, when each member of the suite came to be presented, he also remained standing, but at a few paces distance, and bowing several times. This procedure had been laid down by King

Edward to avoid any question of kissing the papal ring, which, he had decreed, 'would never do'. For all his 93 years, the Pope was quick to see the difficulty, and just as quick to overcome the momentary feeling of stiffness it created. Speaking in French, he declared himself to be so delighted at meeting King Edward's suite* that he wanted to shake each one of them by the hand. And so the papal greeting, like the reception committee, had been made as English as the Vatican knew how. Protocol, which seems so devoid of feeling, can, at times, be charged with it. This was such a time. Each of these mutual gestures, some prepared and some spontaneous, drew another dignified little line under the past.

Before the presentation, King Edward and Pope Leo had spent half an hour privately together. They seem to have talked freely (presumably in French) and about everything under the sun, ranging from the situation in Somaliland to reminiscences of the late Lord Salisbury, and from the Venezuelan problem to the Pope's one visit as a priest to London in 1846. But the Pope himself broached the topic that mattered most. He thanked the King for the way Roman Catholics were treated in contemporary England and added his gratitude for the religious tolerance that prevailed throughout the British Empire.

There was a cordial leave-taking and the King, cheered by a large crowd that had gathered in the great square of St Peter's, then drove out of the Holy City. The Italian Government had done their tactful bit to help by providing, in place of the normal military escort, a tiny protective force of only four civilian policemen, mounted on bicycles. These now pedalled furiously off ahead of the royal carriage. For his part, the King had decided to return not to the British Embassy again, but directly to the Quirinal. This was greeted as a subtle acknowledgement that his meeting with the Pope had been a private interlude in what remained a state visit paid by one king to another. Courtesies were thus delicately balanced all round, to match a delicate situation.

On the following afternoon of 30 May, the Italian visit came to an end when King Edward, wearing his uniform as a British Field-Marshal, embraced Victor Emmanuel on the platform of Rome railway station. In the Italian capital, they spoke of a *redintogratio amoris* or revival of affection between England and Italy as a result of the King's stay. The Italian press of all shades of opinion, from the Socialist *Avanti* to Baron Sonnino's Liberal *Giornale* (as well as, of course, the Right-Wing

---

* Hardinge, who was the nearest thing to a politician in the party, does not appear to have been taken along. As he had been involved in drafting the speeches for the official visit to the King of Italy, this was doubtless a deliberate act of tact on King Edward's part.

Monarchist organs) was loud with praise and enthusiasm. Some over-did it a bit, like the *Tribuna*, which welcomed this new manifestation of British 'power and friendship' as a safeguard for Italy's own future as a Mediterranean country.

The man who had most to worry about over incautious remarks like that, the German Kaiser, was greeted by King Victor Emmanuel on the same railway platform two days later. His visit got off to a damp start, for the rain, which started to fall soon after King Edward left, had continued non-stop. All the street decorations, with their hastily altered flags and coats of arms, were drenched, and the Piazza d'Armi, where yet another military review was due to be held, became waterlogged and unusable.

While the nephew battled with these difficulties, his uncle was approaching Paris, the supreme target of the whole grand tour. In the Holy City he had just shown his Ministers at home how right his instinctive judgement had proved. But the crucial test as to what King Edward's personal touch could or could not achieve lay in the 'City of Light'. And much more was at stake, for what had to be resolved here was not England's religious quarrels of the sixteenth century, but her political destiny in the twentieth.

8

'COMME CHEZ MOI'

King Edward had always realized that he might be in for a difficult time at the hands of the ordinary people of Paris, at least for the first twenty-four hours or so after his arrival in their city. What was impossible to predict was just how hard a time they would give him, and how long it would take for any popular hostility to thaw out. Curiously enough, those same questions, which had been so difficult to foretell as the King's special train rolled into Paris on the afternoon of 1 May 1903, are still among the most difficult to answer. This famous visit of his has been gilded over with so much legend that the hardest thing to recapture today is the real mood of the Parisians when King Edward arrived.

To appreciate the task he was facing, one need only look back a little to 12 March 1899 when his old mother had arrived in Nice for one of the last of her private holiday visits to the Riviera. 'Not a cheer was heard, and only a few people even acknowledged her presence,' observed Count Münster, who happened to be in the town, looking for some holiday accommodation for himself.[1] Münster, then German Ambassador in Paris, was no Anglophobe, who was seeking merely to be spiteful. Moreover, as he well knew, the venerable Queen, who commanded respect wherever she went, was also held in special personal affection by the good people of Nice, to whom the English connection had brought both prestige and prosperity. Yet in March of 1899 the Boer War was still raging, and the 'shame of Fashoda' was only a few months old. French bitterness was still deep enough on that day to smother politeness even towards the royal matriarch of England.

There was a small but very virulent minority at work in Paris four years later, trying to stir up those same feelings of bitterness towards her son. The mouthpieces of these Anglophobe groups were a handful of ultra-nationalist journals, headed by *La Patrie*, *L'Intransigéant*, *Libre Parole* and *L'Autorité*. As their names indicated, they minced neither their words nor their views. In *L'Autorité*, for example, M. Paul de Castegnac had greeted the state visit with an open letter to King Edward, beginning:

'Sir: Your presence in Paris shocks, offends and revolts us patriots
. . .' and the letter went on to recall, by way of explanation, the
'Fashoda humiliation'.

As for the *Patrie*, this had gone to the trouble of bringing out two
special numbers to commemorate, in a negative sense, the royal visit.
These issues carried full-page portraits of King Edward VII, framed
with pictorial reminders of all the Anglo-French quarrels they could
find, going right back to Joan of Arc and the Constable de Richemont.
However, those journals had remained heavily outnumbered in the
Paris press war which had been waging throughout April over the
King's arrival. Obviously, all those papers which reflected official
thinking, such as *Figaro* and *Le Temps*, pronounced themselves in
favour of the visit. But so, as the day drew nearer, did the *Petit Parisien*,
one of the largest circulation newspapers of the capital and often very
anti-British; and even, though with some reserve, the nationalist
Gaulois. Most important of all, the very influential 'League of Patriots'
had itself called a truce a week before the King was due. On 24 April,
Le Temps carried a letter from its General Secretary, M. d'Hurcourt,
calling on all its members to abstain from any hostile demonstrations
against the King, and adding: 'The efforts of the League are directed
against Germany, and Germany alone.' It was a sensible reminder as
well as a significant one. Alsace-Lorraine, after all, was a great deal
nearer to Paris than Fashoda on the Upper Nile.

Lively discussion over how to treat King Edward had also been
going on among the designers of the tens of thousands of special
postcards which were now put on sale for the visit. The bulk of these
were conventional portraits of the King, either shown alone or paired
with Queen Alexandra or President Loubet. However, there were one
or two which suggested either that the artist had no love lost for John
Bull, or that the manufacturer was hedging his bets. There was the
rather cheeky 'Cake-Walk' card, for example, which showed King
Edward and President Loubet prancing about in the Place de la Concorde, with the Foreign Minister Delcassé carrying the King's sword
for him. And inevitably, whenever the Frenchman thinks of history,
there was a 'Carte Napoleon'. The message here was more than cheeky.
It showed the great Emperor crouching on top of his victory column
in the Place Vendôme and shaking his fist at King Edward and Loubet
as they pass below. The caption ran simply: 'Oh, if I were only alive.'
('*Ah, si J'étais de ce monde!*')[2]

But it is in the popular songs of Paris, songs written especially for
the occasion in the spring of 1903, that we find the truest reflection of

all this ambivalence, and also its solution. One, which had a tremendous success and was played by more than fifty orchestras that May-time, was certainly not polite to King Edward, though it was mainly tilted at the President for always 'running after foreign visitors'. The refrain went:

> 'Viens, Mimile, viens, Mimile, viens!
> Viens presser dans tes bras
> Edouard sept, gros et gras.'

There were more in this or a similar vein, and at least one of them was really hard on the King. This, entitled *Les Anglais débarquent*, compared his visit very unfavourably with that of the Tsar Nicholas in 1896:

> 'Quand l'autre vint en France
> C'était pour faire alliance
> L'chourineur de Transvaal
> N'nous réserv' que du mal . . .'

But the song that got it absolutely right, both as regards what the King was banking on and what he finally got away with, was called *Edouard à Paris*. Sung to the tune of the *Pioupious d'Auvergne*, it began by recalling affectionately the King's many private visits to the city as Prince of Wales, 'a good fellow who knew what life was all about and didn't get up from the table until eight hours after he had sat down'.

Then came the lines:

> 'Si nous n'amions guère
> Tes mufles d' sujets
> Edouard, mon vieux frère
> Toi, tu nous allais . . .*
> Combien il nous tarde
> De t'voir revenir
> Car Paris te garde
> Un bon souvenir!'[3]

Everything that the King had sought to convey to his dubious Ministers was in that verse and it was only a pity he had not had it in his hands to show them eight weeks before. The English as a nation were not yet forgiven in Paris and could not be welcomed with open

---

* This first quatrain may be roughly rendered as:
> 'Though there's little joy
> From your people's spite,
> Edward, old boy,
> You, you're all right!'

arms there. But with Edward as one particular Englishman, the case was quite different. The Parisians had nothing to forgive him for. They had always loved him as he had always loved them. *He* could come at any time. In fact, he had kept Paris waiting too long for a reunion as it was. What Edward VII was now setting out to do, during these four days of May 1903, was a conjuring trick: to persuade the Parisians that John Bull, despite all appearances, was really as congenial and pro-French as he was himself.

He started from the moment his special train, with the Union Jack and the Tricouleur flapping side by side over its engine, came to a stop in the Porte Dauphine station of the Bois de Boulogne, precisely at the scheduled minute of 2.55 p.m. The charming little suburban rail terminus had been completely transformed for the occasion. All ticket offices, kiosks and barriers had been removed. Carpets and antique furniture from the 'Musée de la Garde Meuble' covered the humble platforms, and the stone walls had been blotted out behind gold and crimson hangings. As the King alighted, a royal salute of 101 guns thundered away, followed by the two national anthems. President Loubet, freshly tanned by the Mediterranean sun like his guest, moved forward for the historic handshake. Five minutes later, the Porte Dauphine's moment of glory was over as the two men, heading a long procession of carriages, began the journey to the British Embassy.

The standard description of that journey has the King driving into Paris through thin lines of sullen people who offered him more jeers than cheers on the way. Though an understandable exaggeration for any writer* seeking the dramatic contrast later on, it is a very misleading version. If one takes a consensus of eye-witness opinion on this day, both English and French, and of varying political shades,[4] it is clear, first of all, there was quite a good turn-out of people to watch him arrive. Moreover, their manner was certainly no worse than politely reserved, with applause more in evidence than the carefully orchestrated booing of the 'ultras'. As always on such occasions, these demonstrators, though relatively few in number, were concentrated at key points for better effect.

Not that there was anything very political about the fact that the majority of onlookers, without being enthusiastic, were well disposed. Despite gloomy forecasts, that Friday had dawned a perfect spring day, with only a few clouds in the blue sky, a light wind stirring, and not a drop of rain. In weather like that, the Parisians naturally turned out in their tens of thousands to see the show, the ordinary spectators far outnumbering those, like the municipal employees, who had been

* André Maurois is one of the worst offenders in his *King Edward and his Times*, p. 151.

given the day off anyway. The Bois de Boulogne was crammed with people hoping to see the carriages, preceded by a splendid escort of the 1st Cuirassiers, sweep towards the Arc de Triomphe. Along the whole length of the Champs Elysées every window was occupied; the broad pavements were well filled; and the hirers of *pliants*, or folding-chairs, had mostly run out of their wares by lunchtime. Even the vast square of the Place de la Concorde (where the procession turned left up the Rue Royale and so into the Faubourg St Honoré) looked well populated, with the younger and more agile among the crowd climbing on to the square's statues for a better view. *Valenciennes*, for example, nursed a spectator on each of her granite knees, while *Lille*, to the King's great amusement, had an urchin perched precariously right on top of its head.

King Edward, gorged as he must have been by this time with street decorations, also found plenty worth looking at in the carnival Paris had put on for him. Apart from the usual forests of masts, pillars and ornamental arches, erected by the municipal authorities, every private building along the route (and thousands off it) had produced some display in his honour. These ranged from plain flags or portraits hung in the windows to word motifs executed in flowers or lights, of which the most elaborate was one which traced out the motto of his own Garter Order: *Honi soit qui mal y pense*. One of the most satisfactory, however, was the single English word 'Welcome' shown on a huge sign which completely covered the balcony of the Hotel Scribe. It was on this same balcony, only a year or two before, that President Kruger of the Transvaal had stood to take the acclamations of a pro-Boer and anti-English crowd.

But what, precisely, were the onlookers shouting now, on this 1 May 1903? It was a mixture, but the mixture seems to have been not nearly so unpleasant as is usually suggested. '*Vive Loubet*' and '*Vive l'Armée*' had been the cries most heard on this first day, though '*Vive le Roi*' and '*Vive Edouard*' were not infrequent. Of the hostile shouts, the mildest was '*Vive Russie*' (apparently to remind the King that France's basic alliance was with Russia and he had better not try to loosen it), and the strongest were '*Vive Fashoda*', '*Vive Marchand*' (the luckless French hero of that confrontation) and, inevitably, '*Vive les Boers*'. These shouts, however, never appear to have been directed at the King, even when he was riding or walking alone. What did provoke the militants on that first drive in was the sight of Captain Ponsonby's scarlet military uniform as he rode at the rear of the procession. That symbol of Anglo-French rivalry on the battlefields of history was as highly emotive as it was highly coloured. It was literally the red rag to the Gallic bull, and the groups of 'ultras' who started to jeer when they saw it had little difficulty in getting some response from the ordinary bystanders around them. In short, the King's welcome might have been a lot friendlier than it was had his Private Secretary worn a black frock-coat instead of a red military one for the occasion.*

But there were plenty of 'ultras' on the other side too, reinforced by the large British colony resident in Paris and by the flood of English and American† visitors, estimated by the hôteliers at more than 100,000, who had poured into the city for the event. This display naturally reached its climax in the British Embassy building on the Faubourg St Honoré, where the King arrived to take up residence soon after 4 p.m. There could be no question of smothering this building with anything so undignified as pennants or bunting. Instead, the glass *marquise* which, then as now, protected the entrance, had been covered with crimson velvet, dotted with gold stars, while the front lawn showed a tasteful monogram of 'E.R.' picked out in flowers. But Sir Edmund's masterpiece was hanging proudly from the gateway. This was a Royal Standard of truly gargantuan proportions, no less than five yards long and three yards wide, which he had ordered specially from London.

King Edward's rooms, the so-called *petits appartements*, were on the first floor of the Embassy. They contained much of the original furniture and decorations that Napoleon had provided a century before for his favourite sister, Pauline Borghese, whose house this had once been. But amidst all those magnificently uncomfortable appointments of the Empire period, whose sphinxes, swans and *chimères* of gilded wood perched stiffly everywhere, Lady Monson had planted some cosier touches of 'home' for her royal guest. There was at least one large and comfortable leather armchair for him to sit and smoke his cigars in. Silver-framed portraits of his family covered the *marqueterie* tables. A Constable, an Ibbetson and a Landseer were among the paintings on the walls, which also included two portraits of his mother. The bedroom, however, was just as the famous Pauline had last slept in it, the great carved bed still on its dais, draped with the original silk hangings. One imagines the King would have approved.

It was at his comfortable base in the Embassy (after paying his formal call on the President at the Elysée Palace a few hundred yards down the road) that he received his first callers, a deputation from the British Chamber of Commerce. His speech to them gave him the first

---

* King Edward himself showed characteristic common sense when one of his staff, mentioning these shouts, commented that 'the French don't seem to like us'. 'You can't blame them, can you?' was the unruffled reply.

† Several 'Stars and Stripes' were seen hanging among the street decorations, presumably in honour of the American contingent.

chance to exert some political leverage. Its central message lay in these words:

'The days of conflict between our two countries are, I trust, happily over . . . England and France may be regarded as the champions and pioneers of peaceful progress and civilization and as the homes of all that is best and noblest in literature, art and science . . .

'A Divine Providence has designed that France should be our near neighbour and, I hope, always our dear friend. There are no two countries in the world whose mutual prosperity is more dependent on each other.'

He ended with a call for replacing the old 'causes of dissension' with 'a sentiment of the warmest affection and attachment', and he pointedly added: 'The achievement of this aim is my constant desire.' Such a personal commitment, declared during the first hours of his stay, was as large and unmistakable as his own standard flying outside. There was a chorus of approval and flattered surprise in the capital when the speech was reproduced the following morning in all the French papers.

By then the Parisians also had something else to admire, something spread not by the printed word but entirely by word of mouth. For, on that same Friday evening, King Edward had not only gone to the play but had put on a useful performance himself. One must first dwell for a moment, as the people of Paris did, on the phrase 'gone to the play'. While the programme for the visit was being worked out some weeks before, the Comédie Française, who were due to give the performance in his honour, had suggested one of the standard French classics, such as Molière's *Le Misanthrope*. This idea had been given short shrift by King Edward. 'They really must *not* treat me like the Shah of Persia,' was his magisterial comment. 'I would like to see a new play.'

What the King wanted, in fact, was a night out in Paris, or as close as he could get to it as a ruling sovereign on a state visit. The alternative offering suggested by the Comédie Française fitted this bill perfectly; indeed, it was a play that he had already heard about and was curious to see. *L'Autre Danger* was the latest dramatic comedy by the playwright Maurice Donnay. The plot amply accounted for the King's interest; it was daringly novel, especially for this venerable 'House of Molière'. The central male figure, M. Freydières, loses his attractive mistress, Claire, when she marries someone else in order to settle down. Years later, however, they meet again and resume the affair (her husband, in the meantime, having turned 'selfish and sour'). Before turning sour, however, he had presented her with a daughter, and this girl, Madeleine, is 16 and even lovelier than her mother when M. Freydières reappears on the scene. She promptly falls in love with this mature and fascinating bachelor, quite ignorant of the fact that her own mother is his devoted mistress, both past and present. Inevitably, Freydières falls in love with Madeleine. At a ball the daughter learns that it is her mother who is her only rival, at which intelligence she faints clean away then goes into delirium. The situation is saved in the final scene by Claire making the supreme sacrifice and exchanging the role of mistress for that of mother-in-law.

King Edward was as well known in Paris as in London for being an enthusiastic play-goer.* This was just the sort of evening at the French theatre he had enjoyed for more than forty years as Prince of Wales, and the fact that he saw no reason now, as sovereign, to switch to a stuffier form of entertainment had been noted with delight. As though to emphasize that he was determined to have his 'night out', he had ordered that everything should be done as simply as possible and with a minimum of fuss. He himself arrived at the Théâtre Francais (fifteen minutes late, after a private dinner at the Embassy) wearing ordinary evening dress, with only the crimson rosette of the *Légion d'Honneur* and the *Medaille Militaire* as decorations. And though the Administrator-General of the theatre, M. Jules Claretie, was, of course, in the foyer to greet the King and President, he also had donned plain evening clothes and not his gorgeous uniform as a Member of the French Academy. And he did not, as was customary with visits paid by sovereigns to the building, light the way ceremoniously up the grand stairway by walking ahead with a candelabra (a custom dating from the fast-vanishing wax age). Instead, while King and President went up to the first floor by the glass-caged lift, M. Claretie had to sprint at top speed up the broad steps in order to be there and bowing when the lift-doors opened again.

The audience was a hand-picked one. It consisted mainly of Ministers, deputies, senior officers of the government and armed forces, the entire diplomatic corps and leading members of the theatrical and artistic worlds. The lists of other names in the *loges*[5] showed that a few of the King's private and personal French friends had also been invited, notably the Marquis de Breteuil, Count d'Haussonville, and the banker-barons Henri and Gustave de Rothschild with their wives.

Now it really is difficult to believe that an audience of this composition would have given King Edward, as was afterwards rumoured, an 'icy' reception when he entered the Presidential box at M. Loubet's side. There is, in fact, only one French source for this statement, M.

---

* It was once calculated that, for the twelve months between August 1906 and August 1907, he had attended twenty-eight plays, and fourteen of these were in Paris.

Arthur Meyer of the Paris paper *Le Gaulois*. Yet he was writing twenty
years after the event and even he did not claim to have been present
himself on the evening in question.[6]

What *does* seem likely is that a large part of the audience which rose
to its feet at 8.50 p.m. that evening felt a little nervous and stiff. And
that can be easily imagined, with so many *fonctionnaires* among them,
each determined, together with his wife, to look his best and to be on
his very best behaviour under the eyes of the President who had sent
him that coveted invitation. Most of the non-*fonctionnaires* present,
especially the diplomats, the artists and the sprinkling of French
'society', were quite used to such events and were also ardent admirers
of the King.

Whatever stiffness may have existed to begin with was soon dispersed by the combined efforts of the playwright and the guest of
honour. One of King Edward's qualities was a natural zest for life
which he could always communicate to others. Indeed, he had to, for
he could never enjoy himself unless those around him looked happy.
He was never one to applaud, as the French say, *du bout des doigts*.
When he clapped, he clapped; and when he laughed, he laughed. So
it was now. From the moment those three loud knocks sounded out
which heralded the rising of every Comédie Française curtain, King
Edward was seen to be savouring each clever turn of dialogue. As he
knew he was on stage as well, he was also seen to be constantly mur-
muring appreciative comments into the ears of the Presidential couple
who sat on either side of him. And, though the professional actors
could rest once the curtain had fallen on each act, the King was also
hard at it during the intermission. Both the President and, even more
so, the French security police, tried to confine him to the little salon
behind the State Box; but he insisted on going into the main foyer
and greeting all and sundry in the crowd. One such person was Mlle.
Jeanne Granier, a well-known French actress who had appeared in
England. On espying her the King is said to have advanced on her
with hand outstretched in greeting, and the following flattering words:

'Ah, Mademoiselle! I remember how I applauded you in London.
You personified there all the grace, all the *esprit* of France.'[7]

If the words were spoken to Mlle Granier, they were addressed to
those around her, and to the people of Paris outside. The next morning,
through one of those magical processes of the pre-television era, they
had indeed spread the length and breadth of the boulevards.

After the curtain had fallen on the third and penultimate act, the
King asked that the principal actor and actresses taking part (and

especially the enchanting Mlle Piérat, herself only 18 years old, who had played Madeleine) should come to his box. There he congratulated them in French, both as a group ('The play is delightful and I have rarely seen better acting') and also by a few personal compliments paid to each artist individually. When he left, shortly before midnight, he and everyone else in the theatre were all smiles. Outside, the large crowd which had been growing for the past three hours gave the first loud, spontaneous and unanimous cheer of the visit. 'I've had a most enjoyable evening,' were the last words the King was heard to say before he got into his carriage. It had also, from England's point of view, been a most profitable one.

It was on the next day that the King really tipped the scales of French sentiment. That Saturday had been declared a holiday, not just for the municipal employees of the capital, but for everyone. Nearly all the shops were shut and all the schools were closed.* As a result, when the King, at 9.30 in the morning, drove out with President Loubet past the Bastille to the military parade-ground at Vincennes, he found the whole of the suburb out on the streets *en famille* to see him. Despite the fact that this was a working-class area, with violent Republican associations, not a hostile shout was heard, and the cheering was much warmer than that along the elegant Champs Elysées the afternoon before. This was the way he would have wished it. The ordinary man-in-the-street was his real objective.

At Vincennes, the diplomatic corps was already assembled on the packed tribunes. The grandest sights among them were the German and Russian military attachés, each almost submerged under an effulgent mass of gold braid and medals. But the one who attracted most attention was their Japanese colleague, who kept pulling a small camera from his European-style clothes and taking furtive snapshots. For the next hour and a half the King watched the French Army's equivalent of that revue in Rome on the Piazza d'Armi, a parade of 18,000 soldiers of all arms. Even the *grande finale* of the proceedings was the same: a headlong charge of six cavalry regiments, brandishing lances and sabres, which came to a quivering halt, without a word of command being uttered, thirty yards from the stands. The King knew, of course, that it was going to happen, having seen almost as many reviews in his life as there were hairs in each horse's tail. But he did not miss his cue. Affecting surprise, he was seen to turn to the President standing at his elbow and shake his hand warmly in congratulation. More

* Even in the far-distant colony of Pondicherry, in French India, a similar holiday had been declared, in honour of the Emperor of India's visit to the French capital.

cheers from the crowd who, by now, were in a real holiday mood.*

The King's happiest stroke came on the drive back to the Embassy, when they made a prearranged call at the Town Hall. The whole proceedings there lasted barely twenty minutes, for King Edward was back in the Faubourg St Honoré by 12.30 and he did not arrive at the great square of the Town Hall until just after noon. There *had* been some booing on the square before his arrival, but this was directed entirely against the police who, for security reasons, had forced the indignant crowd too far back for their liking. There was a loud cheer as the King removed the grey military overcoat he had worn on the parade-ground and stood in his scarlet Field-Marshal's uniform (this was one British red-coat, at least, they did not object to). Another cheer went up as the Royal Standard was broken on the flag-staff of the Town Hall itself.

Inside, the President of the Municipal Council (most appropriately named M. Deville) gave his prepared speech of welcome in the so-called Chamber of Prefects (Salle des Prevôts), which looked as though it had been both carpeted and wallpapered entirely with fresh flowers. M. Deville's speech, however much work had gone into it, struck a delightfully personal note, with none of the pompous verbosity that might have been expected. He spoke on behalf of the people of Paris who, he said, 'were welcoming the return of a guest they had habitually greeted with respectful sympathy, the return of an old friend who has not forgotten us because we have not forgotten him . . .'

Given such a gracious overture, a man like King Edward was bound to respond. But the few spontaneous words he spoke in reply were among the simplest, shortest and most effective of his life. After thanking M. Deville, and saying how wrong it would have been for him to have come to Paris without having stopped 'even for a moment' at the Town Hall, he ended:

'I shall never forget my visit to your charming city, and I do assure you that it is with the greatest pleasure that I find myself among you again here, where I always feel just as though I am at home.'†

* This spectacular parade-ground manœuvre was done throughout the continent, though not, apparently, by British cavalry. At all events, when King Alfonso XIII of Spain visited England in 1905 this was the only fault he could find with a military review staged in his honour.

† One French version of the speech puts the last phrase as 'where I am *treated* as though I were at home'. Some twenty years later, on the occasion of his retirement from his long tenure of the French ambassadorship in London, M. Paul Cambon claimed that, while the 1903 visit was being prepared, it was he who had first suggested that the King should make a little speech along these lines. But the Town Hall words are such vintage King Edward VII that it seems only fair to leave him the credit for thinking them up as well as delivering them.

At that, he signed a ceremonial parchment, drained a glass of champagne from a crystal goblet ornamented with the arms of Paris, and left. There was a really thunderous acclamation from the square as his carriage clattered away.

That last phrase, *comme si j'étais chez moi*, was aimed at precisely the right target of Parisian pride and emotion and it hit the target slap in the middle. The city did not have to wait to read about the King's felicitous words in the next day's papers. Like his calculated compliment to the actresses of the Comédie Française, the gist of the Town Hall speech was spread up and down the boulevards by the Parisians themselves within a few hours. The tricky part of the visit was over; from now on, it was downhill all the way.

The programme for the rest of the Saturday night might have been planned in advance with relaxation in mind. The luncheon he gave at the Embassy was an informal meal for his suite and for his closest private friends in Paris. He himself sat between two attractive women he had known and favoured for years as Prince of Wales: the Countess de Pourtalès on his right, and the Marquise de Jaucourt on his left. Among the rest of the fifty guests at the large Embassy table were Madame Henry Standish (the elegant and high-born French lady who always insisted that *née des Cars* was put after her American husband's name); Prince d'Arenberg, the President of the French Jockey Club, whose guest the King was soon to be; the Marquis de Breteuil and the Marquis de Gallifet; and Prince Mohamed Ali, brother of the Khedive of Egypt. To the King, one and all were fond and familiar faces of his Parisian scene. Soveral was there as well, and one of the dishes looked as though it had even been named in his honour. Indeed, the whole menu could be construed as a gastronomic tribute to the tour as a whole. Apart from the English courses, there was something for each of the countries the King had visited:

> Oeufs à la Richmond
> Filets de saumon à la Portugaise
> Côtelettes d'agneau aux petits pois
> Jambon d'York aux épinards
> Pâte de mauviettes à la Chartres
> Salade de laitue à la crème
> Petits savarins à la Frascati

Having disposed of that, the King went out with his friends into the sunlit garden. Here he had half an hour for coffee, cigars and gossip before, at 3 p.m. on the dot, M. Loubet's now familiar carriage arrived again on the gravel drive. This time, it was to take them both out to

Longchamps for an afternoon's racing. The night at the play had been for the worlds of Paris officialdom and French culture. The visit to the Town Hall had been for the municipality. The Vincennes review had been for the armed forces. The drive between the two for the humble people of Paris. On Saturday afternoon at Longchamps, for the first and last time during his stay, all sections were present at once, dispersed somewhere on the famous course. Understandably, the *beau monde*, which had taken a back seat so far, was in total command here.

The afternoon was filled with sunshine, feminine beauty and good sport. It was also marked by a chain of Anglo-French courtesies and compliments. Some of these had been prepared in advance, while others were happy accidents on the day. In the former category came the special gold cup which King Edward had presented for the winner of the principal race on the card, the *Prix Persimmon*, named, of course, after the King's own English Derby winner. As an extra touch of delicacy, the cup had been filled with roses, of the variety *La France*.

The ladies of French society had paid their own compliment to the King (who, in many cases, knew not only the mothers but their grown-up daughters) by sporting the so-called *Edouard Sept* hat. The distinguishing mark of this creation was a great plume or set of plumes usually in white, but sometimes, just to be different, in black. For the rest, a fashionable floppiness seems to have been the order of the day, and the paddock swam with dresses of white tulle, trimmed with yards of lace or enormous feather boas, all rather like some untidy ballet scene out of *Swan Lake*.

The only thing that irked King Edward, the target of all this feminine magnificence, was that he couldn't get a really close look at it. When he arrived (a little late at 3.35 p.m.) to a tremendous ovation which lasted for nearly five minutes, he was whisked almost straight away to the Presidential box. This was a rather daunting-looking pavilion, shaped like a baroque Swiss chalet, and submerged for the occasion under a suffocating display of hydrangeas and rhododendrons. Even more suffocating was the company. Madame Loubet, who was of course seated next to the King, had done her best to compete with Paris society. But she was not exactly a vision of beauty. Moreover, she did not know a thing about the finer points of horse-racing, and neither did Mme Dubois, the wife of the Governor of Paris, who was next to him on the other side.

After a while, the King could stand it no longer. He summoned his secretary and told him in an imperious whisper: 'Get me out of this!' As usual, he had thought out an irreproachable way of doing things. The secretary was to slip over to the Committee Stand of the French

Jockey Club and persuade Prince d'Arenberg to ask the King if, 'as a special favour, he would come and inspect the new wing they had built'. This invitation was duly brought over within a few minutes by a three-man delegation. The King, with polite apologies, left the Republican ladies to themselves and went across to the other stand, dwelling a while in the paddock, to inspect everything on display there. This little subterfuge was greeted by the crowd as though it had been a dutiful demonstration of King Edward's 'true democratic spirit'. It was indeed a day on which nothing could go wrong.

The same applied to the actual race-meeting itself. The well-known French owner M. Deschamps had done his best to help the results in advance by withdrawing two of his horses from the card. One was called 'Kruger' and the other 'Boer', and it really would have been awkward had either of those won the King's gold cup. But even M. Deschamps could have neither arranged nor anticipated the happy results which did come up that day. The first race, the *Prix Perdita*, was won at the useful odds of 7–1, by Chrysothemia, a filly out of Venia by the King's very own Persimmon. The second, the *Prix Diamond Jubilee* (named after Queen Victoria), had one horse running in it called 'Imperator', which would have made quite a suitable winner for the Emperor of India who was the guest of honour. But even more appropriate was the relative outsider who came first past the post at 8–1. He was called, of all things, 'John Bull', and a great shout of laughter mixed with cheering greeted his victory. Almost as appropriate, and even more unexpected, was the winner of the main race, the Persimmon Cup, which King Edward watched from the Jockey Club Stand. This was the 16–1 outsider 'The Tsar', named after the ruler who was linked to France by an alliance and to the King by marriage.

The French Head of Protocol, M. Mollard (who had greatly irritated the King the day before by sending him a list of the clothes the French Republic expected him to wear) could not have arranged the meeting at Longchamps any better had he bribed all the jockeys himself. As a beaming King Edward said on leaving:

'What better could I have expected? I've seen my stables win with Persimmon's daughter, my people win with "John Bull", and my family win with my nephew, the Tsar.'

That Saturday evening, the President and his Ministers had the stage to themselves again at a function that was the climax to the formal hospitality of the visit. One hundred and twenty-six people sat down to dinner in the *Salle des Fêtes* of the Elysée Palace and, on this occasion,

ight: de Soveral and, *below,*
he celebrations during the
King's visit to Lisbon which
e engineered.

Above: The King salutes the French colours at a review at Vincennes and, *below*, in the Presidential box with Madame Loubet at Longchamps just before making his escape to the Jockey Club.

The historic private audience with Pope Leo XIII.

everyone except the *beau monde* seems to have been present. All the King's suite had been invited, together with all the senior members of the British Embassy. From the rest of the diplomatic corps, only the so-called 'family ambassadors' had been asked, that is, the envoys of those countries* to whose ruling houses the King was related. (This gave King Edward the chance to be particularly amiable to the German Ambassador, Prince Radolin, in case he might be reporting the wrong things back to his imperial master in Berlin.)

The Cabinet were there in full, and so were other members of the French establishment such as General Florentin, the Grand Chancellor of the Legion of Honour, and M. Pallain, Governor of the Bank of France. There was a Lafayette touch about the list of senior naval and military officers present. The former included Admiral Cotton, commander of an American naval squadron which had happened to be in Marseilles harbour to salute President Loubet when he had passed through earlier in the week on his way back from Tunisia. Finally, Paris being Paris, the French Academy was there, represented by such distinguished figures as Gabriel Hanotaux and Albert Sorel. The composers Massenet and Saint-Saens were among those who turned out for the French Institute, and works by both were included in the musical programme, offered by the band of the Republican Guard from the discreet distance of the winter garden.

The ten-course menu lived up to the company. After starting off unpromisingly with Brown Windsor soup as a tactful gesture to the King, it never looked back. Lamb was King Edward's favourite meat; indeed, it was the only meat he really enjoyed. He can rarely have had it more grandly presented than in the *Baron d'agneau de Pauillac aux morilles* which formed the centre-piece of this meal. The wines chosen were among the legends of the day, including a Château d'Yquem 1874 for the fish and a Château Haut Brion 1877 for the lamb.

When it came to the toasts, President Loubet (reading from a prepared text clipped to a candlestick in front of him) could do no better than the well-worn theme of 'strengthening the ties of friendship between our two countries'. King Edward's reply, on the other hand, was impromptu, and in it he returned to the simple, personal themes which had scored such a success at the Town Hall that morning.

'I have known Paris since my childhood. I have returned here many times and I have always admired the beauty of this unique city and the *esprit* of its inhabitants. I shall never forget the welcome I have received at your hands, M. le Président, and from the government

---

* Notably Russia, Germany, Greece, Sweden and Denmark.

and the people . . . Our great desire is that we should advance together in the path of civilization and peace . . .'

Prince Radolin could scarcely object to that. Much less could someone seated a few places away from him, the French Foreign Minister, M. Delcassé. He, like King Edward, had rather special ideas about what the words 'advance together' really meant.

A gala performance at the Opera rounded off this long and memorable day. Unlike the Friday evening at the theatre, this was a formal affair, with two powdered flunkies with torches to light the King's way even on the few yards from the vestibule to the lift. By knocking down the partitions, three boxes of the Grand Tier had been made into one great Presidential *loge* for the occasion. The distinguished audience around and beneath them ranged from the Grand Duke Boris to M. Monod, Director of Public Assistance, and from the great novelist Anatole France to the delectable Mlle Piérat, the Madeleine of *L'Autre Danger*. When the King and President left, two hours later, after a mixed programme of music and ballet that was easy on both the eye and the ear, they found the square in front of the Opera and all the surrounding boulevards packed solid with waiting crowds. The midnight drive back to the Embassy via the Place Vendôme, the Rue de Castiglione, the Rue de Rivoli and the Rue Royale was a triumphal procession. It is doubtful whether, by now, even the hardiest Anglophobe had the courage left to shout '*Vive Fashoda*'. It seems certain he would not have been heard above the cheering if he had done. The mood of Paris that Saturday night had settled the argument.

As at Lisbon, Sunday was a 'rest-day', with the usual Sabbath programme. After breakfast, King Edward walked with his suite to the small English church in the Rue d'Aguesseau to attend divine service. The distance was only a few hundred yards and, as the weather was still fine, nothing could have been more natural to English eyes. But in France, where the Republican President had adopted much of the life style of the departed emperors, such informality among rulers was a novelty. The sight of this sovereign of an immense Empire strolling down the Faubourg in black tail-coat, top-hat, grey trousers and yellow gloves to pay a private call on his God caused much appreciative comment. It was, they reflected, just what he would have done at home; and that, perhaps, was the message King Edward wanted to convey.

The day before, the King had said to the English chaplain, Mr Noyes: 'Do your normal service. You will simply have one more in the congregation.' It was an impossible command. The 930 specially

invited worshippers who jammed the little Gothic church to the eaves
were, of course, several times the chaplain's normal Sunday morning
flock. They played 'Onward Christian Soldiers' as the King marched
down the aisle to his seat near the chancel, and the service started the
moment he sat down. The text for Mr Noyes's sermon (which, on the
advice of the King's suite, he was keeping shorter than usual) was from
St Matthew 13. The first verse chosen was highly apposite: 'Whence
hath this man this wisdom and these mighty works?' But then came:
'Is this not the carpenter's son?' Well, hardly.

From church the royal party went, via the Embassy, to the Quai
d'Orsay, where M. Delcassé, who had done so much towards bringing
England and France together, gave a luncheon. After the meal, the
King withdrew for nearly half an hour's private conversation with the
French Foreign Minister. No written record of this was kept on either
side. But to judge by the comments made later by Soveral (who, of
course, was present on this occasion too, described on the official
guest list as *ami personnel de Sa Majesté*), the talk was not merely of
pushing ahead as fast and as far as possible on the Anglo-French political plane, but of bringing Russia into the combination as well.[8]

Like Lisbon, Paris had a large English colony, and the King spent
the rest of the afternoon with them. In the gardens of the Embassy
were gathered 150 boys and girls from the 'British and American
School' at the Rue des Acacias; and, seated in front of them, twelve old
English ladies from the 'Victoria Home' at Neuilly-sur-Seine. They
had been grouped on the lawn to watch the King plant a chestnut tree
in commemoration of his visit. He did so, with the words, 'May it
grow large and splendid, and remember me,' at which several of the
old ladies burst into tears. This great day in the evening of their lives
was rounded off with a slap-up tea which had been specially prepared
for them at one of the best restaurants of Paris, the *Ambassadeurs* on
the Champs Elysées.

The King's dinner at the Embassy in honour of President Loubet
rounded off the day, the visit and, indeed, the whole tour. As though
to emphasize this, the eighty-two guests included not merely those
'family ambassadors' we have met with already, but also the envoys
in Paris of the other countries King Edward had visited: M. de Souza
Rosa, the Minister of Portugal, and the Italian Ambassador, Count
Tornielli. To judge by the careful *placement*, the King had drawn the
necessary moral from that very boring sojourn he had endured in the
Presidential box at Longchamps before his escape to the Jockey Club
stand. There was no such flight possible now, from his own dinner
table. So, though Madame Loubet had to be placed on his right, at his

left hand was the Countess Wolkenstein-Trostburg. If she had a husband, he did not appear on the guest list. One can only conclude that
the King had picked her, before all the wives of official notabilities
present, because he was determined to have a good looker and a good
talker at least on one side of him. The meal also reflected King Edward's
preferences. A plain saddle of mutton was the only meat course. His
own royal house was represented this time not in the soup but in the
Windsor Pudding. Among the wines, Sir Edmund's cellars had produced a claret every bit as good as the President's Haut Brion 1877: a
Margaux of the same fabulous year. There was music during dinner
and a concert of more light music afterwards. But there were no toasts
on this last evening. Everything had already been said.

The King was to have left very early the following Monday for
Cherbourg, where the *Victoria and Albert* was waiting to take him
back to England. However, by the time he had said good night to M.
Loubet at midnight on the Sunday, even he was wilting under the strain
of the past few days. At his request, the departure time of his train was
accordingly put back until 11.30. Tens of thousands of Parisians had
taken the morning off to bid him farewell, encouraged by a sky that
was still mainly blue. (Ten minutes after his train pulled out, the beautiful weekend weather was to break, with a violent hailstorm descending
over the city.)

This last drive in the Presidential carriage went along the Avenue
Marigny, the Avenue Nicholas II and so across the Alexander III
bridge to the Rue de Constantine and the Western Station. There was
the same atmosphere of open-air carnival along the route as on the
Saturday, but with some significant differences. The sellers of souvenir
pins and brooches bearing pictures of the King had their best day yet.
Indeed, the cry most heard from them now was *'Qui n'as pas son petit
Edouard?'* which suggested that those people who had still not bought
a royal memento were somehow out of it.

It is unlikely that King Edward heard these street hawkers' shouts
as his carriage rolled by. But among the steady roar of applause that
he certainly did hear there was one sound which must have given him
a particular glow. For the first time, the cries of *'Vive Loubet'*, *'Vive
l'Armée'* and *'Vive le Roi'* were almost matched by the cry of *'Vive
l'Angleterre'*. That told the whole story of the visit. His conjurer's trick
had come off. For the Parisians, at least, that *sale pays*, England, had
become identified with *nôtre bon Edouard*, its King.

* * *

That the 1903 tour in general, and the Paris visit in particular, had

represented a purely personal triumph for King Edward was not disputed at the time; nor has it been since. It had been a one-man show
on the diplomatic stage which he had planned, produced and directed,
with himself as the central actor. All over the Continent, it had laid the
foundations for that legendary (but not mythical) reputation he soon
acquired as the most influential diplomatist in Europe. At home in
England, it loosened still further any ministerial restraints which might
have prevented him actually operating as such. He rarely ever differed
with his governments over the broad fundamentals of British foreign
policy, a fact which caused many historians to draw the highly illogical
conclusion that he therefore exerted little influence upon them. But
there were often differences with his Ministers as to the 'how' and the
'when', and these are both elements of the political equation which can
be almost as important as the basic 'what'. For the rest of his reign,
whenever such discussions arose with his Cabinets, whether Conservative or Liberal, 'Remember 1903' would be in the back of their minds,
and in the back of his. That had been the year when these issues of
timing and method had first divided the King from his advisers. He
had been proved right and they had been proved wrong.

In later years, the question of what influence the 1903 visit had on
the development of the Anglo-French Entente became rather muddled
up by the claims of various politicians to be considered as the 'real
architects' of that Entente. But at the time there was near-unanimity
among observers that those four days in Paris might well go on to
produce a transformation of European politics, and that it was King
Edward who had done the transforming.

The Belgian Minister in Paris in 1903 declared: 'Seldom has such a
complete change of attitude been seen as that which has taken place in
this country . . . towards England and her Sovereign.'[9] For his French
colleague Paul Cambon in London, the King's visit was the one event,
above all others, which was to make the Entente possible. Looking back
on it four years later, Sir Eyre Crowe of the Foreign Office, in one of
those incisive and very influential memoranda of his,[10] stressed the
psychological importance of the visit. It had, he wrote, caused the
French to shed their suspicions of 'English designs and intentions' and
develop confidence in what he placidly called 'England's straightfor-
wardness and loyalty'. Normally, such confidence would have been
slow to evolve, but:

'That it declared itself with unexpected rapidity and unmistakable
emphasis was, without doubt, due, in the first place, to the initiative
and tactful perseverance of the King . . .'

Those who had accompanied King Edward on his triumphal progress were, naturally enough, even more emphatic in their verdicts. For Hardinge, the Entente which now developed was due 'entirely to the initiative and political flair of King Edward who, had he listened to the objections of his Cabinet, would never have gone to Paris'.[11] Ponsonby was more dogmatic still. 'Any clerk at the Foreign Office could draw up a treaty, but there was no one else who could have succeeded in producing the right atmosphere for a *rapprochement* with France!'[12]

Though the Foreign Office clerks (who, by implication, included the Foreign Secretary himself) come off rather roughly there, Ponsonby's verdict is accurate for the paradoxical reason that no treaty of alliance ever *was* drawn up between England and France. The strange relationship which now developed between them, and which was ultimately to bring them together into the First World War, was based, not on formal political commitments, but on a general climate of trust and understanding. This climate *was* the treaty. In a very special sense, therefore, King Edward VII had created the second with the first in May of 1903.*

Ironically, in view of what was to come, the only people who did not immediately grasp the significance of the King's visit to Paris were the Germans. They had been strangely complacent from the moment it was announced. On 15 April 1903, for example, Bülow, in a comment to the Kaiser on the impending visit, even thought it might do Germany some good. As England was Russia's rival and France was Russia's ally, the King's wooing of the French could, he thought, 'lead to a cooling of Russian-French relations and so to a drawing together (*heranreichen*) of Russia and Germany'.[13]

The same note was struck immediately after the event by both official and press comment in Germany. The Berlin *Post* of 3 May wrote, for example:

'A real Anglo-French entente is in the long run impossible because in the colonial sphere differences will invariably arise. Indeed, they will arise again very soon and these artificially spun threads will be severed with a jerk.'

The German Foreign Office itself was prodded into making a considered verdict by a memorandum composed in Berlin on 10 May 1903 by the former Chargé d'Affaires in London, Baron Eckhardstein.[14] In

---

* The King himself was characteristically modest about his role. When a formal Anglo-French understanding was concluded a year later, all that he would say to Paul Cambon in London was that his 1903 Paris visit had 'cleared the ground'.

this, he argued that the real danger for Germany was not that France and Russia would be driven apart by England's sudden initiative in Europe but that, on the contrary, all three countries would eventually come together in a Triple Entente. (This, as Eckhardstein may have suspected, had been the long-term aim of both King Edward and Delcassé for years past.)

Bülow read the Baron's analysis of the situation and then sent sceptical telegrams off to the German Ambassadors in St Petersburg, Paris and London, asking for their comments. All three envoys from all three capitals poured scorn on Eckhardstein's conclusions. It was 'much too far-reaching', replied Count Bernstorff from London. It was 'music of the future' declared Prince Radolin from Paris. The old dispute over a Russian 'warm-sea port' in the Mediterranean would always prevent any Anglo-Russian alliance, reported Count Alversleben from St Petersburg. Summing up, Chancellor Bülow confidently told his Emperor on 20 May 1903 that Eckhardstein 'stood alone with his ideas about the possibility of a new French-English-Russian grouping'.[15] 'A verdict based on common sense,' the Kaiser wrote approvingly on the final telegram in this long exchange, and the file was complacently closed.

As the German Emperor was to demonstrate himself, and in the most bizarre fashion, neither the common sense nor the complacency was to last for long.

PART IV

1903-1907

9

MARIENBAD

King Edward's Europe, and the way he dominated it, can never be understood simply through the formal world of embassy banquets and state visits. Edward VII became the leader of European diplomacy so effortlessly because he had always been the leader of European society. For him, this society comprised villas as well as palaces, and scented envelopes as well as cyphered telegrams. These two trails, the social and the political, often criss-crossed in confusing style. But if there was one place where, year after year, they ran neatly and sweetly in parallel, it was at a spa tucked prettily away in the Eger Valley of Bohemia. More than any other regular station on the King's travels, Marienbad demands a chapter in its own right.

The continental court he established there during seven successive summers was quite unlike anything that Europe had known before. It seems safe to predict that Europe will never know anything like it again. Edwardian Marienbad became a gold-rush town, with statesmen and princes for prospectors and prestige for nuggets. As with so many Eldorados, its reign was brief; but, during this brief hey-day, Marienbad was established as the unofficial midsummer capital not merely of Bohemia, or of Austria-Hungary, but of the entire Continent. For three weeks each year, usually from mid-August onwards, the spa guests came to include almost everyone in Europe of rank and importance whom the King wished to see there. Unavoidably, they also included a great many more who just wanted to be seen with him.

Their variety reflected not only the King's passion for international affairs but also the rich mixture of his personal friendships and tastes. The Prime Minister of Republican France trying to talk the King into building a bigger British Army against Germany would brush shoulders on the hotel stairway with a Hungarian horse-breeder trying to sell that same monarch some racehorses for his stables. The Foreign Minister of Imperial Russia, in Marienbad to get the King of England's help over some dangerous Balkan muddle, would have to elbow aside on the promenade tailors from Berlin busy sketching the cut of his latest coat, to copy in their autumn catalogues. Inventors with a patent to proclaim; financiers with a scheme to float; famous journalists who had the King's ear for their news and views; humbler colleagues who never spoke a word with him but still made a summer's living by writing a few lines each day about his movements; a special muster of chefs, doctors, police chiefs, musicians, actors and sundry other entertainers – all these formed the busy cosmopolitan background against which the King's party moved. It was more Byzantine than central European. Yet, at the same time, it preserved, through King Edward, a homely informality that was essentially English.

Then there were the ladies, either illustrious or witty or beautiful, and preferably all three together. They were always at the centre of King Edward's private stage and at Marienbad they positively jostled for the spotlight of royal favour. Here again, the variety was as dazzling as the individuals themselves. Some who came specially over from England were mementoes of his younger days: the actress Lily Langtry, for example, that famous 'Jersey Lily' who had been his mistress as Prince of Wales in the '80s and '90s. Greying now, she was a reminder of romance rather than an invitation to it.

Not so another Englishwoman who caught the King's eye at Marienbad and whom the gossip-writers of the day discreetly referred to as Mrs X. This lady was 30 at the most and her beauty was quite distinctive in that, though her cheeks were rosy, her hair was white. The King would visit her at her house, which was not far from his hotel, and would sometimes take her for a drive in an ordinary carriage and pair to the Café Nimrod, a dairy tucked away in the woods outside the town. On these occasions, he would understandably dispense with a retinue, or even a single equerry. But he could not dismiss the Austrian police commissioner detailed to watch over his safety twenty-four hours a day. This worthy would follow him in another carriage at a distance that reconciled surveillance with discretion. Then, at an even discreeter distance, he would prowl dismounted in the woods. Eventually, the unusual beauty of Mrs X was outshone by the arrival in Marienbad of an American actress. The dethroned lady promptly left by car with 'a certain Foreign Minister' for Germany and, for the rest of the season, her rosy cheeks and white hair were to be seen constantly at his side at Baden-Baden.

Such was the King's amorous reputation that candidates for his favours took to turning up in Marienbad, as though they were applying for an official post. His secretary, the hard-worked Ponsonby, describes one such applicant, who arrived at his office at the end of an arduous day of interviews. His appointments had begun with an Austrian Countess, who wanted him to provide a special pass to exempt her dogs from quarantine on a journey to England. Then had come in succession an American tourist complaining about his treatment by some British consul; a sculptor wanting to do a bust of the King; and an army officer who had devised a new telescopic scabbard for swords which the King might perhaps sponsor. Finally, the lady was announced, a beautiful Viennese, who told him quite simply that she wanted to have the honour of sleeping with the King. Ponsonby replied that this was quite out of the question. She considered this rebuff for a moment and then suggested that, in order not to waste the money she had spent on her train fare, she might as well go to bed with the King's secretary instead. This offer too was declined, at which the lady got up and left in a huff. She must have thought the English very ungallant.

But it was not only the unescorted ladies who came to Marienbad each August to seek their luck. What would nowadays be called the 'jet-set' of the Continent turned up in force, simply to see and to be seen at this improvised open-air English court eight hundred miles from Buckingham Palace. The King, who was both loyal to old friends and yet always eager to make new ones, welcomed them all.

Madame Waddington, who was marching towards her eighties during the Marienbad era, was a ripe example from the first category. An American by birth, she had been married to a French politician and diplomatist who had spent the last ten years of his life, from 1883 to 1893, as his country's Ambassador in London.* There had been few embassies during that decade where the Prince of Wales had been a more frequent and more happy guest; and the King always found time for the aged widow Waddington now. She was distinctly old-fashioned. Even King Edward could not persuade her to come to the bridge table after dinner; the game, she complained, had been the ruin of good conversation.

As for new friends, there was simply no knowing whom the King might not take a fancy to on his walks round the town or his trips to the surrounding cafés and beauty spots. One day, for example, he produced a 'M. et Madame de Varrue' at his lunch table. She was identified as a faded Parisian beauty married late in life to a much younger man who had bestowed upon himself the title of Baron. Another surprise guest was a Mrs Dale Lace, described by Ponsonby as a lady 'with an eye-glass, short skirts and a murky past'. Like the bogus baron, she amused the King, however much she may have shocked some of his friends.

When we last saw King Edward at a spa, he was comfortably in-

---

* He seems to have been a dullish man, of whom the wags said that he was 'much wadding and very little tone'.

stalled at the Ritters Park Hotel at Homburg in Germany in 1902. One might well wonder therefore what it was that had persuaded him, the year after, to move permanently to Marienbad. He never gave his reasons in any records that have survived; but they are not hard to guess.

To begin with, Homburg, though a pleasant enough place, was, not surprisingly, very German. As such, it could easily irritate a sovereign who had deliberately dropped the Albert from his title in favour of the Edward. In 1901, for example, the Directorate of the spa had brought in new rules under which, in the interests of hygiene, every partaker of the waters had to possess 'a glass of his or her exclusive property'. With true Germanic thoroughness, the regulations were enforced to admit of absolutely no exception, though it was admitted that to ask the King of England to buy his own glass would have been somewhat awkward. Accordingly, on that last visit of 1902, King Edward had found himself presented by the municipality with a special tumbler emblazoned with the arms of England and neatly scaled down the side like a medicine bottle so that he could measure each and every gulp. (His uncle, the Duke of Cambridge, was given a similar one, painted with the Lion and Unicorn.)

That was hardly the King's idea of informality, which, for him, was one of the supreme pleasures of life, especially when on holiday. And though it was a little enough thing in itself, that heraldic measuring tumbler, when contrasted with the plain glass mugs that everyone carried around with them at Marienbad, must have summed up the difference between the prim fussiness of Wilhelminian Germany and the easy-going, relaxed atmosphere of Franz Josef's polyglot monarchy. Moreover, when he recalled his two visits to Marienbad as Prince of Wales,* the more tolerant moral atmosphere of the Bohemian spa must have seemed another attraction. Indeed, already by the end of the Victorian era, Marienbad had achieved something of the 'fast' reputation of those Indian hill stations like Simla which had helped to sweeten the summer months of another Empire.

The English Liberal leader and future Prime Minister Campbell-Bannerman had (for quite different reasons) become devoted to Marienbad in the early '70s, when indeed it was still a tranquil summer resort and anything but a royal mecca. But by 1899, which was two years after the Prince of Wales had put it on the English social map with his first visit there, Campbell-Bannerman was already writing sorrowfully home:

* He had been a guest of the Metternichs in those days at their nearby castle of Königswart.

'We have seen a new realization of the true saying that, wheresoever the eagle is, there will the carcasses be gathered together. Whether on account of the Prince's presence or not, the English and American society here has contained an extraordinary number of tainted ladies – including five divorcées and about ten others of varying degrees of doubtfulness. The decent people were almost in a minority and we thought of wearing our marriage certificates as a sort of order outside our coats . . .'

But however much King Edward appreciated the gay and tolerant ways of Austria-Hungary in general and of Marienbad in particular, what probably clinched the matter was the simple fact that Bohemia was not under the German flag. At Homburg, he was in his nephew's kingdom and thus totally at his mercy when it came to submitting to those lightning visits, with military parades conjured out of the ground. To King Edward, the Emperor William spelt instant death to any idea of jollity or relaxation, especially as the Kaiser acidly and sometimes publicly disapproved of the King's personal friends and private morals. The thought of having every August holiday on the Continent ruined by his exhausting and sanctimonious nephew was more than the King could face. True, Marienbad was not far from the German border; but it did lie in a different Empire, and that surely afforded some protection. (In fact, though there was one nasty scare in the local *Marienbader Zeitung* that the German Kaiser was about to descend on the place, and another even nastier scare at the Foreign Office that Chancellor Bülow was heading there, neither of them ever did turn up at any time during the King's annual stays.)

* * *

And so, launched by all these considerations, King Edward's seven-year 'reign' at Marienbad began when, at 2.30 p.m. on the afternoon of 13 August 1903, he stepped out of his special train at the local station. His nephew had given him a taste of what he was escaping from by stage-managing a brief meeting *en route* across Germany at Frankfurt, complete with guard of honour and the usual swarm of officials. And although the King had expressly forbidden any such formal ceremonies at Marienbad, he could not, of course, be allowed to arrive as a private individual. Sir Francis Plunkett, the then British Ambassador to Austria-Hungary, had to be there to welcome his sovereign, even though the plumed hat had been left behind in the Metternichgasse embassy in Vienna.

Moreover, it was really too much to expect that the spa dignitaries would not be present on this, the most auspicious moment in Marienbad's history since the great German poet Goethe had arrived to take these waters eighty-two years before. Their leaders were all there on the platform, including the mayor, Dr Nadler, and his principal assistant, Town Councillor Metzner. And, despite the fact that the time of the King's arrival was supposed to have been kept a secret, the good people of Marienbad, natives and visitors alike, were also determined not to be left out. Crowds had been lining the streets since the morning and they now waved and cheered and curtsied and saluted (according to their rank, sex, nationality and profession) throughout the King's brief carriage ride to his hotel.

This was the Weimar; and as it was to be the scene of several important political events, as well as of numberless unimportant social ones, during the next seven years, it is worth a closer look. It was an imposing, yellow-washed building, typical of those Grand Hotels that were sprouting up in the '70s and '80s at mountain and seaside resorts the length and breadth of the Continent, all of them designed, in the very layout of their suites, attics and box-rooms, for stays of at least three weeks by demanding guests accompanied by flocks of servants. The Weimar was more elegant and handsome than most, a successful cross in style between a baroque Bohemian shooting-lodge and a French provincial opera house.

The rooms that the King went up to (having first greeted the hotel-keeper, Herr Hammerschmid, who was waiting, bowed almost double, in the foyer) were a suite of five on the first floor. At their centre was the so-called 'study', in reality a spacious reception-room nearly twenty-five yards square. Like the rest of the suite, it had been decorated and furnished in what the proprietor and the city fathers hoped would be a style fitting for this English King. To the left of the entrance door, for example, an open fireplace with a red mahogany mantelpiece had been installed, flanked by two leather armchairs that might have come from Sandringham. A huge Smyrna carpet, red with blue borders, covered the floor and added to the welcoming feel of the room. The only incongruous touch was the oil-painting which had been chosen to hang over the writing-desk. It was a scene by the artist Ernst Stanton entitled 'Solitude'. That was the last thing King Edward sought in life, least of all on holiday in Marienbad.

What he did seek there, among other things, was fresh air and mountain scenery, and in this respect, the Weimar served him perfectly. A stone balcony, the breadth of several hotel corridors put together, ran the length of the suite. Here he could sit or stroll; see and be seen; and look out on to the tiny park beneath and so across the

216

town to the panorama of the wooded valley stretching beyond it.

The King's private rooms opened out to the left of the main *salon*: bedroom, dressing-room, a tiny *Kabinett* for his valet and, finally, a bathroom with a brand-new American bath of which Herr Hammer-schmid was immensely proud. As well as taking great care over his arrangements, the proprietor was also shrewd enough to renew the entire collection of carpets, furniture and paintings every year. The outgoing items apparently fetched double their value with the souvenir-hunters. Recording this, the King's secretary comments, with that sublime disdain of the Edwardian English gentleman: 'I never had the slightest wish to buy any of them.'

Though the King's accommodation sounded very grand, it was in fact modest compared with the style in which his mother had lived on her much rarer private excursions to continental resorts. She had often taken an entire hotel, not just one suite, to ensure her privacy, and as she travelled abroad with anything up to a hundred servants, this was just as well. As for an entourage, though Marienbad was soon to seethe with all manner of persons bobbing about in the King's political or social wake, on this first visit in 1903 no personal friends were invited out from England, and his doctor and his secretary were the only two court officials in attendance. He had also travelled *incognito* as the Duke of Lancaster. This, of course, did little or nothing to conceal his identity, though it did cause the English biologist Professor Roy Lankester some embarrassing special attentions when he turned up himself at Marienbad one day.

But *incognito* or not, and informal or not, the King ran immediately into the same problem that had plagued him at Homburg, the smother-ing curiosity of the general public. Dreading this, the municipality had put out special pleas for restraint in advance. But it was all to no avail. As at Homburg, from the moment the King showed his face outside the hotel early on the first morning of his stay, he and his two com-panions were mobbed, in Ponsonby's words, 'by a dense crowd of several hundreds' who jostled him with their clicking Kodaks when-ever he sat down. He thundered his disapproval and the rumblings were transmitted via the Mayor and the Provincial Governor to Vienna. Swift action was taken, including the strengthening of his police guard under the remarkable Hans Schober. (This man was destined one day to become Federal President of the Republic of Austria in a future world suddenly and strangely bereft of Habsburg double-headed eagles, a world which no one in Marienbad in 1903, and least of all Herr Schober, could have envisaged.)

Thanks to Schober and his detectives, the crowds were brought under acceptable restraint. True, this public pestering was liable to get out of hand again at any time. It got so bad three years later, for example, that on 16 August 1906 the Mayor was driven to the desperate step of nailing great warning notices to the trunks of the trees on the main promenade. These appealed to all spa visitors 'not to annoy our exalted guest from England by crowding in on him or hurrying after him or by any other demonstrative behaviour'. This worked wonders and the placards (which had embarrassed the King even more than the crowds) were removed at his request a day or two later. Always bearing public curiosity in mind, he soon evolved a regular daily routine for himself.

Despite the intensive social and, later, political activities that the King developed at Marienbad, he followed with remarkable obedience the medical discipline of the spa. All his life he had been an early riser, and it was no hardship for him to be awakened between 6 and 6.30 every morning to take his first glass of spa water in his bedroom.

A letter the King wrote to Soveral on 27 August 1905, during his third stay at Marienbad, takes the story of his daily routine and his companions on from there, in his own words:

'I appear at the "Kreuzbrunnen" at 7.30 on and get through 3 tumblers of the rather pleasant water by 9, when *le café au lait* is very welcome. Luncheon at 1, dinner at 7.30. Bridge frequently but always to bed by 11. Sometimes I go to the theatre, which is much improved.

'Princess Joachim Murat and Marquise de Ganay are here – both charming women. Then we have the Goschens,* Sir H. Campbell-Bannerman, Madame Waddington and Mrs King (both very amusing), Sir S. McDonnell, the *ancient* Col. Swain (!) Lord and Lady Clanwilliam, Mrs Hall Walker, Mrs A. Pike, Mrs Horton, Mr and Mrs C. Matthews, Captain and Lady Lilian Boyd, Mrs Bacons and her very pleasant daughter . . .

'I have a splendid Mercedes Motor and take constant drives which are delightful . . .'

It is the letter of a man enjoying a well-ordered rest in pleasant but (with the exception of the two French ladies) socially unspectacular company. That was doubtless just what he wanted, though neither the smart *demi-monde* or the gossip-writers would ever believe him.

The so-called *Kreuzbrunnen*, which the King mentions, was, with its broad avenue, lined with trees on one side and a handsome colonnade on the other, Marienbad's great social promenade. Here, for an hour

* By 1905 Sir Edward Goschen had succeeded Plunkett as British Ambassador in Vienna.

or two, the waters were taken quite literally on the stroll. The gentlemen mostly followed the King's example by wearing town suits in mid- or dark grey with soft felt Homburg hats curled upwards at the brim, though a few sported straw boaters. Spats (to judge from the many contemporary photographs that have survived of these *Kreuzbrunnen* mornings) seem to have been an optional item. But the men carried, one and all, a walking-cane or a slimly furled umbrella in the one hand and, in the other, a mug of Marienbad's sulphurous water, from which they took sips between strides and bouts of conversation. (The soda sulphate in the water, incidentally, was particularly recommended by the medical authorities of the day for 'persons of luxurious habits', which seems apt enough.)

Their ladies, who were dressed to kill in huge hats and elaborate long dresses, also carried their little mugs. In addition, they were equipped with parasols to guard against sun as well as rain, for to get sunburned, in Edwardian times, was more distressing than getting drenched.

Occasionally there would appear at the *Kreuzbrunnen* strange apparitions that darkened this brilliant mirror of Edwardian elegance. These were the Polish rabbis, with whom Marienbad had long been popular, not, one presumes, because of their 'luxurious habits' but because Galicia, from where most of them hailed, was a nearby province of the same Habsburg Empire. Dressed in black from head to foot – black caps, or hats with flat brims wide enough to stand a teapot on; long black caftan-like garments buttoned up to the neck; black boots and black (unrolled) umbrellas; even black beards, and greasy black ringlets down their cheeks – they look, in the photographs, like spectres of doom come to haunt this social feast. One wonders what the *beau monde* made of them; or, perhaps more to the point, what they made of the *beau monde*. Like the white-robed monks of Tepl, with whom they formed an almost operatic contrast, the Galician rabbis got up at the crack of dawn and took their first drink at the *Kreuzbrunnen* before 6 a.m. So the two worlds of spiritual and temporal did not often collide.

As for food and drink, the King also tried his best to remember that Marienbad was supposed to be a health cure as well as the social and political jamboree it developed into. He was never a great one for meat, and he hardly touched spirits. But he was immensely fond of food and wine in general, and he also loved his cigars, which were the size of capstan bars. Marienbad's desire to tickle his gourmet's palate was therefore constantly at loggerheads with its mission to trim his ample waistline. The King himself was pulled between the two. Champagne, for example, was strictly 'forbidden' because of its fattening properties; but the King had not been more than ten days in Marienbad on his first visit when the Marquise de Ganay, giving a lunch for King Edward and the King of Greece (who had also turned up), passed temptation all round the table in the shape of the delectable wine. King Edward was in torment, but probably took a sip.* His fellow monarch was seen to fairly gulp it down.

Even without champagne, however, there were plenty of temptations. The local brook trout and the fried aubergines (his favourite vegetable) were harmless enough. On the other hand, a luncheon menu provided in that 1903 season for these same two monarchs at the Café Rübezahl, a famous restaurant in the Marienbad forests, was full of danger for their waistlines. Proceedings commenced with grilled *Fogosch* (then, as now, the most delicious fish to be caught in the Danube). This was followed in succession by lamb cutlets *à l'anglaise*; roast partridge; Prague ham in aspic; and finally a *compôte* of fresh fruits, the whole repast being irrigated by the finest Austrian wines. It was a meal that was the epitome of 'luxurious habits' rather than an antidote for them.

But despite all this, the spa authorities proudly claimed in the local paper that, after fourteen days of his first Marienbad cure, the King of England had lost over 11 lbs (5 kilos) in weight. The most that the King himself is on record as claiming (in his many Marienbad letters to Cassel and Soveral) is a loss of 'more than 8 lbs in a fortnight', and the amount was underlined in triumph. Weight was, in fact, an obsession of his, and not only his own, but other people's. Thus in 1904 we find him urging Soveral to persuade his own very stout King Carlos 'to go to Carlsbad next year, or his health will suffer for it'. King Edward's own weighing ceremony at Marienbad was regularly conducted by one Fräulein Senft. She was the manageress of the cake shop near the Hotel Weimar, and appeared with her scales every day in the royal suite for this purpose. The King, gallant enough at all times, was so pleased with her first year's statistics that he presented her with a handsome pearl brooch.

In August 1903, King Edward was, of course, fresh from the political triumphs of his spring tour. Yet there was hardly any diplomacy about this first sojourn in Marienbad. Apart from the *Kreuzbrunnen* routine, the chronicles had little to report about the King's doings beyond walks, excursions into the countryside, shopping trips and, in the evenings, small dinner-parties or attendances at Marienbad's town

---

* When champagne was called for and he himself was the host, the King chose a natural wine without the fattening sugar. This happened in August 1908, for example, when he gave his usual dinner to honour the Austrian Emperor's birthday. The wine King Edward wanted for the occasion, a Veuve Clicquot Brut, 1898, was not to be found in Marienbad, so the Austrian Jockey Club rushed him a special supply of it from Vienna.

theatre or open-air concerts. However, from the very start, he never missed a trick where England's 'public relations' were concerned.

On the second day of his stay, for example, he had driven to a nearby beauty spot in the hills, the Podhornberg, from where a lovely panoramic view of the surrounding peaks and valleys could be enjoyed. One Michael Wurtinger, 78 years old and a well-known local character, acted as the King's guide. He had donned all his medals for the occasion, including those dating from Radetsky's brilliant campaign against the Italians nearly forty years before, a victory which all Austrians particularly savoured, as it concerned their traditional enemy. The old man had often worn these medals before, so often, in fact, that the ribbons and clasps were almost falling apart. The King noticed this and asked the guide, to whom he had taken anyway a great fancy, to call on him at his hotel. When the veteran soldier duly turned up on parade at the Hotel Weimar he was presented with money with which to renew all his clasps and ribbons, as well as with an extra medal to go with them. This little gesture was soon the talk of Marienbad. The King of England, already residing in the Austrian Emperor's domains, had now put himself in Field-Marshal Radetsky's historic camp. There was no surer path to Austria's affections than that.

It was in a shower of medals and personal gifts (dispensed by himself) that, on 31 August 1903, the King left Marienbad after his first stay. We have seen, the year before, how an English decoration had meant so much to the Shah of Persia that he had travelled all the way from Teheran to Portsmouth to try and get it. It needs little imagining, therefore, how these humble dignitaries of a Bohemian watering spa were overwhelmed by other, if lesser, honours. The King forgot nobody; and, as the Victorian Order was his to dispose of, he consulted nobody either.

The Provincial Governor, the Mayor, the station-master, the postmaster, and Dr Ott (who had supervised the royal cure) were all made commanders or officers of the order. The Victoria medal, in silver or bronze, was handed to lesser lights in the railway and the post office, as well as to the detectives and gendarmes who had guarded the royal visitor. Others, whose functions were essentially non-official, were given presents. The hôtelier, for example, received a pair of diamond cufflinks, which had doubtless been bought from Marienbad's chief jeweller Herr Richard Spitz. The jeweller received a parting present better than diamonds: the right to display the King's coat of arms and the magic legend 'By Appointment' in his shop. And perhaps the happiest thought in all their minds was the prospect that this portly twentieth-century 'Sun King' was to be a regular visitor. Indeed, his last words as he boarded his train (for a visit to Vienna) were: 'Marienbad can rest assured it will soon see me again.' As if to prove the point, fifty bottles of the spa's spring water had been loaded on to the royal train at his request.

King Edward kept his word. His return the following August of 1904 marks the beginning of Marienbad's resplendent hey-day. By now, English society had taken note of the fact that a stay at this Bohemian spa was on the King's annual itinerary, and of the 3000 extra guests that Marienbad registered that year, a goodly number were English. That list of names already quoted shows that, despite the extravagant claims of the spa directors, the innermost circle of English aristocracy never joined the trek to Marienbad. Some may have felt that, if they had no weight problems, such a pilgrimage was unnecessary, for they entertained the King later in the year in their great houses at home. Furthermore, those Marienbad weeks came right at the beginning of the grouse-shooting season, so the natural pull of the calendar would be north to the Scottish moors, not east to the Bohemian forests. However, in 1904, both King Edward and Marienbad were to greet their most illustrious visitor of all, the Emperor Franz Josef himself.

The relationship between these two rulers was an intriguing one. If Edward was the restless uncle of Europe, the Austrian Emperor was its sedentary grandfather. He had already sat fifty-six years on the throne by the time this meeting took place, and was destined to outreign Edward VII by ruling for another twelve. He had long since abandoned state visits abroad as exhausting fripperies for a sovereign who anyway had more than a dozen different nations and races to cope with in his own domains. So he welcomed the chance of a meeting in Marienbad, partly because it would be an easy substitute for the invitation he had been given to go to Windsor, and partly because he genuinely liked this remarkable English King.

Franz Josef, like his imperial German ally, may have found King Edward's private life a great deal too permissive for his tastes. But, unlike the tactless William, one suspects that the old Austrian Emperor would have disapproved with a twinkle in his faded blue eyes and always with a finger pressed tightly on his lips. What linked Franz Josef and King Edward above all else was their dedication to the mission of kingship and their passionate concern for the rights and duties that went with it. Each, in his very different way, was a polished professional at the game. That, in itself, was enough to set them apart from any other European ruler.

How different those ways were was exemplified again during this brief meeting. The King, wearing an Austrian Field-Marshal's uniform, was on the station platform with a small suite to greet the Emperor when he arrived at Marienbad on 16 August. The two sovereigns then drove to their respective quarters through triumphal arches festooned with Habsburg double-headed eagles and English Lions and Unicorns, decorations over which the city fathers had been sweating blood and spending treasure for months. The Emperor's apartments were modest enough by any standards, let alone those of contemporary monarchs. They consisted of three rooms in the villa of the late Herr Halbmayer, an industrialist who had left his house to the spa authorities on the extravagant condition that it should only be used by visiting royalty, a condition which, for once, could be fulfilled. Apparently unaware that the Emperor always slept on a military field-bed in his thousand-room Palace of Schönbrunn in Vienna, the municipality had bought a large and magnificent bed, made of finest English brass, for the occasion.

What was so totally non-English, however, was the ceremony with which this spartan old monarch now greeted his Marienbad subjects. Even in this informal watering-place, Spanish court etiquette, combined with the rigid corporate class structure of the monarchy, ruled the roost. Nineteen separate groups, in strict sequence of protocol, lined up in the Spa Rooms that afternoon to present their respects to their sovereign. First, and described as such on the programme, came 'The Aristocracy', led by the heads of the Bohemian houses of Lobkowic, Nostitz, Zedwitz, Berchem, and those late-comers from the Rhineland, Metternich. The army officers paraded, of course, in one group. Then came the municipal authorities (just before the provincial government officials); the local mayors and their councils, and the evangelical pastors (just before doctors, schoolmasters and the *Kultusgemeinde*, which meant the Jews). The last four groups to march forward were made up of the local medical charities (with Red Cross coming before White Cross and Green Cross); and finally, as Group 19, the War Veterans and the Fire Brigades. The English party with the King must have been rather tickled by this strict compartmentalization, which contrasted so strongly with the much more mobile divisions of Edwardian life. Perhaps the more percipient among them felt some unease as well. A society as rigidly built as this would surely topple over and crash into fragments the moment its foundations were shifted by as much as one inch.

That, however, was not a suitable thought for this sunny tranquil August in Bohemia. In any case, the spectators' eyes that day were fixed not so much on the Spa Rooms as on the 'Weimar', where King

Edward, doing the honours for his guest in his guest's own Empire, gave a dinner that night in the new restaurant of the hotel. All thoughts of diet were thrown to the winds for the occasion. The King had arranged every detail of the menu himself, even to the grouse rushed from far-off Scotland. Here, as wherever and whenever King Edward was in control, his personal brand of dignified informality set the tone. The mood was relaxed and the toasts exchanged between the two rulers were short and unrehearsed. The old Emperor enjoyed himself immensely, especially after that familiar and wearying routine with his own subjects. King Edward too was in high spirits, though it is likely that, at the back of his mind, he was carefully totting up England's political credit in Vienna with every jovial gesture. Those courtiers and outside commentators who hailed this Marienbad meeting* as being of 'great historical importance' were, admittedly, shooting over the mark. But it *could* have been a significant one, had the course of European politics not cut across the two rulers and their two Empires a few years later.

There is one anecdote from this same year, 1904, which is worth recording because it shows King Edward's growing tendency to keep himself at the centre of events and abreast of world affairs throughout every hour of these Marienbad visits. The Foreign Office telegrams and other state papers were, of course, brought to him here, as they were to any other station of his continental travels. But though a special King's Messenger arrived in Marienbad three times a week, the news was often out of date, and this was something from which another Marienbad visitor, the well-known Vienna correspondent of *The Times*, Henry Wickham Steed, drew advantage. Steed was due in Marienbad that August to report on the meeting between the two sovereigns and had sent a telegram in advance of his arrival to a British diplomat who was already installed there to await the King. Steed's message was really about his hotel booking, but he added an item of information he had just read on the Reuter's machine in his Vienna office: the Russians, then at war with the Japanese, had just suffered a serious naval defeat. This was duly passed on that same evening to the royal suite at the Hotel Weimar.

The next morning on the *Kreuzbrunnen* promenade, the King was thus able to bring that monstrously smug and self-important little man, Prince Ferdinand of Bulgaria, up to date on the Far East situation. As 'Foxy' Ferdinand always took immense pains in knowing everything

---

* It was commemorated, three summers later, in a special memorial stone which was erected in the park of Marienbad with portraits of the two sovereigns in bronze medallions.

first (and usually succeeded), King Edward's delight can be imagined.

Steed, who was no stranger to the King, found himself greeted with royal smiles when he arrived. Every evening of his stay he continued his service by telephoning Vienna for up-to-the-minute news which he then transmitted to the Hotel Weimar in time for dinner. This gave the King a thirty-six-hour lead on the Foreign Office telegrams, and he sent his 'special correspondent' a warm message of thanks when the visit was over. But that was not the happy end to the story. When Steed, in due course, sent his newspaper a bill for the few pounds he had spent on rushing the Far East news to his King, he was both sobered and astonished to get a rebuke back from his home office. 'Albert Edward,' *The Times*' manager wired tartly, 'ought to have paid for the telegrams himself.' And, to add insult to injury, Steed was cautioned by his newspaper to 'find a way of refusing' any decoration the King might want to bestow upon him. That must have been a rare command indeed in Edwardian Europe.

Royal dinner-parties and royal bounty were all very well, but the King was also an Englishman abroad, and what the general public, here as elsewhere on the Continent, expected from any Englishman was that he should be an effortlessly versatile and expert sportsman. This presented problems for King Edward's 'image', for he was now a 62-year-old gentleman whose mobility had been severely reduced by a good forty years of high and fast living.

There were no local racetracks where the King could at least be seen leading a winning horse by the reins into the unsaddling enclosure; nor could he be admired as a deckchair yachtsman, for Bohemia (*pace* Shakespeare) had no oceans. That still left golf and shooting, however, so Marienbad and its surrounding landowners now concentrated on putting King Edward at the centre of these.

At home, the King had once been quite an enthusiastic golfer, with an imperious habit of regarding bunkers as something intended only for his subjects to play into. He had had his own course laid out in the private park at Windsor (originally one of eighteen holes had been ordered, but when his staff worked out that, at the King's leisurely pace, that would take them a good three hours to cover, they persuaded him to settle for nine). Yet however much the King enjoyed the game, his portly figure and his erratic tee-shots both argued against him trying to enjoy it too often in public, especially here, in full view of Marienbad's cosmopolitan crowd. That did not prevent him from being the presiding genius when, on Monday afternoon, 22 August 1905, the great day dawned, and Marienbad's golf course, beautifully laid out along the forest's edge on the road to Abaschin, was formally opened by the King of England to the strains of his own National Anthem. He signed himself in as the club's first member but did not (for the reasons mentioned above and doubtless to the disappointment of the select gathering) drive the first ball down the fairway of the first hole. Instead, after taking tea with those inescapably familiar locals, the mayor of the town and the Abbot of Tepl Monastery, he walked the course sedately with a party of players.

Quite apart from the King's own august presence and patronage, Marienbad's golf club had a predominantly British flavour. The professional, Mr Doig, was a Scotsman; the course had been designed and the clubhouse built on British lines; and Ponsonby, the King's secretary, effectively ran the whole operation, becoming, in 1908, the club's official manager. But though the English 'High Life' (as the Marienbad papers described them) were also the biggest national contingent of players, the membership was as polyglot as Marienbad itself during the summer season. This constantly confronted Ponsonby with delicate problems. On one occasion, for example, he found himself summoned to the links to adjudicate among a crowd of agitated members and bystanders, each of whom seemed to be shouting in a different tongue. The cause of the fuss was a Russian nobleman who had invented for himself a special club for getting out of trouble whenever he landed in the rough: a mashie fitted with prongs which swept through the long grass. The trouble this time was that, in playing his shot, he had actually impaled the ball on one of the prongs. What should he do – shake the ball off; remove it and drop a penalty; or just go on playing? Ponsonby the oracle simply disqualified the Russian for using an illegal club and then marched off, leaving an even louder babel of argument behind him.

There was a croquet ground attached to the golf course, and croquet the King did play. Moreover, as befitted one whose political reputation was that of the shrewd old tom-cat of Europe, he seems to have been quite a cunning hand with the mallet. It was not exactly a virile game with which to maintain the legend of the English outdoor sportsman; but then, the King was himself no longer the Prince Hal of former years. One of his favourite croquet partners at Marienbad was a lovely French lady, Madame Letellier, whose skill through the hoops matched her elegance. One afternoon they had a match against Ponsonby and Harry Chaplin, who was an old devotee of Marienbad's and an old friend of the King's, which produced situations both amusing and instructive.

Ponsonby loathed croquet, and was yearning to get back to the golf course. So, both to end the business as rapidly as he could and to persuade the King not to 'draft' him again, he walloped the King's ball to the far end of the ground whenever he got the chance. The King became steadily more furious. Eventually, his beautiful partner could stand this no longer. When the King was safely out of hearing, chasing his ball yet again, she cornered Ponsonby and pleaded, with tears in her eyes, for a little more consideration. Surely, she asked, courtiers always allowed their monarchs to win at all games?

Not *this* courtier with *this* monarch, the King's secretary replied, adding that he personally made a point of beating any member of the royal family at any game he could. Having abandoned the Bourbon approach, Madame Letellier fell back on her skill. After two and a half hours' play, she and the King just managed to beat their opponents to the post. Ponsonby, who was hoping he would never be summoned to the croquet-lawn again, was horrified to hear his exultant master propose a return match for the following day.

Shooting was the only other sport in which King Edward indulged with any regularity while at Marienbad; and this too produced its fund of anecdotes.

Marienbad was, of course, not East Anglia, as the King was to discover in the most delightful way. He shot most frequently on the estate of Prince Trautmansdorff at Bischofsteinitz near Pilsen, and here the company was conventionally aristocratic and the bags appropriately large. On one occasion, for example, a small party of guns accounted for what the local press described as '718 partridge'. The King alone was credited with 210, which suggests that he was either in uncommonly good form or that (as was customary on the Continent) the beaters had had instructions to amass in front of the royal stand as many dead birds as they could collect from anywhere. In 1908, writing to Sir Ernest Cassel, the King himself rejoiced at 'a capital day's shooting' on the same estate, where they 'only shot after luncheon with five guns and got about 300 brace of partridge and 100 pheasant'.

But eventually the Abbot of Tepl decided to play the sporting host. He was, after all, on good terms with the King, and large areas in and around Marienbad belonged to his monastery. What a Prince Trautmansdorff could do, surely a great dignitary of the Roman Catholic Church (with two millions' sterling invested in English securities) could do just as well, even though, as in the case of His Grace the Abbot, he had never fired a shotgun in his life. An invitation was accordingly sent to the Hotel Weimar and the King, greatly tickled by the idea, accepted with alacrity.

The monastery game preserves had never been driven; all they had known were modest and informal walking shoots for the Abbot's table. So the first problem was to collect enough birds. This was solved by sending one of the senior monks, Father Bernard Gnad, with a large posse of gamekeepers, to net as many partridges as they could find in the nearby monastery lands of Tuschkau, Lochuzen, Mirschowitz and Gottowicz. The wretched birds were then popped into baskets, loaded on to trains, and brought back to Tepl to be released in the field there.

The next problem was to stop them flying home before the shoot was held, and at this point the churchmen overreached themselves. It was decided to hoist two huge kites, one on either side of the main coverts, which the partridge would hopefully take for some monstrous birds of prey and thus stay put. Unhappily, when the great day arrived and the King, with six other guns (mostly members of his suite), took up their positions, nobody thought of hauling the kites down. As a result, most of the bewildered partridge refused to fly at all, even when prodded into activity by an army of keepers, behind which marched one aged monk, bearing an even more ancient fowling-piece.

To make matters worse, the Abbot, quite correctly numbering his guns from the right, had incorrectly assumed that Number One was the proper place of honour for the sovereign. This, of course, put the King out on the flank, from where he could scarcely expect to fire many shots at such birds as did fly. Oblivious to this, the Abbot, wearing a short shooting coat over his white cassock, with a 'wide-awake' hat set at a rakish angle on his head and a huge cigar in his mouth, planted himself in the King's butt. Horns were sounded and the Tepl Monastery partridge shoot began.

At the end of the afternoon, it was reckoned by those who had done the actual firing that 36 brace had been killed. This was not nearly enough for the Abbot, but he was equal to the challenge. By counting all the birds that had died on the train journey to Tepl, as well as all those knocked on the head by the beaters at Tepl, he managed to construct a round figure of 150 brace. A special game-card was drawn up accordingly. As the shoot had been preceded by a splendid luncheon at the monastery, with the choicest food and wines, nobody was very concerned, and least of all the guest of honour.

However informally the King's days at Marienbad were passed (and Abbot Helmer's partridge shoot, to which he was driven in his claret Mercedes, was a typical example), he was nonetheless a reigning monarch, abroad in a Europe where anarchy was rife. Superintendent Quinn – tall, lean and monosyllabic – and his assistant, Inspector Hester, always travelled out from London as the King's own bodyguard. On the Austrian side, the Empire's foremost policeman, Herr Schober, who had been assigned to Marienbad primarily to control that vexatious public, was also given a staff of six detectives to mount a twenty-four-hour watch over the King's safety as well as his comfort. Yet throughout the Marienbad era, even when the political leaders of Europe began to converge on the Hotel Weimar to discuss the troubled issues of the time, not a shot was fired, nor a knife ever flashed.

Indeed, things seem to have been too quiet for the liking of some of the Austrian security officials, whose names would have been made had there only been one assassin around, with a plot to foil. Schober's successor at Marienbad, Franz Brandl, tells a delightful story in his memoirs of how the tranquillity became too much for one of his ambitious colleagues. This was the head of the security branch of the Prague Police Directorate, who called on Brandl in Marienbad one day to suggest that they might liven things up a bit, and improve their own promotion prospects, by having a little bomb planted somewhere in the King's entourage. Indeed, the Prague policeman even had a tame 'assassin' ready at hand to do the job, in return for a fat and secret award, coupled with a light and prearranged prison sentence. The horrified Viennese inspector rejected the scheme outright, but stayed on his guard for weeks afterwards, in case of 'plots' hatched by his own colleagues.

Night life at Marienbad, or evening entertainment as it was styled in those days, was fairly sedate on the official surface, as befitted a health spa. Here too, the King's personal tastes soon struck the keynote and helped to liven things up, if only because every second entertainer who made the August pilgrimage to Marienbad thought that liveliness was what the King wanted. They were treading a narrow plank, as some of them soon realized.

At Marienbad, as at any other station in the King's European travels, boredom was the supreme enemy. His passion for international politics, witty company and beautiful women all helped to chase it away, and if music or drama were enlisted as well, it followed that they had to be the opposite of stuffy. Yet, extremely broad-minded though he was, the King drew his own boundaries of good taste and never allowed himself, nor anyone in his presence, to step one inch beyond them.

As an example of someone who kept daintily an inch or two inside the limits at Marienbad was an English dancer named Maud Allan who, at the King's request, had been asked to perform at a private dinner-party given in his honour. The King's staff made their routine enquiries about the young lady and got distinctly nervous when they heard that she usually appeared clad in 'two oyster shells and a five-franc piece'. But after the Marienbad press corps (who included several special correspondents of English papers) had been sworn to secrecy, the performance went ahead. Miss Allan lived up to her reputation as a scanty dresser but – especially as Salome brandishing the head of John the Baptist – exceeded all expectations as an artist. The King was enchanted; his equerries (as well as his hostess for that evening) were much relieved; and everyone agreed that another blow had been struck against prudery.

But it was another matter when a famous Vienna cabaret singer (it was usually the Viennese ladies who caused the trouble) insisted on doing her regular programme uncensored at a guest performance in Marienbad which the King was attending. The programme included a skit about a Catholic priest who is sorely tempted by a licentious Countess. 'Were it not for my holy robes,' he sings at one point, longingly. 'Then take off your holy robes,' the temptress replies, and the priest obliges. This, at a public performance in the town of Marienbad which was owned by the good monks of Tepl, was clearly too much. King Edward, furious, stalked out of the theatre. The tactless diva was bundled back to Vienna after being made to pay a heavy fine. Like that other Viennese lady who had travelled all the way to this Bohemian valley to help the King of England justify his reputation, she must have been puzzled as well as angry.

It is worth adding, however, that though the King had firm ideas about good and bad taste, he never became sanctimonious or hypocritical (which, in his case, would have been two words for the same thing). One episode that the papers did get hold of concerned another display of royal displeasure at Marienbad on 29 August 1907, when a touring cabaret from Vienna appeared at the local theatre. Their songs turned out to be full of double meanings that were more lewd than witty; and, once it was clear that the second act was going to be in the same vein as the first, the King again stood up and left. When news of this incident reached England, the Bishop of Ripon sent a flowery letter to his sovereign, praising him for his Christian stand against obscenity. This, in the King's eyes, was leaning too much the other way. When he was approached by his secretary about the draft for a reply, he said simply: 'Tell the Bishop the exact truth. I have no wish to pose as a protector of morals, especially abroad.'

King Edward's approach to the arts was that of the *bon vivant* seeking distraction rather than the aesthete seeking enlightenment; and nothing typified this more than his taste in music. He was fond enough of Wagner, provided it was ladled out in melodic spoonfuls. Indeed, the Sunday afternoon Wagner concerts in the open air at the Café Bellevue were just about as far as he wanted to plunge into the foamy seas of grand opera. The overture to *Rienzi* or to *Tannhäuser*; Walter's Prize Song from *The Mastersingers*; the 'Liebestod' from *Tristan*; and even (if played with a little *brio*) the Funeral March from *Götterdämmerung* – all went charmingly with the rattle of teacups and the chatter of his equerries and lady companions. The Wagner concerts at Bayreuth itself he never attended, though they were within fairly easy reach by car. His true preference was for something lighter altogether, and the Monarchy of Franz Josef had enough of this to offer, notably the operettas of Johann and Oskar Strauss, of Franz Lehar, and of all their imitators, good and bad. Edwardian Marienbad was itself a waltz rather than a pavane.

Rather, perhaps, to their surprise, the politicians and diplomatists who came to the spa to talk matters of state with the King found that this gay tempo eventually came to suit them quite well. These statesmen and their grave preoccupations belong in other chapters. We need only note here that, whatever their political preoccupations were, they brought these to Marienbad in August for an airing with King Edward and his entourage.

In the case of tiresome Balkan jokes like Prince Danilo of Montenegro or Prince Ferdinand of Bulgaria, little more than a search for prestige – exemplified, perhaps, by a British decoration – was at stake. It was a very different matter with Clemenceau, the Prime Minister of France, and Isvolsky, the Foreign Minister of Russia, both of whom became regular visitors to Edwardian Marienbad (or to Carlsbad, which served in this respect as its ante-chamber) from about 1906 onwards. These were the decisive years in the construction of the Triple Entente between England, France and Russia. Though the foundations of this historic alliance were being laid, notably by King Edward himself, far away from Bohemia, each summer at the Hotel Weimar in Marienbad he would add a little cement or knock an awkward brick or two into place.

Inevitably, the knowledge that this was happening drew the leaders of the rival diplomatic camp to the spa in August, men like Count Aehrenthal, the Foreign Minister of Austria-Hungary, and his German and Italian counterparts, Kiederlen-Wächter and Tittoni. Those who were watching from the wings of European politics, such as Hakki Pasha, the Grand Vizier of Turkey, or Pasic, the Prime Minister of Serbia, also became regular summer visitors to the Bohemian resorts. Ambassadors, Princes, Grand-dukes and Archdukes buzzed around their respective political leaders like swarms of attendant midges, too numerous to mention. Such importance as they had at Marienbad depended, quite simply, on how well they knew King Edward and how highly he thought of them.

And finally, because the Eger Valley in August was gradually turned, by King Edward's presence, into an annual open-air diplomatic bazaar, his own advisers flocked there in increasing numbers. Some of these, like Admiral Sir John Fisher, were even older devotees of Marienbad than the King. Among the prominent newcomers to the scene were Lloyd George, the rising young Chancellor of the Exchequer, and the Minister of War, Lord Haldane, who came to Marienbad for talks with the King in 1906, on his way to attend army manœuvres in Germany. As the scholarly Haldane was steeped in German culture and almost slept with Goethe under his pillow, he must have felt quite at home at the *Kreuzbrunnen.*

But whatever the stature and whatever the nationality of the visiting statesman, when he came to Marienbad to talk to King Edward it had to be done in a holiday setting and atmosphere. This led to some odd situations. On 15 August 1909, for example, Clemenceau came over from Carlsbad to lunch with the King. It was a small party for six, two equerries plus the French and British Ambassadors in Vienna (M. Crozier and Sir Fairfax Cartwright) being the only others present. As the weather was fine, the King decided that afterwards they would talk on the balcony that ran in front of his suite of rooms at the Hotel Weimar – in full view and almost within earshot of the promenaders in the park below. Clemenceau expressed polite concern: was this not a little too public? Quite the contrary, his host assured the Frenchman. For them to be seen talking like this was the best possible protection against alarmist gossip. Nobody would imagine that world affairs would be debated on an open-air hotel balcony in full view of the world at large.

Part of the conversation was, indeed, harmless enough. Talking of the local golf course, Clemenceau maintained that, for the English, golf was like croquet and tennis – simply an excuse to bring the two sexes together and, in the case of wooded golf courses, to give them the chance of actually making love. (Clemenceau was every bit as devoted to the fair sex as his royal host. His own long chain of passionate affairs reputedly began when, as a young teacher in an American girls' school, he had sired four illegitimate children with one of his pupils.)

If all this was merely racy, what followed when Clemenceau became serious and turned to politics was highly sensitive. After some discussion of the Near East problem and the necessity for France and England to support Greece against any move by Turkey, he launched into the real purpose of his visit. It was also the purpose of his political life: how to contain and, if possible, crush the menace of German militarism. Clemenceau was nervous that the Liberal government of Campbell-Bannerman (which, for him, was uncomfortably pacifist and pro-German) would not, in a crisis, honour its tacit undertaking to land an expeditionary force of some 110,000 men in France to fight a German invasion. Even this scale of military effort, he now proceeded to argue, was quite inadequate. It was not enough for England to build up her fleet against Germany. She must expand her army as well, rapidly and substantially, in order to be ready to do battle at France's side in the war that was coming. He grew so heated that eventually the King pulled him off the balcony and led him back into his study to continue the talk.

It was an extraordinary episode, though by no means untypical. Marienbad was in the middle of the Austro-Hungarian Empire, which was the faithful (eventually almost servile) ally of Germany. Yet here, on the balcony of the Hotel Weimar, was Clemenceau, the dedicated enemy of that Germany, urging the King of England to expand his army in order to ensure the defeat of both the Central Powers in battle. One could argue that this was an odd way for King Edward to repay the Austrian Emperor for the annual use of his Bohemian spa. The answer, of course, was that in August 1909, though the holocaust in fact lay only five years ahead, world war still seemed a matter for philosophical debate rather than an imminent reality. King Edward would have felt he was discussing, not plotting. Be that as it may, it was as well that the Emperor's loyal subjects strolling past below imagined the illustrious balcony scene to be as harmless as it looked.

For all the King's ideas about camouflage, the truth is that the people of Marienbad could, and did, quite as easily read the signals upside down and so get the message just as wrong. A classic case of this concerns Campbell-Bannerman himself. One year an illustrated paper reproduced an artist's drawing of the Prime Minister talking to his sovereign in the Kurhaus gardens at Marienbad, with the crowd keeping their distance. The mien of both men is grave and the King is seen driving some momentous point home by striking his fist in the palm of the other hand. Everything seemed to bear out the title underneath: 'Is it Peace or War?' Campbell-Bannerman smiled when he was shown the picture. He recalled that particular conversation exactly. What the King had been debating with his Prime Minister was whether halibut tasted better baked or boiled.

Those two scenes, the one on the balcony of the Hotel Weimar and the other in the Kurhaus gardens, sum up the phenomenon of Edwardian Marienbad. One is the mirror image of the other. They contrast completely, yet complement perfectly. This was a little Bohemian town where, for three weeks every summer, King Edward persuaded everyone around him to mix the trivial and the vital, the gay and the sombre, and the art of living with the art of politics. It was just as much fun, and by no means as difficult as it sounds.

Marienbad today is part of the People's Republic of Czechoslovakia and, except to the older German-speaking generation, is known only by its true Bohemian name of Mariánské Lázně. Yet though the hammer and sickle has long taken over from the double-headed eagle, the memory of the spa's most faithful royal patron still lingers on, and is, moreover, still respected.

The Hotel Weimar is nowadays a workers' sanatorium; and the King's splendid suite on the first floor has been split up into ordinary bedrooms. But on the front of the great yellow-washed building, above the entrance and just below that balcony where he used to stroll up and down, there is still the original black and gilt memorial plaque which records, in a mixture of English and German, that 'King Edward VII of England' stayed here each year from 1903 until 1909. The inscription, kept spotlessly clean with the rest of the building, gazes out on to the same little park and the same octagonal church. However, the square itself is now named Namesti Klementa Gottwalda, after Czechoslovakia's first Communist President.

On the back road from Marienbad which leads through the pine woods to Karlsbad (now Karlovy Vary), King Edward's golf course soon appears, set in the brilliant green meadows which stretch away on the left-hand side. True, the clubhouse he frequented so often for tea with the Abbot and Madame Letellier has been partly demolished, but only to make way for something more up-to-date. And opposite the clubhouse, on what was the croquet-lawn, is the second of Marienbad's memorials to him – a plaque sunk into a large boulder to commemorate the summer day in August 1905 when he opened these links. Moreover, this plaque is new, and engraved in near-perfect English.

He even manages to linger on in some of the spa's once elegant restaurants and hotels (most of them now youth or workers' hostels) which he used to patronize seventy years ago. The Fürstenhof, for example, which today rejoices under the name 'A. Zapotocky Trade Union Recreation Centre', still has, in its dining-room, an enormous oil-painting* which depicts King Edward on the *Kreuzbrunnen* promenade, surrounded by dozens of those easily identifiable European cronies who flocked each year to Marienbad to be with him. The picture is

---

* Reproduced between pages 296-297

referred to simply as 'Historical Portrait', so there is no danger to the appetites of the Communist faithful from North Korea, China, Cuba and Bulgaria who, each day, eat away underneath it.

He has survived, on stone, on canvas and in spirit because, like the monks of Tepl who donated their healing springs to the public, he is still regarded as one of the founding fathers of Marienbad's fame. Considering that this recognition bridges an ideological gulf that is wider even than the two world wars put together, he could never have wished for a greater compliment, however little he would have expected it.

ALLIANCE UNDER FIRE

For some months after King Edward's conquest of Paris, the Germans went on believing that nothing had changed on the political map of Europe. The Kaiser, not unnaturally, resented the fact that his uncle had put the Republican capital of France before the imperial Berlin of his Hohenzollern relatives on his travel agenda, and that resentment came out in many a spiteful word. In June of 1903, for example, when an English torpedo boat accidentally exploded off Cherbourg, the Emperor William could not resist remarking to the French Naval Attaché in Berlin: 'I'm glad to see that you are always ready to give a proper reception to your good friends and neighbours.'[1]

Three weeks after that remark was made, M. Loubet arrived in London to reciprocate King Edward's visit of May. The Kaiser was now given another demonstration of what Anglo-French ideas of a 'proper reception' really were. This four-day (6–9 July) return visit showed that France, personified by the red-cheeked and ever-jovial President Loubet, was becoming just as popular in England as John Bull, in the elegant guise of King Edward, had already become in Paris. The reception that London put on for the French visitor was hailed in the British press as 'one of the greatest welcomes ever extended to a Republican ruler in a monarchial state'. Londoners even overcame their linguistic inhibitions and ventured boldly out into French for the occasion. *Bienvenu à Loubet à Londres* proclaimed one placard on the route from Victoria Station to Buckingham Palace. Clubland went one better. Along St James's Street they had fashioned a very tasteful *Vive la France* entirely out of *La France* roses. Any members in Pall Mall's military clubs who, only six years before, had marched with Kitchener against the French in the Upper Nile, must have sat in their leather armchairs that day and asked themselves whether the world had gone quite mad.

Though King Edward was not responsible for the street decorations, every detail of the programme had, as usual, been decided by him. His modest guest had crossed the Channel in an ordinary cruiser, the *Gûichen*, for he seemed to be the only head of a first-rank power who did not possess an official yacht to sail about in. King Edward made up for any resultant lack of pomp by marshalling a column of British men-of-war two miles long off Dover, each unit of which fired a twenty-one-gun salute as the President steamed into harbour. The King had also decided that, despite its unfortunate associations for crowned heads, the *Marseillaise* should not, on this occasion, be given that skimpy treatment so common with foreign bands. He forbade the usual trun-cated version, confined to the first four bars only, and laid down that it should be played throughout the visit from start to finish, whereas the British National Anthem was to be restricted to the first six bars. For any Frenchman, this was the stuff of which any entente was woven.

At the various banquets, the King hammered home, in impromptu speeches, his simple Paris theme: France and England, always such close neighbours, must now become close friends as well. At the Guildhall, the Lord Mayor, Sir Marcus Samuel, went a step further by posing the rhetorical question, when he spoke of the new Anglo-French spirit: 'Who can predict how far-reaching such an example might prove?' That question, by now at the back of everybody's mind in London and Paris, was still being dismissed as of no consequence in Berlin. Despite the spectacular success of this return visit (which King Edward had made his absolute priority for that summer),[2] Chancellor Bülow continued to believe, like his great predecessor Bismarck, that a republican France could always be isolated within a monarchical Europe. These state visits were pure window-dressing, the Germans argued, behind which there still stood the harsh and immovable reality of Anglo-French colonial conflicts.

It was only after the rapid conclusion of a treaty which formally put an end to those conflicts that German eyes began to open to this entirely new constellation on the European horizon. Though Bülow shrugged even this pact off as simply 'another symptom of the peaceful evolution of the world situation',[3] the Kaiser was not so sure. He was cruising in the Mediterranean when the news reached him and, soon afterwards, he cabled his Chancellor from Syracuse that this Anglo-French agreement had given him 'a lot to think about'. England, having settled her differences with France, had acquired 'a new mobility' and would be less ready than ever to 'spare Germany's feelings'.[4] And, in an attempt to contrive a meeting with both the King of Italy and with President Loubet in Monaco to restore German influence, the Kaiser hung around on his yacht until he had to be almost bowed out of the Mediterranean.

Despite the complexity and the variety of issues at stake, the famous 'Convention between the United Kingdom and France respecting Newfoundland, and West and Central Africa' (to give it its proper name)[5] was signed in London between Lord Lansdowne and M. Cambon on 8 April 1904, less than a year after the King's Paris trip. The two men who wrote their signature under the pact could (and did) rightly claim credit for the many months of diplomatic donkey-work needed to superimpose the spirit of the entente on the physical map of the world. But to infer from this that King Edward had now been relegated to the back seat would be to go sadly astray.

It was no part of a king's business (and least of all of this king's) to argue whether, and under what terms, France should renounce the Newfoundland fishing rights bestowed upon her by the Treaty of Utrecht; whether the tribes of Tessaoua-Maradi and Zinder should be left in French territory along the River Niger; or how the basin of the Menam River should be used to divide British and French zones of influence in Siam. King Edward's world was the classical world of the European continent, despite the fact that he ruled over a quarter of the twentieth-century globe. With the single exception of America, he soon got bored with anything farther afield than the Mediterranean, so one can well believe, on that count alone, that he took little interest in these remote territorial minutiae. For him, and for most of his generation, the 1904 treaty was important, not for its repercussions on England's black or brown subjects overseas, but for its effect on big-power relations in Europe itself. As Europe was then both the power-house and the powder-keg of the world, this was not 'reactionary' (if not visionary either). It was merely, in contemporary terms, realistic.

Significantly, the one part of the treaty text that we know King Edward did work on himself concerned the division of interests in the Mediterranean. Apart from being the King's home territory, it was on a settlement here that the whole future of Anglo-French relations depended. In essence, this agreement was a thirty-year pact under which France bowed out of her long-established position in Egypt in return for getting as free a rein as England could give her in Morocco. Here the King corrected, in his own hand, Lord Lansdowne's draft on two substantial points, and both of his corrections were reflected in the final text. His first intervention was to delete any reference to his country ever 'annexing Egypt' in the future, even though England was only promising, in Lansdowne's draft, to do no such thing. Better not even mention that dread word, was the King's view. Accordingly, Article I of the final text ran: 'His Britannic Majesty's Government declare that they have no intention of altering the political status of Egypt.'* The King's second intervention was to

* France gave a guarantee in identical language in respect of Morocco.

strengthen the language in which assurances of absolute commercial liberty were to be guaranteed in the open ports of Morocco. In view of what his imperial nephew was soon to get up to in one of those self-same ports, King Edward's anxiety about outside interference might almost have been clairvoyant.

* * *

But before the Kaiser could indulge in any mischief-making, King Edward first had to protect his new entente as best he could from a crisis at the other end of the world. In February of 1904, while the formal Anglo-French agreement was nearing completion, war between Russia and Japan had broken out in the Far East.* The immediate repercussions must have made some Ministers in London hanker after those uncomplicated, if vulnerable, days of splendid isolation.

Japan, England's ally since 1901, was now fighting Russia, with whom the King was aching to get on closer terms. Moreover, France, with whom England was about to seal a pact of friendship, had been Russia's ally for the past ten years. There was little danger of England and France being dragged militarily into the Far Eastern conflict on opposing sides. But the war had put them on opposing sides politically. In an attempt to ward off any damage, King Edward made personal interventions in both the Russian and the French capitals.

Within a week of the outbreak of the Russo-Japanese war, Count Benckendorff, the Russian Ambassador in London, was off to St Petersburg, carrying personal letters to the Russian royal family from King Edward, Queen Alexandra, the Tsar's aunt, and even the Prince of Wales, his cousin. Benckendorff told his French colleague in London, Paul Cambon, in the strictest confidence, the purport of this family barrage of letters, and also what King Edward's parting words had been. According to Cambon's report,[6] the King had told the Russian envoy:

'I don't bother much if the (Russian) newspapers or an ignorant public accuse us, but I do care what the Emperor thinks. He is my nephew. He knows my feelings. He must know I would do nothing against him . . . How can anyone imagine we would get up to anything behind his back with the Japanese? We have a treaty with them, that's true. But it's only a treaty and that doesn't mean that we have intimate relations with them.'

And the King went on to assure the Tsar that he himself would

---

* The principal cause was the rivalry between the two powers in Manchuria, though Korea and indeed China itself were also disputed spheres of influence.

see to it that England stayed 'strictly neutral' in the conflict. The King's appeal to France for patience and understanding went to the man he had fêted in London six months before. Baron Eckhardstein (now retired from the German diplomatic service* but still an active observer of the English scene) wrote to Count Bülow at the time:

> 'The King of England is very concerned about revived resentment in France against England, and consequently has today dispatched a long letter by courier to Persident Loubet . . .'[7]

There were other problems arising from the war that summer, notably the passage of Russian warships through the Dardanelles, and the seizing of British vessels on contraband charges. But again, the family link between Windsor and the Winter Palace helped to keep the two courts and, through them, the two countries, in friendly contact. In August, the Tsar was at last presented by his wife with a son and heir and, across all the confusion of the war, he wrote to ask his English uncle to be one of the god-parents. In accepting, King Edward deputed Prince Louis of Battenberg to go to the christening on his behalf, and sent him to St Petersburg with the express mission of tackling the Tsar and his government on current problems the moment the infant Grand Duke had received his baptism. Prince Louis found the Tsar personally well disposed and reported in this sense to King Edward at Marienbad on his way back to England.

Everything then continued on these correct and amicable lines until the night of 21 October 1904 when the Baltic Fleet of Admiral Rozhdestvensky, ploughing its way through the North Sea on the immensely long haul to the Far East, opened fire on a group of British fishing trawlers which it had somehow managed to confuse in the dark with enemy Japanese ships. One trawler went to the bottom, others were damaged, and the trawlermen suffered both deaths and injuries. To make matters worse, the Admiral sailed on into the night without even stopping to see what it was he had hit, let alone whether there were any survivors.[†]

This Dogger Bank crisis was by far the worst that the Far East war threw up between England and Russia and, consequently, the sharpest threat it produced to England's new friendship with France. In

---

* Eckhardstein had married the daughter of England's wealthy furniture manufacturer, Sir John Maple. According to Bülow (II, p. 287), King Edward later boycotted Eckhardstein after the German deserted his wife and gambled away a lot of her father's fortune.

† He reached Japanese waters with his fleet six months later only to be wiped out, within a matter of weeks, by the Japanese Navy under Admiral Togo at the great naval battle of Tsushima.

London, wild talk of war sprang up almost overnight. That this mood died down almost as swiftly as it had arisen was, yet again, largely due to what a later generation would have termed King Edward's personal 'hot line' to his nephew, the Russian Emperor. Admittedly, Tsar Nicholas did not make things too difficult for his uncle. The moment the first unofficial news of the incident reached St Petersburg, it was clear that the Admiral was guilty of, at the least, an unprofessional error and, more probably, an appalling blunder. On 25 October, the Tsar cabled his condolences to King Edward, deploring the 'loss of lives of innocent fishermen', and expressing the hope that the tragedy would cause 'no complications to arise between our two countries'. The only explanation he could advance (and that rather defensively) was that Russia had received 'many warnings that the Japanese were lurking (among) fishing smacks . . . for the purpose of destroying our vessels'.

In his reply, which he first showed to Lord Lansdowne, the King wisely avoided an issue that could not be substantiated and concentrated instead on one that could. What had pained both him and the British people, he replied to the Tsar, was the undeniable fact that the Russian warships, who must have seen by their searchlights what had happened, did not stop and help the stricken fishing fleet.

Despite all the further apologies and excuses which came in from the Russians during the next forty-eight hours, both the King and his Foreign Secretary were agreed that, apart from the obvious question of compensation, the Russian Admiral and his officers responsible for the firing must be punished. It was King Edward who then drew his government back. By now, he had seen the official Russian report in which Admiral Rozhdestvensky did, indeed, claim that it was a Japanese torpedo-boat he had been trying to sink when the trawlers were hit. The British newspapers, some of which were howling for vengeance as though the Home Fleet itself had been destroyed, sobered the King down even more than the official Russian statement. In both a telegram and a letter to Lord Lansdowne, he urged that England should not now press for the public punishment of the Admiral. 'Russia,' he said, 'could not accept such a humiliation.'

They were wise second thoughts, and they were followed. The unhappy affair was formally wound up four months later with an award, by an International Commission of Inquiry, of £65,000 damages against Russia. The two countries would probably have reached some sort of peaceful settlement in the end, even without King Edward's influence. But there is little doubt that the King, who had set the pace for his government from start to finish, had been mainly responsible for the crisis ending as rapidly and as smoothly as it did.

The Dogger Bank settlement of February 1905 removed the last menace posed by the Far Eastern war to King Edward's entente policy in Europe (and the war itself was brought to an end only six months later, thanks largely to the very capable mediation of President Theodore Roosevelt). But barely was this indirect strain on the Anglo-French Entente removed than Germany put it under direct and deliberate pressure. The arena selected by Berlin was Northern Africa, which had formed the cornerstone of the 1904 Conventions.

*   *   *

Quite how the Kaiser's dramatic descent upon Tangier in March of 1905 was planned is still something of a riddle. As the time-lag indicates, it was far from being an automatic *riposte* to the Anglo-French Treaty of April 1904. Bülow, in his own suave and rather too disarming account of the crisis,[8] claims that he had only grown concerned about the Anglo-French deal in North Africa during the winter of 1904–5, when Delcassé 'showed his claws' by trying to turn Morocco into a French vassal state on the pattern of Tunisia, thus threatening Germany's established trading interests.

But the real reason for Germany's about-face of 1905 was that there were now far bigger prizes on the board than Moroccan commerce. That same winter, France's sole official ally, Russia, had been disastrously defeated in her war in the Far East at the hands of the Japanese. Meanwhile, in Paris, the signs were growing that Delcassé's high-handed methods were stoking up bitter opposition towards him, among party opponents and ministerial colleagues alike. In Berlin, the time seemed ripe for a master-stroke that would destroy at one blow the entire skeleton structure of this Anglo-French-Russian alignment which, by now, was beginning to haunt the Germans in their nightmares. The weapon chosen by Bülow for this operation was the most august one in his armoury, the All-Highest himself, who was to convert a 'holiday cruise' in the Mediterranean into a political expedition on Moroccan soil. Normally also the most willing, the most compulsive even, of diplomatic instruments, the Kaiser on this occasion seems to have had his doubts.* Even in retrospect, Bülow had none. Though he fully realized that his action might lead to war with France, he described his feelings (and his larger aims) at the time in these words:

---

* At least that was what he claimed later on, grumbling to Bülow that, in the 1905 escapade, he had 'risked his life, riding through the streets of Morocco with my bad arm', all to serve his Chancellor.

'I did not hesitate to confront France with the possibility of war, because I had confidence in my own skill and caution. I felt that I could prevent matters coming to a head, cause Delcassé's fall, stem the flow of aggressive French policy, knock the continental dagger out of the hands of Edward VII and the war group in England and, at the same time, ensure peace, preserve German honour and enhance Germany's prestige.'[9]

That would have been an ambitious programme for German diplomacy to have tackled inside twelve months all over Europe. To try and achieve it all at one go, simply by putting the German Emperor ashore at Tangier for a few hours, was both naïve and foolhardy, especially in view of the Kaiser's notorious unpredictability. He was scarcely the ideal tool for a calculated provocation which, even in Bülow's words, demanded 'skill and caution' if it was not to lead to catastrophe.

That mischievous demon that always hovered behind the Kaiser's shoulder was waiting for him again now as his ship (the German *Hapag* liner *Hamburg*) dropped anchor in Tangier harbour at nine o'clock on the morning of 31 March 1905. The demon on this occasion came in the person of the young German Chargé d'Affaires in Tangier, Herr von Kühlmann. The steamer had been one and a half hours late in arriving and the sea in this notoriously tricky harbour was so rough that the Kaiser had spent another two hours deliberating whether it was safe enough to land in a small pinnace boat or not. In the middle of this dithering, Kühlmann skimmed across the choppy waves to pay his respects to his imperial master. He had donned the uniform of the Bavarian Lancers for his audience and, clad in this – complete with shiny black high boots and the *tchapka* on his head – he leapt like an agile monkey up the rope ladder which was dangling down the heaving flanks of the liner. The Kaiser was immediately impressed by this.*
Truly, there seemed *nothing* that German military might could not do when he could watch one of his Bavarian cavalry officers suddenly shooting out from the coast of Africa and cutting through the rough ocean with the same easy contempt he might have shown in a charge against some native rabble on land.

At 11.45, still nervous, but with the heroic spark now fatally kindled inside him, the Kaiser landed. Drawn up on the quayside to salute him was a company of Moroccan troops commanded by a French officer and, in front of these, a famous Scottish soldier-of-fortune, the Caid

---

* Kühlmann rose to be Secretary of State in the German Foreign Office, his career helped considerably by the Kaiser's patronage.

Maclean, who had become one of the greatest powers in the Sultan's land. With the Bavarian lancer by his side and this Anglo-French military ensemble in front of him, the Kaiser's heroic mood could only sharpen. The white Barbary stallion that the Sultan had sent him to ride on probably did the rest.

The Kaiser was seen to be sweating profusely on his ride to the German Legation, but when he got there his restraint had gone as well as his nerves. He saluted the handful of German officials and merchants assembled at the Legation to greet him as 'the brave pioneers of German commerce'. Nothing wrong with that. But then he added that his aim, with their help, was to maintain and develop, in a free Morocco, the interest of the German Fatherland. The German Empire, he declared, had 'great and growing interests in Morocco'. He concluded:

> 'Commerce can only progress if all the Powers have equal rights and respect the independence of the country. My visit is the recognition of this independence.'

He addressed even sharper words on the subject in a brief talk with the local envoy of France, Count René de Chérisey. But these remarks, though duly reported to Paris,[10] were made in private. The speech to the German colony was in public. It was echoing throughout the world almost as soon as the Kaiser, refusing all official Moroccan invitations, had ridden straight back to the harbour again and sailed away in the *Hamburg* for Gibraltar. While at Gibraltar, the Kaiser, who was by now relishing the *furore* his escapade had caused, rubbed salt in the Tangier wound in a talk with Prince Louis of Battenberg.* He was determined, he said, to stop France swallowing Morocco as she had swallowed Tunis.[11] As the Prince was one of King Edward's favourite nephews, the German Emperor could be sure that his words would be passed on to Buckingham Palace, as they duly were.

King Edward hardly needed reminding of the gravity of the challenge the Kaiser had just made, for it was tacitly accepted in Europe that Morocco would become a French protectorate. Moreover, the pact on North Africa was the very hilt of that Anglo-French 'continental dagger' which Bülow was seeking to knock out of Edward VII's hand. It was also the one weak spot in this new and, so far, untried weapon. Everything the uncle had achieved in four days in Paris two years before could now be undone by what his nephew had stirred up in less than four hours in Tangier. The King's immediate reaction was

---

* Prince Louis, who became the Marquess of Milford Haven in 1917, had married the King's niece, Princess Victoria of Hesse.

more of anger than alarm. A letter which his Principal Secretary, Francis Knollys, penned to Soveral from Windsor Castle a week after the news of the Tangier speech had reached England shows us the mood of the King and his court:

'The German Emperor talked at Tangier in the most arrogant way, and quite in the strain of the first Napoleon . . . His falseness in *everything* is almost beyond belief, but fortunately he is almost always found out . . .'[12]

And in a letter to Lord Lansdowne on the incident the King did not mince his own words.

'The Tangier incident,' he wrote to his Foreign Secretary, 'was the most mischievous and uncalled for event which the German Emperor has ever been engaged in since he came to the throne . . . He is no more nor less than a political *enfant terrible* and one can have no faith in any of his assurances . . . His annual cruises are deeply to be deplored, and mischief is their only object.'[13]

That last sentence was somewhat ironical, for it was written while King Edward was himself in the middle of the Mediterranean on one of his own annual cruises. Mischief was not the pennant which the *Victoria and Albert* flew on these occasions (pleasure would always loom larger with the uncle than with his nephew). But, seen with Berlin's eyes, anti-German mischief was what the English royal yacht left in its wake. The Kaiser, who went on from Gibraltar to meet the King of Italy at Naples, was doing almost a carbon copy of his uncle's Mediterranean voyages. Moreover, he was travelling with an identical political purpose, to strengthen the prestige and influence of his crown and country.

Yet King Edward's wrath was not entirely misplaced, much less hypocritical. These annual exercises of diplomacy by the royal yacht had their own conventions; and, in view of the private nature of nearly all the calls made *en route*, those conventions had to be both genteel and restrained. It was this accepted framework of behaviour that had just been smashed. Had the roles of uncle and nephew been reversed at Tangier, with King Edward seeking to check a German thrust there, he would have driven around the town in an ordinary carriage, wearing ordinary clothes, and, at the right moment, would have spoken a few quiet words in the Sultan's ear. '*C'est le ton qui fait la musique.*'

Yet though the challenge was immediately recognized, the damage was not. In that same letter to Lord Lansdowne, King Edward dismissed the Tangier landing as 'a theatrical fiasco' which would do his nephew no good at all in the eyes of the world. In Paris, Delcassé's first reaction had been even blander. 'Nothing,' he declared to his closest collaborator, Paléologue, 'could be better calculated to produce a salutary effect on the English.' Whereas a German provocation say, at Strasbourg, would have left the ocean-minded English indifferent, a German challenge in Morocco, right opposite to Gibraltar, would surely turn them even more to France.

This became the crucial question as pressure from Berlin rapidly mounted, and complacency disappeared on both sides of the Channel. Would Germany push matters to the brink of war and, if she did, would England stand firm by France's side? It was to their friend and champion, King Edward, even more than to British Ministers, that the French now looked for clues, and for reassurance. By a coincidence, on the very day that the Kaiser dropped anchor in Tangier harbour, the King had sent word to Delcassé that he would soon be passing through Paris on his way to board the *Victoria and Albert* at Marseilles. The King wanted to cross the French capital 'without being met at the station or any fuss'.[14] But the French, who had quickly grown uneasy at the Kaiser's 'blackmail', had other ideas. On 4 April, President Loubet sent urgent word to London asking whether, 'as a great favour ... His Majesty would allow him to be at the Paris station on the arrival of the train from Calais so that he might pass a short time with His Majesty'.[15] Such a meeting, however informal, 'would in the present circumstances be a good thing'. In the event, the King spent thirty minutes alone with the President in Paris on 6 April. He found M. Loubet in two minds as to whether to regard the Kaiser's action in Tangier merely as a calculated insult or as 'a direct menace to France'.[16] Though no longer relaxed, the mood in the French capital was still one of scandalized concern rather than of panic. The King echoed this in his own verdict to the President:

'The way my nephew behaves defies description. He neither knows what he is doing nor what he is after; and anyway he is completely at odds with his Ministers . . . The crisis you are going through is only a storm which will pass by.'[17]

President Loubet replied that the Tangier storm might nonetheless cause a great deal of damage while it was still overhead. It was a gloomy comment, and also a prophetic one.

The atmosphere in Paris was indeed much more tense when King Edward arrived there again three weeks later on his way home from the Mediterranean. Moreover, the King, by an extraordinary personal intervention, was by now up to his armpits in the crisis himself. It was a situation that only Edward VII would have dared to get himself into, or have managed to get himself out of.

A debate on the Moroccan question in the French Chamber on the morning of 19 April had started things in motion. Delcassé came under heavy fire from several quarters, and particularly from the French Socialists led by Jaurès, for his stiff-necked policy of refusing to negotiate with Germany. For once, the Foreign Minister was hesitant and unconvincing in his reply. No vote was taken, but he got an icy reception. Talk of his impending resignation was all round Paris by the afternoon.

Four days later the rumour reached King Edward on board the *Victoria and Albert*, just as his yacht was putting in at Algiers. Without any hesitation (and apparently without consulting his government at home) he sent, through the French Governor-General, a personal message in his own name to Delcassé in Paris, calling on the beleaguered Minister to stay at his post. King Edward, this message of 23 April said, would be 'personally distressed' by M. Delcassé's departure from office. He 'strongly urged' the Foreign Minister to stay on, not only because of the authority he still commanded but also because of the 'loyal and trusted relations' between the Minister and himself.[18]

The King's own Foreign Secretary, Lord Lansdowne, was later to call this a 'very unusual step'. It was more than unusual. It was a totally unprecedented action for a constitutional monarch to take, or even a non-constitutional one for that matter. Whether the Ministers of foreign governments stayed at their posts or not was no earthly official business of the King of England. Moreover, if he had felt compelled to intervene, this should have been done only with the approval of his own Cabinet and then only through a private message to the French President, whose responsibility it was to accept or reject resignations. In fact, unbeknown to King Edward, M. Loubet had already talked Delcassé out of resigning on 22 April, the day before the royal message arrived. But this does not diminish the audacity of the King's action. He was, quite plainly, meddling in the domestic politics of another country, in an attempt to preserve the sacred cause of the Entente. He relied on his unique prestige to get away with it. It was the greatest tribute to that prestige that he succeeded. There was not a murmur in either London or Paris. Indeed, when King Edward heard that Delcassé was staying on, he topped things off by sending him another telegram, this time of congratulations.

It was in this charged atmosphere, with talk of a European war very much in the air, and with the French capital still politically divided over how to handle the Morocco affair, that the King arrived in Paris, for the second time in a month, on 29 April. It was supposed, of course, to be another purely private visit, an informal transit stop on his way back to England. And, in fact, the King did do his traditional social round as though no international crisis existed.[19] On Sunday, 30 April he lunched with his old friends, the Standishes, at a table which reunited other fond and familiar Paris faces like the Breteuils and the Gallifets. The next day he inspected a racing stud and attended the St Cloud races. Other private engagements included a visit to the Paris Salon and an evening at the Théâtre Français, the scene of his own great solo performance two years ago almost to the day.

Yet, interspersed between these amusements (and, to some extent, camouflaged by them) came a great deal of high politics. On the Sunday afternoon, after a long private session with Delcassé, King Edward discussed the crisis *tête-à-tête* with M. Loubet, and he then returned to the Elysée that evening for a dinner given by the French President. This had originally been planned as a quiet 'family affair'. But, in honour of the crisis as well as of Edward VII, it had swollen on the night to a banquet of eighty guests. Though the King sensibly declined to make even the most anodyne of speeches, the presence of the German Ambassador gave him the chance of appealing also to Berlin for moderation.

As Sir Francis Bertie wrote to Lord Lansdowne the next day:

'After dinner the King, having a cold and not having any inclination to smoke, remained for some time in a corner of the room – where all the ladies were penned together like sheep – and had a long and animated conversation with the German Ambassador, Prince Radolin. All eyes were fixed on the two and I have no doubt that much more than probably passed was and will be credited to the conversation . . . H.M. told me this morning that Radolin was very sensible and regretted the misunderstanding but argued that Germany had all along felt sore at being left out of account by England, France and Spain. H.M.'s impression is that the storm will blow over . . .'

Certainly, the German interpretation of this Paris visit – namely, that the King had done all in his power to foment the conflict[20] – was sadly wide of the mark. There were a few firebrands, even in London, who felt the moment had already come for a showdown with Germany. Sir John Fisher, for example, the swashbuckling First Sea Lord, had given the following advice to Lord Lansdowne only a few days before: 'This seems a golden opportunity for fighting the Germans in alliance with the French, so I earnestly hope you may be able to bring this about.'[21] But to King Edward, the idea of fighting a European war over the privileges of a score of German merchants in Tangier seemed a monstrous irrelevancy. All he wanted was to wipe the slate clean, as swiftly and decorously as possible. Indeed, it was a German class-room phrase he used about the crisis to another old friend he met in Paris. '*Schwamm darüber! Schwamm darüber!*',* he told Baron Courcel, a former French envoy to his own court of St James.

King Edward had a final private meeting with Delcassé on Wednesday, 30 April after a small informal luncheon-party at the Breteuils'. Delcassé's staff at the Quai d'Orsay found that their Minister was much calmer afterwards, both in himself and in the tone of the instructions he was sending to the French mission in Tangier. One can assume, therefore, that the King was beginning to carry both conviction and reassurance with his arguments for moderation. It was a strange situation. During these few days, Delcassé seemed to be closer to this foreign monarch than to his own colleagues. He was behaving almost as though he were one of King Edward's own Ministers. Indeed, he clung to the royal visitor till the last possible minute of his stay.

As the King wanted no formalities at all at his departure, it had been arranged that only members of the British Embassy should see him off. Delcassé made a special point of asking, the day before, whether this meant that the King did not expect him to be at the station, and the British Ambassador made a special point of assuring him that this was indeed the King's wish. Very well, said the Foreign Minister, he would not come. But the next morning, not only did Delcassé turn up himself to bid the King farewell. He brought with him a naval officer to represent the President, as well as the Head of Protocol.[22] For a France in crisis, King Edward *was* the Entente. For Delcassé personally, he was the one firm lifeline in the storm.

But soon after the King's departure, the political storm in Paris blew up into such a hurricane that no lifeline, at home or abroad, could save the Minister. Bülow, pursuing his campaign of calculated pressure, allowed more threats of war to seep out of Berlin. 'Be friends with us, or fight,' was the ultimatum various 'unofficial' German messengers conveyed to Paris. The French capital was thrown into an agony of indecision. Was there to be a repetition of 1870, or were the Germans this time only bluffing?

On 2 June, Bülow played his trump card, or rather persuaded Morocco to put it on the table for him. The Sultan informed the French that he had now decided to reject their programme for internal reforms in his country. Instead, the future of Morocco was to be decided by

* 'Sponge over it! Sponge over it!'

convening an international conference of all the powers represented at his court. To have 'stood firm' now, the French would have had to have mounted, or at least threatened, military intervention from neighbouring Tunisia. In case that thought was in French minds – and even if it was not – the Germans made it plain that the moment French troops entered Morocco the German Army would invade France. The French Government could already hear the guns. In the Cabinet, the Prime Minister himself, M. Rouvier, now led the movement against his Foreign Minister with the cry 'Delcassé is leading us into war.'

On 6 June, having failed to persuade a single one of his colleagues to resist this German-inspired move to 'internationalize' Morocco, Delcassé resigned. There was jubilation in Berlin over this resounding, if short-lived, diplomatic triumph. A delighted Kaiser, who had forgotten all about his earlier doubts over Tangier, made his Chancellor, Count Bülow, a Prince.* In London, King Edward was silent. For the moment, there was nothing he could do.

*   *   *

As no one realized better than he did, however, something had to be done before long. The work of constructing the Entente was little more than two years old. The ground floor of the edifice was scarcely built, and the mortar was still wet even on those few bricks when this massive blow had fallen. The confidence, and the masonry, would need rapidly restoring if the King's dream of a lifetime was not to be shattered on both sides of the Channel. For it was not only French morale that had taken a knock. Although it was clear to inside observers in Paris that Delcassé had largely engineered his own fall by playing too much of a lone hand for too high stakes, to the outside world his eclipse appeared simply as a capitulation to German might and German blackmail. As Lansdowne wrote sorrowfully to the Paris Embassy: 'Recent events have, I am afraid, undoubtedly shaken people's confidence in the steadfastness of the French nation.'[23] The Prime Minister, Balfour, went even further in his gloomy verdict to the King.[24] The surrender of the French Cabinet over Morocco, he wrote, showed that France 'could not at present be counted on as an effective force in international politics'. At the critical moment, there was always the danger that she would 'yield to threats'.

---

* It is only fair to point out that Bülow himself always claimed that the honours had been bestowed on him a few hours *before* the news of Delcassé's fall was announced, and that the occasion for it was the marriage of the German Crown Prince in Berlin to the Duchess Cecilie of Mecklenburg-Schwerin. This also took place on 6 June. It seems highly unlikely, however, that the Moroccan affair, in which Germany seemed clearly to be heading for a victory, played no role. Bülow was a Chancellor, not a courtier.

For a while, the King was thoroughly down in the dumps and at a loss what to do. Then, as so often, he turned to the Navy, that apparently non-political weapon of his which, in fact, packed the force of a dozen treaties on its quarter-decks. Already on 28 March 1905, that is, three days *before** the Kaiser's landing at Tangier, an official invitation had been delivered in Paris for a detachment of the French fleet to visit Spithead in August. That this had been the King's own idea emerges from the unusual wording of the invitation, which was from 'King Edward and his government.'[25] Two weeks later, on 9 April, the First Sea Lord, Admiral Fisher, had started discussing plans for this, and the linked visit of the British Atlantic Fleet to Brest, with the French Naval Attaché in London. The Admiral made it plain that he was talking on his sovereign's behalf. The King, he said, was determined that the French sailors should take away *un bon souvenir* from their stay.[26] It was to this idea that, in the troubled midsummer of 1905, the King returned. He would himself be at Cowes in August (which was why that particular timetable had been proposed); and he now took personal charge of a programme that was to turn that *bon souvenir* into a major political demonstration of Anglo-French strength and friendship.

It is unlikely that any group of foreign sailors had ever had a welcome to British shores to compare with that given to the officers and men of the six French cruisers and six French destroyers under Admiral Caillard which anchored at Portsmouth on 7 August. King Edward set the example himself by scurrying round the harbour like a plump water-beetle. He was forever boarding the French ships to lunch with the captains, confer instant honours, dispense compliments, and propose toasts to France, and his good friend, the President.

Even more exceptional festivities were arranged for the visitors on land. They were taken to London where there was one lunch in their honour at the Guildhall and another, given jointly by the Lords and the Commons, in the sacred precincts of Westminster Hall itself. Both the Conservative Prime Minister, Mr Balfour, and the leader of the Liberal opposition, Mr Morley, were in attendance. The latter may well have been drawing rather too long a bow when he declared that, of all the great events that had been witnessed in this ancient hall, 'none had such importance for Western civilization as the extraordinary reunion taking place today'. But, even if exaggerated, this was just the theatrical effect the King had sought to achieve. When the French warships sailed away on 14 August, they left new confidence behind

---

* It is thus incorrect, as is often done, to portray these fleet exchanges of 1905 as the result of the Tangier crisis. What that crisis did affect was how they were handled.

them in England as well as taking a massive dose of it with them across the Channel. The King's formal messages exchanged afterwards with President Loubet were enthusiastic. So were his private letters to his friends, though he was characteristically modest about his own role.

To Sir Ernest Cassel he wrote from Marienbad the following month:

'Nothing could have gone off better than the visit of the French Fleet to England. The results will be good, I am sure . . .'[27]

From Berlin, they were watching this rapid resurgence of the Entente spirit with some disquiet. In June they had thought to have destroyed Delcassé's policies with the man himself. Now, only two months later, they were not so sure. The Germans would have been even more alarmed had they known the highly secret instructions which General Brun, the Chief of the French General Staff, had sent to his Military Attaché in London during that same month of August 1905. These were to examine what concrete help the British Army could give to France in the event of war with Germany. Would it be possible, for example, to land 100,000 British soldiers at between the fifteenth and twentieth day after mobilization? It was the first tendril in that web of staff talks and 'understandings' which, eventually, was to bind England and France as closely together as any formal military alliance.

* * *

Meanwhile, there was Morocco to be sorted out. Delcassé's fall meant that the German demand for an international conference would now have to go through. This duly convened at Algeciras, the little Spanish port close to Gibraltar, on 16 January 1906, and sat there for three and a half months. The agreement finally signed by the twelve interested maritime powers* on 6 April showed that much of the ground Germany had won twelve months before by brandishing her military sabre had been gradually lost in the minute cut-and-thrust of diplomacy. Though certainly not routed, she had lost on balance. The independence of Morocco was reaffirmed, and so was the freedom of commerce. But, apart from such face-saving devices as the appointment of a Swiss Inspector-General over the police force, French predominance in the country was left unchallenged.

And so, after some initial successes and a tense testing-time, Bülow's plan to destroy King Edward's 'continental dagger' had failed. Germany had hoped to drive the wedge of Morocco between England and France. Instead, the wedge had only pushed those two powers closer

* England, France, Germany, Russia, Austria-Hungary, Italy, Spain, the Netherlands, Sweden, Belgium, Portugal and the United States.

together and deepened the split between them and Germany. Though the Kaiser never knew it at the time, the proof of this lay not so much in what was going on in public between the Entente powers at Algeciras as in what was being discussed between them in the deepest secrecy in London while the conference was actually in progress. Here, throughout the winter and spring of 1905–6, England and France began seriously to prepare for the awful eventuality of a common war against Germany. Naval and military experts from both countries got down to their semi-official contingency planning while, above them, at the political level, the new Liberal Foreign Secretary, Sir Edward Grey, soon showed he was not going to lag behind Lord Lansdowne in a pro-French stand.*

Indeed, the historic importance of the Moroccan crisis of 1905–6 was that it had helped to fix those great power alignments which Europe took with her into the First World War. The dialogue between new political friends which King Edward had opened up less than three years before in Paris had now become, to all intents and purposes, a dialogue between new military partners. Thanks to a German inspired crisis, the Entente Cordiale was already changing out of its frock-coat and into uniform.

King Edward's own attitude to this transformation was probably ambivalent. There was hardly a monarch on earth less militaristic at heart. His whole approach to world problems was the peaceful one of the diplomat, not the warlike one of the grand strategist. But though it is unlikely that the King ever favoured any formal defence pact with France, we do know that, from 1905 onwards, he used all the influence at his command to tighten the informal military links across the Channel.

Paul Cambon, in London, who had his ear very close to what went on at court, probably got it right when, at the end of January 1906, he reported on a weekend of discussions which the new Liberal Prime Minister, Campbell-Bannerman, and his Foreign Secretary, Grey, had just spent with the King at Windsor Castle. According to Cambon, King Edward had agreed with his Ministers that, though there could be no question of 'the identity of interests between England and France in the event of a German aggression', it would be best for the moment to maintain official silence on the subject and simply 'continue discreetly' with the vital Anglo-French staff talks.[28] This suggests that, even if King Edward did not exactly welcome all this secret planning for war

---

* There had been vague French fears, and definite German hopes, that the arrival of the Liberals under Campbell-Bannerman to power on 10 December 1905 might swing England back into a more uncommitted position between Paris and Berlin.

against his imperial nephew, he fully accepted the need for it in the circumstances. Cambon's report also shows that the new Liberal Cabinet, like the previous Conservative one, did not merely inform their constitutional monarch what they proposed to do in foreign policy. They discussed their ideas with him as a political equal, seeking first his agreement and then his support.

*   *   *

One more thread of future history was spun out of the turmoil of this crisis. For the first time since its creation, the United States intervened in an attempt to settle the quarrels of Europe. That remarkable man, President Theodore Roosevelt, whom King Edward came greatly to admire, was responsible for this pioneer effort of the New World 'to redress the balance' of the Old. When the Tangier incident had first occurred, the President had jumped in straight away in April of 1905 with an offer of his services as mediator, fearing that the dispute which had just broken out might lead to a general war. The initial response he got from London was a haughty one. Even if Lord Lansdowne shared these White House fears, he was not going to allow an American President to do his worrying, and much less his thinking, for him. 'We have not, and never had, any intention of attacking Germany,' the Foreign Secretary replied to Roosevelt, 'nor do we anticipate that she will be so foolish as to attack us.'[29]

But the President aroused much more interest with his offer where it counted most, in both Berlin and Paris. For the next few months he was busy, in talks with French and German diplomats[30] and through personal letters to the Kaiser, in finding a formula acceptable to both sides on which the conference could be launched. Edward VII, who, as always, responded to the personal approach, now took a hand and sent several messages of encouragement to the American leader, messages which, at the same time, contained warnings about the Kaiser's unpredictability. This led President Roosevelt to draw a clear distinction (in a talk with M. Jusserand, the French Ambassador in Washington) between the King's government, of which he had no great opinion in this matter, and the King himself, to whom he gave the highest praise.

When, in March of 1906, the Algeciras conference reached its most critical stage, with both France and Germany refusing to give way over the degree of future French control in Morocco, King Edward and the President acted in parallel to bring them back to the table and sign. Roosevelt reminded the Kaiser of his personal promise to accept any solution that was 'fair and reasonable', a pledge which he now held up to the German ruler to honour. The King and his Ministers worked mainly on M. Cambon in London, whose word, they knew, was almost as good as law in Paris. That the deadlock was broken, and the Algeciras Treaty duly signed a few weeks later, was due in no small measure to these august pressures, exerted from behind the scenes on opposite shores of the Atlantic.

Nothing, therefore, was to be quite the same again after this first Moroccan crisis.* England and France, though not yet fully fledged military allies, had become something more than good-neighbourly political friends. England and Russia, through parallel action at Algeciras, had also moved closer. America, though not yet acting as a world power, had realized, for the first time, that her own frontiers of peace lay across the ocean in Europe as well as around the shores of her own continent. As for King Edward himself, the Tangier escapade seems to have settled any remaining doubts he had about the emotional instability of his nephew, and the perils that this instability might one day bring with it for Europe. Soon after the crisis erupted, the King was discussing the political problems posed by the Kaiser's character with a group of friends, who included the Marquis of Soveral. He pointed to the dangers of so vain a ruler being constantly assured by his courtiers that he was the greatest sovereign on earth, with a divine mission to make Germany the greatest power on earth. The King went on:

'But he is even more cowardly than vain, and because of this, he will tremble before all these sycophants when, urged on by the General Staff, they call on him to draw the sword in earnest. He won't have the courage to talk some sense into them, but will obey them cravenly instead. It is not by his will that he will unleash a war, but by his weakness.'

It was not a bad forecast of what was to go on in Berlin during the first days of August 1914.

---

* The second, which lies outside the scope of this book, was touched off by the visit of the German warship *Panther* to Agadir in 1911.

UNCLE AND NEPHEW

In the summer that followed the settlement of the Moroccan crisis, all Europe was smiling over a Berlin cartoon that had dealt with another, and more permanent, aspect of the Anglo-German problem. The drawing, which appeared in the *Berliner Lüstiger Blätter* of August 1906, satirized King Edward's notorious reluctance to meet his imperial nephew. It tilted both at the King and the Emperor, whose absences from his own imperial capital had become so frequent that he was nick-named the *Reisekaiser, Reise* being the German for journey. King Edward is shown poring over a map of the Continent, pencil in hand, trying to plot the most convenient route to reach his beloved Bohemian Spa.

> 'How can I get to Marienbad without meeting my dear nephew?' he asks. 'Flushing, Antwerp, Calais, Rouen, Madrid, Lisbon, Nice, Monaco – all are very unsafe. I have it! I shall simply go via Berlin. I'm sure not to find him there!'

In fact, by the time that caricature appeared, arrangements had at last been made to bring uncle and nephew together again and, ironically, the King's annual pilgrimage to Marienbad was the pretext. It was Count Metternich, the much-tried German Ambassador in London, who first sounded out the ground. On 4 May 1906 he observed, in a letter to Chancellor Bülow:[1]

> 'The Germans are without doubt most unpopular among the upper circles of English society. This is due to a great extent to the attitude of the Court and to the personal relations between the two sovereigns. If an amicable meeting could be arranged between them, this would change things greatly for the better . . .'

When Bülow sent this message on to his imperial master, the Kaiser fairly snorted in a marginal comment:

> 'I don't believe it! Two years have passed since Kiel.* Meetings with Edward are of no lasting value because he is so jealous!'

* In June of 1904, King Edward had attended the Kiel Regatta as his nephew's guest. It was an amicable occasion, but the Kaiser had not endeared himself to his English visitors by gathering every German warship he could lay his hands on and parading them in the road-stead.

That, of course, was only William II getting something off his chest. In truth, there was nothing he wanted better than a meeting with his uncle, preferably in England, but, at the very least, on the King's next journey to Marienbad. Various sweeteners were already in the air. Groups of German artists, German burgomasters and, most important for the general climate, German journalists, were visiting England, and return visits were planned. Then on 24 May, less than three weeks after receiving Metternich's letter, the Kaiser invited Haldane, War Minister in the new Liberal Cabinet, to come to Berlin in August. Haldane had been partly educated in Germany, spoke fluent German, and was thought to have pro-German sympathies.

With all this in train, a reunion between the two sovereigns fell naturally into place, so when, on 7 June, Sir Edward Grey was formally asked 'whether the King would be willing to meet the Emperor', he could only accept on King Edward's behalf.[2] The Kaiser thereupon suggested Friedrichshof, the former castle of the King's sister near Cronberg, where the two rulers had met earlier in the King's reign. As it lay close to the direct route to Marienbad, mid-August was fixed as the most convenient time.

King Edward was distinctly unenthusiastic, not to say a little un-gracious, about the plan, modest though it was. 'I suppose that means I shall have to sleep at Friedrichshof,' he grumbled to Lascelles, his Ambassador in Berlin. To do him justice, however, there was more to it than just a reluctance to give up twenty-four hours of his Marienbad cure for an exhausting spell of his nephew's company *en route*. The French were already getting distinctly worried over these little signs of an Anglo-German *rapprochement*; and what worried the French usually worried the King. Two years before, when he had last visited the Kaiser at Kiel, King Edward had deliberately included in his entourage both the Prince of Monaco and the Baron d'Estournelles as travelling symbols of the new Entente. This had been a simple enough matter to arrange for a trip made on board his own yacht. But there could be no question of taking a couple of Frenchmen with him now on the train to Cronberg, simply to allay French suspicions.

That the French were growing uneasy was shown by the behaviour of that level-headed ambassador of theirs in London, Paul Cambon. During a weekend at Windsor Castle, he felt obliged to warn the King personally on 25 June that French public opinion might well be dis-turbed by the news of the forthcoming Cronberg meeting. There was also the prospect that the German Emperor might now expect, or be entitled to, an autumn visit to Windsor Castle itself, which, after all, he had not entered since his grandmother's funeral in 1901. Lascelles in Berlin was all for such a visit. The Foreign Secretary, Sir Edward Grey, was, on the other hand, dubious about the wisdom of two such meetings within the space of a few months, in view of French reactions. Cambon, needless to say, was doing all he could to reinforce those doubts and drive them home to the King.

For King Edward, it was the same old tight-rope between those distasteful family duties he owed to Berlin and the much more congenial feelings he had towards Paris. He simply could not make up his mind about issuing an invitation for the Kaiser to come to Windsor. Everything would depend on how things went at Cronberg. But that meeting, he now realized, would have to take place. As the King told Cambon:

> 'If I go through Germany I cannot avoid the Emperor. Perhaps people will talk about our meeting. But they would talk a great deal more if it did not take place.'[3]

A few days later the man who received that report, the then French Foreign Minister, M. Bourgeois, was given a lot to talk about and think about himself. At his annual reception for foreign diplomats, the German Ambassador in Paris – still the same Prince Radolin – had approached him out of the blue to ask how France would react if England and Germany were in fact to reach an agreement. Not only Paris, but London as well, buzzed with speculation. Were the Germans planning to turn the Cronberg meeting into a major political event? Were they trying to scare the French for the fun of it? Or had the solemn Prince Radolin simply had one glass too many, for a change? No one could think of a convincing explanation and all eyes turned to Cronberg, the English ones with curiosity, the French ones with apprehension. Suddenly, that will-o'-the-wisp of an Anglo-German 'understanding' had popped up again.

Compared with this advance build-up, the reunion of uncle and nephew on 15 August 1906 proved something of an anti-climax. As always, however, the presence of the Emperor William prevented things ever becoming dull. He was there at Cronberg Station to meet the King's train, wearing the inevitable military uniform and attended by the customary swarm of army officers and courtiers. After lunch at Friedrichshof Castle, the Kaiser piled his guests and his entourage into motor cars and drove them all to the ruins of the Roman camp at Saalburg, which lay nearby. A more accurate description would be 'the former ruins', for the Emperor had devoted a great deal of energy and money to having the entire site rebuilt as he imagined it must have looked when the Roman legions were garrisoned there. Among the exhibits were machines for shooting arrows which, he claimed, were exact reproductions of the original weapons. Even a car journey with the Kaiser could not be quite normal. His own vehicle was equipped, apart from the Hohenzollern standard, with a special box at the rear from which a trumpeter sounded long blasts on the bugle as they approached each corner. In this way, the surrounding populace in general and all road traffic in particular were warned of the All-Highest's approach. King Edward's reaction to this can be imagined.*

They got down to politics after dinner at the castle. Bülow was unable to be there due to illness. It was that terrible fellow Holstein, the Kaiser went around saying, who had laid the Chancellor low, by piling too much work on his shoulders. In his place there had appeared State Secretary von Tschirschky of the German Foreign Office; not an ideal choice, for he had made a name for himself during the Boer War as one of Berlin's leading Anglophobes. King Edward's political adjutant was Charles Hardinge of 1903 fame, with, of course, the Ambassador to Berlin, Sir Frank Lascelles, who was distinctly put out that he did not have the King's ear to himself.

He must have grown more frustrated as the meeting progressed, for Hardinge now appeared on the scene as something much more than a royal adviser and confidant. At Cronberg in 1906 he acted, for the first time at such a major political occasion, as the unsupervised spokesman for both King and government. The guidelines of what he was to say had, of course, been laid down by Sir Edward Grey and the Cabinet in London. But Hardinge was left to play the hand more or less by himself. It had been agreed that the King would avoid, as far as was possible, getting involved in any detailed discussion with either the Kaiser or his Ministers. Instead, King Edward would merely introduce the general themes and, for the rest, concentrate on keeping his nephew happy and the whole occasion harmonious. This was to set the pattern for future Cronberg meetings. The arrangement had one drawback, though this was not to reveal itself until later.

So far as this 1906 gathering was concerned, the division of labours on the English side worked out well and all the first-hand accounts from both sides suggest that, on the surface, everything passed off fairly smoothly.[4] The Kaiser reported to his sick Chancellor that the two sovereigns had spent some time discussing their own professional worries, namely, the conditions prevailing in Europe's other empires. The Kaiser had found his uncle particularly worried about the parlous

---

* It must be noted, however, that at Biarritz the following year King Edward did ask to have a distinctive multi-tone motor horn fitted to his car there, in imitation of another motoring device used by the Kaiser.

state of affairs in Russia, where the Tsar's refusal to grant liberal concessions could only be stoking up trouble for the Romanovs and for everyone else who sat on a throne. King Edward said that he had twice written to his imperial nephew at St Petersburg, urging him to see sense, but had apparently received not one word in reply. Nor, according to the Kaiser's report, was the King much happier over the outlook for that other great land empire, the Habsburg Monarchy. Did the old* Austrian Emperor still have enough strength left in him to stand up to 'subversive elements'? Furthermore, once he died and was succeeded by his heir, Franz Ferdinand,† what should be done about the Archduke's morganatic wife Sophie, who had been denied any rank higher than that of Princess? Surely, King Edward reasoned, it would be better for everyone concerned if the Vienna court faced facts and recognized her as Empress? The Kaiser absolutely agreed with all this and told his uncle how pleased he was that the two of them could act according to their 'common understanding' of these problems.

This was the talk of monarchs, debating the affairs of their own select if shaky European club. At the 'lower' political level, King Edward, as arranged on the journey out, had had a short talk with Tschirschky before the German Minister closeted himself with Hardinge. The King referred to recent suggestions‡ that England and Germany might conclude an entente similar to that signed two years before with France. He brushed these suggestions gently aside with the same arguments that the Foreign Office had used with German diplomats in London. An *entente* had been possible with France precisely because so many specific points of friction had existed all over the globe between her and England. But Anglo-German relations were quite different. 'There are no frictions between us,' he told Tschirschky blandly, 'there is only rivalry.' It was an impossible argument to penetrate. The Germans must have felt, at Cronberg as in London, that they were thwacking away at an eiderdown.

Tschirschky's talk with Hardinge, which then followed, could do little more than survey the whole chequered course of Anglo-German relations, from the Boer War to Algeciras, with polite hopes of improvement being expressed as the two men went along. But Hardinge made it crystal clear that, in his own words, 'friendly relations with us cannot be at the expense of our *entente* with France, but that, if they are to

---

* Franz Josef was already 76 years old by August of 1906.
† This, of course, never happened. The Archduke and his wife were assassinated at Sarajevo in June 1914, and the aged Emperor survived them for nearly two and a half years after that.
‡ They had been floated in London earlier that summer, as well as in Paris.

exist at all, they must be co-existent with that *entente*'.[5] This robust statement seemed to have been accepted by the German side and the discussion of specific questions such as the Anglo-German 'press war' and Britain's strategic interest in the German project of the Baghdad Railway all went off amicably enough.

Indeed, when the gathering broke up on 16 August – with the Emperor and his suite returning to Berlin, Hardinge going back to his desk at the Foreign Office, and King Edward proceeding pleasurably to Marienbad – everyone agreed it had been a great success. The Emperor told Bülow that things had gone 'to my complete satisfaction'. Tschirschky thought that the meeting of the two monarchs at Cronberg had been a step on Germany's path 'towards a more trusting and more friendly *rapprochement* with England'. Even the matter-of-fact Hardinge noted with relief and approval that 'no tiresome question nor discordant note was raised'.

Hardinge had spelt out why, in the delicate state in which the Anglo-French *entente* stood in 1906, no dramatic move closer to Germany was possible for England. French susceptibilities had to come first. The Cronberg meeting was less than a fortnight old when something happened which showed how delicate those susceptibilities were.

One of King Edward's political guests at Marienbad that summer was his War Minister, Mr Haldane, who was on his way to Berlin in response to the Kaiser's invitation. Between 27 and 30 August, at picnics taken in the woods of the Eger Valley surrounding the spa, Haldane explained to his sovereign the sweeping reforms being planned for the British Army; indeed, it was at Marienbad that the King signed the first Army Order implementing those reforms.* The two men also discussed the recent Cronberg meeting, the King saying how much it had helped general relations and how he hoped that Haldane's presence in Berlin would carry the good work further. But almost as they were talking in Marienbad, trouble was brewing with the French in London over the War Minister's trip.

The French Government had got hold of a report that the Kaiser had invited Mr Haldane to attend the so-called 'Sédan Review' while he was in Germany. This was a spectacular military parade staged by the German Army each first day of September, to commemorate the anniversary of its crushing defeat of the French in 1870. M. Cambon, who had been about to leave London on holiday when the news got out,[6]

---

* The second stage of those reforms, which received the Royal Assent four months later, provided for the raising of a British Expeditionary Force of 120,000 men. This was too little to satisfy the French and not big enough to scare the Germans. But it showed the continental commitment that flowed from the Entente with France.

postponed his departure to tackle Sir Edward Grey personally on the matter. He found the Foreign Secretary 'surprised and upset' by the news.[7] Pressing home his advantage, the Ambassador pointed out that the invitation must have been a calculated trick on the part of the Germans and warned that, 'if the British Minister of War associated himself with a display so painful for France, the very next day articles inspired by German agents would be appearing in French newspapers attacking both Mr Haldane and the British Government'. In the event, Mr Haldane saw his review the day before the Sédan commemoration and all was well. But the whole incident showed what high hopes the Kaiser held out for the 'pro-German' Mr Haldane and his Liberal Cabinet. It also, of course, demonstrated once again the Kaiser's disastrous sense of tempo. Even when he was reading the music correctly, he was always too fast on the beat.

*   *   *

Perhaps to smoothe these ruffled French feathers (and perhaps also to give his wife a rare treat), the King suddenly decided to go over to Paris for the first week of February 1907, taking Queen Alexandra with him. They travelled, theoretically incognito, as the 'Duke and Duchess of Lancaster', and most of the week was spent in a gay round of pleasure that any pair of distinguished tourists might have followed. There were visits to art galleries and theatres (including a new play with Sarah Bernhardt), shopping expeditions, dinner-parties in friends' homes, and even some meals taken *en ville* in Paris restaurants. The Parisians were delighted, impressed and perhaps slightly amused by *le bon Edouard*'s display of domesticity in the very capital where he had had so many love-affairs during the more than forty years of his married life. It would all have been in dubious taste had anything been done awkwardly or badly. But the King did it exquisitely, and his friend Lord Esher gives us a touching picture of the tonic effect the outing had on that rather tragic Queen. Her joy during that week in Paris, he noted, was 'the joy of a girl. She cried it from the house-tops.'[8]

Yet politics, as ever, lay just under the surface even of this genuinely private visit. A lunch at the Elysée with the French President could not be avoided, and there the King met and talked with the new Prime Minister of France, Georges Clemenceau. The famous 'Tiger' of future years was already rattling the conservatives of Paris with his impetuous methods and his radical ideas. The King, at first sight, seems to have shared their concern, though something of a meeting of minds between the two men was to develop later on.

Prince Radolin, the German Ambassador, was also at the luncheon, and the King worked hard on him in order to convince the Germans that there was nothing sinister about his presence in Paris. The Ambassador, of course, reported this conversation to Berlin,[9] and the Kaiser's remarks on the dispatch are more interesting than its contents. When Radolin, for example, quoted the King as saying that he had simply wanted to show Paris to the Queen 'in order to relax for a few days after the opening of Parliament', the Kaiser scornfully commented: 'Relax from what? And far better at Sandringham!'

At the end of the dispatch, where King Edward's hopes for an overall improvement in relations between England, France and Germany had been aired, the Emperor wrote simply: 'Words! Words! Words!' The mere presence of his uncle in Paris angered the Kaiser just as the mere presence of King Edward in Germany worried the French. It was a sickening political rocking-horse for the King to have to ride.

* * *

There are times, even with a drama, when operetta gets closer than grand opera to the spirit of things. An Anglo-German row which broke in the autumn of 1907 was a good example. It concerned, of all things, the Military Band of His Majesty's Coldstream Guards. By then, there had been another (and, on the personal level, fairly harmonious) August meeting between nephew and uncle at Cronberg. True, the Kaiser had not helped matters at the start by staging another of his mammoth military reviews by way of welcome (which meant that the famished guests, who had arrived on empty stomachs, had to wait until mid-afternoon for their lunch). But at the political talks, during which the dreaded naval question was not even raised, all was sweetness and light. Accordingly, the Kaiser had been formally invited to pay that long-postponed and much-debated visit to Windsor and had accepted with real pleasure. Then, even before certain last-minute personal complications arose which almost cancelled the visit,* came the row over the Military Band.

A continental tour had been planned for the band of the 1st Battalion Coldstream Guards, and the King had envisaged that it would give performances in both Germany and France, as a token of England's 'open-handedness' towards these quarrelling neighbours. Indeed, the Germans had already been told of the musical joys awaiting them when

---

* On 9 November, just as the Kaiser was preparing to leave for England, his most intimate friend, Count Eulenburg, was involved in a public homosexual scandal and threatened with criminal proceedings. The Kaiser feigned illness to avoid showing himself in England, but was talked out of it by both his uncle and his Chancellor.

the Foreign Office discovered what appeared an insuperable obstacle to the whole project.[9] In June of 1907, the Army Council in London had, for some reason known only to itself, laid it down that English military bands were not to play in France. At that, the French had refused to allow the band of the *Garde Republicaine* to accept an invitation to appear in Manchester in September. This ridiculous war of the bandmasters was still in force when the question arose of the Guards' Band performing at Mayenne in France during their proposed autumn tour, and the concert accordingly had to be abandoned. Then the Foreign Office, in its wisdom, maintained that if the musicians of the Coldstream Guards performed in Germany without performing in France, the French would be offended and the Entente would be injured. So they called the entire tour off.

King Edward was livid. Not only had he sponsored the band's visit to Germany, but the whole question seemed none of the Foreign Secretary's business. Foreign Office interference, he wrote,[10] was 'hardly consistent' with his own position as 'head of the Army and Colonel-in-Chief of the Guards'. Furthermore, it was decidedly awkward for anything to be done in this way which might 'offend the Germans on such a small matter, especially on the eve of the Emperor's visit'. But bureaucracy proved more powerful than either monarchs or Ministers. The tour remained cancelled and the King, much put out, left it to the Foreign Office to make the necessary apologies to Berlin.

Despite all these last-minute alarms and irritations, the Kaiser's state visit of November 1907 passed off well. He arrived at Windsor with the Empress on the 11th and stayed a full week instead of the five days originally planned. For amusement, there were the usual Windsor pheasant shoots in what the Kaiser had affectionately described as 'the dear old park I know so well'. As usual, the Kaiser turned out looking more like a Ruritanian cavalry officer than a sportsman, his black knee-boots and square-cut tunic contrasting sharply with the soft tweeds and homely woollen stockings of his host. But the sport was good and the mood was jovial.

Inside the Castle were assembled a collection of crowned and royal heads the like of which even Windsor had rarely, if ever, seen. No fewer than twenty-four of them sat down as luncheon guests at the Castle on 17 November. They included, apart from the German Emperor and Empress, King Alfonso and Queen Ena of Spain (who were on a private visit), Queen Amelia of Portugal, Queen Maud of Norway, and a cluster of former French royalty who had gathered in England to celebrate the marriage of Prince Charles of Bourbon to Princess Louise of Orleans. Though it is unlikely that King Edward had made any special effort to collect them all at one table, he can scarcely have been displeased with the effect. In an innocuous but convincing way, he was reminding his nephew that Windsor was still the summit of royal prestige, just as London was still the centre of world power.

At a Guildhall luncheon given in his honour on 13 November, the Kaiser had used one of his most famous and most effective phrases. Speaking of the need to strengthen all the natural Anglo-German links, he had declared: 'Blood is thicker than water.' The cynic might have observed that, unlike water, blood congeals. In any case, the visit had shown that, whatever its qualities as compared with water, blood was not thicker than international politics. The German Emperor should not be denied full credit for making another personal effort to bring the alignments of England and Germany closer together. Nor, for that matter, should King Edward's role be forgotten, for it was he who, in April of that year, had first raised with his Ministers the desirability of a visit by the Kaiser to Windsor that autumn. But there was no escaping the fact that, by the end of 1907, England was measuring her every act by its likely effect on her deepening alliance with France and Russia.

The year thus closed with Anglo-German tensions lying too strong and too deep beneath the surface to be eased by any family gathering at Windsor Castle, or any appeals to its Hanoverian and Coburg links. European politics were indeed out-growing the clasp of European dynasties, great and small, and were soon to destroy several of them for good.

BIARRITZ AND BEYOND

King Edward's second regular continental 'court' was at Biarritz, where, from 1906 onwards, he stayed each year for at least three weeks, usually from early March to early April. It thus took its place in the fixed royal calendar between the end of a winter passed in England (the whole of February itself being normally spent at Buckingham Palace) and the beginning of those cruises in the Mediterranean in a combined search for spring sunshine and political allies.

Unlike that other Edwardian court of his, held every August at Marienbad, these stays at Biarritz were private rather than political. There were, as we shall see, some interesting international side-effects of his love for this fashionable resort in the Alpes Maritimes, while his mere presence there was a token of his, and England's, interest in the whole of southern Europe. As the 'wise arbiter' or 'chief mischief-maker' of the Continent's affairs (depending on which extreme view his contemporaries took), King Edward could not go anywhere without becoming the focus of their curious or suspicious eyes. But even when he kept to one tiny patch of Europe, as he did at Biarritz, he was like a diplomatic 'fleet-in-being', as powerful at anchor as it was out at sea.

Basically, however, Biarritz itself was, for him, a pure holiday resort, and he went there for its relative peace and quiet as well as its strong air (a mixture of Atlantic salt and Pyrenean pine) which always seemed to clear the cigars and the London fog from his chest. As Prince of Wales, he had been the uncrowned monarch of the Riviera, and the hôteliers of the Côte d'Azur were distressed at losing his custom. But as he once told his French-Corsican bodyguard:* 'I no longer go to Cannes and Nice because you meet too many princes there. I should have to spend all my time paying and receiving visits, whereas I come here to rest.' Though at Biarritz, in contrast to Marienbad, he was not constantly surrounded with potentates, grand dukes, archdukes, and the statesmen and diplomatists of half a dozen European powers, his 'rest' was, as always, a fairly active one. King Edward's day was seventeen or eighteen hours long, whether on business or pleasure or both

* Xavier Paoli, whose memories, *Leurs Majestés*, tell us a lot about the King's Biarritz days.

combined, and he did not let up here. Though he rarely got to bed till around midnight, he was up soon after seven each morning in his first-floor suite of rooms in the great Hotel du Palais, rooms which were regularly reserved and specially appointed for him from year to year,* like their counterparts in Marienbad's Hotel Weimar.

After a warm bath and a glass of milk there came a preliminary look at state papers or newspapers, an examination of the day's programme and of the wardrobe to match it. Breakfast was served at ten o'clock. This was substantial (as was every meal King Edward ate), consisting usually of bacon that was grilled, eggs that were boiled, and small fresh trout from the nearby mountain streams. The King then got down to his correspondence which, as his many surviving letters from Biarritz show, was copious, and political in content as well as personal. Most of it was done in that perfectly appalling handwriting of his (a blend of all the worst faults of German and English orthography), and, if his letters were half as laborious to write as they are for a later generation to decypher, he must have spent quite a time each day at his writing-desk. The morning stint there normally ended at 12.15, when he would leave the hotel for a walk with his friends along the cramped sea promenade and harbour of the town. Lunch followed at one; then, almost regardless of the weather, would come the speciality of those Biarritz stays, the afternoon excursions in his claret-coloured motor cars† to explore the surrounding region in all its infinite and (in those days) unspoilt variety. Here, too, he was endlessly looking for something new: an unfamiliar lake or château or ruin on those flat *landes* which stretch northwards to Bordeaux, or a new village perched in the Pyrenees above him; a mountain pass into Spain they had not yet tried, or a new beauty spot inside Spain itself. Even the picnic sites chosen for these trips (the hot food from the hotel having been placed in deep dishes which were then sunk into a large heavily padded box) had to be constantly changed. The King had his favourites; but his greatest love, in this as in so much else, was for variety.

Back in Biarritz by the late afternoon or early evening, the King would then have another session with his equerries who would have opened and sorted the red-sealed canvas bags which came regularly by courier from London with their piles of letters and government dis-patches. Then, at 8.15, came dinner. This was taken either at the Hotel

---

* One novelty the King insisted on was a telephone in his rooms, from where he would place calls to all over Europe.
† They left England about a week ahead of the King to do the long journey by road and never failed to arrive on time.

du Palais, the floor waiters bringing the trolleys to the door of the King's suite, where his footman, Hoepfner,* would take over, or at one of the dozens of villas owned by the local notabilities or specially rented for the period by the monarch's English friends.

Whereas the top drawer of English society – the equivalent of the Austrian *erste Gesellschaft* – never made its way in any strength to Marienbad, it sent plenty of representatives to keep the King company at Biarritz. A typical example was a party of guests which he took by car on 21 March 1906 to lunch at the Spanish village of Fuentarabbia (having deliberately bamboozled both the detectives and the newspaper reporters by pretending he was going to Pau). The party consisted of Consuelo, Duchess of Manchester, the Earl and Countess of Dudley, the Duchess of Roxburgh, and the Duke of Devonshire. Not one of those names crops up in the King's own letters describing his circle in Marienbad, and there was certainly never a lunch-party given in that Bohemian spa with such an all-British, blue-blooded look. The time of the year may have had a lot to do with this. In March – for this was the era before winter sports – Biarritz provided a delightful escape from the English winter, even if the region was not always as reliable climatically as they always imagined. Another reason for their presence was perhaps that that other sun, a sun which shone quite reliably and predictably at the centre of the King's private life, was always here at Biarritz and never at Marienbad – Alice Keppel.

Quite why the King never took her with him to Bohemia (or why she decided not to go) is not certain. The most likely explanation offered today by survivors of that era is that, at Marienbad, King Edward was, after all, an honoured guest in the dominions of His Most Apostolic Majesty, the Emperor Franz Josef. Though Vienna had a lively enough *demi-monde*, and Austrian court society had no worse or no better morals than most, the Emperor himself had always lived an austere life and had an unrelenting eye for appearances. It would not have done for the King of England to parade his famous mistress each day and every summer at Marienbad, especially in view of the King's life-style there, which was more high diplomacy than high jinks. Quite possibly, Alice Keppel herself, with that unfailing tact and shrewd common sense of hers, had seen this difficulty without ever being told. Perhaps, in the midsummer holidays, she wanted to be not only with her children but also with that rather sad figure of a husband of hers, who never accompanied them on the so-called 'Easter holidays' in Biarritz.

---

* His first valet, Meidinger, was also an Austrian by birth, while the Swiss-born Mr Fehr handled all his travel arrangements.

If March was more propitious as a time of year, Biarritz was even more propitious as a place. Not only was it situated in a republic, whose President would never have raised a whisper against the King's goings-on, but that republic was France, which had a unique historic tradition and a unique national sympathy for such matters. By copying the French pattern of openly adopting an 'official' mistress, King Edward, while causing his Queen no extra hurt, had created a greater comfort for Alice Keppel in English society, as for Lily Langtry before her. But to the French, this declared and unchallenged favourite of a monarch did not merely have a social position. She almost had a constitutional position as well. There is, at any rate, no doubt that when Mrs George Keppel stepped into her sleeping-car at Calais (having been swept through customs by the *Chef du Gare* in person) it was as though Mesdames Pompadour and Dubarry rolled into one were being helped into their gilded coach. French state officials had been deprived of this sort of thing for more than a century. Even if they had to look these days to the White Cliffs to maintain the tradition of a King's faithful infidelity, it was better than nothing, especially when that King was their very own *bon Edouard*.

But however much fuss the French railways made of her, Mrs Keppel travelled down to Biarritz discreetly (never dining in the restaurant car, for example), whereas, officially, she never arrived in Biarritz at all. It was natural that her presence there should never have been recorded in court circulars or any other formal accounts of the King's movements and company abroad. What was more remarkable was that her name rarely, if ever, cropped up in those English newspaper reports which covered, usually in dispatches from special correspondents, the King's daily activities in and around Biarritz. Everyone knew she was there and everyone spoke of her there. But not a word was printed. The English had given their own refinement to the Pompadour legend.

It was Sir Ernest Cassel who, in this, as in so many aspects of the King's private affairs, provided the indispensable cover for such an operation. Just as, in Paris, Alice Keppel would often put up at Cassel's magnificent apartment in the Rue du Cirque, so in Biarritz she (and her children whenever they were with her) would stay in the house he had rented there, the Villa Eugenie, where his sister did the formal honours. Who the Villa Eugenie belonged to, and how much it cost Sir Ernest to render this particular annual favour to his sovereign, is not recorded. But it is clear from passages about Biarritz in some of the King's letters to his protégé and friend that the owners, or their agents, were not easy people to deal with. Indeed, one winter the King lets out a sigh of relief on paper that tiresome difficulties about the leasing have been overcome and that the villa is theirs again for the coming spring. For him, Biarritz without Mrs Keppel soon became as unthinkable as her presence there was unprintable.

He would have been hard put to it to decide which of his two regular continental resorts he loved the more. But, especially as he grew older, Biarritz in March probably just held the palm over Marienbad in August, if only because Alice was there.* For her, it must have seemed the nearest thing to a family life they could enjoy together: natural despite its anonymity because it was free from all those embarrassments and pinpricks of protocol that their long love-affair inevitably had to endure in England. There was no question here as to whether Count Mensdorff could or could not invite *La Favorita* to a formal banquet at 14 Belgrave Square because of those awkward problems of '*placement*' she might create around his Embassy dining-table. There was even less question as to whether 'Mrs G.K.' should be asked to stay for the weekend at Eaton because both the King and Queen Alexandra were coming as well. For three weeks in Biarritz, Alice Keppel *was* Queen.

A relatively minor advantage that this Atlantic resort had over Marienbad – though it was not in itself to be despised – was that the Biarritz public, both French and international, was far less obtrusive. If the tourists' Kodaks appeared, they came, to invert Shakespeare's phrase, in single spies rather than in battalions; and the mayor of the town was never driven, like his opposite number in Marienbad, to plastering posters on every tree of the promenade with appeals to leave their 'illustrious guest' in peace. For all that, King Edward was, as usual, the central figure around which the local universe revolved. High and low took their cue from him and set their watches by him, often literally.

Among the lowly examples of this was a pair of blind beggars who posted themselves soon after noon every day on the road from the Hotel du Palais to the beach where they would be sure to catch the King on his regular stroll. Caesar, who, of course, went on these walks as well, developed a particular dislike for these tattered creatures and would start barking as soon as he spotted them. For them, however, this was a most convenient signal to warn them of the King's approach and, at the dog's first bark, they would put on their most pitiful look

---

* His passion for Biarritz led to one of the most unorthodox and most criticized decisions he took in English domestic politics, namely the summoning of Mr Asquith, Prime Minister elect, all the way from England, to kiss hands in the Hotel du Palais on 8 April 1908.

and extend their bowls for money. The King never failed to drop a handsome contribution into each bowl and to give them what must have been a most warming greeting: '*À demain*.' One day, only one of the beggars turned up. The King's concern that one of his faithful sentinels might be unwell turned to curiosity when the missing man appeared as usual the following morning. Had he been ill? he asked the beggar. No, sire. Late then? This second question threw the poor man into great embarrassment. Finally he blurted out:

'Pardon, *monsieur le Roi*, it was not me who was late but you who were early!'

The King roared with laughter and offered profuse apologies together with his normal contribution.

Though the general public was much less of a nuisance than at Marienbad, the problem of guarding the King on these Biarritz visits was, if anything, greater. It was mainly those afternoon (and sometimes day-long) excursions into the surrounding countryside that caused the headaches. The sedate tea-picnics were, from the security point of view, fairly harmless, despite the King's occasional preference for a roadside site, where the dust of passing cars and carriages was liable to settle with the paprika on the plovers' eggs. The worst hazards here were those socially aspiring English mothers, their cars laden with débutante daughters, who would contrive to break down at the precise spot where the King had halted.

But the journeys into the interior, much of it primitive Basque country where the people could be as wild as the scenery, were a different matter. Nor was security the only problem in the explorations of the tiny mountain roads above Cambo and St-Jean-Pied-de-Port. Sometimes, herds of cattle made the way impossible; sometimes the spring snow still blocked the passes. And, as regularly as a royal salute, at least one tyre would burst on the rough surface and the many spares which the Mercedes always carried had to be put into service. This was a process which, like most things mechanical, the King would watch with almost incredulous curiosity.

Fortunately for both the chauffeurs and the police, they did not always head for the mountains. He grew fond of watching the pelota matches at nearby Anglet (where he would always congratulate the reigning champion, Chiquito); he occasionally patronized the racecourse at La Barre; he always made a point of visiting the British military cemetery (from the Napoleonic wars) at Bayonne; and, on his last visit, he even attended an aviation meeting at the small aerodrome of Lachiste, where those great French flying pioneers,

Leblanc and Blériot, both made ascents and were presented to him.

* * *

It was from across the Pyrenees that the greatest excitement came to Edwardian Biarritz. Most appropriately, it concerned another royal romance.

Quite why the young King Alfonso of Spain was *so* determined to marry an English Protestant princess is something of a mystery. The massive combined weight of Spanish history, tradition and religion was all piled up against it. So was the narrower pressure inside his own family. His widowed mother, for example, herself an Austrian Arch-duchess by birth,* wanted nothing more than that her son should also go to the Habsburg court at Vienna for his bride, and was constantly telling him so. And even if the Habsburgs failed to appeal, there was no shortage of other Catholic princesses for the young monarch to marry. France had quite an assortment of them which, though staunchly republican, her government would have been very glad to sponsor. As for the Kaiser, whose German Empire included mediatized dynasties both Catholic and Protestant, he had long been angling to make the King of Spain his nephew by marriage. The truth was that, compared with Portugal, which, through the English alliance, was tied quite firmly to the Entente side, Spain was still something of a floater on the diplomatic ocean. The bride of King Alfonso's choice could act as an anchor.

Edward VII's delight can be imagined, therefore, when it became plain that the 20-year-old monarch, impervious to his mother's en-treaties and indifferent to other continental offers, was quite set on an English marriage. At first, his fancy was caught by Princess Patricia, daughter of King Edward's brother, the Duke of Connaught, and a granddaughter, therefore, of Queen Victoria. But that romance came to nothing for the good reason that the princess was just as determined, as was her Spanish suitor, to marry the person of her choice, and her heart did not happen to be set on Don Alfonso, King or no King.† If his feelings or his pride were hurt, King Alfonso soon got over it. That same summer of 1905, when on his first visit to England, he pursued his quest on the spot and, this time, was more successful. At a ball given in his honour at Buckingham Palace, his Latin eye alighted on, and stayed on, Princess Victoria Eugénie, the daughter of

---

* Queen Maria Christina had, in fact, acted as Queen Regent until Alfonso was 16 years of age. He had been born King of Spain on 17 May 1886.

† In fact, she married a sailor, Admiral Sir Alexander Ramsay, and only died on 12 January 1974, aged nearly 88.

King Edward's youngest sister, Princess Beatrice of Battenberg, a widow. The Spanish King left England looking for all the world like a love-sick swain, and Princess Ena, as she was always known, did not seem disinclined. To avoid any repetition of the Princess Patricia affair, it was decided that the two young people should be given a good chance to get to know each other, away from all the constraints of court life. At this point, Biarritz comes into the picture, positioned as it was just across the mountain frontier from Alfonso's own kingdom. But this granddaughter of Queen Victoria and niece of King Edward had to be suitably and non-committally housed there, as well as properly chaperoned. She could not very well stay along the corridor from her uncle in the Hotel du Palais. The Villa Eugénie, with Sir Ernest and its other inhabitants in residence, would have been even less suitable.

There was, however, another house in Biarritz, the Villa Mouriscot, which had admirable royal connections. Indeed, it was the permanent home of Princess Frederica of Hanover, daughter of the claimant to that kingdom which Bismarck had obliterated and a kinswoman, of course, of King Edward. True, he had regarded her marriage to the Austrian Baron Alphons von Pawel-Rammingen* as something of a *mésalliance*, and whenever the couple were asked to Buckingham Palace the Court Circulars referred to 'Princess Frederica of Hanover and Baron von Pawel-Rammingen' as though they were two quite separate people on the guest list. But the good baron, who was devoted to his Hanoverian princess and took the loftiness of her royal relatives in good part, now came in extremely useful. It was arranged that Ena should go with her mother in January of 1906 to stay at the Villa Mouriscot and to remain there, for months if need be, until she had quite decided whether she wanted to become the Queen of Spain, with all that the choice entailed. The very day after she arrived, King Alfonso turned up at the villa, and started the speculation buzzing. Miss Minnie Cochrane, a lady-in-waiting to the Battenbergs, who was also with the party from England, was asked straight away whether there was a royal romance in the air. 'It will be decided here,' she replied, with a glance at the villa and the luxuriant gardens which surrounded it.

During the next few weeks King Alfonso came almost every day, usually arriving from San Sebastian at ten in the morning, having driven over the border at breakneck speed at the wheel of his Panhard phaeton car. As he had to return again by the 10.30 train each evening, it was a strenuous routine. But he was sustained by a breakfast of eggs, rump steak and potatoes, salad and fruit before leaving his kingdom, and with excellent lunches and dinners provided by Princess Frederica's

---

* Much of what follows was provided by his great-nephew of the same name.

old Hanoverian cook, Fräulein Zinska, at the Villa Mouriscot. For extra energy, there was always his favourite beverage, *zucharillos*, the white of egg beaten up with sugar and poured into a glass of water.

On fine days they could drive around the countryside (with Miss Cochrane as chaperone) or walk in the garden. But in bad weather which kept them indoors, the house, which was somewhat cramped for visitors on this scale, had its disadvantages.

Fifty years later, that bride-to-be of 1906 was standing, as the widowed Queen of Spain, in the same salon of the Villa Mouriscot where Don Alfonso had paid her his courtship. She told the present Baron Pawel-Rammingen:

> 'On that little corner seat they used to leave us discreetly alone. The King would edge a little closer to put his arm around my waist and crash! one of those countless framed photographs or other souvenirs and figurines with which the entire room was covered would go tumbling on the floor, making everybody look at us and ruining the moment completely. There were so many of these objects that, wherever one sat, it was almost impossible to avoid upsetting one of them with your elbow. More than once, this happened just as the King seemed to be on the point of putting the question, and we had to give it up until the next day. When, at last, everything was settled and we felt so wonderfully relieved, we took our revenge on all this bric-à-brac. We pelted each other with some of those superfluous bits of porcelain and smashed them up, to make quite sure they would not get in anybody else's way in future.'

Already by February of 1906, the bric-à-brac had been subdued long enough for King Alfonso to propose to Princess Ena, and to be gladly accepted. They seemed genuinely in love, and decided to mark the event and, at the same time, to say their thanks to the Villa Mouriscot, by planting with their own hands two fir trees side by side in the gardens. Both were still there and flourishing when the house passed out of the hands of the Pawel-Rammingen family after the Second World War.

It was now time for King Edward – who, back in London, had been receiving regular reports from his niece about the romance – to step into the picture. There had been unrest in the Church of England the year before when the possibility that Princess Patricia might become Queen of Spain had arisen. He knew this difficulty would arise again, coupled perhaps with wider criticism once an official announcement was made, for any English bride of King Alfonso's would have to abjure her Protestant faith and become a Catholic. To lessen any sense of public shock, he now decreed that this ceremony had best take place as quietly as possible and be held neither in England nor in Spain but in one of the smaller chapels at Versailles. In the meantime, Princess Ena was to return home to take the appropriate religious instruction from Monseigneur Brindle, the Catholic Bishop of Nottingham. This was done and, in due course, the King dealt firmly with protests from both the Protestant Alliance and the Church Association in Britain.*

On 6 March 1906, King Edward himself descended on Biarritz (preceded, by a few hours, by Princess Ena) to supervise the formal arrangements for the announcement. On Wednesday the 7th, while he visited Princess Frederica at the Villa Mouriscot (her self-effacing husband was not mentioned), Princess Ena had crossed into Spain, where, at the Miramar Palace of San Sebastian, she received her First Communion as a Catholic. Monseigneur Brindle had travelled specially down to officiate (another sop to British popular feeling). Before he set out for Nottingham again the next day, he had been decorated by King Alfonso with the Ribbon and Grand Cross of the Order of Isabel the Catholic for his services.

Two days later, on 9 March, the engagement was officially made public. The announcement from Madrid was conventionally formal. King Alfonso informed the Pope by telegram, assuring the Supreme Pontiff that the bride-to-be was 'happy to call herself a devout daughter of the Catholic Apostolic Roman Church'. A formal Bill was then read to Spain's Parliament, the Cortes, which allotted to Princess Ena, as Queen of Spain, the sum of 450,000 pesetas (then roughly £18,000) a year.

In the English newspapers the engagement was made known in the oddest way. Ena's mother happened to hold the post of Governor of the Isle of Wight and it was to the mayors of Newport and Ryde on that island that Princess Beatrice's legal adviser, Mr Paget Cooke, now sent telegrams officially announcing the engagement of their Governor's daughter to His Majesty the King of Spain. One would not be surprised had King Edward been behind this extraordinary approach as well. They could not have trodden more gently on British Protestant toes. The announcement was not even directed at the mainland.

Princess Ena was now bundled back to England to prepare for her wedding, while on 10 and 11 March, King Edward and King Alfonso exchanged visits at San Sebastian and at the Villa Mouriscot. There

---

* They called on the King to veto the match under the Royal Marriages Act of 1772. King Edward got out of this by declaring that, as Princess Ena belonged to the 'foreign' house of Battenberg, he had no right to interfere.

was a bizarre occurrence when they sat down to bridge at the Biarritz house. A brand-new pack of cards was unsealed and found to contain two kings of spades, to match the two kings at the table. They were proudly collected by the good baron and preserved in a special picture frame, to replenish his somewhat reduced stock of mementos at the villa.

The wedding took place in Madrid that 31st of May in the ancient church of Los Geronimos. Centuries-old state carriages and the blaze of heraldic uniforms made the procession look like a pageant from an almost vanished world. But a new world, which was determined to speed up that vanishing process, was also represented. An anarchist's bomb was hurled at the royal carriage as the newly married couple were driving back to their palace, and they narrowly escaped death on the spot. Others nearby were killed, and some of the blood was spattered on the bridal gown. Throughout this terrifying initiation into Spanish life and politics, the new Queen of Spain managed to retain her native calm, to the boundless admiration of the crowd. In fact, this bomb, which was intended to wipe the marriage out with both its partners, only served to give it an unexpected popular boost.

Writing about this 'dastardly and fiendish' event to the Tsar a fortnight later, the German Kaiser could not resist a dig at England. It was there, he told his cousin, that sanctuary was given to such anarchists, enabling these 'beasts' to 'live undisturbed and plot against the lives of anybody'. The Kaiser's asperity towards England was, of course, nothing new, yet he probably felt particularly sour at this moment. There was no denying that, in marrying his niece to the King of Spain, Uncle Bertie had gone one up on Berlin yet again.

There is no written evidence, either in the Royal Archives themselves or in the Battenberg/Mountbatten family papers, that King Edward had actively promoted this match for political ends. But there would seem to be little doubt that he welcomed it because of those same ends. Indeed, there is strong circumstantial evidence that he may have done all in his power to promote the romance from the sidelines for its diplomatic dividends. At all events when, three years later, another Battenberg girl, Princess Louise, was proposed to by another Iberian monarch, the boy-King Manoel of Portugal, and refused him, King Edward was highly indignant. He told her sternly that she should have a 'more patriotic approach to marriage, as it would be a great thing . . . if the Queen of Portugal was British'.* It is pretty obvious that Edward VII would have had that same 'patriotic approach' in mind with Princess Ena in 1906. Indeed, in the year that followed the

* Information kindly supplied to the author by Earl Mountbatten of Burma.

wedding, King Edward took a leading part himself in strengthening the political as well as the dynastic ties between London and Madrid.

This process was neither solely nor deliberately directed against Berlin. But in Spain, as in almost every other country of Europe where King Edward and his government were active, a plus for England meant a minus for Germany. One really cannot blame the Germans for confusing the aims with the results. At times, the English themselves cannot have been too clear about the difference. The Kaiser himself had scented high politics behind the Spanish marriage from the moment Princess Ena's engagement was officially confirmed. On the day of the official announcement, the German Chargé d'Affaires in Madrid, von Stumm, reported to Berlin on the growing belief in the Spanish capital that the forthcoming marriage, coupled with the talks King Edward was constantly having with King Alfonso in Biarritz, would lead to 'an imminent closer relationship between Spain and England'. On this dispatch the Kaiser wrote one of his vintage comments, which deserves to be quoted in full. A little of its vituperative impetuosity is unfortunately lost when translated:

'The whole of these pathetic and degenerate Latin races are becoming tools in England's hands, tools with which to block German commerce in the Mediterranean. Not only do we no longer possess a friend among them. This eunuch people bred from the ethnic chaos of ancient Rome hates us from the depths of its soul . . . they all betray us left, right and centre, and leap into the open arms of the English, who will use them against us! A fight right across the board between Teutons and Latins, with the former, alas, divided among themselves!'[1]

The Kaiser's fury can only be understood when it is realized how hard and how long he personally had been striving to draw King Alfonso into the German net. This campaign had reached what seemed to be a promising climax only four months before, when King Alfonso paid a visit to Berlin. Characteristically, the Kaiser had been trying, throughout the summer of 1905, to make the visit overlap with the great annual military review staged at the beginning of each September to commemorate the German Army's historic victory over the French in 1870. But his guest had refused, partly because of his sympathies towards France and partly because he had no desire to appear as 'a vassal of the Kaiser's'.[2] However, when King Alfonso did arrive for a week's stay in November, he found himself under heavy siege to become, if not a vassal, then at least a blood-brother in peace and war.

To begin with, there was the important matter of the young

monarch's hand in marriage, already rejected by Princess Patricia of Connaught but not yet, at that time, entwined with Princess Ena of Battenberg's. The Kaiser paraded the finest filly in the German stables, the 22-year-old Duchess Marie Antoinette of Mecklenburg-Schwerin. Admittedly, she was two years older than Don Alfonso. Yet she had all the other requisites that would be demanded: high birth, good looks, vivacious wit and, above all, the Catholic faith from birth and not by adoption. That, at any rate, was what the Berlin press, with semi-official nudges from on high, concluded after King Alfonso had been carefully led to the young lady's table and left there at a dinner-party given by the German Crown Prince.[3] With one voice, the Duchess was proclaimed the ideal person to become the next Queen of Spain.

The Duchess (and the Kaiser), of course, had no luck. Had they but known, King Alfonso was already in constant and tender communication with Princess Ena. Indeed, the very day he had left Madrid for Berlin, he had sent her an affectionate postcard to England. What is more, a copy of it had been made by a Spanish post office employee in the pay of a prominent newspaper editor who was nonchalantly producing it at a diplomatic party in Madrid on almost the same evening that the little German Duchess was being put into the paddock at Berlin![4]

Nor did the Kaiser have much more luck with his political overtures to his young visitor. These, according to King Alfonso's own account afterwards, were nothing less than hair-raising. After returning home via Paris (a route which the German Emperor had done his level best to persuade Don Alfonso not to take),[5] the King decided to confide in the French Military Attaché in Madrid, Cornulier-Lucinière. What the Attaché heard sent him straight to his Ambassador and then the pair of them straight to their cypher room, to get parallel secret reports off to the Quai d'Orsay and the Ministry of War in Paris.

The nub of King Alfonso's story was that, while in Berlin, the Kaiser had asked him outright whether, in the case of war breaking out between Germany and France, he would be prepared to concentrate enough Spanish troops along the Pyrenean border to immobilize French army units in the south. The inference that Germany might be contemplating an attack alarmed the French Government even more than the blatant attempt to drag Spain into any war on Germany's side. The Tangier crisis, and the Franco-German rivalry in Morocco which lay beneath it, was still acute, and the notion of a German invasion of France could never be dismissed out of hand.

But the most interesting thing about these urgent reports from Madrid was what happened to them when they reached Paris. M.

Rouvier (who had by now succeeded the fallen Delcassé as Foreign Minister) sent them on to the French Embassy in London with instructions to the Ambassador, Paul Cambon, to show them instantly to King Edward and discuss their significance with him *before* even informing any British Minister of their existence. His telegram enclosing the two reports[6] indeed ended with the words:

'A discussion with the King of England on the subject of this dispatch appears to me to be necessary and urgent. It would, I think, be premature to raise it with the British Cabinet.'

It was a striking example of the faith that continental statesmen had in the King's judgement, and also of their habit of placing him above his own constitution. In fact, when Cambon had his audience two days later, King Edward tried to put everything back into perspective. He immediately told the envoy to inform both the Prime Minister and the Foreign Secretary about the Madrid reports, while keeping King Alfonso's name out of it as the source. As for the reports themselves, the King felt that, on balance, they were only German bluff and military blackmail. But he did add:

'When we are dealing with anyone with a temperament like the Emperor William's, I realize one can never be sure about anything.'[7]

King Edward's assessment proved correct, and German invasion talk remained only words. Yet the Kaiser's frontal assault both on King Alfonso's domestic plans and on the alignment of Spain in any future European war does explain why Edward VII was so anxious to bring both into the Entente camp instead.

King Alfonso's Anglophile sympathies – never in real doubt – were finally sealed by the marriage. The political pact with Spain followed only a year later. Like the marriage, it was consummated with powerful help from King Edward. Moreover, this time he was present in person at the ceremony.

The setting was a bizarre one, the harbour of the Spanish port of Cartagena in April of 1907. The King had left Biarritz on the 6th and travelled by train across the neck of France to Toulon where the *Victoria and Albert*, with Queen Alexandra on board, was ready to set out on the annual spring cruise. Almost the only source of personal friction with King Alfonso had been King Edward's adamant refusal to visit the Spanish monarch in his own capital. Fears of anarchist activities in Madrid had been lively enough in King Edward's mind even before the wedding-day bomb tossed at his niece. But after that outrage, they were insurmountable. Despite what King Edward himself described as 'very pertinacious'[8] pressure from King Alfonso, exerted from September of 1905 down to January of 1906, the refusals from London were polite but adamant.

Yet though the King's life could not, the Cabinet all agreed, be risked, it seemed imperative for him to meet King Alfonso somewhere in Spanish territory, and for Spain herself to be put beyond Germany's eager political grasp. The Entente powers had already blocked two German thrusts: a project to lay an ocean cable line between Vigo and the Canaries,[9] and a more alarming offer to construct a naval dockyard and arsenal at Ferrol, *provided* both were leased for use by the German Navy after completion.[10] It was against this political background that the meeting afloat at Cartagena was contrived.

Anarchist bombs were not the only peril. By the time everyone reached the rendezvous on 8 April, a typhoid epidemic was raging in the port. Even the Military Governor of Cartagena, General Aldarve, had had to remain on shore in quarantine as two of his daughters were down with the fever. The warships and yachts, however, reprovisioned with large supplies of fresh water brought from the interior, merely retired a few extra cable lengths away from the shore. Then, for two days, the festivities, mixed with hard diplomatic bargaining, went on undisturbed.

King Alfonso had set the scene for both by transporting the treasures of his Madrid Palace to his yacht, reasoning that if his guest could not come to the capital, he would bring the capital to him. As a result, the *Giralda*'s state rooms were covered with priceless tapestries and oil-paintings from the Escorial on the walls and with the famous carpet designed by Goya on the floor-boards, making it a tiny palace on the water. Historic Spain was also represented by the great array of admirals present, each carrying his huge, gold-topped Malacca cane. The only person missing, and sorely missed, was Queen Ena. But as she was expecting her first child, there was cause for joy even in this.

Between the fireworks and the banquets, Hardinge slogged away with the Spanish Prime Minister, M. Maura, on the text of the draft declaration, approved by the King, which the English side had prepared. They were, in fact, acting for the French as well (with whom the Spaniards were not on very happy terms). The highly satisfactory outcome was an agreement by which France and England would exchange simultaneous and identical notes with Spain, pledging the maintenance of the *status quo* in the western Mediterranean.

This, in King Edward's view, was an excellent result but it was still not quite good enough. He accordingly made one of his fairly rare interventions into the detailed mechanics of diplomacy by persuading

YACHT DIPLOMACY

Edward and Alexandra at Cowes.

Left: Aboard the Czar's yacht, the King wears Russian uniform and Nicholas that of The Royal Scots Greys.

Far right: The Queen's camera catches the King and de Soveral on the *Britannia*.

Below: The King and the Czar at Reval in 1908. Among the party are Admiral Fisher and General French.

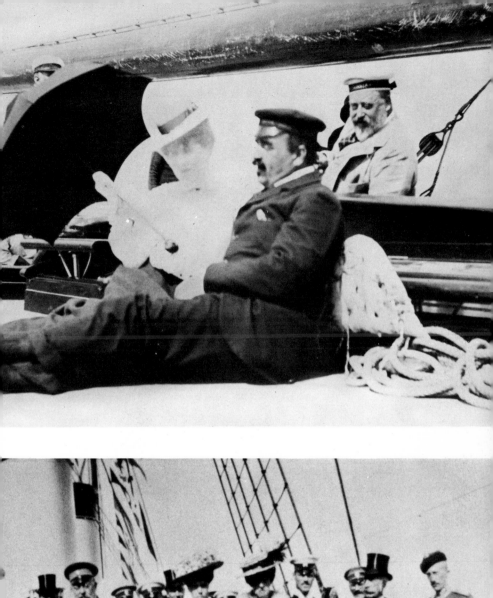

Above: 'Soveral Überall'.

Below: The King at Gaeta, 1907.

both his own government and the French to link their own notes to Spain by a third exchange of notes between themselves. In this way, he argued, Spain would be tied to the Entente as such, and not simply to its two partners. It was his own Cabinet that presented the King with the greatest trouble over this, but by 17 May, the Prime Minister had given way. As a delighted Paul Cambon, who gave full credit to King Edward, reported that day to Paris:

'The link is now established between the three governments . . . Spain has been snatched from German influence . . . yesterday's arrangement ties her henceforth to France and England.'[11]

One more contemporary verdict is worth giving. Commenting on that meeting, the Madrid paper *Correspondencia* wrote:

'Germany wants Don Alfonso's horse to ride two lengths behind the Kaiser's, whereas England puts King Edward's horse right alongside that of the King of Spain. This is something Spain will never forget.'

It would be difficult to find a more succinct tribute to the royal technique that had triumphed or a more pointed criticism of the imperial approach that had failed.

*   *   *

After that highly successful anchorage at Cartagena, the *Victoria and Albert* continued its diplomatic foray around the Mediterranean with a visit (via Malta) to the King and Queen of Italy at Gaeta. This meeting, as Hardinge makes plain,[12] had been entirely at Edward VII's initiative, and his Foreign Secretary had fallen in gladly with the plan.

There was no thought in the minds of either the King or his Ministers of drawing Italy right into the Entente's landing-net, as they had just done with Spain. But, to pursue the fly-fishing metaphor, the King was resolved to go on making trial casts over her head every now and again, just to register interest and to mark the response. This, and no more, was in his mind when he steamed into Gaeta harbour on the morning of 18 April. King Victor Emmanuel, who had arrived the evening before in his own yacht, the *Trinacria*, was there to greet him with a massive escort of twelve Italian warships and their accompanying torpedo-boats. So also was a vast concourse of visitors, who had thronged to the ancient harbour* from far and wide. Indeed, a spare bed in Gaeta was so hard to find that Sir Edwin Egerton, the British Am-

---

* Near Gaeta was the island rock of Circeo, where Ulysses and his companions had been confronted by the enchantress Circe.

bassador in Rome, had been searching for hours the day before, while Signora Tittoni, the wife of the Italian Foreign Minister, had to be given the spare room in the mayor's house.

Unhappily, it was pouring with rain when the *Victoria and Albert* steamed in, and though the Italians consoled themselves with the thought that 'the English were used to it', the weather put paid to any idea of going ashore. It also hampered the efforts of Queen Alexandra who, now as ever, wanted to get busy with her camera. But the rain could do nothing to dampen the gay mood on board the *Trinacria*, where the King and Queen of Italy gave a lunch for their visitors, with *rosbif à l'anglais* as the main course. The meeting was not quite without politics. Tittoni, who had been partly educated at Oxford and was a strong Anglophile as a result, talked freely with Hardinge about Italy's relations with England becoming closer without giving any offence in Berlin. Hardinge agreed that cordiality between London and Rome was directed at nobody and would hurt nobody, and they left it at that. King Edward seems, on this occasion, to have concentrated entirely on being affable to King Victor Emmanuel. He knew that the King of Italy had unpleasant memories of his meeting with the Kaiser aboard the *Hohenzollern* when the German yacht had anchored at Naples in March 1904, and was quietly emphasizing the same contrast in style which had proved so effective with Don Alfonso. According to Tittoni's enthusiastic words of farewell, King Edward made his point.[13] After lunch, the *Victoria and Albert* steamed off for purely private calls at Naples and Palermo. It left to the strains of the National Anthem, rendered from the ramparts by a chorus of English ladies who had come specially to Gaeta to salute their sovereign. They were observed to be in a highly emotional state, though perhaps, from the rail of the yacht, some of the raindrops were taken for tears.

Back in Rome the next day, Signor Tittoni was describing this highly successful lunch-party to the French Ambassador, M. Barrère. The Italian Minister passed this verdict on the King of England:

'King Edward is not in the least bellicose. His nephew gets terribly on his nerves, that is clear. But he himself wants to live on good terms with the Germans. He is, and this one cannot deny, the arbiter of Europe's destiny, the most powerful personal factor in world policy. And, as he is for peace, his overall approach will serve above all to maintain harmony between the nations.'[14]

Even allowing for Latin exaggeration and, in Signor Tittoni's case, for a mild dose of Anglomania, this was a remarkable tribute to be paid by a statesman in what was, technically, the opposite camp. It was in marked contrast to another comment on King Edward's Mediterranean activities which had earlier appeared in that famous Vienna paper, *Neue Freie Presse*:

> 'If the King of England has a meeting with the King of Italy without . . . any . . . obvious explanation, then it must be a question of serious politics. The fact that he travelled by sea from Spain to Italy does not lessen the deliberate . . . character of the meeting . . .
>
> 'This meeting at Gaeta is another facet of the burning jealousy between England and Germany . . . Everywhere, people are already posing the anxious question: what is the meaning of these continuous political efforts . . . whose object is the complete encirclement of Germany (*Deutschland gänzlich einzukreisen*)?'

The famous charge against Edward VII of 'encirclement' had had one of its earliest airings. Though at first only a distorted reaction to a luncheon-party on a yacht, it eventually assumed the proportions, and the strength, of a full-blown legend.

*   *   *

The fact is that, though King Edward called fairly regularly at Italian ports on these annual Mediterranean cruises of his (they were, after all, in the middle of that sea), only one occasion can be traced when he even as much as hinted that Italy might do something of which her German allies would not approve. This was when, meeting with King Victor Emmanuel again at Baiae near Naples on 29 April 1909, he took Signor Tittoni aside and, to the latter's astonishment, started talking of the alarming expansion being planned for the Austro-Hungarian fleet. This, King Edward indicated, was a development to which he personally attached 'great importance'.[15] It was a shrewdly planted blow, even if the Italian Minister did manage to duck it, for, at heart, Italy and the Habsburg Monarchy remained deadly rivals, especially in the Alto Adige and along the northern Adriatic.* Given the Austrian Emperor's unfailing courtesy and hospitality towards King Edward, it was also rather a cheeky blow. But it was, of course, the German Navy that, indirectly, he was seeking to contain.

That meeting at Baiae (his last with the Italian monarch) also saw one of King Edward's very rare slips of the tongue. In one of those impromptu toasts which, almost invariably, he brought off to perfection, he referred to the 'alliance' between England and Italy, when he should, of course, have used a more general word such as 'friendship'.

---

* Indeed, one of the Italian officers on the yacht told a member of King Edward's suite that the only reason he had joined the army was the chance of fighting the Austrians.

His Ambassador in Rome (now Sir Rennell Rodd) alerted Hardinge, who alerted Sir Edward Grey, who in turn alerted the Prime Minister, Mr Asquith. They all agreed, with the alacrity of those who rarely have the chance of such criticism, that it had been an 'unfortunate' or 'tactless' lapse.[16] Happily, on this occasion, the King's words did not get out into the press, or the uproar in Berlin and Vienna, the two capitals who really were allied to Rome, would have been considerable. As it was, the Kaiser could not fail to note that, at least in terms of personal standing, he had lost the competition with his uncle for Victor Emmanuel's favour, just as he had earlier lost it with Don Alfonso. The Italian monarch had devoted an entire day to his cordial meeting with King Edward at Baiae. Yet he only gave the Kaiser a very formal four hours – the bare minimum demanded by protocol for an allied sovereign – when the German ruler (whose yacht, the *Hohenzollern*, was as usual sniffing around in the *Victoria and Albert*'s wake) put in at Brindisi the following week.[17] The truth was, as one of King Victor Emmanuel's courtiers had complained after an earlier visit of the *Hohenzollern*: 'The Kaiser still acts as though Italy is still under his heel, as in the days of the Hohenstaufen.'[18]

It ought, perhaps, to be added here that King Edward's suite, well aware of the importance their master attached to keeping fellow-sovereigns like King Victor Emmanuel in the best of tempers, gave their own unfailing help. Here, for example, is an anecdote of Ponsonby's about that 1909 cruise:

'It was the custom for an ordinary mortal like myself, when taking a photograph of a monarch, to salute before pressing the catch and again after doing so, but no one had told me what the etiquette was when the monarch was the photographer and oneself was the victim. When the King of Italy expressed a wish to photograph me in uniform, I sprang to attention and saluted. When I heard his camera click, I again saluted. I consulted Seymour Fortescue* as to whether this was not overdoing it, but he said that with foreign monarchs you could never do too much saluting.'[19] By such tiny drops of oil was the wheel kept turning.

*　　　*　　　*

Finally, Greece, for the other Mediterranean monarch to be visited by Edward VII on these spring cruises was his brother-in-law, King George of the Hellenes. By the standards of most of those foreign royalties imported during the nineteenth century to sit on Balkan

---

* Naval Equerry to King Edward.

thrones, Queen Alexandra's Danish brother was a success. Moreover, in addition to being good at his job, he was also shrewd enough to have few illusions about its long-term security. Indeed, before accepting the throne, he had persuaded the great powers to guarantee him a 'pension' of £20,000 a year should he ever be toppled off it. When the King and Queen visited him at Athens in April of 1906 – King Edward, as usual, having bade farewell to Alice Keppel in Biarritz to greet his wife in Marseilles – the only danger that this might happen seemed to lie in Crete.

Since 1898 this island, nominally still part of Turkey, had been governed by Prince George, the second son of the Greek King and, therefore, yet another of Edward VII's royal nephews. Even backed as he was by British and other foreign troop contingents, the Prince's task as High Commissioner was no easy one, and he had repeatedly written to his 'dear Uncle' in England for advice and help as to how Crete's rival factions of Greek and Turk could best be kept quiet. Crete was a strategic Mediterranean island and Prince George was a fairly close relative, so, on both grounds, King Edward had always done all he could. His biggest contribution (and, in itself, another striking example of his power to influence British foreign policy) had come in June 1904, when his government was seriously considering withdrawing the British forces as part of a general military evacuation by the European powers concerned. In a memorandum that came as close as a constitutional monarch could get to a highly unconstitutional veto, King Edward declared that 'British troops *will not* be withdrawn from Crete, as Prince George leans on England more than any other country – and especially for advice.'[20] The Prime Minister, Mr Balfour, thought again, and British troops were not withdrawn.

But by the time King Edward landed in Athens two years later, things had changed, at least as regards Prince George, who by now was putting everyone's back up by trying to rule Crete like a petty dictator. His uncle discussed it with his father, and Hardinge discussed it with the Greek Prime Minister, M. Skouzes. They all agreed that Prince George would have to go, and go, three months later, he did. As a result, tranquillity returned to Crete.

However, the respite was short-lived and, three years later, it was the King of Greece himself who thought he might have to go (and claim that £20,000 pension), so violent had the Cretan quarrel grown between Greece and Turkey. Since the beginning of 1909, Queen Alexandra had been pressing King Edward about her brother's personal safety, and when a new crisis boiled up, in August of that year, the King stretched out a protecting arm accordingly – all the way from Marienbad. He telegraphed his government in England asking that the Royal Navy should stand by in case of emergencies in Athens. From Sir Edward Grey, a rather nervous message came back to the 'Duke of Lancaster' at the Hotel Weimar. While instructions were being given, he said, for units of the Royal Navy to be ready to embark the Greek royal family if necessary, the Foreign Secretary added that the impression should not be given that England was intervening in the domestic political crisis at Athens.

From Marienbad King Edward crisply replied:

'I never for a moment dreamt of my Government in any way interfering in the internal affairs of Greece. I only wished to point out the importance of the safety of King George, my brother-in-law, and therefore thought that the fleet should not be too far off.'[21]

As it turned out, the British warships were not needed. But the other Mediterranean powers, and above all Italy and Turkey, had doubtless taken note of the fact that they had edged closer to the Greek coast while the crisis in Athens was at its height.

Like the movements of his own navy, King Edward's presence each year, first at Biarritz and then on his spring cruises, served as a palpable reminder of England's interest in what went on both in the Iberian peninsula and throughout the whole Mediterranean area. The effect is impossible to quantify. No one can say what contribution his dynastic diplomacy as conducted, for example with the Kings of Spain and Italy, made to the behaviour of their respective countries when the First World War broke out. All that seems clear is that, without all King Edward's personal efforts, England's political position in the area would not have been so strong, or Germany's so doubtful, as they were when the test of alignments came in 1914. Diplomacy, as the King fully realized, was not just a matter of those great and spectacular heaves like the Paris visit of 1903. Much more often, it consisted of a series of small and hidden nudges, patiently planted over the years in the right place and at the right time.

PART V

1907-1910

1907-1910

THE AUSTRIAN OPTION

The most venerable among the doomed European dynasties, the Habsburgs, had now begun to enter King Edward's political calculations for the first time. His respect and affection for the Emperor Franz Josef had been deepening steadily throughout the forty-odd years they had known each other. But by 1907, with the hammers clanging ominously twenty-four hours a day from every naval dockyard in Germany, a practical thought arose as well. Perhaps the patriarch of Europe might succeed where the uncle of Europe had, so far, failed, and talk some restraint into the head of his German ally.

Ever since his accession, King Edward had been preparing the ground for a contact with Austria far closer than anything that had existed during all those pleasure-trips he had made to Habsburg domains as Prince of Wales. His immediate thoughts about Vienna after coming to the throne were largely personal. He still felt a warm glow of gratitude for the way the Austrian Emperor had behaved during the dark years of the Boer War. Alone among all the major European rulers (and almost alone among his own people), Franz Josef had steadfastly refused to indulge in that orgy of John Bull baiting which was sweeping the Continent. Indeed, he had openly condemned it. 'As far as this war goes, I am completely English,' he had once declared at a court ball, where plenty of foreign diplomats could hear him.

But to King Edward there was a principle involved, as well as gratitude. In the eyes of this great believer in human relations, a dialogue simply had to be opened between the greatest of Protestant and the greatest of Catholic courts. Admittedly they could not marry each other and share each other's beds. Yet that was no reason why, especially in this Republican-tinged age, they should not trust each other and share each other's thoughts.

It was primarily with this in mind that on 31 August 1903 Edward VII arrived at Vienna for his first (and only) visit to the Austrian capital as King. His four days there were mainly devoted to dynastic courtesies and, with two such past masters of the art as King Edward and the Austrian Emperor, it was not surprising that it was a resounding success. At a banquet at the Hofburg on the first evening, for example, King Edward sprang a complete surprise on his host by announcing his appointment as a Field-Marshal of the British Army. Normally such a move would have been signalled to Vienna in advance, as well as cleared with the political and military authorities in England beforehand. The King rode blandly over both conventions, calculating that the effect of the gesture would be immensely increased if he produced it instead like a conjurer out of his Hofburg wine-glass. He had calculated correctly. The old Emperor was enchanted both with the honour (which revived old Anglo-Austrian memories of the Duke of Marlborough's campaigns with Prince Eugene) and with the unorthodox way it had been presented. Determined to get even in this battle of flowers, he dispatched, the following morning, personal telegrams of comradely greetings to all other Field-Marshals on the British Army list. The Field-Marshals must have been surprised at this. So were the Emperor's personal staff. They had rarely seen that dry, gilded old stick who was their master unbend so far.

When it came to their talks *tête-à-tête*, King Edward had only two specific points to raise with the Emperor. The first was a delicate personal matter. The closest thing to a family link between the two men had been the marriage of the Emperor's only son, Crown Prince Rudolf, to Stephanie, daughter of Leopold of Belgium who, as a Coburg, was in turn related to King Edward. After the Crown Prince's suicide at Mayerling, his wife, after some flaunting of her widow's weeds, had eventually got herself remarried to a Hungarian nobleman, Prince Lonyay. King Leopold, who was as pompous as he was obnoxious, declared this match to be beneath his royal dignity and had cut off his daughter without a penny. She had been bewailing her plight up and down the Continent ever since. Though King Edward had neither the desire nor the justification to intervene at Brussels himself on her behalf, perhaps, he now suggested, the Austrian Emperor could put in a word for his ex daughter-in-law? It was a typical gesture of the King's, an attempt to help this remnant of an imperial ménage from which he had enjoyed so much hospitality in happier days. As far as we know, however, it led to nothing.

The only matter of international politics that King Edward raised at Vienna was the brutal treatment still being meted out by the Sultan of Turkey to his Christian subjects in Macedonia, and the turbulence in that disputed province of the Ottoman Empire generally. Concern over Balkan atrocities had, of course, become a traditional eccentricity with both the English crown and the English nation during the nineteenth century. Like condemnation of the slave trade, it was the touchstone of a liberal conscience in an illiberal world. But King Edward's own interest in Macedonia went beyond conventional outrage. He dreaded the policy of 'muddling through' which all the Great Powers, including England, tended to adopt. Indeed, later in 1903 he was to urge on his own Foreign Minister, Lord Lansdowne, the idea of a Royal Navy demonstration in Turkish waters, not as a prelude to any act of aggression, but simply to shake both Turkey and other European powers out of their apathy.

Before leaving Vienna, King Edward also discussed Macedonia with the Austrian Foreign Minister, Count Goluchowski. An account of that conversation has survived[1] which is of more than local interest. After urging on the Minister an energetic but pacific attitude towards Turkey in the Balkans, the King continued:

> 'Our policy is the same as yours: preserving for as long as possible the *status quo* in the Near East, and avoiding a war which would have incalculable consequences for Europe.'

In other words, the Habsburg Monarchy was the lid on the Balkan powder-keg, and could count on England's support as long as she kept that lid in place. It was an injunction the Austrians were to ignore five years later.

*   *   *

Having once re-established personal contact between the two dynasties, King Edward was determined not to let go. Reciprocal visits to London and Vienna were arranged for the heirs to the two thrones, and when the Archduke Francis Ferdinand came to England, the King piled compliment upon compliment over his head in an attempt to penetrate the armour of suspicion with which that difficult and ill-fated man surrounded himself. There remained the problem of the Emperor. Try as he might, the King could not lure the 73-year-old ruler to London. In these circumstances the King could hardly go himself a second time to Vienna. So, as a happy substitute for both sovereigns, there developed instead the habit of informal summer holiday meetings, either at Marienbad or, later, at the Emperor's favourite hunting spa of Bad Ischl in the Salzkammergut.

The first of these Bad Ischl meetings was in August of 1905, and such by now was the King's reputation for mixing politics with pleasure that premature rumours arose that King Edward was already trying to exert strong leverage on the Emperor. One of the worst among the contemporary offenders was that ponderous chatterbox, Baron Albert Margutti. As one of the Emperor's *aides-de-camp*, Margutti was in attendance at Bad Ischl whenever the two sovereigns met there, though he was not present at any of their private talks. According to him, it

was as early as this 1905 meeting between the two monarchs that King
Edward started on his supposed campaign of enticing the Emperor
away from the German alliance, offering him, in vain, unspecified
'compensations', and generally reducing the aged monarch to such a
state of nervous collapse that he could barely utter a word at dinner that
evening.[2]

This account, which was widely quoted, was every bit as wide of the
mark. King Edward himself gives quite a different impression of that
sunny afternoon when the two rulers took a pleasant carriage drive
together from Ischl to Halstatt. In a letter to Sir Ernest Cassel sent
from Marienbad on 17 August 1905, he writes:

> 'I stayed a few hours at Ischl on my way here to pay the E. a visit
> and found H.M. in excellent health and we had some very interesting
> conversations. Would to God that some other sovereigns were as
> sensible as he is! I was very much struck with Ischl, wh is a lovely
> place surrounded by mountains . . .'[3]

This is hardly the language, or the mood, of a man who has just
emerged from a frustrating struggle to persuade a stubborn old monarch to change his views about the world.

*   *   *

Their next Bad Ischl meeting, which took place on 15–16 August
1907, had much more than one leisurely carriage ride to it. For the first
time, an Anglo-Austrian political 'summit' was staged, with both the
two sovereigns and their chief diplomatic advisers coming together
for parallel talks. Mensdorff's diary makes it plain that this was all
done at King Edward's initiative. On 14 July 1907, the Austrian Ambassador in London noted:

> 'The King said to me last night that, if the Emperor is agreeable to
> him paying the Ischl visit, he would like to take Hardinge along and
> that perhaps Aehrenthal* might also be present at Ischl so that he
> (the King) could see him there and that, at the same time, Hardinge
> and Aehrenthal could have talks together. A splendid idea. I hope
> it comes about and I have telegraphed Aehrenthal today about it.'[4]

Six days later Mensdorff was able to record that the King's plan had
been approved in Vienna and that King Edward, who was personally
supervising all the arrangements, had had 'a lengthy conversation
about everything concerning Ischl' with him. Macedonia was still the
problem at the top of the agenda. No one could solve the riddle, yet

---

* Baron Alois Aehrenthal had succeeded Count Goluchowski as Austrian Foreign Minister
in October 1906.

no one dared to leave it alone. For two years past the particular debate between London and Vienna had turned on the merits or demerits of energetic intervention to clean up the administrative mess in the province.* The English case, of which King Edward himself was the most emphatic spokesman, was that Turkish injustice must be pulled out by the roots if the racial and religious violence was to cease, and with it the threat to peace in the Balkans. The Austrian case was that once you started tugging anything up by the roots anywhere in the Ottoman Empire you might well bring down the entire petrified forest over your head. It was the Habsburg Monarchy which would have to live with the consequences of such a collapse on its southern frontiers, and so, not unnaturally, the Austrians were reluctant to let well-meaning English liberals dictate the pace for them.

This argument had been going on, through ambassadors and special envoys, throughout the summer of 1907. Aehrenthal, it was clear from the exchanges, was a much tougher and more determined customer than his easy-going predecessor. He also seemed much more of an ambitious careerist (or *Streber* as his own countrymen would have put it) and, as such, more prickly and more suspicious. Yet no one at the Foreign Office had ever met him as Austrian Foreign Minister. It was high time, in King Edward's view, that somebody did. And as Sir Edward Grey could never be persuaded to budge outside Britain, that meant the King's own diplomatic *alter ego*, Charles Hardinge.

Bad Ischl was an incongruously delightful place at which to discuss Turkish atrocities and Balkans powder-kegs. The little spa (asthma and bronchitis; complaints of the heart, liver and gall-bladder; nervous diseases, skin diseases, rheumatism and even female sterility, were all said to be curable by its mud baths and sulphur waters) was one of Austria's most genial holiday resorts, prettily perched, nearly 1500 feet up, in a ring of forest-clad mountains. The Emperor adored it, as much and probably more than any spot in his vast and varied domains, and it was those mountain forests, rather than the medicinal waters, which drew him here summer after summer.

When, in 1514, his ancestor Maximilian I had bestowed a new coat of arms on the rebuilt town (the original 'Markt Ischl' had been laid waste by fire), they had picked a chamois astride two mountain tops, with a green tree sprouting from a third peak in front of his nose. Bad Ischl was, and is, a hunter's paradise, and stalking, next to work, was the ruling passion of the old Emperor's life. He had visited Ischl every

* Since 1904, an attempt had been made, at England's insistence, to internationalize the administration of the disputed province, with British, French and Italian officials working alongside those of Russia and Austria.

summer as a child and, for a wedding present, had been given a splendid residence there, still standing today and still known as the *Kaiservilla*. In and around this sprawling, yellow-washed house, both the imperial family and the imperial Ministers gathered each July and August. It was to the *Kaiservilla* that King Edward and Hardinge were now heading on 15 August 1907, direct from that relatively harmonious meeting with the German Emperor at Cronberg.

A bigger contrast with Cassel the previous day, when the German Emperor had roped in 50,000 soldiers from their summer manœuvres just to line the streets in his uncle's honour, could hardly be imagined. There was scarcely an Austrian soldier to be seen as, a few minutes before midday, the carriage which had collected the two monarchs from Ischl's little railway station entered the town. Instead, the streets were lined with men from the local voluntary fire services (a prestigious organization in the Austrian countryside); with workers from the nearby salt mines at Hallein; and, most delectably, with two hundred of the prettiest girls of the neighbourhood, each dressed in her traditional peasant *dirndl*. As the carriage passed, they bombarded it with little bouquets of alpine flowers. The schoolchildren of Ischl joined in, as did all the English and American holidaymakers, complete with their Kodak cameras, who had flocked to the town for the event. Their shouts of 'Hip! Hip! Hooray!' mingled with the 'Hochs!' of the Austrians. A total of twelve gendarmes at the salute represented the only vestiges of formality along the entire route. It was more like a village carnival than a diplomatic conference. King Edward, beaming with delight, was in his element.

The carriage stopped at the Hotel Elisabeth where a suite of rooms on the first floor (the same King Edward had used on his brief visit two years before) had been made ready for him again. In the hall, another bunch of alpine flowers awaited him, this time presented by the small daughter of the hotel proprietor, Herr Seeauer. King Edward found the child so irresistible that he swung her high up in his arms and kissed her on both cheeks. One wonders how long it was before she was allowed to wash her face.

The King, like most royal visitors, had been accommodated at the hotel because the *Kaiservilla* had been designed, doubtless deliberately, without any large apartments for state guests. Indeed, at lunch that day, they did not even use the dining-room of the main building. The meal was taken instead in the so-called 'Cottage', a tiny house in the wooded park high above the villa with a magnificent view of the surrounding mountains, stretching right away to the distant Dachstein. It was a family lunch, given only for the two monarchs and the Emperor's other royal visitors and relatives (the Duke and Duchess of Cumberland, as the House of Hanover was now known, had arrived, together with Princess Marie Louise of Baden, Princess Olga of Braunschweig, and the Prince of Schleswig-Holstein).

While this select gathering were eating at the 'Cottage', Aehrenthal and Hardinge were taking each other's measure* at a lunch for eighteen more ordinary mortals (the so-called 'Marshal's Table') served in a private room of the hotel. The two men had an hour together, while the Emperor and King Edward set out for a carriage drive by themselves to Laufen.† When the monarchs got back from their drive (still, from all appearances, in the best of spirits) each received the diplomatic adviser of the other – Hardinge going for a private talk with the Emperor, while the Austrian Foreign Minister came to the King.

Bad Ischl took over again from Macedonia in the evening. As a treat for King Edward (who had asked to hear it) the little spa theatre had staged a special performance of Oskar Strauss's operetta, *The Merry Nibelungs*. Then, after supper, the two sovereigns went for a carriage ride around the town, which was not only bathed in moonlight but lit by the glow of thousands of lamps and torches up and down the valley and by three hundred mountain fires ignited at the same instant on the peaks above. As at Rome and Paris in 1903, the fine weather just held out for King Edward. When he left the next morning for Marienbad, having embraced the Emperor warmly on both cheeks twice at the railway station, it was pouring with rain, and the *dirndls* had to stay indoors.

In that relaxed, almost idyllic setting, it would have been almost impossible to quarrel, and difficult not to agree. Indeed, official communiqués and commentaries issued afterwards all spoke of 'complete accord' having been reached in the policy of the two powers towards Macedonia, both as regards the nature of the reforms to be launched in the province and the measures necessary to combat terrorism. It was far from a permanent arrangement; but then, nothing even remotely connected with an international witches' cauldron like Macedonia ever was or could be. But what the Bad Ischl talks had succeeded in doing was to clear the air between England and Austria and remove – for the time being at any rate – Aehrenthal's image as an intractable trouble-maker. As Mensdorff noted:

---

* It was not the first time they had met. They had both served together in St Petersburg as Ambassadors for their countries.
† This had been the Emperor's own suggestion. It disposes of any idea that he was dreading another private political 'hammering' from King Edward.

'Very good news yesterday from Ischl about the King's visit. I'm extremely happy about it. May the good Lord help things further along so that A. loses his distrust of England and that they get used to him at the F.O.'[5]

King Edward had done his best to help things along in this respect. On the morning of his departure from Ischl it was announced that he had bestowed upon Baron von Aehrenthal the Grand Cross of his Royal Victorian Order.

Other matters had, of course, been touched on during the Bad Ischl talks. They had examined the state of the world in general and of the Mediterranean in particular, where the Austrians were somewhat suspicious about King Edward's constant initiatives. But what there was still no sign of in August 1907 was any attempt by either the King or Hardinge to drive a wedge between Austria and Germany. All the evidence we have points, indeed, the other way, as would be natural in this particular summer when the tension between London and Berlin had, for once, noticeably slackened. Referring to the successful meeting that had just taken place at Cronberg, Aehrenthal told Hardinge that he 'rejoiced in the improvement of Anglo-German relations'.[6] For their part, German diplomats reporting on the Ischl meeting, quoted King Edward as saying that any weakening of the alliance between Austria and Germany 'would be a great misfortune'.[7]

Given the climate of the time, there is no reason to suppose that either statement was insincere. It was the following year that brought the change. For when the Austrian Emperor and King Edward met the next time at Bad Ischl, England's relations with Germany had sunk to their old depths of rancour and mistrust. The flashpoint had moved from Macedonia to Berlin. As a result, Austria as the ally of Germany seemed, for the moment, even more important to England than Austria as the peace-keeper of the Balkans.

* * *

The Anglo-German barometer started to plunge again in February of the new year, though the fall was only registered by the public at large a month later. It was the same old storm at sea that started things off.

On 16 February 1908, the Kaiser took the unusual step of writing[8] directly to the First Lord of the Admiralty in London, Lord Tweedmouth, about what he called the 'battle royal' being waged between the Press of the two countries over Germany's Third Naval Act. (As this measure provided for another twenty per cent increase in future German expenditure on the fleet, there was plenty to argue about.)

UNCLE OF EUROPE

Left: King Alfonso XIII of Spain and Princess Ena of Battenberg at their betrothal in Biarritz 1906.

Below: Windsor 1907 – *l. to r.* The Queen of Spain, Edward VII, The Empress of Germany, Emperor Wilhelm II, Queen Alexandra, The Queen of Portugal, The King of Spain and the Queen of Norway.

Above: The King and the Emperor Franz Josef inspecting their stags at Lobau.

Above right: King Edward takes Franz Josef for his first ride in a car at Bad Ischl, 1908.

Below: Edward VII at Marienbad – among the group round the King are, *l. to r.* King Ferdinand of Bulgaria, George I of Greece, the Marquis de Soveral and Sir William Harcourt. Among the crowd to the left of the Royal group can be seen Abbot Helmer and Hakki Pasha.

Above: An informal visit to the Kaiser in 1906.

Below: Berlin at last – the State Visit in 1909.

Though the Emperor had privately informed King Edward about his action forty-eight hours beforehand, he does not appear to have told his own Chancellor what he was up to. King Edward was none too pleased about this latest venture of his nephew's. In a reply sent a week later, he said:

> 'Your writing to my First Lord of the Admiralty is a "new departure", and I do not see how he can prevent our press from calling attention to the great increase in the building of German ships of war, which necessitates our increasing our navy also.'[9]

This was, in fact, precisely the argument which the Kaiser had been trying to deal with in his letter to the British Minister. The German Navy, he told Lord Tweedmouth, was being built solely to protect Germany's 'rapidly growing trade'. It was directed against nobody, least of all against 'the great British nation with its world-wide Empire and its mighty navy which is about five times the size of the German navy'. In any case, any nation had the right to build as many warships as it felt it needed. If England suddenly announced she wanted '60 or 90 or 100 battleships', that would not affect Germany's plans, and all she asked in return was to be left in peace to construct whatever fleet she needed.

So far, no great harm had been done. There was nothing new, and certainly nothing menacing, in the Kaiser's words. Moreover, his uncle, who had himself sent personal messages directly to foreign statesmen (Delcassé, for example), was really in no position to object too strongly to the Kaiser using the same methods, especially as he had given him advance warning.

But now Tweedmouth committed an appalling indiscretion. Though he showed the Emperor's letter both to King Edward and to the Foreign Secretary, Sir Edward Grey, and presumably got from both some guidance as to how he should react, he enclosed in his reply to Berlin 'a proof of the paper I have prepared as my statement to be issued next week to Parliament, with the detailed estimates for the year 1 April 1908 to 31 March 1909'.[10] In other words, the Kaiser was being given the details of England's forthcoming naval programme before they had even been announced to the House of Commons. This particular aspect of the matter, which would have caused a national uproar, fortunately never got out at the time. The Cabinet shrewdly made a clean breast of it in confidence to the leaders of the Conservative Opposition (Balfour and Lansdowne) and everyone agreed to close ranks and keep Lord Tweedmouth's blunder a secret.

But the noble lord himself, who was, in plain language, going dotty,* ensured that the exchange of letters as such would leak out by gossiping about them at clubs and dinner-parties for days on end. He even read the full text of the Kaiser's letter to the assembled company when staying for the weekend with Lord Rothschild at Tring.[11] Not content with that, he also circulated its contents among his lady friends (who seem to have been numerous), and finally gave the original to one of them as a personal keepsake. The King and his Cabinet were at their wits' end to know what to do. Finally, Hardinge was instructed by the Prime Minister to try and get the letter back and was authorized to offer up to £200 to the lady in question. But, for once, this accomplished negotiator failed in his mission. His go-between, the Prince of Teck, reported that the owner of the letter was evidently not short of cash as she appeared to have bought herself six new hats shortly before he called on her. The Kaiser's letter eventually found its way back into the Admiralty archives, though by another means and in a later reign.

King Edward's main concern was that this embarrassing correspondence should not be made public, as *The Times* had demanded on 6 March. When that danger had passed, it was with an audible sigh of relief that he wrote to Hardinge: 'Thank God, the German Emperor and Tweedmouth incident is at an end.' But the King's fears that Lord Tweedmouth was not quite right in the head were only strengthened when, a few weeks later, he received the most extraordinary invitation from him. On 20 May, the Minister† wrote to inform his sovereign that he had 'about 15 young unmarried nieces' and suggested that the King should join them in staging a little amateur variety show, 'very bright but very proper', with supper afterwards. Compared with this effort, even Lord Tweedmouth's letter to the Kaiser seemed rational, though, as the King commented with a sorrowful shake of the head, the one did help to explain the other. It had also been a rare incursion of buffoonery on to this sombre Dreadnought scene.

The spring and summer of 1908 only brought more friction. The German mood was not helped, for example, by the elaborate official reception given to President Fallières of France when he came to London in May. Though not as well liked, either by the King or by the British public, as his genial predecessor, M. Loubet, the new President was fêted as though he were an official, as opposed to an informal, ally. Hardinge felt obliged to assure the German Ambassador Count Metternich, that 'England was not even thinking of getting involved in European alliances'.[12] One could hardly have blamed this

---

* He died of a brain disease the following year.
† He had by then been removed as First Lord of the Admiralty but still held the relatively harmless post of Lord President of the Council.

congenitally gloomy envoy if he regarded that assurance as being, in the circumstances, little more than word play.[13]

There was also a personal uncle-nephew aspect to the Fallières visit, for it once again underlined the fact that King Edward had still not balanced the protocol scales by going himself to Berlin. After that relatively successful visit which the Kaiser had paid to England in November of 1907, King Edward had, in fact, accepted a return invitation to the German capital for himself and his wife in the spring of 1908. But the New Year had barely dawned before the visit was called off by the Palace; the King's distaste for the whole idea, coupled with Queen Alexandra's positive hatred of 'Berlin and the Prussians', were thought to be the real reasons.[14]

Another problem that had come to a head that summer was finding a suitable replacement for Sir Frank Lascelles as British Ambassador in Berlin. It was very much of a parallel issue to that of the royal visits, not only because it intimately concerned the two sovereigns in person, but because it was very much linked, in the Kaiser's mind, with the importance King Edward really attached to the German court and capital. Ideally, the Kaiser would have liked Lascelles to have stayed on at the post, for he had found him increasingly sympathetic, amenable and pro-German. For the same reasons, however, both King Edward and the Foreign Office had decided that it was time for Sir Frank to go. Yet who could be found to replace him on this bed of Prussian nails?

Their first choice was Fairfax Cartwright, then Minister in Madrid. He knew the Kaiser personally from his earlier service as an Embassy Secretary in Berlin; moreover, both his mother and his grandmother were of German blood. On 16 June 1908 the King had pointed all this out to the Kaiser in a letter sponsoring the proposed appointment, which he hoped would 'find favour'.[15]

It found precious little. If Lascelles had to be moved, the Kaiser replied, could he not be replaced by someone outside the diplomatic service altogether, 'somebody . . . who plays a prominent part in your country. For instance, a person of the calibre of Curzon, Cromer, Rosebery or Bryce'. A future Viceroy of India, a retired suzerain of the Nile, and both of them peers of the realm and renowned public figures: they were the Kaiser's idea of the British envoy whose credentials he would like to receive. Needless to say, it did not appeal to the Foreign Office who, already in the Edwardian age, had become enough of a professional closed shop to want to keep the best appointments for its own men. Nor, one may be sure, would any of the Kaiser's four candidates themselves have relished dancing attendance on him at his Potsdam court, which managed to combine stuffiness with hysteria.

The matter could best be thrashed out by a personal meeting between the two sovereigns, and this was what King Edward now suggested. The annual journey to Marienbad came in handy again: could his nephew give him 'a *rendezvous*' on 11 August at Friedrichshof? He could arrive in the morning and stay till after dinner, on his way to visit the Emperor Franz Josef at Bad Ischl to congratulate the Austrian monarch on the sixtieth anniversary of his reign. The Kaiser replied that he would be delighted, and so this important meeting came about.

Its importance was not, of course, to be measured simply by the relatively minor problem of finding a new British Ambassador for Berlin but by much more heated discussion over far greater issues. The Cabinet were now so alarmed by Germany's unchecked naval expansion that they agreed to use the Cronberg *rendezvous* as a forum to thrash it out with the Germans once and for all; furthermore, the King's Ministers suggested that he himself should act as their principal spokesman. The King was quite agreeable to the first part of the proposition which he had, in fact, helped to inspire. His friend and financial adviser, Sir Ernest Cassel, who had a finger in all sorts of political pies, had long been urging him to try for some top-level settlement of the naval dispute, and the Cronberg meeting seemed a natural opportunity. But, from the very first, King Edward was none too happy with the second part of his government's proposal, namely that he himself should do the talking.

Despite this royal reluctance, the Cabinet went ahead with their idea. On 23 July, Sir Edward Grey furnished his sovereign with a long guidance memorandum for use during the forthcoming discussions with the Kaiser, and followed this up with another document, delivered on 6 August, just before the King's departure.[16] Both papers only repeated the arguments that British Ministers, Grey prominently among them, had been putting to the Germans for months and even years past. The central strategic point was the familiar one that the crushing superiority of Germany's land forces was only acceptable to English eyes as long as that army could not be transported overseas. Once Germany acquired the sort of fleet capable of doing that, no one in England could sleep soundly in their beds, whatever they might think about German professions of friendship.

*　　*　　*

The King arrived at Cronberg as planned on the morning of 11 August, accompanied only by the familiar trio of Hardinge, Ponsonby and Sir Stanley Clarke, his personal physician. Almost immediately he went into a *tête-à-tête* session alone with the Kaiser, from which the two sovereigns did not emerge until three hours later. All the time, King Edward had in his pocket those memoranda on the naval problem, for use as he thought fit, as and when the occasion arose. But when the meeting finally broke up, King Edward gave Hardinge the rather surprising news that though he had had an extremely cordial talk with his nephew about every subject under the sun, they had never managed to get down to the one subject that really mattered. The King had once tried to bring it up by mentioning that he had with him a paper setting out his government's official views on the naval problem. But, uncharacteristically, his nephew had displayed not the slightest curiosity over the document, nor indeed any interest in pursuing one of his very favourite topics.* In view of that, the King told Hardinge, he had felt it unwise to press the matter further and risk clouding such a friendly exchange. Hardinge was also informed by his sovereign, just before they went into luncheon, that it was now up to him to tackle the All-Highest on the vexed question.

It was an intriguing situation. Perhaps for the first time in history, a British sovereign had been officially briefed by his government to act as their spokesman in a matter of the highest political and military importance. But that same sovereign who in 1903 had sailed clean away from the Foreign Office on a self-charted diplomatic course of his own, now made no real attempt to lead the field, and seemed content to leave this tricky bit of navigation to a professional pilot. Why? Was he, in plain language, ducking it?

For answers, we can only draw on inferences rather than evidence. Though supremely self-assured, and endowed with both a powerful personality and a strong temper, King Edward always loathed scenes. In diplomacy, he can be likened to an eighteenth-century swordsman who welcomed any duel but abhorred a common brawl. Moreover, in any debate on something so highly technical as battleship construction, King Edward faced the prospect of seeing his nephew make circles round him.

But perhaps more important than all this to King Edward was the fact that his nephew, tiresome or not, was a fellow-sovereign and that all matters relating to armed forces fell, second only to decorations and the like, pre-eminently within the personal preserve of sovereigns. If the King himself could have made so much fuss, only the previous year,

---

* Commenting, a month later, on a report from London that, at Cronberg, the original intention had been for King Edward to discuss the naval problem, the Kaiser wrote ironically: 'How nice that would have been!' (G.P., Vol. 24, No. 8247, Kaiser's annotation.)

about the Coldstream Guards military band having its itinerary cancelled without reference to him as 'head of the Army', how could he,
in all conscience, now try and tell the Emperor of Germany how many
warships he should or should not build for his own navy? King Edward
was prepared, in an emergency, to ignore constitutional restraints which
were not of his creation. But he could not ignore monarchical restraints,
because these were the rules of his own exclusive club.

Just how formidable the Kaiser could prove to be on naval questions
was something Sir Charles Hardinge learned to his cost that same afternoon. We are fortunate in having the fullest accounts of their conversation from both the English diplomat and the Kaiser himself.[17] If, as
usual, the Kaiser's version may well have been somewhat over-pitched,
the Englishman's report may equally well, on this occasion, have
suffered from rather too much under-statement. The truth about this
very heated and very important talk at Cronberg probably lies somewhere between the two descriptions.

Hardinge (whose account is not contradicted at this point by the
Kaiser) started off with a firm but calm statement from the British side
of the poisonous effects German naval construction was having on
Anglo-German relations. He expressed the fears in London that 'if the
present German programme is completed, the German navy will, in a
few years' time, be in a superior position to the British navy as regards
the largest type of battleship, and British supremacy at sea would thus
be endangered'.

The two men then embarked on a detailed examination of the
German fleet build-up (which would have left King Edward, aptly if
only metaphorically, quite at sea), and here the first clash came.
According to Hardinge's bland account, which does not have a single
direct quotation in it, the Emperor had maintained that, in a year's
time, England would still have sixty-two first-class battleships to
Germany's twenty-four, so why all the fuss? Hardinge had questioned
this comparison, saying the Emperor must surely be talking about
'every obsolete vessel that could be found floating in British harbours'.
The Emperor had thereupon sent for a copy of the latest German
Nauticus handbook to prove his assertions; and, when the volume was
put in front of him, Hardinge had commented only that he 'wished
very much' he could accept the statistics it contained, which would be
studied.

This should be compared with the Kaiser's sentence-by-sentence
report sent to his Chancellor, Prince Bülow:

He: [Hardinge] Your construction of Dreadnoughts is now being

so accelerated that . . . say in 1912 you will be equal or even
superior to us.

I: That's complete nonsense. Who has been telling you such
ridiculous tales?

He: It is not nonsense, but authentic evidence from our Admiralty.

I: It's still nonsense, even if your Admiralty produces it . . . I
can prove I'm right out of the *Nauticus*.

He: You cannot have figures which are more authentic than those
the Admiralty have given me.

I: Your documents are wrong. I am an Admiral of the British
Navy which I know all about and understand better than you,
who are a civilian with no idea of these matters.

After all allowances have been made for embellishment and exaggeration, that sounds a not unlikely description. Indeed, the Kaiser had
used some of the same language only the day before, in a talk with Sir
Frank Lascelles. There is no mistaking the authentic flavour of the
All-Highest.

This also applies to what, in the Kaiser's account, was the most
dramatic exchange of all. It does not even receive a mention in Hardinge's version, who merely records that he had hoped 'moderate
counsels will prevail' when the two men made their final observations
on future naval expenditure.

But, according to the Kaiser, the climax to their argument went
like this:

He: Can't you put a stop to your building, or build less ships?

I: Germany's maritime construction is measured by her own
interests and needs. It is defensive and is directed against
nobody, least of all against England . . .

He: But an arrangement must be reached to limit this construction.
You must stop or build slower.

I: Then we shall fight, for it is a question of national honour and
dignity.*

At this point, Hardinge, according to the Kaiser, went brick-red
with embarrassment, bowed, and asked the Emperor to regard his
last words as a regrettable lapse in a private conversation, which he
hoped would be forgiven and forgotten. If the tone and the language
had been anything like what the Kaiser recorded immediately afterwards, the apology was certainly called for. It was no way, especially in the year 1908, for a Foreign Office official who was not even

* This sentence the Kaiser spoke in English, to give it added emphasis.

a Minister of the Crown, to address the Emperor of Germany.

According again to the Kaiser's account, Hardinge did his best to make up for the afternoon's unpleasantness when they all met again that evening. He was, the Emperor noted, 'a changed man, friendly, relaxed, and spicing his conversation with anecdotes'.* And when the Emperor (who was certainly playing his part in the process) conferred on him after dinner the Order of the Red Eagle, Hardinge solemnly declared that it would be preserved in his home 'as a holy relic'. He pointed out that his own grandfather had also held this same order for services to Prussia when, serving on Wellington's staff in the Napoleonic campaigns, he had been seconded to Blücher's command.

On the surface, therefore, harmony had been restored by the time King Edward and his party left Friedrichshof Castle. Between all the earnest talk about Dreadnoughts and *détente*, two personal matters had been settled to the apparent satisfaction of both monarchs. It was agreed that the King, accompanied by Queen Alexandra, would pay his long-debated and oft-postponed state visit to Berlin early the following year. The tedious question of the new British Ambassador to Berlin had also been decided. It had already been conveyed to the Kaiser that, while Cartwright's name was being withdrawn, there was no prospect of someone like Cromer or Curzon being offered in his place. The Foreign Office had been racking their collective brains for weeks to find a candidate eminent enough to meet the Kaiser's demands. They had proposed another career diplomat, Sir Ralph Paget, from their own ranks, and had even, in desperation, sponsored a distinguished outsider in the person of Lord Selborne. Finally, after nothing had come of either suggestion, they worked out an elaborate game of envoys' musical chairs, as part of which Sir Edward Goschen would be switched from Vienna to Berlin.

Nobody, at heart, was too happy about this arrangement. According to his colleagues, Goschen himself, despite his German origins,† was positively miserable. The German Foreign Office seems to have been satisfied with his selection, though without feeling unduly flattered. Their strictly professional attitude was best summed up by a memorandum sent by State Secretary von Schoen to Chancellor Bülow at the time. This described Goschen as 'not an important diplomat but . . . an open and honourable character, not disposed in any way to intrigue'.[18]

---

* It is only fair to point out that, according to Hardinge (*Old Diplomacy*, p. 162), it was the German Emperor who first introduced the friendly spirit at dinner.
† The Goschens were a family of Leipzig printers who moved to England early in the nineteenth century to make their homes and careers there.

The Kaiser, who had started all the fuss in the first place, did one of his characteristic somersaults. When he had first heard Goschen's name mentioned, more than a fortnight before the Cronberg meeting, he had shown a distinct lack of enthusiasm, even muttering some offensive remarks about the diplomats' origins.[19] King Edward can have been none too confident, therefore, at putting the name forward when the two monarchs met. However, to his delight, his nephew now declared Goschen to be just the man he would have selected himself. King Edward might have been excused for wondering why, in that case, the Kaiser had not included the name in his earlier list of candidates. However, the main thing was that the matter, which had been a major irritation throughout the summer, was settled at last.

All this, of course, was but small compensation for the fact that the central aim of the entire meeting from England's point of view had failed. They had not come to Cronberg just to get a new ambassador installed at Berlin, convenient pretext though that had been, but to trim those menacing black silhouettes lined up in the German naval tables. Here, there had been worse than deadlock. Quite apart from rejecting every argument and disputing every figure put forward from the English side, the Kaiser had served clear notice that the German fleet was his business and he would brook no interference. There was no prising him loose. At Cronberg, the English chisels had broken off. What was to be done?

*   *   *

It was probably only at this point that the King and Hardinge finally decided to tackle their next hosts, the Austrians, on the subject, and ask them outright for their help. They knew, of course, that it would not come as news to the Austrians that the fleet-building programme of their German allies had become a nightmare in London, and that the English would snatch at anything within reason to banish it. But there is no record of any such appeal to Austria being discussed either between the Palace and Sir Edward Grey or within the Foreign Office before the King set out on this eventful progression to Marienbad. The visit to Bad Ischl, where they were now heading, had been arranged long before Cronberg, and quite independently of it. Mensdorff's diary makes it plain that it was King Edward who had again taken the initiative to turn his next midsummer meeting with the Austrian monarch into another political gathering. But this had been seen solely in the context of Anglo-Austrian relations, and with the hope of improving the still strained relations between London and Vienna over Macedonia.

It was on Good Friday, 17 April 1908, that the King had summoned his friend, the Austrian Ambassador, to Buckingham Palace to start things in motion. Describing the audience in his diary two days later, Mensdorff wrote:

'[The King] talked about politics and of the coolness between Grey and Aehrenthal. There is no doubt that our Aehrenthal rubs people up the wrong way . . . The King would like to visit the Emperor in Ischl again . . .'[20]

Early in July, as the event drew nearer, Germany did, it is true, come into King Edward's calculations, but only in the familiar context of balancing one royal visit against another. Thus on 8 July (after the King had expressed the wish to make the Ischl meeting as festive as possible, in view of the Emperor's Diamond Jubilee) it was the Austrian monarch who had himself suggested moving the whole thing to Vienna, with a banquet at the great summer palace of Schönbrunn. But when Mensdorff put this up to King Edward, he would have none of it.

'The King, however, prefers Ischl,' he recorded.[21] 'If he goes to Schönbrunn, the Emperor William would be offended that he is not also going to Berlin . . .'

That little episode, in itself, again disposes of stories that King Edward's 1908 visit to Austria, like his trip the previous year, was a calculated move to break up the Austro-German alliance. Had that been his aim, surely he would have leapt at the suggestion of a second state visit to the Austrian capital, where all the German federal princes had recently been received in a display of Teutonic solidarity. There were other, and typically human, reasons for the King's choice. He liked Bad Ischl, both the place and its atmosphere. Moreover, he was on his way to Marienbad and this was much the simplest and pleasantest way of getting there. So Ischl it was, on 12 August 1908.

There were a number of changes, not all of them improvements, compared with 1907. This time, King Edward's train came directly to Ischl, instead of stopping at nearby Gmunden,* and the little village station, in contrast to the previous year, was now almost blotted out under military uniforms. A long line of officers, headed by the then Commander of the 14th Army Corps, Archduke Eugene, was assembled on the platform among all the other dignitaries.

A lot of other people had tried to get on that platform as well, to watch the King of England arrive. He was due at 9.45 and, early that

* This had, in fact, been the King's suggestion, a thoughtful move to spare his venerable host the fatigue of an extra journey.

morning, the local stationmaster noticed that a record number of tickets had been sold for trains all of which were due to leave Ischl for Aussee or St Gilgen between 10 and 11 a.m. It was a gallant effort on the part of hundreds of would-be gate-crashers to the ceremony, but it failed. Fifteen minutes before the royal train was due in, all other services were suspended and the station was cleared by police.

The saddest comparison with 1907 was, however, the weather. Instead of the brilliant sun of the previous August, it was raining in buckets as the Emperor, wearing a British Field-Marshal's red uniform (with the blue band of the Garter under the chain of his Golden Fleece) greeted his guest with a warm embrace. Either due to the rain or to the greater formality of the occasion, the King this time had to go without that curtseying line of local damsels, dressed in their pretty *dirndls*, along the route. As some compensation, a contingent of young English and American holidaymakers (principally girls) had again turned up from all over the Salzkammergut to cheer him.

The weather brightened up after lunch, and the political talks themselves seemed to reflect this mixture of sunshine and showers. On the personal level, for example, Aehrenthal* seemed to grow much more relaxed and understanding over Macedonia. The position there, and throughout the Ottoman Empire, had anyway just been transformed by the successful revolt, in July 1908, of the so-called 'Young Turks' against the Sultan. It looked as though that old Anglo-Austrian dispute about the nature and the pace of reforms in the Sultan's Balkan domains might now be settled by new and more liberal measures enforced by the Turks themselves.

So far so good. But when they came to the matter which had just cropped up again at Cronberg, it was a different story. Different, but still neither as depressing nor as dramatic as most Austrian versions would have us believe.

It is not known precisely how, when, or in what words the King tackled his host on the subject of German fleet building, for no first-hand account of their private conversations was ever made. Tradition has it that King Edward made his move on the afternoon of his arrival, after the two monarchs had rearranged their programme in view of the suddenly improved weather. The Emperor suggested a carriage ride, like the previous year. But as they had been discussing automobiles at luncheon, and as King Edward had noticed one or two of these machines, belonging to distinguished visitors, driving around the village, he managed to persuade his host to take one of these instead.

* Mensdorff's comment on this: 'With all his merits, Aehrenthal lacks suppleness, and insists on his views like a pedagogue. He has no *suaviter in modo*.'

Horses and trains had always been good enough for the Austrian Emperor until this day. But now, in the eightieth year of his life and in the Diamond Jubilee year of his reign, he was talked into taking his first-ever ride in a motor car. The vehicle in question was not, as is often said, King Edward's own; that was, as usual, making direct for Marienbad from England under the care of the faithful motor-engineer, Stamper. It was, in fact, a Züst,* belonging to Prince Leopold of Bavaria, who had brought it with him to Ischl.

The excitement as the old Emperor prepared to mount this gently simmering steed outside the Hotel Elisabeth was intense. A beaming King Edward asked him to climb aboard first. 'No, no, you go ahead. You know much more about it,' came the cautious reply. Installing the Emperor alongside his guest was a performance in itself. Blankets were put aboard in case it should prove too chilly for him, and Princess Gisela (wife of Prince Leopold and the Emperor's own daughter) offered him cotton wool for his ears. Then she and her son climbed in behind the two monarchs and off they all went for a spin down the Traun Valley to Weissenbach, reaching, on one stretch, a speed of more than thirty miles an hour.

The whole trip lasted eighty minutes. That would have given plenty of time for the King to have tackled the Emperor with his most pressing problem, but somehow it seems unlikely. Apart from the chauffeur, the Emperor's daughter and grandson were also in the vehicle, which was hardly therefore the place for a highly delicate and secret discussion. Moreover, one cannot envisage King Edward trying to take advantage of his venerable host in this way. Despite his frequent expressions of astonishment and pleasure during the drive, the Emperor was probably concentrating on getting back to Bad Ischl in one piece. It was really not the moment to bring up Dreadnoughts.

Sometime that day, the question was brought up, however, and the King is known to have got a courteous but firm refusal to his plea for Austrian intercession in Berlin. Whether, in this connection, the old Emperor really used the words† 'After all, I am a German prince' cannot be proven. Even if he did, they do not tell the whole story. To His Apostolic Majesty, being a 'German prince' meant being a sovereign of the vanished Holy Roman Germanic Empire as much as being a blood brother to the Hohenzollern Kaiser in Berlin. That being

---

* A joint German-Belgian product which has long since vanished.
† One often quoted source for this does not exactly inspire confidence. The Emperor is said to have confided this to his favourite ghillie on a deer stalk at Ischl, who in turn passed it on to a friend, Eugen Ketterl, the Emperor's valet. (See Cissy Klastersky, *Der alte Kaiser*, Vienna, 1929, p. 140.) The Emperor was just about the last person on earth who would discuss state secrets with a gamekeeper.

said, however, he obviously would have been reluctant, as would any Austrian ruler of his day and age, to do anything which might impair that alliance with Germany which, for exactly thirty years now, had been the central pillar in the foreign policy of his Empire.

But there may well have been other factors in his refusal to intervene; and if, as is possible, he mentioned these to King Edward, they would have been all too convincingly familiar to his guest. The Austrian Emperor, like the King of England, was a stickler for the rights of fellow-sovereigns, and it went against his grain to question them on what they did about their own armed forces. Furthermore, Franz Josef knew far less about naval affairs than King Edward did, and unlike the King, was not even very interested in them. Though Austria-Hungary was herself building up quite a respectable fleet,* its ruler was never to be seen in naval uniform, and was happy to leave this side of things to his heir, Archduke Franz Ferdinand. Indeed, it is unlikely that either the Emperor or his guest knew that, while they were talking naval matters in 1908 at Bad Ischl, the first air pilots the Austro-Hungarian Navy ever possessed were receiving their initial training – in England. The King was not a technical man, the Emperor not a maritime one. Even had they wished, they could not have probed very far into the intricate problem of the German fleet.

If we are still in the dark as to what exactly passed between the two monarchs about Dreadnoughts, we have two accounts, one from the Austrian side and one from the English, as to how their political advisers tackled the subject that day. Hardinge's version, as usual, is the blander of the two:

'As regards the question of Germany's naval armaments, I pointed out to Baron d'Aehrenthal that Austria, the ally of Germany, could contribute effectually to the cause of peace by acting as a drag on any ambitious naval policy which the German Government might be tempted to pursue. In reply to his inquiry as to whether the question of naval armaments had been discussed at Cronberg, I told him briefly what had passed. He finally admitted that the attitude of the German Government, if persisted in, might, in a few years' time, bring about a very critical situation between England and Germany which it was to everybody's interest to avoid. He wished, however, to tell me privately, and as a friend, that he had received certain

---

* The Monarchy went into the Great War six years later with a fleet of fifteen battleships, nine cruisers, eighty-six destroyers and torpedo boats (some of the latter British built), and six submarines. Sokol, *Seemacht Oesterreich* (Molden, Vienna, 1972), is the best modern work on this subject.

indications of an undercurrent in Germany which was strongly opposed to the German naval programme, and this current, fortified by the serious financial difficulties which the German Government had now to contend with, was daily growing in strength, and he was hopeful that . . . the German Government might find themselves compelled to modify the law which they had made . . .'[22]

The Austrian version of the exchange is given by Mensdorff. It tells basically the same story but suggests that the talk was rather more lively than Hardinge indicates:

'The English approaches to achieve a sort of understanding with Germany over her naval programme were rejected. I regret that greatly, for in my opinion that is the only basis on which an agreement could be reached. Aehrenthal told Hardinge . . . that at least the pace of [German] armaments construction would not be increased as he didn't believe the naval programme was really popular in Germany and, quite apart from that, Germany's financial position was none too brilliant . . .

'For the rest, we are loyal allies of Germany and shall remain so. We take no part in her squabble with England over the fleet and so on. That is no concern of ours. A. spoke in this vein both to Hardinge and to the King and, I believe, met with understanding.'[23]

That final phrase of Mensdorff's is very important. Neither in these contemporary eye-witness accounts nor in any later material[24] is there a scrap of evidence to support stories that King Edward attempted to 'break up the Austro-German alliance' at Ischl, much less that he departed in a bad temper after having failed. The problem of the German fleet had certainly cast its shadow over Bad Ischl as it was doing over the European scene in general. But the two sides had clearly reached an agreement to differ over it. This is reflected in the mood of all concerned as the meeting broke up. The King left for Marienbad on the morning of 13 August in the best of spirits and after a very warm leave-taking from his host. Hardinge, in his report, summed up the visit as 'entirely satisfactory in every respect'. Quite independently, for he was by then in Wiesbaden, Mensdorff echoed this verdict: 'The course of the meeting was emphatically satisfactory' [*entschiedend zufriedenstellend*].

Strong, if indirect, confirmation of this mood is given by King Edward himself, in what was possibly the only account he ever put on paper of the Cronberg and Ischl meetings, and certainly the only one to survive. This was in a letter,[25] hitherto unpublished, which he sent to Sir Ernest Cassel from Marienbad on 15 August 1908 when both events were still quite fresh in his memory. The King had evidently not written to his old friend and regular correspondent for several weeks, for he begins by bringing Sir Ernest up to date with the close of the season in England.

The King's letter then continues:

'On 10th I departed for Cronberg and spent the whole following day and evening in the company of the G. Emperor . . . who I found in excellent health and spirits. He and I had a long talk on international politics but the subject of the Navy was not broached! [*Sic*] though Sir C.H. had some conversation with him and I regret to say that he did not see his way to diminish his ship building programme. This I greatly regret as we have no other alternative but to go on building.

'I arrived at Ischl on morning of 12th and found the kind old E. of Au. in the best of health, and much interested as well as agitated regarding the news from Constantinople . . . I took the Emperor for his first motor car drive wh he greatly enjoyed, and will I hope in the future not object to that mode of locomotion . . .'

And that is all. The King had great trust in Sir Ernest's judgement and discretion, and there were few major developments, on the political as well as the financial scene, he did not discuss with him. That letter had passed on the central point about the failure of the Cronberg meeting, which was information of a highly secret nature. It seems inconceivable that had the King been smarting under the failure of another and closely related mission at Bad Ischl, he would not have gone on in his letter to say so. Instead, he continues with a report on the Marienbad weather, which was 'bitterly cold and wet alas!' on his arrival, but which had just 'greatly improved'.

The conclusion, as regards Ischl, seems to be that the King was in no way downhearted over this first approach to the Austrians because neither he nor the Foreign Office intended at the time to let the matter rest there. The démarché of August 1908 was visualized only as the first step in a campaign to reduce Austria's supposed subservience to Germany in what was thought to be the general interest of European peace.

M. Crozier, the French Ambassador in Vienna, got it dead right when he reported:

'However cordial the personal relations are between the two sovereigns, the Ischl meeting did not produce any political results. The Emperor of Austria did not feel able to intervene with his [German] ally on the delicate question of [naval] armaments . . .

'King Edward is said to have aimed at achieving at least a modification in the political line of the Monarchy . . . He will certainly try again . . .'[26]

And it was precisely this gentle long-term effort (as opposed to one quick and brutal wrench) that Hardinge himself had indicated to Mensdorff before they parted company at Ischl:

'Hardinge told me he was very glad to have talked things over with Aehrenthal, as our advice concerning Germany might well be important in the years ahead.'[27]

Whether this gradual pressure to soften up the rigid Dual Alliance into a more elastic form of Austro-German Entente would ever have succeeded so long as a conservative monarch like Franz Josef sat on the throne, and a dedicated pan-German like Conrad von Hötzendorf remained in charge of his army, is a debatable point. From King Edward's point of view, it was obviously worth a try.

* * *

What stopped his campaign dead in its tracks was something totally unexpected and quite unconnected with either Germany or Dreadnoughts. In October of 1908, the Habsburg Monarchy both astounded Europe and endangered its peace by announcing the formal annexation of Bosnia and Herzegovinia, those two Balkan provinces of the Sultan's which, under the international Berlin agreement of 1878, had been allotted to Austria to occupy and administer.

Characteristically, King Edward's first reaction was one of dismay and indignation that the monarchs of Europe appeared to be letting each other down, for that, in his view, would spell the end of everything. Long before the Austrian *fait accompli* of October, he had responded in this fashion to what he held to be mere rumours of trouble ahead. The services which that remarkable journalist Mr Wickham Steed performed for King Edward as purveyor of special intelligence at the annual Marienbad court have already been mentioned. But Mr Steed's greatest 'scoop' was destined to fall on obstinately deaf ears.[28]

On 15 August 1908, only forty-eight hours after the King had arrived in Marienbad from Ischl, Steed warned his sovereign that Austria was 'getting ready' to annex Bosnia-Herzegovinia. The King dismissed the idea. His first reason was that such a move would upset the whole of Europe. But his next, and equally emphatic objection, was that the Emperor Franz Josef, whom he had just left, had 'given him no hint of anything of the sort'. And when Steed cited an unnamed senior Austrian official as his source, a man who had approached him specially on behalf of the Austrian Cabinet to sound out his reactions to the plan, King Edward would still have none of it. 'Surely the Emperor would have said something to me,' he protested, and that was that.

In fact, the decision to go ahead with the annexation was taken by the Joint Council of Austrian and Hungarian Ministers in Vienna just when Steed had predicted – three days later, on 18 August 1908, the Emperor's seventy-eighth birthday.* That it was intended in some measure as a Diamond Jubilee birthday present seems beyond doubt. But there was much more to it than that. During the second half of the nineteenth century, the Austrians had been driven from most of their Italian domains to the south, and also ousted by Bismarck from the German Confederation to the north. Only to the south-east, against a Turkish Empire that was in far worse shape than its own, could the double-headed Habsburg eagle still use its talons. But, like so many attempts to display masculine virility at an advanced age, this belated effort of the Austrians to prove their manhood turned out to be costly – in energy, reputation and after-effects. For, whatever the background to the annexation, in diplomatic terms it was, and remained, an act of irresponsible folly. In the eyes of every other power in Europe, whether ally, friend, or rival, the Habsburg Monarchy had one supreme role to fulfil: to prevent the Balkan powder-keg from overturning or igniting. Now, after decades of caution, she had made one unprovoked move that threatened to do both.

It was not until 29 September that Franz Josef wrote personal letters to all his European fellow-monarchs and Heads of State, informing them of Austria's impending action. Not only was King Edward made, in this way, merely one recipient among many of an imperial round-robin. To rub salt into the wound, he did not get his letter actually delivered to him by Mensdorff until the late afternoon of 5 October, forty-eight hours after the President of France had received his. Mensdorff's trepidation when he arrived at Balmoral can be imagined. But on that day, the King was even more distraught than offended. Lord Redesdale, who was one of his house guests at the time, wrote later in his memoirs:

'No one who was there can forget how terribly upset he was. Never did I see him so moved . . .'[29]

The King's first two questions after he had skimmed the Emperor's message went right to the bone. Had Austria squared this with the Turks, from whom she had seized these provinces? How was Russia,

* How far the Emperor was himself aware of the plan, and the likelihood of its being adopted, when talking to King Edward at Ischl the week before, is a debatable point.

her main rival in the Balkans, likely to react?* Then came the recriminations which, in Mensdorff's own words, the King somehow managed to put 'in the friendliest form'.[30] Did Austria realize she had threatened the peace of the entire Continent? Could she not understand that, whatever justifications she pleaded, a major international treaty like that of 1878 simply could not be 'unilaterally put aside' in this way?[31]

It was in precisely this same tone, filled more with sorrow than anger, that, on 11 October, King Edward replied to the Austrian Emperor:

'I cannot help conveying to You all my regrets at seeing such a decision taken, particularly at a moment when developments in Bulgaria have already complicated the situation among the Balkan states.

'Furthermore, I will not hide from You how much I hold to the principles laid down in the Protocol of 17 January 1878, according to which the Treaty of Berlin should not be altered without the consent of the contracting powers . . .'[32]

Not until the beginning of April 1909 was that series of crises which Austria had precipitated – connected one to the next like a diplomatic firecracker – finally mastered. The Turks, who had lost two provinces on paper which they had not possessed for thirty years in reality, were eventually bought off by Vienna for the sum of £2,500,000 Turkish pounds. Serbia, who had long dreamt of uniting those same provinces into a new South Slav bloc under her own control, was not so easy to satisfy. The fact that Russia stood, menacingly if rather ditheringly, behind these aims, gave that European dimension to the crisis that King Edward had dreaded from the start.

For weeks after the Turks had been paid off, Serbia, hoping for full Russian backing, demanded her compensation from Vienna, and demanded it in territory, not in cash. But the Habsburg eagle, relishing the first kill it had made for many a long year, was in no mood to let anything go. At the end of February 1909, it looked indeed as though the Austrians were determined to march on Belgrade and 'annex' the Serbian capital as well. It was only after Germany had persuaded

---

* By a private pact struck at Buchlau on 15 September 1908, Aehrenthal had agreed to support Russia's drive to open up the Mediterranean to Russian warships in return for her support over the Annexation. The outcome of this deal between the two political adventurers was that Aehrenthal got what he wanted but gave Russia nothing in return. A desperate Isvolsky went to Paris and London for reassurances. King Edward could not open the Bosphorous Straits for him but, in the interests of Anglo-Russian friendship, he did open all doors in the capital, including those of Buckingham Palace, where he gave a great dinner in the Russian's honour on 19 October.

Russia to climb down and after Sir Edward Grey in London had produced more compromise proposals[33] that, on 31 March, Serbia formally accepted the new situation, and the threat of war subsided.

Far from putting the Austrians up to their coup, as was suspected in London at one time, the Germans knew as little about it beforehand as the English did, while the Kaiser was every bit as offended as King Edward had been at being left out. 'I personally, as an ally, am wounded in my deepest feelings that I was not taken, in the slightest degree, into H.M.'s [i.e. Franz Josef's] confidence,' he minuted to Bülow when he heard the news.[34] Nonetheless, at the height of the crisis three months later, the Kaiser was writing to the Austrian Emperor:

> 'Germany's place will, for sure, always be at Austria-Hungary's side, a solid bloc in the heart of Europe which the other powers would be well advised not to tamper with.'[35]

That fateful 'blank cheque' eventually handed over to Austria by Germany was being drafted. Historians are still disputing who was more to blame when it was used five years later – the banker who had issued it, or the customer who had cashed it.

THE RUSSIAN PACT

It is a moot point whether King Edward, who had a relaxed approach to religion, felt that he ruled by divine right as well as by dynastic right. But, unlike so many of his fellow-sovereigns on the Continent, he was convinced that no prerogative existed which could justify any monarch of the twentieth century trying to stop the clocks of progress. Reactionary rule dismayed and appalled him wherever it prevailed. This was not merely because, as in the case of the Turkish treatment of Macedonia, it ran counter to his own liberal views; he was also well aware that, in the long run, it could only weaken the institution of monarchy as such. The Romanovs had been his main worry on this score ever since his first visits to St Petersburg as Prince of Wales, and there was still no sign that the Russian royal house had come to its political senses. Yet, when the next mortal blow was struck against the European old order, the victim came from a dynasty both more modest and more innocuous.

On 1 February 1908 a group of left-wing assassins opened up with rifle fire from both sides of the road on an open carriage in which the Portuguese royal family were returning to Lisbon. King Carlos and his eldest son, the Crown Prince, were killed outright. Don Manoel, the younger son, was wounded in the arm. Quite possibly he had been saved from worse injury by the brave action of his mother who, with an instinctive eye on the succession, had stood up to shield him. Queen Amélie herself escaped unhurt.

The news struck London, and Buckingham Palace in particular, like a bombshell. Count Mensdorff, the Austrian Ambassador, wrote in his diary:

'Everyone shaken to the core here. The King and Queen feel it very badly. Everything has been cancelled.'[1]

For his Portuguese colleague, the Marquis of Soveral, the catastrophe had brought with it the moment to use both England's ancient alliance with Portugal and his own intimate friendship with King Edward for all they were worth. Fearing that civil war would sweep his homeland and that the monarchy itself would be toppled, he pleaded both with the Foreign Office and with the King for a British naval squadron to be sent to the Tagus to steady the situation.

A copy of a letter found among Soveral's papers when they were opened sixty-four years later perhaps shows us why he made this particular request in that dark February of 1908. The letter, on Foreign Office stationery and marked 'Private and Confidential', was from the then Prime Minister, Lord Salisbury, to Sir Hugh Macdonell, and was dated 15 March 1896. The extract which Soveral had carefully preserved ran:

'It is impossible to speak with absolute certainty about future events, but I cannot imagine the case in which we should not be willing to send a fleet to the Tagus if such a measure were likely to help in maintaining the Throne of Portugal against foreign or domestic insurrection.'

Precisely that threat to the House of Braganza had now arisen, but those British warships of which Lord Salisbury had spoken were not forthcoming. The Foreign Office's case in 1908 was that, to make a naval demonstration in the turmoil following upon King Carlos's murder might easily make matters worse and result in the deposition of his successor, the boy-King Manoel, as well as threaten the lives of the thousands of British subjects resident in Portugal. Edward VII seems to have been in two minds, torn between prudence and loyalty, and between the cool reasoning of his Ministers and the passionate pleading of his friend.

Soveral kept a private log of the telegrams he sent back during this period to his government. They suggest that, at one point during that first week of February, King Edward favoured positive and even drastic action. Thus, late on 5 February, Soveral cabled Lisbon that the King had just had him to dine alone at Buckingham Palace, to discuss the crisis. Edward VII had specially asked him, Soveral stated, to tell the boy-King that 'England will help Portugal with all means at her disposal'.[2]

That was clear and uncompromising language and it is unlikely that King Edward would have used it just to cheer up his distraught friend. But either the King had, for once, promised more than he could deliver, or he was later persuaded by his Ministers of the inherent hopelessness of the Braganza cause. Elsewhere in Soveral's papers there is a letter which the King wrote to him later that same month which shows how the mood at Buckingham Palace had changed. One sentence in it reads:

'The attitude of the [Portuguese] people is not favourable towards a Monarchy and I fear the country is rapidly drifting towards Republicanism!'³

Indeed, the very evening after that dinner alone with Soveral, King Edward had given a hint of this when talking with a few friends at Lady Savile's. Soveral was not there but Mensdorff was, and the Austrian noted in his diary two days later that the King had been 'distinctly pessimistic about conditions in Portugal'.⁴ On 8 February, as a mark of the particular grief King Edward felt about the murders, he, accompanied by Queen Alexandra and other members of the royal family, attended a Requiem Mass in King Carlos's memory at St James's Church, Spanish Place.* It was the first time since the Reformation that an English sovereign had worshipped in a Catholic Church in Britain. The Protestant Alliance duly protested. Their Protestant King duly ignored the protest.⁵

The rest of the tale is told in Soveral's own record of messages to and from Lisbon. The gaps are as significant as the entries. There is nothing more about the crisis until 13 February when he receives instructions from his government to ask for the services of 'six English detectives' to help the Portuguese police track down the assassins. Four days later there is a note that Mr Quinn had left for Lisbon – alone.⁶ Superintendent Quinn, personal bodyguard to King Edward himself, was not a person to be trifled with. But he was not quite the same thing as a squadron of British warships. Moreover, there is no indication in Soveral's official telegrams – which are silent about the crisis from this point on – that Mr Quinn ever found the murderers.†

*   *   *

The disaster to the Braganzas turned all royal eyes in Europe once again towards the Romanovs. One Russian Emperor, Alexander II, had been assassinated already within living memory. The grandson of the murdered man, the King's nephew Nicholas II, still ruled in open

---

* They had already attended a memorial service held at St Paul's Cathedral the day after the murder by King Edward's own wish.
† A British naval squadron did eventually enter the Tagus, but only as a courtesy visit in July of the following year, when the position of the Portuguese monarchy seemed a little more secure. That same November, the young King Manoel himself visited England, to be given a state banquet at Windsor and the Order of the Garter. Yet King Edward's growing pessimism about the Braganza's prospects for survival proved only too well founded. Within a year of the Windsor Castle banquet, a republic was declared in Portugal, and King Manoel came to live in exile in England. Princess Louise of Battenberg must have been glad that she had resisted her uncle's efforts to make her marry him. She ended up, in fact, as Queen of Sweden.

conflict with the liberal forces of his empire. Moreover, especially after the murder in Lisbon, he was now barricaded in his palaces in a state of permanent siege against the anarchist elements who stood on the dark fringes of Russia's reformist movement. Would he too go the way of the King of Portugal, and of his own ancestor? And if he did, would the Romanov Empire itself collapse, and bring general chaos with its fall? That summer, King Edward was able to go and see something of the problem for himself.

The *Victoria and Albert* had been on some remarkable political forays since Edward VII became its master. But the most extraordinary of all its voyages began at 3.50 p.m. on 5 June 1908, when it cast off from the Port Victoria Pier at Sheerness – royal standard flying at the main mast, the Admiralty flag at the fore, and the Union Jack at the mizzen – to take the King on his only visit as sovereign to Russia.

Everything was strange about this expedition. To begin with, this was the first time in history that an English monarch was to set foot in Russia. Moreover, it was not Russian *terra firma* that he was going to set foot upon even now, but only Russian territorial waters that he was going to anchor in. Because of the new flare-up in anarchist activity, his nephew had suggested that they should hold their meeting afloat, in the Estonian harbour of Reval.* Finally, despite the fact that this was supposed to be only a family gathering, the *Victoria and Albert* had never sailed for anywhere with so many political guns on board. True, the purely private aspect of the cruise was reinforced by the presence of Queen Alexandra (whose sister, Marie, was now Dowager-Empress of Russia), and that meant that there were ladies-in-waiting on the yacht as well as the usual clutch of male courtiers and equerries. But on the 'business' side the King had with him (apart from Hardinge, in his usual role of diplomatic mentor) Sir John French, the Inspector-General of the British Army, as well as the First Sea Lord, Admiral Sir John Fisher himself. Not unnaturally, all over Europe they were scratching their heads in perplexity. In Berlin they were frowning as well, and none more so than the Kaiser.

For years past, he had been pounding the Tsar with advice as to how Russia should behave on the world stage. With flattery and gifts, with exhortations and innuendoes, the Kaiser, like some imperial Svengali, strove to establish a hypnotic influence over the Russian ruler. There is little doubt that he sometimes succeeded. Indeed, on one occasion he had got agreement for a Far Eastern port for the German Navy out of Nicholas II by a few casual remarks exchanged between the monarchs

---

* Later renamed Tallin.

when they were alone on a tennis court and resting between sets.*

In the aftermath of Russia's defeat by Japan, the Kaiser had moved in for the kill, using the technique so successfully practised by his English uncle. He arranged a meeting with the Tsar for 23–24 July 1905 at the port of Björkö, on the Gulf of Finland, the two sovereigns to travel there in their respective yachts, ostensibly for nothing more than a look at the midnight sun and an exchange of family gossip. In confirming the arrangement, the Kaiser had stressed that he would be coming 'as a simple tourist'. Thus duped, the Tsar had arrived at Björkö in his yacht the *Standart*, with no thought of politics in his head and nothing more than sailors and an aide-de-camp on board. But when the *Hohenzollern* came to drop anchor alongside the Russian yacht, the 'tourist' had brought with him not only State Secretary von Tschirschky of his Foreign Office but also, in his pocket, a Russo-German treaty of alliance, all ready for the Tsar's signature.

There was nothing outlandish about the idea of a treaty as such. According to Bülow, the Tsar himself had suggested one the previous autumn, in a sudden fit of alarm after the Dogger Bank flare-up with England. A brief draft for a mutual defensive pact, consisting of only three clauses, had accordingly been drawn up in Berlin and forwarded to St Petersburg by the Kaiser, who added a considerably longer and more flowery covering letter of his own for the Tsar. What was, however, outlandish about this Björkö venture was that the Kaiser had not even discussed the new project with his own Chancellor (whom he had been at pains to leave behind), let alone clear the revised terms of the draft treaty with him. The Kaiser was determined to land this *coup* in his own individual style, as the wretched Tsar was to discover.

As we only have the Kaiser's own account (first made public some twenty years afterwards) for what happened when the two rulers were alone in their state-rooms, the customary grain of salt must be taken with his words. On the other hand, they were penned with all the events still vivid in his mind, and even the theatrical touches he describes match what we know of his character and temperament.

In a long, handwritten report[7] to his Chancellor, who was unsuspectingly enjoying a holiday at his favourite summer resort of Nordeney, the Emperor began with his first conversation, held with the Tsar before dinner on the German yacht. Unless the Kaiser was simply inventing things, the two cousins appear to have had some severe things to say about that English uncle of theirs, to whom they were always sending such affectionate letters:

* The Chinese base of Kiao-Chou which Germany had seized in 1898.

'The talk turned to England, and it was soon clear that the Tsar was personally very angry with the country and its King. He described Edward VII as the greatest "mischief-maker",* as well as the most deceitful and dangerous intriguer in the world. I could only agree with him, with the remark . . . that the King had an absolute passion for starting something up with every country everywhere and making a "little agreement". At that, the Tsar interrupted me and, banging his fist on the table, declared: "Well, I can only say, he shall not get one from me, and never in my life against Germany or you – my word of honour on it." '

After some discussions of their uncle's latest bout of 'mischief-making' on their own doorstep in Scandinavia (namely King Edward's attempts, which were to prove successful, to place his Danish son-in-law Prince Christian on the throne of Norway), the two sovereigns rejoined their suites for dinner at the advanced hour of 10.30. The brief midsummer Nordic night had ended and it was broad daylight when the Kaiser saw his cousin off the *Hohenzollern*, his own spirits as sparkling as the early morning sea around him.

It was now the Kaiser's turn to visit the Tsar on the *Standart*, where he hoped to press home his advantage. As always at dramatic moments in his life, the All-Highest mobilized the Almighty. In his report to Bülow, he describes how, just before boarding the pinnace-boat to take him across to the Russian yacht, he had opened at random his handbook of holy texts. 'Each shall receive his reward according to his labours' were the words that met his eye. It sounded encouraging and, in the short term at least, it even proved prophetic.

All that the Kaiser had to angle for now was the chance to flourish the draft Russo-German agreement he had tucked away in his tunic. Edward VII – who else? – provided the pretext, for the two men could not talk politics for five minutes together without their uncle's name being mentioned. It cropped up this time when the Tsar waxed indignant about the fact that his French allies – without even informing him – were exchanging naval visits with the English.† Perhaps, the Kaiser put it slyly, Uncle Bertie was preparing another of his 'little agreements'?

'What shall I do in this disagreeable situation?' asked the Tsar despondently. There would never be a better opening than that. 'Why don't we make our own agreement?' the Kaiser suggested.

---

* Parts of the Kaiser's report are in the original English in which his talks with the Tsar were held.
† The Brest and Portsmouth visits; see *supra*, pp. 251–2.

As he wrote the next day to Chancellor Bülow:

'I drew the envelope out of my pocket and unfolded the paper on the writing-desk of Alexander III, in front of the portrait of the Tsar's mother . . . I prayed to God that He would be with us now and influence the young ruler. It was as still as death. There was no sound but that of the sea . . . Right before me, glistening white, lay the *Hohenzollern*, the imperial flag fluttering aloft in the breeze. I was just reading the letters *Gott mit uns* on its black cross when I heard the Tsar saying next to me: "That's quite splendid. I entirely agree!" '

After the Tsar had signed,* the Kaiser appears to have been literally drenched with emotion. The beads of perspiration already trickling down his forehead and his back, he told Bülow, were now joined by 'tears of joy' that welled from his eyes. He invoked the blessing of all his illustrious ancestors who were surely 'looking down from above' and blessing this 'turning-point in European history'.

Whatever blessing the ancestors may have been bestowing from heaven on the new treaty, it got pretty short shrift from the Ministers of both capitals when the two sovereigns got back on dry land again. Bülow promptly offered his resignation in writing. In St Petersburg, the Russian Foreign Minister, Count Lamsdorff, was just as emphatic when the Tsar sheepishly revealed his secret a few weeks later. It was, the Minister declared, a flagrant and unacceptable breach of Russia's treaty with France, a treaty which the Tsar's own father had concluded for the long-term profit and protection of their country. The Prime Minister, Count Witte, agreed, and so did most influential voices at court. There was much head-scratching as to how the Tsar might best beat a retreat, until finally it was agreed that he should write to the Kaiser suggesting that their private pact should be kept in abeyance 'until we know how the French will look upon it'.[8]

The Kaiser sent him one final appeal, claiming that 'What is signed is signed!'[9] When that produced no response, even he gave it up. Björkö had gone back to being simply the name of a pretty little northern harbour.

Though nothing is inevitable in foreign affairs, the odds were strongly on an eventual Anglo-Russian *entente* after the Kaiser himself had closed off the Berlin option for the Tsar. Even before the Björkö escapade, King Edward had made the maximum gesture of goodwill to St Petersburg by sending Hardinge himself to do a spell as ambassador there. When, in May of 1906, Isvolsky, the ardent Anglophile

---

* The 'Treaty' of Björkö bound Russia and Germany to come to each other's aid in Europe only if either were attacked by another European power.

and protégé of King Edward's, became Russian Foreign Minister, the forward momentum grew well-nigh unstoppable.

Indeed, the only brake that could now check it was not so much diplomatic as what we would nowadays call ideological. There was a Liberal government in England presiding over what was the nation's traditionally liberal conscience, and both, like the King, were revolted by the blind oppressiveness of the Tsar regime under that well-meaning weakling, Nicholas II. It was sensibility on this score which caused King Edward to abandon his first project to visit his nephew, and so set the seal on that dynastic policy he had pursued with St Petersburg for so long.

There had been a plan for such a visit as early as the summer of 1906.* But the violence and political turmoil inside Russia – which had led to the inauguration of Russia's first Parliamentary Duma on 6 May of that year – ruled this out. A memorandum he wrote[10] on 22 March 1906 makes it plain that the postponement of the trip was the King's decision and not that of his Ministers:

> 'I honestly confess that I can see no particular object in visiting the Emperor in Russia this year. The country is in a very unsettled state and will, I fear, not improve for some time to come. I hardly think that the country at home [England] would much approve of my going there for a while. I have no desire to play the part of the German Emperor who always meddles in other people's business. What advice could I possible give the [Russian] Emperor as to the management of his country? What right have I to do so, even if he were to listen to me, which I much doubt . . .'

So the project was dropped, despite a remarkable letter to the King's Private Secretary from Sir Edward Grey six days later, pleading for the matter to be left open. Provided there was no more revolution and bloodshed inside Russia, the Foreign Secretary argued, the King might manage some sort of meeting at sea in the Baltic. 'An *entente* with Russia . . . is the thing most to be desired in our foreign policy,' Sir Edward went on. 'It will complete and strengthen the *entente* with France and add very much to the comfort and strength of our position. But it all depends upon the Tsar and he depends on the King.'[11]

That was a plain enough statement and, from that source, a striking acknowledgement both of the value of Russia to England in the

---

* The Tsar Nicholas, accompanied by the Tsaritsa and their small daughter, had paid a private visit to Balmoral in the autumn of 1896, and though he had not been to England again during King Edward's reign, technically it was the King's turn. The last time the two sovereigns had seen each other was at a family reunion at Copenhagen in 1901.

diplomatic game and of the value to England of her own King on the European chessboard. Edward VII had always heartily agreed with both propositions; but concern for public opinion at home still held him back. That gap in popular feeling he had been the first to bridge with France had been essentially a nationalistic one. Now, though he was dealing with a fellow-monarch and not a republic, the gap was almost an ethical one. For a while, the struggle for liberty was thus replacing the struggle for the Himalayas as the great barrier between the two countries.*

It was the conclusion of the long-awaited Anglo-Russian agreement the following summer (the actual signing took place on 31 August 1907) which overcame this last obstacle. Though kept informed and giving constant encouragement, King Edward took no part in the actual drafting of the complicated Anglo-Russian agreement.† This, like its Anglo-French precursor, was a detailed job for the professionals, and the King was happy to leave it to them. What the Convention represented on paper was important enough: the settlement of all those long-standing Anglo-Russian rivalries in Tibet, Afghanistan and Persia, through a complicated balancing of spheres of interest. But the political message of this 1907 pact was even more significant than its strategic implications. When the King finally set sail to meet his new political partner, the basic structure of a Triple Entente between England, France and Russia was now standing, even if, in parts, the mortar was still wet and many of the bricks were still loose. For King Edward, a personal vision he had cherished since his youth was becoming reality.‡

*　　*　　*

* There were also worries on the other side. When the Tsar called off a visit that the Royal Navy was due to pay to Cronstadt that same summer, the danger of having 'free' English sailors mix among his own restless fleet was one of the reasons reported to be behind the move. (See *D.D.F.*, Série 2, Vol. 10, No. 152, 13 July 1906.)

† The Russian Prime Minister, Count Witte, claimed in his Memoirs that, as early as September 1905, he received personally from King Edward the draft of an Anglo-Russian agreement. There is however no confirmation of this in any British source, documentary or otherwise.

‡ There was political controversy about the visit even now. Radical and Labour M.P.s joined in calling on the King to abandon the trip and, on 4 June 1908, 59 out of the 284 Members present in the House of Commons actually cast their votes against the Reval meeting. What infuriated King Edward about that division (however much he had anticipated the debate) was that the new Liberal Member for Stirling, Mr Arthur Ponsonby, had been among those to oppose him. The Ponsonbys were gentlemen and, moreover, gentlemen whose family served at court. It was really too much. The miscreant was punished, with others, by being temporarily denied access to those outermost fringes of royal favour, the lawns of a Buckingham Palace garden-party.

When the curtain finally went up on the Reval meeting of 9–10 June 1908, the brief performance there more than lived up to this long and eventful overture. To begin with, the security precautions taken to prevent them all being blown out of the water by anarchists had to be experienced to be believed. The Russian secret police, who were very worried men at the best of times, had been thrown into an even greater state of agitation by the Tsar's last-minute decision to alter all his travel plans. This, in turn, had been caused by some violent changes in the weather. On the eve of the rendezvous in the Reval roadsteads, the mercury had fallen to freezing-point in St Petersburg and a snow-storm had raged in this first week of June, ravaging the fruit blossom in the orchards. The soothsayers of ancient times would have called off the entire venture at such a bad omen. Nicholas II, who was an indifferent sailor, merely called off the crossing by sea from his own capital to the 'capital of Estland', as Reval was known. So whereas his advisers (notably the Prime Minister Stolypin and the Foreign Minister Isvolsky) put out as planned in the cruiser *Almaz*, the *Standart* crossed without the imperial family, who went by train instead.

This, of course, redoubled the dangers of a terrorist attack *en route*, and the authorities quadrupled their original precautions accordingly. It was estimated that a force of nearly seven thousand Russian soldiers was spaced out the length of the railway line to guard their ruler against harm, while more than half of the passengers on the royal train itself were detectives or policemen. At 8 a.m. on the morning of 9 June, this contingent poured out at Reval station with their imperial charges, to add to the considerable security forces already assembled there. These latter, commanded offshore by Admiral Iretzky from the cruiser *Asia*, had already searched every house in the town and every vessel in the harbour and thrown a tight cordon around all approaches by land and sea.

But at least the ordinary people of Reval had something to be happy about. They had known that King Edward would not set foot on shore, and they had assumed that that also applied to their own Emperor. Now, on this, the greatest day in Reval's history since Peter the Great had seized it from Sweden two centuries before, they had been able to glimpse the present Tsar, the Tsarina, the Tsarevitch and the four little grand-duchesses, as they drove hastily through the town and boarded their yacht to the sound of a thirty-one-gun salute.* For the remainder of the time, the good people of Reval had to rely on gossip and, in

---

* This was the normal welcoming salvo for a sovereign. Characteristically, the German Emperor had added one extra for himself, making it 32 whenever he came aboard.

the case of the wealthier ones, on field-glasses and telescopes trained out to sea for twenty-four hours a day.*

The royal vessel they were all looking for had had to endure a variety of tribulations *en route*. The weather across the North Sea was so rough that one of the waves to strike the yacht threw Queen Alexandra flat on her back in her cabin below, surrounded by cakes and sandwiches, an emptied teapot and, more dangerously, an urn of boiling water. By the time they reached the Kiel Canal, through which, of course, the convoy was routed, the sea had calmed down, to be replaced by other irritations on shore. The Kaiser, who was viewing this Reval meeting with a very beady eye, had decided to give his uncle another reminder of Germany's power. There was an enormous turn-out of troops at Kiel harbour and relays of German cavalry then trotted along each bank during the yacht's entire passage through the Canal itself. It was a military warning-shot against what the Kaiser firmly regarded as his uncle's hostile military expedition.

Yet, for all that, the Reval meeting did, in fact, remain essentially an informal family affair. Contrary to all expectations, the weather turned out to be brilliantly sunny as the *Victoria and Albert*, with the British cruisers *Achilles* and *Minotaur* and four destroyers as her escort, dropped anchor on the Tuesday morning in Reval harbour. For the next forty-eight hours, the pinnace-boats were kept busy as the royalties and their advisers were ferried ceaselessly backwards and forwards for luncheons, teas and dinners between the three yachts.† There were one or two awkward moments, as when Hardinge discovered the Tsarina sitting all by herself in a corner of the deck one night, dissolved in floods of tears. But as she was a German married to a Russian, such fits of *Weltschmerz* were nothing extraordinary. In general, the atmosphere was relaxed and, given the shadows of anarchy which lay across the water, even gay. Admiral Fisher, for example, seemed just as anxious to execute the *Merry Widow* waltz with the Grandduchess Olga on deck as he was to discuss grand strategy with the Ministers below. The King, as usual, gave excellent extemporate toasts, and delighted the Emperor, as he had done Franz Josef in Vienna five years before, by conferring a surprise honour (in this case, Admiral of the Fleet) at the dinner-table. He had also won the heart of the Russian sailors on board by addressing them earlier that day in their own language, with the traditional greeting: 'Good morning, my children.'

---

* Dawn followed almost immediately on sunset in the midsummer 'white night' of the north.

† In addition to the *Standart* with the Tsar on board, the *Polar Star* had come to Reval with his mother, the Dowager Empress.

The question of entertainment presented problems in more senses than one. There were three distinct ethnic groups in Reval: the Estonians, the Germans and the Russians, each with its own band and folk-singers. They had been squabbling for days over the artistic tributes to be offered to the royal visitors, and could agree only to singing the two national anthems in unison. Apart from that joint effort, each had insisted on serenading the sovereigns with their own programmes.

Security presented even more headaches than nationalist pride. These were, after all, the only ordinary citizens of Reval to be allowed to approach the Tsar, his family and his guests. It had been agreed that they would not be allowed actually to board any of the royal yachts, but would perform from a special steamer hovering nearby. Yet, for the performance to have much merit, they would have to hover fairly close, as the groups contained dancers who had to be seen as well as the singers, whose voices could be expected to carry farther across the water. What if one of the girls had a pistol tucked somewhere in her embroidered peasant's blouse, or one of the men had a bomb concealed in his *balalaika*? The Russian police assured Mr Quinn, the King's detective, that, with this in mind, they proposed to strip and search everyone, including the women, before they boarded their steamer. On hearing this, Ponsonby, with characteristic perception, thought straight away of possible newspaper stories in England, attacking the Tsar's despotic policemen for humiliating innocent female artistes. He succeeded in getting the women spared from the body search with, as it turned out, no subsequent danger to royal life and limb. After all this trouble, it would be nice to be able to record that Reval's three-pronged folk entertainment was a success. But all that Ponsonby himself has to say about it is that:

> 'After dinner the two monarchs and their suites stood on deck while a steamer full of some choral society came and sang weird Russian songs.'

As for King Edward, the British Ambassador, Sir Arthur Nicolson, evidently thought he was bored by the whole business.

Sir Arthur, who had sailed out with the royal party from England, had been squeezed remorselessly by his sovereign for information and guidance on every possible aspect of the coming talks. The King's queries ranged from the names of leading Russian scientists and musicians to the state of Russian finances; from conditions in the army and navy to the prospects for the next harvest; from the exact provisions and scope of the previous year's Anglo-Russian convention to the aims of Russia's present policy; from Russia's railways to the foreign languages, if any, spoken by her Prime Minister.*[12] It was an exhaustive and (for the envoy) an exhausting interrogation, and the King made full use of it in his conversations with the Russian statesman.

The most ticklish personal problems on the King's agenda arose from approaches made to him before his departure by some of his Jewish friends in England. The Rothschilds had formally approached him in writing to intervene with the Emperor on behalf of the Russian Jews, who were being subjected to increasing pressure and discrimination. The King's own Jewish financier, Sir Ernest Cassel, may have sympathized with the appeal, but there is no evidence that he supported it or associated himself with it in any way. Perhaps this enigmatic man wished to obliterate his Jewish descent as well as his German origins. At all events, the memorandum that he had sent to his sovereign was on a very different subject, and one evidently much closer to his heart: would King Edward help him at Reval to float a Russian loan?

The King's advisers, and the King himself, could not help but be struck by the contrast between these two requests. The leaders of the established English Jewry, who had preserved their faith, forgot about money and made only a disinterested appeal for their fellows. But the first-generation Englishman (who had, in fact, abjured his Jewish faith to speed up his assimilation) had thoughts only for another business deal.

The King, as usual, did his best for everyone concerned, though on this occasion he exerted himself a great deal more on the Rothschilds' behalf than on Sir Ernest's. He raised the question of the Russian Jews himself, in a talk with the Tsar's Prime Minister, M. Stolypin, and then prodded Sir Arthur Nicolson to demand outright whether the pogroms would be stopped. All he did for Cassel was to ask the Tsar to receive his financier friend if he ever visited Russia. The loan itself was not mentioned. (The Kaiser, who inevitably heard about Cassel's manœuvres, was, as usual, grossly over-shooting the mark when he declared that the whole Reval meeting was dominated by money and had turned King Edward into 'a stock-market jobber, acting principally on behalf of the French'.[13] But he was by no means the only observer who found the episode distasteful.)

For the most part, the King's talks (and the parallel discussions held between the advisers and Ministers) were of a general and non-sensitive nature. The King's purpose was to create at Reval an atmosphere of trust and to secure, if that were at all possible with the Russians, a meeting of minds as well as a meeting of yachts. When the *Victoria and Albert* weighed anchor and headed for home again on 11 June, he

---

* M. Stolypin spoke both English and excellent French. The King conversed with him in the latter.

had, to a large degree, succeeded in both aims. Moreover, both the King and his advisers had succeeded without trying, or at least without seeming to. Nothing could have been more of an overwhelming relief for the Tsar, after that other famous rendezvous of yachts in Björkö with the Kaiser, than to find English admirals who were as merry as midshipmen, and sovereigns who had nothing more formidable than decorations to produce out of their pockets. It made this strange new partnership between the lion and the bear seem the most easy and natural thing in the world. That, from the English side, was the object of the voyage to this tense little Russian port.

Nonetheless, moments of grim earnest sometimes entered, almost uninvited, among all the pleasantries. Admiral Fisher described one of these, writing his memoirs ten years afterwards. He recalls how, on one occasion at Reval, Stolypin had asked him outright what he thought Russia now wanted most in the way of aid from England. If the Russian Prime Minister had imagined that the English sailor would inevitably talk of providing battleships for Russia's decimated navy,* he was mistaken.

The Admiral replied instead:

'Your Western Frontier is denuded of troops and your magazines are depleted. Fill them up, and then talk of Fleets.'[14]

Fisher, as he found out in later years, was pushing at an open door. Stolypin's one obsession, right down to his death, was to strengthen Russia's border with Germany.

King Edward returned to an England well satisfied with yet another royal expedition that seemed to have been a smooth success; even the Radicals who had publicly opposed the visit were content to let matters rest. It was in Germany that the violent reaction came.

To some extent, this had been anticipated in London. Indeed, the Foreign Office had been applying soft and soothing soap on the Germans from the moment the visit had been announced.[15] But the Kaiser was not to be mollified, and perhaps understandably from his point of view. Before the exact composition of the King's suite was known, his nephew had growled: 'If Fisher goes, then the visit is very dangerous and we can look to our rearming.'[16] Once the presence in the royal party of that notorious anti-German firebrand was established, the Kaiser feared the worst, and was not to be persuaded that the worst would not happen.

---

* The *Almaz*, which was lying in Reval harbour as a floating hotel for Russian Ministers, was the only major warship to survive from the fleet that had been wiped out by the Japanese two years before.

On the day the Reval meeting started, he recieved from Count Pour-
tales, the German Ambassador in St Petersburg, a somewhat pessimistic
verdict on Russia's probable intentions. On this dispatch, the Kaiser
commented sourly: 'Now we know what we must expect from these
scoundrels.'[17] Commenting on the same envoy's report to Berlin after
the meeting had taken place (a report which had mentioned the dread
word 'encirclement'), the German Emperor was even more emphatic.
'We must now overhaul our state finances! Heavy indirect taxation; a
strong navy, a strong army and our powder dry!' was his conclusion.
And a few days after that, in a speech to his Cavalry Guard at Döberitz,
the Kaiser himself, in a clear reference to Reval, spoke of a provocative
ring being thrown around Germany, a ring he was resolved to smash.

In London, Sir Edward Grey himself took over the task of allaying
German suspicions. But he had little better luck with Count Metternich, the Ambassador, than Hardinge had enjoyed before him. Metternich defended all the suspicions being voiced in Berlin as being quite
natural and added pointedly that all King Edward's visits abroad 'were
regarded very searchingly since several international agreements have
already been linked with his travels'. Grey blandly replied that the
German Emperor had visited the Tsar three times, so surely no one
could object if the King of England went once.

Though Germany's suspicions were never dispelled, they were,
during the next few weeks, temporarily covered by a thin screen of
Anglo-German cordiality. Yet there was one secret order which the
Kaiser issued soon after the Reval meeting which showed the way the
wind could so easily start blowing from Berlin. No English officers,
he directed on 2 July 1908, would in future be admitted to the German
Army, while henceforth such officers would be allowed to attend
German military manœuvres as foreign observers only at his own
express and personal invitation.[18]

It was a petty decision on a petty issue, and was, in any case, soon
side-tracked by the Kaiser's Ministers. But it symbolized the great
military divide that was to come only six years later. The war of 1914
was not simply the product of accidents, blunders and miscalculations.
That tragedy was spun also out of a web of alliances and a skein of
suspicions. King Edward had not gone to Reval either to add to these
or to split the Continent into two great rival groupings. But in the
nature of things, the Russians could not move into the Anglo-French
camp without pitching their tents opposite the Germans. England's
settlement with Russia had not, in itself, made a European war more
or less certain. What it had done was to ensure that, if a conflict broke
out, the whole Continent would be engulfed.

BERLIN AT LAST

King Edward knew that, barring catastrophes, he would have to go to Berlin in 1909, even if they had to carry him around the German capital on a stretcher. As it turned out, catastrophes were just avoided in those six months between agreeing to the state visit at Cronberg in August 1908 and carrying it out in February of the following year. Yet the whole period was an extremely tense run-up to this event that was supposed to open a new era of Anglo-German friendship or, at the very least, to end the old one of bitterness and suspicion. Those familiar feelings seemed to be simply ineradicable, not only as between the two sovereigns, but also between the two nations. One of the most interesting illustrations of this is to be found in the Zeppelin mania which was sweeping Germany at the time.

Count Zeppelin's first great 'dirigible balloon' had been destroyed that summer near Stuttgart. With one accord, the Kaiser, all the Princes both imperial and federal, the major cities, and thousands of private individuals, poured money into a fund to build, not one, but several replacements. A frenzy of excitement seized the country, a feeling, unknown since the days of Bismarck's great triumphs nearly forty years before, that Germany stood on the threshold of a magical new age. Even sober professional observers were impressed by the phenomenon.[1]

Two things strike one as particularly significant about it. The first is the way in which the Zeppelin was promptly converted into a *Wunderwaffe* in popular imagination, thus joining that long line of mystical Teutonic weapons of salvation, which had begun with Siegfried's sword in the ancient sagas and was to continue right down to the rockets of Adolf Hitler. Already supreme on land, and already challenging England at sea, there emerged in 1908 the prospect of German superiority in a third element, the air. It was no coincidence that the balloons themselves were soon called *Luftkreuzer*, or 'air cruisers'.

The second all-too-typical aspect was the way the Zeppelin, once envisaged as a weapon, was automatically pointed at England. Count Seckendorff, a well-meaning and pro-English courtier of the Kaiser's, was disturbed to find that many people in Bavaria regarded their subscriptions to the Zeppelin fund as an outright 'retort to King Edward's political activity'.[2]

Nor were there voices lacking to spell out the strategic use of the Zeppelin in any Anglo-German conflict. At a public meeting of the 'German Society for Motor Balloon Travel', the Society's President, a retired government official called Rudolf Martin, gave a lecture entitled, quite simply, 'The German Landing in England'.[3] Thanks to Count Zeppelin's machines, he declared, Germany could succeed where Napoleon had failed. England's island security was now a thing of the past. One thousand Zeppelins could land 100,000 soldiers there in one trip. Martin was, admittedly, a bit of a crank. But the fact that his large and enthusiastic audience for that lecture included several German officers in uniform and that his proposals led to no official rebuke, suggested that, among people in high places, his ideas were not thought as peculiar as he was himself.

It must be added straight away that, Zeppelins or no Zeppelins, German invasion talk was just as prevalent and just as unrestrained at the time in England, with personalities far more important than a retired *Regierungsrat* as the spokesman. On 23 November, for example, Field-Marshal Lord Roberts had again sounded the German alarm-bells in a public speech. Germany was now a far greater danger to England than, in a previous era, France had been, he warned. She could easily concentrate a force of 150,000–200,000 men at the Channel ports and then 'load them into waiting steamships and hurl them against the English coast'.

An interesting point about this speech was that King Edward was thought to have personally intervened beforehand to try and get it toned down. Knowing Lord Roberts's reputation as an anti-German firebrand, the King is said to have sent his secretary, Francis Knollys, to plead with the old Field-Marshal not to mention Germany by name. Our only source for this report is the German Ambassador in London, Count Metternich, who sent a long private letter on the incident to his Chancellor, Bülow.[4] But it does not sound in any way implausible. King Edward, whatever he may have thought and said in private about his nephew's Germany, was never one for dotting the 'i's' too obviously in public. And, in any case, there was his approaching visit to Berlin to be considered.

This same consideration may well have been one of the perfectly innocent, and indeed well-meaning, motives behind a far greater scandal that had just erupted from the Kaiser's side: his notorious *Daily Telegraph* interview of 28 October 1908. In this, the German

Emperor, speaking through the mouth of an anonymous interviewer at some unstated date, had tried to remove English 'misconceptions' about him and his country. The source and the date were soon established,* and that did not help matters; but what caused the real damage were the Kaiser's remarks in themselves. Having roundly declared the English to be 'mad, mad as March hares', he then, in this synthetically constructed 'interview', paraded his familiar arguments and complexes, all in the most unfortunate language imaginable.

Thus, it was 'a personal insult' that his 'repeated offers of friendship' had been rebuffed. Germany's new fleet was not being built against England but rather with 'eventualities in the Far East and the Pacific' in mind, which, in fact, meant Japan, England's ally since 1902. Even the Boer War was dredged up again. Reviving what must have been (for King Edward particularly) painful memories of those imperial *Gedankensplitter* of 1901, the Kaiser told his English audience that, when things had looked their blackest for England in 1899, he had kindly worked out for the English how they could best win the war. He had sent his written suggestions to Windsor, where they were still enshrined, 'awaiting the serenely impartial verdict of history'.

The entire 'interview' (which had been a put-up job between the Kaiser and the Colonel, with Chancellor Bülow being shown at least the first draft)[5] caused uproar in England and astonished amusement in the rest of Europe. But where it did perhaps the most damage was inside Germany itself. There, for once, all sides were up in arms against the Kaiser: the small pro-English group because of the damage done to Anglo-German relations; the anti-English majority because of the excessive sympathy their Kaiser appeared to have harboured for his Anglo-Saxon cousins; and the politically uncommitted because they were uncomfortably aware that the Kaiser had made a universal laughing-stock of himself and his country. There was a threatened resignation by Bülow (who, as so often, tried to slip out of his share of the responsibility) and a tense debate in the Reichstag before this storm in an ink-well died down. It had all been yet another classic example of the Kaiser's good intentions being turned against him by his own ham-fisted methods. 'Of all the political gaffes which H.I.M.

---

* After the Kaiser's amicable visit to Windsor in November 1907, he had expressed the wish to stay on in England privately for a whole month. This caused some concern to King Edward who feared (as it turned out, prophetically) that his nephew could not possibly last for four weeks without doing something dreadful. After the Kaiser had abandoned a plan to stay with his friend, Lord Lonsdale (the 'Yellow Earl'), Highcliffe Castle in Hampshire was rented for the German Emperor's use from its owner, Colonel Montagu-Stuart-Wortley. He was the source of these belated disclosures of the Emperor's table-talk the previous autumn.

has made, this is the greatest,' King Edward wrote to Hardinge from the Jockey Club on 30 October.[6]

A month later, the Kaiser again put his foot in it in the Western press, and, this time, not even the excuse of good intentions could be advanced. In November 1908, Dr William Hale, the Literary Editor of a New York paper (who was also an ordained minister of the Anglican Church), was granted a three-hour audience and interview with the German Emperor in Berlin. According to a memorandum drawn up by one of his colleagues after Hale's return to America,[7] the Kaiser had declared that he was 'most bitter towards England', and that Germany was 'ready for war at any moment with her, and the sooner it came, the better'. There was a great deal more in this vein, dealing with England's misdeeds in Egypt, India and Southern Africa. America was, however, a horse of a very different colour. The Emperor expressed great interest in, and friendship for, his visitor's native land, 'because the march of progress and the degeneration of Great Britain showed that the two dominant forces of the future would be Germany and the United States'.

Fond as it naturally was of sensational 'scoops', the American press deemed Dr Hale's story too explosive to publish, at least textually. The *New York Times* declared outright that it was 'so strong that it cannot be printed'. Even when a censored synopsis eventually appeared in the *New York World*, there was an outcry. The German Foreign Office intervened in Washington to prevent further distribution (branding the whole affair as 'an invention') and also exerted pressure in London to prevent the *Daily Mail* picking the story up. Everyone had done their best to smother the explosion, but the shock-waves could not be stopped. As the *New York Times*' own confidential report on the incident ended:

'If he [the Kaiser] is in such a frame of mind that he opens out to an American clergyman at the first time of meeting him, there is a danger of something happening before long.'

Almost at the same time as that was being written by a newspaper editor in New York, the British Foreign Secretary, in a private letter to Paris, was saying, on exactly the same theme, and with characteristic acumen:

'I am not confident about the future . . . When she [Germany] has recovered from the effect of the Emperor's latest vagaries, she will resume not only her self-respect, but the tendency to resent anything being done without her leave, or any friendship between other countries in which she is not included. Then there will be trouble.

She has reached that dangerous point of strength which makes her itch to dominate.'[8]

Uncle and nephew had uttered equally typical verdicts on these newspaper incidents. King Edward had been sent a letter from the German Ambassador in London, Count Metternich, reporting the Kaiser's 'emphatic denial' that he had ever spoken to Dr Hale in the terms being quoted. The King replied to his secretary:

'. . . I am however convinced in my mind that the words attributed to the German Emperor by Mr Hale are perfectly correct. I know the German Emperor hates me and never loses an opportunity of saying so (behind my back) whilst I have always been kind and nice to him . . . This American incident is by no means over. I don't think our American cousins will be pleased or satisfied by the Imperial denial . . .'

That was perhaps a shade hard on the Kaiser, whose feelings, deep down, for both England and her King might more fairly be described as those of love-hate. Indeed, the Kaiser's own comment on all this upheaval is, for once, rather more winning than his uncle's. Early in December, it had already been reported[9] to London that, at a shoot with Prince Fürstenberg at Donau-Eschingen, the Emperor was giving vent to 'fits of fury alternating with hysterical weeping' even when out with the guns and, presumably, in full view of the beaters. Buckingham Palace soon had its own confirmation of this Foreign Office report. During the same week, Queen Alexandra, replying to a solicitous enquiry from the Kaiser about her husband's health, said that the King had recovered from his cold, but that she understood that the Emperor had now caught one himself. To this the Kaiser engagingly replied in a telegram sent *en clair* for all the post offices to read:

'I am not suffering from cold, but from complete collapse.'

His uncle's only comment on that was:

'We do live in marvellous times.'[10]

But a great deal more was going on during these strange weeks before the Berlin visit than imperial blunders in newspapers or exchanges of telegrams about royal colds. England was taking two fateful steps to counter that German 'itch to dominate' which Grey thought he could glimpse on the political horizon. One of these steps was taken, deliberately, in public. The other was perhaps the most closely guarded military secret in the kingdom. It concerned the key question of how much help, and what sort of help, England's armed forces should give to France in the event of war against Germany. Both the Cabinet and the Imperial Defence Committee were divided over this argument which, by November of 1908, had reached its climax. King Edward himself was fully engaged in the debate, though operating entirely from the sidelines.

There is no account of this personal involvement of the sovereign's in the contemporary British records or royal archives. But a very full and fascinating description lies buried in the French diplomatic documents of the day.[11] On 8 November 1908, the French Military Attaché in London, Colonel Huguet, was invited by Lord Esher to come to Orchard Lea, his house near Windsor, for a long private talk on the problem. The significance of this, as Huguet pointed out, was that, apart from being a leading member of the Imperial Defence Committee, Esher was also a close friend of the King's, and the monarch's *alter ego* on military matters. The French therefore regarded this initiative as coming either directly from King Edward or with his full knowledge and approval.

What Esher had to say was that the Liberal government was now split into two camps over the question of actually going to battle at France's side. The stronger group, headed by Asquith, the Prime Minister, Haldane, the Minister of War, and Grey, the Foreign Secretary, were in favour of fighting with everything that England could provide. They had put it to their Cabinet colleagues that if England did not support France in this way in a war with Germany (no other conflict was even envisaged in this context), French bitterness at being abandoned would never die down and 'the bad faith and selfishness of England could be exploited again'. Such exploitation could easily take the form of a demoralized France being dragged into the German camp in a coalition directed against England. And, in any case, these 'activists' had argued, a conflict with Germany seemed inevitable for England, sooner or later. Better to fight it 'today, and remaining faithful to our policy' than put it off and alienate England from France, with all the dreadful consequences this might bring.

The opposite group in the government were described by Lord Esher to the French officer as 'the progressive and pacifist elements, with Winston Churchill* at their head'. Their case was that it was better to stand aside in any war between France and Germany, who would then mutually exhaust themselves, leaving England 'intact and with a dominating position in Europe'. King Edward, Esher said, would 'most certainly' exert all his influence against this group and in favour of intervention. But the Frenchman was warned, on this occasion, not

* Then President of the Board of Trade, and passing through a marked 'socialist' phase.

THE LAST YEAR

Above: The Derby 1909. *L. to r.* The Duke of Connaught, the King,
Lord Beresford and George, Prince of Wales.

Overleaf: The Last picnic – Edward with Alice Keppel and Caesar at
Biarritz about a fortnight before his death.

to expect too much from the King's efforts. Only the government could take the decision because only the government had the power and the responsibility in a matter like this.

Lord Esher then described the parallel debate that was going on in his own Imperial Defence Committee. Here the issue was not whether to help France in a war, but how. Several of his colleagues, he told Huguet, favoured a simple division of labour: England would take charge of the war against Germany at sea, while France would look after the land fighting. Esher (and by implication the King) were of the opposite view. England ought to fight also on land at France's side, not merely because this was a moral obligation; but because, in any campaign, the German Army would certainly try to overrun the Low Countries, and that was something England would anyway have to resist, in her own strategic interests.

Summing up this particular argument, Cambon was optimistic:

'Even if all the members of the Cabinet without exception do not favour giving us the help of both the British Army and the British Fleet, we have on our side, together with the King, all the most influential Ministers . . .'

The British Fleet was the subject of the other, and contrastingly public, argument of that month. On 23 November, Asquith defined anew in the House of Commons England's doctrine of the 'two-power navy standard'. England's policy, according to this, was to possess ten per cent more tonnage in principal warships than the combined strength in such vessels of 'the two next strongest powers'.* However, so far from being ten per cent up on this basis, England in November 1908 was three battleship units down, and would be six units down by the time Germany had completed her naval programme for 1909. The only answer to that, as King Edward had sorrowfully written to Cassel from Marienbad three months before, was that 'we must go on building'. Asquith's statement sparked off the great debate as to whether England needed four, six, or (as was eventually demanded) eight extra Dreadnoughts to match Germany's latest naval expansion.

The debate was still at its height, and still undecided (with the King personally intervening to get the maximum British increase possible), when the time came for him to set off with his Queen for Berlin. This visit, which was supposed to be symbolizing a new spirit of trust and

---

* What this formula meant in 1908 was that the Royal Navy needed one-tenth more battle-ships of the *Dreadnought* and *Invincible* classes than Germany and America (!) taken together.

friendship between both the courts and the governments of the two countries, thus took place against an intensely gloomy background:* the unresolved Bosnian crisis; the Kaiser's disturbing outbursts in the Anglo-Saxon press; the secret debate in London as to how England should fight a war alongside France against him; and the semi-public argument as to how the growing menace of his navy could best be held in check.

*   *   *

Few sovereigns can have set out for a foreign capital with less illusions than did King Edward, when he crossed the Channel in the *Alexandra*, the smaller of the two royal yachts, on 8 February 1909. He had never been eager to go, and his Queen, as he well knew, loathed the prospect. To make matters worse, he was feeling distinctly out of sorts and pining for the early spring sun of Biarritz.

In these circumstances, what was needed, apart from reasonable weather in the German capital, was a programme that went off without a hitch. The King was destined to get neither. Indeed, it was as though an army of mischievous gremlins had boarded the train at Calais alongside the King and his large suite,† and then had stuck to them throughout the journey.

They first showed their hand, in a very harmless way, at dinner on the train that night. A footman, thrown off his balance by a sudden lurch of the royal dining-car, upset a dish of quails right over the Queen's head, leaving one clinging to her hair. This was taken as a great joke, however, and the Queen set the whole company laughing by declaring that she would arrive in Berlin *coiffée de cailles*.[12] Perhaps offended by this levity, the gremlins gave the carriage another jolt, upsetting the claret all over the table.

The next mishap was much more irritating. It took place, ominously, just as they were entering Brandenburg at the frontier town of Rathenow. A Prussian guard of honour with a Prussian military band were waiting on the platform, and the bandmaster had been ordered to strike

---

* Morocco was the only area of tension where there was any relief. On the day of King Edward's arrival in Berlin, Germany and France finally reached an agreement which recognized the commercial and political interests of the two countries respectively.

† The King had reluctantly agreed to Cabinet pressure that he should be accompanied in Berlin by a Minister of the Crown, and Lord Crewe, Secretary of State for the Colonies, had been designated. Hardinge was also in attendance in his usual role, however (Grey having declined to come). In addition, the King took his own Lord Chamberlain (Lord Althorp) and the Queen's (Lord Howe); Field-Marshal Lord Grenfell, to represent the Army, and Admiral Sir Day Bosanquet for the Navy; Sir James Reid as his physician; and various Grooms and Ladies-in-Waiting; and Ponsonby, his Assistant Private Secretary.

up 'God Save the King' as the train stopped and to go on playing it
until the King stepped out. Unfortunately, the King's valet had got the
times mixed up and had only started dressing him when the train came
to a halt. As a result, his suite, and everyone else on the platform, had
to endure the British National Anthem played non-stop for ten minutes
before the angry monarch himself appeared, ready at last in the uniform
of a German Field-Marshal.

That was not a very auspicious welcome to Prussia, but worse was
to follow when they arrived, an hour or two later, at Berlin's Lehrter
railway station.[13] The imperial reception committee was waiting for
the King to alight at the precise spot, marked on the platform, where his
carriage was supposed to stop. Nobody had apparently informed them
that he intended to disembark instead with the Queen from her carriage,
which was to the rear of the train. As a result, the Kaiser, with his wife,
and all the imperial and royal princes with their wives, had to scuttle
more than a hundred yards down the platform in full regalia to bid
their guests welcome.

From that point the soldiery took over (in the shape of a massive
escort headed by the *Garde du Corps* which clattered ahead of the
carriages) and the Kaiser must have thought that, with the army in
charge, his troubles were now over. But it was not to be. As the procession got under way, one observer noticed that the carriages were
not keeping their proper distances, 'the horses of one being almost in
the legs of the footmen standing up behind the preceding one so that
the poor men kept turning round to see when they would be bitten'.
But the worst thing happened at the worst possible time, just as the
cavalcade was approaching the palace, where the dutifully cheering
crowd was at its thickest. The ceremonial coach containing Queen
Alexandra and the German Empress suddenly stopped altogether and
the horses drawing it reared up and then refused to move another yard,
despite all the coaxing and whip-cracking of the coachmen. There was
nothing for it but for the two royal ladies to dismount and get into an
ordinary carriage behind. This vehicle had to be emptied of its occu-
pants and so the process continued right down the line. Whether the
last two passengers in the procession had to enter the palace courtyard
on foot we are not told. And, as if this was not humiliating enough,
two of the cavalrymen of Prince Salm-Salm's escort were thrown off
their horses which then galloped around loose, causing havoc throughout the squadron. One explanation offered afterwards was that the
artillery salute had sounded unnaturally loud in the cold air, and had
frightened the animals.

The wretched Kaiser, who had reached the courtyard of his *Schloss* with the King, only to find no procession behind him, was, under-standably, furious ánd disinclined to accept any excuses. The Master of Horse, Baron von Reischach, was summoned to the presence to receive the stiffest reprimand of his life. Of all people, his Emperor asked him despairingly, why must it be the English, who are so proud about their horsemanship, who have to witness such a shambles? It was rumoured that the one person to be secretly delighted at all this confusion was Queen Alexandra. Presumably, she felt it was some consolation for all the damage that this same legendary Prussian war machine had once inflicted on her native land.

It is impossible not to feel somewhat sorry for the Kaiser over all this, especially as, inside the palace, he had done his level best to make both Queen Alexandra and King Edward feel 'at home'. The Queen's suite of rooms during her stay, the so-called *Königskammer* on the first floor, had been specially equipped with a concert piano for her use, and the Kaiser had personally seen to it that some works in Danish had been included among the books, while pictures of both Copenhagen and Sandringham had been hung on the walls. And in the study of the King's suite (the *Wilhelmsche Wohnung*) his nephew had placed not only a portrait of Queen Victoria, but also, propped up on a large easel, a coloured print of 'British Naval Victories', decorated with the figures of Nelson, St Vincent and Howe. He really could not have tried any harder to please.

One reason why the Kaiser had suggested the visit at this particular time was that it marked the height of Berlin's social season, which was, as usual, crowded into the few winter weeks from January to Lent. Everyone who wanted to be taken as anyone always flocked to the capital then from their country houses or castles; and the muster in February of 1909 was especially brilliant, in view of the English royal visit. But if the King was hoping for any charming female company at the State Banquet given in his honour on this first evening, he was to be disappointed. Among the two hundred guests who sat down at table, almost the only German ladies present, apart from the Empress and the Crown Princess, were the so-called *Palastdamen*. These were the Ladies of the Imperial Household, each of whom wore a special enamelled locket on her dress as an official badge to signify she was 'on duty'. It would be hard to imagine anything farther removed from King Edward's idea of a jolly supper-party. The King did his best to be affable, but one sure sign of the nervous strain he was under was his speech in reply to the Kaiser's formal toast of welcome. The King read it from a prepared text, a complete break with his tradition of extempore performances on such occasions. Not surprisingly, by his standards, it sounded lifeless. It was also quite clear to everyone that night that he was not in the best of health. He was constantly coughing, and looked drawn.[14] Even the question as to which German should be given what Order failed to arouse his interest.*

The following day, a Wednesday, was the big day in the programme. The success it brought – which was also the one unqualified success of the entire visit – came about quite unexpectedly. As at Paris in 1903, the scene was the Town Hall of the capital. Bülow claims it was he who had persuaded the King to include in his programme a reception at the Rathaus, in view of the unique importance of this building, and all it symbolized in the way of civic pride and German commercial power and wealth. Certainly, the Kaiser was not keen on the idea (for him the Rathaus was the 'Red-House', forever opposing his policies) and he did not accompany his guest. Nor had the King been too eager to go at first, in view of the virulently anti-British reputation of Berlin's city fathers. Yet, once inside that enormous pseudo-Gothic building, itself so typical of the Wilhelmian cult of the massive, King Edward found himself far more relaxed among these German aldermen than at the Kaiser's martial court. They, for their part, soon fell under the charm of this portly and prosperous-looking figure who, with his perfect German and his civilian garb, might almost have been one of themselves.

The great hall had been decorated with a forest of earthy fir trees. Here the King drank the traditional *Ehrentrunk* of 25-year-old Steinberg wine out of an ancient golden cup, while, from the gallery, a chorus sang *Gott Grüsse Dich*. It was the nearest Berlin could get to Bad Ischl, and the King responded with tactful speeches and compliments all round. There was even occasion for one of those spontaneous personal touches in which he specialized. As the list of City Councillors was being read out by Bülow, the King caught the name of Dr Renvers. He rightly guessed that this was the same physician who had cared for his sister Vicky, the late Empress Frederick, during her last painful illness. Renvers was called over, shaken warmly by the hand, and thanked in words that obviously came from the heart. When the King left, after a stay of some forty-five minutes, the good burgesses of the capital were all smiles. Rather like those Parisians six years before, they had begun to wonder whether John Bull could be such a dreadful fellow after all if he had a King like this.

From the Rathaus, the King went on to the British Embassy, where

---

* In fact, far too many German officers and officials were expecting far too much, and Ponsonby had a difficult time in making it plain that the Order of the Garter was not something one showered among foreign generals.

a large luncheon was given in his name to the diplomatic corps of the capital. The meal passed off smoothly enough, but it was barely over before something alarming happened which, in Ponsonby's words, was like 'the forerunner of disaster'. Too tired to make formal conversation with any of the ambassadors, the King was chatting on a sofa with Daisy Pless, an English society beauty* who still regarded him as being very much *her* King, despite the fact that she had married a German prince. King Edward was wearing a tight-fitting Prussian uniform, which did not help matters, and smoking one of his usual huge cigars, which helped even less. Princess Pless wrote in her diary that night:

> 'Suddenly he coughed and fell back against the back of the sofa, and his cigar dropped out of his fingers, his eyes stared and he could not breathe. I thought: "My God, he is dying; oh! why not in his own country." I tried to undo the collar of his uniform . . . then the Queen rushed up and we both tried; at last he came to – and undid it himself . . . Please God, this dear, kind, able Monarch is not in for a serious illness!'[15]

Everyone withdrew as Sir James Reid, the King's physician, was fetched from an adjoining room. He took the whole incident casually – perhaps too casually – and, after fifteen minutes, everything was pronounced to be in order. The King himself sent back a telegram to Lord Knollys at Windsor that afternoon which ended with the words 'All well'; and the Principal Secretary was soon at pains in a letter written the following day to the British Embassy in Berlin[16] to assure them that King Edward had long suffered from spells of giddiness, 'and always after luncheon', which, he said comfortingly, could only 'proceed from indigestion'. But no one who had heard the almost unconscious monarch gasping to draw breath on that embassy sofa could have been in much doubt that he was already wrestling with severe and chronic bronchitis.

It was just as well that King Edward was not expected to take the floor at the Court Ball, which was given in his honour that night in the so-called White Hall of the Palace. This was a vigorous affair, executed in the military style that seemed to govern the Kaiser's court. The Hall was ablaze with army uniforms: the Cuirassiers in white, the Dragoons and Hussars in brown and green, the Uhlans with their splashes of orange, all of whom outshone in every sense the Ministers and envoys in their gold braid. It was reckoned that not more than five or six gentlemen were present in the entire gathering who were wearing ordinary evening dress. They must have felt quite naked.

* Née Cornwallis-West.

The opening was marred by yet another technical hitch. The royal party was supposed to enter the Hall, to the strains of 'See the Conquering Hero comes', preceded by twenty-four court pages. At the first attempt, the pages duly advanced, but no Majesties appeared behind them. The music died out to a buzz of concern; the pages retreated; and they tried it all again. The procession now came in as planned, with the Kaiser dressed as a British Field-Marshal and poor King Edward tightly buttoned up again in another Prussian tunic, this time that of the Stolp Hussars. Polkas, lancers, quadrilles, galops and gavottes then followed in strenuous succession, as they had done for decades past. One of the German royal princesses had, it appeared, once attempted to bring these Berlin dance-cards into the twentieth century by introducing the two-step. But the Kaiser had squashed the idea flat. As he commented that evening: 'People do not come to a Court ball to amuse themselves, but to learn deportment.'[17]

A visit to Potsdam had been planned for the following day, but in view of the King's condition and the bitingly cold weather, it was abandoned. Instead, the King went round the royal stables, which were opposite the main palace building, and inspected the three hundred-odd horses they contained, as well as his nephew's collection of pale-yellow automobiles. The King then lunched with the officers of the 1st Dragoons, of which he was Colonel-in-Chief. (There is a photograph of the occasion on which his grave white-bearded figure appears quite isolated amid all the grinning Prussian subalterns.) The King also took things very easily that evening at the opera, letting the Queen move around the house on his behalf between acts, while he remained quietly in his box. The programme consisted of a ballet, *Sardanapulus*, said to have been devised by the Emperor himself. Certainly, it combined that ruler's passion for the dramatic with the national fascination for the *Götterdammerung* theme. In the final act, the monarch of the title sat on his pile of treasures and destroyed both himself and them in a blazing funeral pyre.

On the final day, a Friday, the Kaiser personally conducted his guests on an inspection of his real treasures in the Hohenzollern Museum. They were an extraordinary mixture. There were mementoes on display of his own student days in Bonn, with the originals of the 'Yellow Peril' cartoon. There were souvenirs of Prussia's great military triumphs, such as General von Moltke's writing-desk and death-mask, or the Buhl table on which, in 1870, Napoleon III had signed that rash declaration of war. The showpiece, as regards both artistic beauty and value, was Frederick the Great's famous collection of jewelled snuffboxes. So far from wanting to set fire to these, the Kaiser had had them housed in a special steel case which rose up from underground on a signal and then sank back again after inspection.

'They are worth millions,' he told the party. 'You may go close and look – but hands behind backs, please!'

It was still the tone, and even the language, of the self-conscious *nouveau riche*.

What had been achieved when the King and Queen of England left Berlin by train again at five o'clock that afternoon? The most important thing about it all had been the plain fact of King Edward's presence. Not because it was the first time (or so it was said) that any British sovereign had been in Berlin for nearly two hundred years, but because this was the first time this particular British sovereign, who travelled around Europe as though he were strolling around Windsor Great Park, had ever come to his own nephew's capital. It was not so much a case of breaking the political ice (for that soon formed again) as of breaking a private taboo.

Nobody had expected, and nobody had wanted, to use the visit for serious discussions. While it was being planned the month before, Count Metternich had warned from London that any attempt at such talks would be 'highly inappropriate'.[18] Sir Edward Grey, defending his decision not to go, had written that, apart from the navy question, there were 'no big issues to negotiate' in Berlin.[19] Yet, somewhat surprisingly in the light of all this, King Edward took it into his head to raise personally with the Kaiser the one crucial matter that he had always been so anxious to avoid – the threat of Germany's naval programme. Why he should have suddenly tackled in Berlin in February 1909 what he had avoided at Sandringham, Windsor, Kiel and Cronberg during the previous seven years is a bit of a mystery. Perhaps he sensed, especially after that fainting fit, that he might never see either Berlin or his nephew again. Perhaps he merely felt that the decorum of a full-blown state visit, with the Kaiser as his host, was sufficient guarantee against any unpleasantness. Whatever the reason, he picked the very end of his stay in the German capital (presumably on the drive to the station or even on the railway platform itself) to take the initiative. This, at any rate, is what the Kaiser minuted on the evening of that 12 February to his Chancellor, and the Kaiser's version is the only one we have.*

Even allowing for any exaggerations and distortions, the Kaiser's

---

* Curiously, Hardinge, who had been in the thick of the naval debate at Cronberg the year before and who was also acting in Berlin as the King's right-hand man, makes no mention at all in his Memoirs of this discussion between the two monarchs.

account, written only an hour or two after the conversation took place, must command attention:

'H.M. King Edward VII held his first political talk with me in the last minutes before his departure. He expressed his thanks and deep satisfaction with his reception here. The day in the Town Hall had pleased him very much. Then he came to the relations between our two countries which, he hoped, would henceforth move into safer and calmer channels of mutual trust. On the naval question he said:*

"I hope people will grow sensible . . . and take a quieter view. We are in a different position from other countries; beeing [*sic*] an island, we must have a fleet larger than all the other ones. But we don't dream of attacking anybody, only we must make sure that our shores are quite safe from danger.

I: It is perfectly natural that England should have a Navy according to its interests and to be able to safeguard them and its shores. The same thing is with us. We have laid down a naval Bill . . . adequate to our interests. This implies no aggressive [*sic*] against any Power, certainly not against England.

He: Oh quite so, quite so, I perfectly understand it is your absolute right; I don't for one moment believe you are designing anything against us.

I: This Bill was published 11 years ago; it will be adhered to and exactly carried out, *without any restriction.*†

He: Of course that is quite right, as it is a Bill voted by the people and their Parliament, I know that cannot be changed.

I: It is a mistake on the part of some Jingos in England that we are making a building race with you. That is nonsense. We only follow the Bill.

He: Oh, I know that is quite an absurd notion, the situation is quite clear to me and I am in no way alarmed; that is all talk and will pass over." '[20]

There is no other record against which that very detailed report can be checked. It is likely that, if the Kaiser were writing true to form, he would have overplayed his own attacking role and have underplayed any points scored by the King. Yet the general impression which is conveyed, of King Edward being both conciliatory and defensive, was probably correct. To begin with, there was no sense in having a row

---

* Here the Kaiser's report goes over from German into English in the original. The mistakes have been left unaltered.
† Kaiser's italics.

on the platform of the Lehrter railway station just before the train's whistle blew. Moreover, whenever and wherever that talk had taken place, the King would have felt the same personal constraint at trying to tell a fellow-sovereign what to do with his own armed forces. As regards the great Anglo-German contest, this was the one blunted arrow in his quiver.

Off the train went, enveloped in clouds of relief as well as clouds of steam. Then came the postmortems. The new British Ambassador in Berlin, Sir Edward Goschen, was letting his enthusiasm run away with him when he reported that same evening[21] that the visit had passed off 'without a hitch of any sort'. He was also a little premature in claiming that the tone of the German press now 'left nothing to be desired'. His dispatch had barely landed in London before the *Berliner Tageblatt*, while admitting that the royal visit had done some good, raised the perennial fleet problem again and deplored the fact that even the Liberal government of England was 'afflicted with the German invasion bacillus'. However, little as he liked his new post, Sir Edward cannot be blamed for trying to make the best of it.

As for King Edward, he was certainly in high spirits as he bade his farewells and headed with his equally relieved Queen for home. His good temper was only improved by an incident which happened at Spandau along their route. The station there was near one of the many Pless properties, and Princess Daisy had hit on the bright idea of having the royal train specially halted there so that she could bid a solo farewell to 'her' King. This good lady's Anglomania had, long since, grated on the Kaiser and his court. Not unreasonably, they felt that it was high time she stopped behaving like a starry-eyed débutante at Buckingham Palace and settled down to the staid responsibilities of a German princess at Potsdam. And, fond as he was of her, King Edward may also have found that her efforts to hog the limelight and wave the Union Jack were becoming a little embarrassing. Whether he now tried to be as accommodating as he could or slightly malicious towards her is not clear. The instructions he gave to his staff when her request had been submitted the previous morning rather tend to support the second interpretation. The train, he said, was not to stop at Spandau but to proceed instead 'at a snail's pace' through the station.[22] Intentionally or unintentionally, Princess Daisy herself was led to believe that her wish was being granted. As a result, her elegant figure, swathed in furs, was observed standing alone on the platform, the expression of radiant expectation on her face changing to one of bewilderment and then of dismay as the train slid slowly past. The King was observed peeping out of the drawn curtains of his saloon car with a smile on his face. Even if it had been imprudent of her, this was rather naughty of him. Needless to say, the incident does not appear in her own account of the visit.

*   *   *

Five weeks later, installed at last in the Hotel du Palais of his beloved Biarritz, the King wrote another of his regular letters to Sir Ernest Cassel, bringing his friend up to date.* Part of his report went:

> 'Since you left England, we have had many dark days relating to the state of affairs in the Balkans! I however hope that matters may yet be settled without going to war . . .
>
> 'I arrived here on the 6th and though our weather has been changeable and strong it has done me much good as I left in deep snow and intense cold with a bronchial catarrh which was not improved by my visit to Berlin, though that visit was in every respect a great success . . .'[23]

The 'great success' was, in reality, nothing more than that this controversial event had passed off without ructions; above all, it was the simple fact that it was behind him at last. Looking back at Berlin from his gay window on the Atlantic, the King was rather like a patient who has finally paid that much-dreaded and oft-postponed visit to the dentist, and has emerged, to his delight, with his head still on his shoulders. With the journey, he had paid an overdue personal debt to his nephew, and felt all the better for it. But, as the King well knew, if only from that last-minute talk on the navy, the grim political balance sheet between their two countries was quite unchanged.

---

* The correspondence makes it clear that Sir Ernest had been in Constantinople on financial business while the King was in Berlin.

'A FULL STOP'

The enigma of the German challenge, which had confronted King
Edward from the first day he had sat on the throne, thus remained
unsolved to the end, despite renewed attempts to tackle it in the aftermath of the Berlin visit.* But if the deadlock with the Central Powers
continued, King Edward was able during that last summer of 1909 to
go on reinforcing his own rival camp of the Triple Entente.

On 2 August, Tsar Nicholas came to visit him at Cowes, having
already met with President Fallières at Cherbourg on the way. The
Cowes meeting was, of course, intended to reciprocate the King's own
journey to Reval the year before; but that was about as far as the
comparison got. Instead of the stifling secret police atmosphere of the
Russian port, with anarchists' bombs suspected under every cushion,
there was the free-and-easy mood of Regatta week, with nothing more
than the weather for the imperial guests to worry about as they sat
about on their deck-chairs. Instead of a home fleet denuded by recent
war disasters of all but one battleship to grace the harbour, the Tsar
could now witness, as his yacht entered his uncle's waters, one of the
greatest displays of naval might ever assembled in the Solent. No
fewer than twenty-four battleships, sixteen heavy cruisers, forty-eight
destroyers, and fifty other warships greeted the *Standart* as she steamed
in. If either the Tsar or his Foreign Minister Isvolsky (who was among
the suite) had needed a reminder of what British naval supremacy
really looked like, this was it.

So 1910 came round. At home, it was to be marked by the gravest
political challenge the King had ever faced, the constitutional crisis
over the Liberal government's campaign to reduce the powers of the
House of Lords, if need be by flooding it with several hundred new
Liberal peers, and to draw new dividing lines between the two legis-
lative chambers. But abroad, it was as though the great dividing lines

* The most extraordinary of these, which is set out in detail in the Cassel papers, was a
bid by Sir Ernest (doubtless sponsored by Edward VII) to reach an Anglo-German
naval agreement through private talks with the influential German Jewish shipping
magnate, Albert Ballin. The financiers found it more difficult to rule the waves than to
rule the Stock Markets, however, and this first joint venture of theirs had petered out
by mid-August 1909.

had already been drawn. With one Balkan crisis disposed of and the next not yet on the horizon, Europe was settling into a natural lull. For King Edward, at any rate, there were no more Great Power *ententes* or agreements to encourage, nor was there any fresh quarrel with Germany or its ruler to be faced. Indeed, during this final phase, he was not even to show the royal standard (and the Union Jack) to the smaller powers along the Mediterranean again with another spring cruise. Quite appropriately, the last of all his many journeys was to his beloved France, where he had made his very first trip abroad as a wide-eyed child fifty-five years before.

On Monday, 7 March, he crossed to Calais *en route* for Biarritz, escorted by the torpedo-boats *Mohawk* and *Corsair*, which were deemed sufficient for a holiday voyage of this nature. He dined quietly and early that evening in his usual rooms at the Hotel Bristol in Paris with the Ambassador, Sir Francis Bertie, as his only guest. They then went to the Porte St Martin theatre to see Edmond Rostand's new allegorical play, *Chantecler*. The King had been greatly looking forward to this, so much so, indeed, that he had ordered two stage boxes ten days before, even offering to arrive in Paris twenty-four hours later if the seats were not available on that particular evening. Obviously, they were available, and, at 8.20, the King settled himself pleasurably in his box (having cabled the theatre beforehand to fix an arrival time that would be 'the most convenient' for both management and audience).

Though afterwards he complimented M. Hertz on the production and urged him to bring it to London, the King seems to have acted more out of politeness than conviction. At any rate, looking back on the evening a week later, he wrote to his eldest son that he had been 'dreadfully disappointed' with the play, which had turned out to be a 'stupid and childish' form of pantomime. Moreover, the heat in the theatre had been so stifling that, on top of a miserable night's entertainment, he had 'contrived to get a chill with a threatening of bronchitis'.[1]

Despite this, however, he was evidently feeling sprightly enough the next day in Paris to complete another of those typical programmes of politics and pleasure mixed. He had two talks with President Fallières, one in the morning and one in the afternoon and, in between, attended a private luncheon in his honour given by the indestructible Madame Waddington, who had mustered several of his dearest French friends around the table. After dining again at the Bristol that evening, he was even prepared to forget the *Chantecler* disappointment and to give the Paris stage another chance by seeing a play at the Gymnase Theatre.

All in all, there seemed no cause for concern when he got off his special train at Biarritz late the following day, to be met at the station by the obligatory reception committee headed by the Mayor, M. Forsans, and the British Consul, Mr Bellairs. His first two days also passed normally enough, with strolls on the beach, motor excursions, and visits to, among others, Princess Frederica of Hanover and Queen Amélie of Portugal, who happened to be holidaying there. Then, after a weekend during which the weather turned suddenly cold and windy, came the first official sign that all was not well. On 14 March, it was announced that, on the advice of his physician, Sir James Reid, the King was remaining for the day in his apartments, owing to the storm. The announcement ended with the soothing words: 'His Majesty's health is, however, excellent.'

How misleading those words were is shown by a hurried note that Alice Keppel, who had arrived at the Cassel villa a day or two ahead of him, wrote to Soveral, who was also at Biarritz:

'The King's cold is so bad that he can't dine out but he wants us all to dine with him at 8.15 at the Palais, SO BE THERE.

'I am quite worried *entre nous* and have sent for the nurse . . .'[2]

So it went on throughout the following week, with Soveral (duly announced in the daily reports) calling on the patient almost every day and Alice Keppel (never announced) constantly coming and going. If the proprietors of the Hotel du Palais had known in advance that the King was going to be laid up, they could not have rearranged his suite better. Weeks before his arrival, the spare bedroom had been converted into a small private dining-room, and his own bedroom had been moved to the end of the apartments, where it was even quieter. But though they had no doubts that their royal guest was comfortable, the people of Biarritz were nonetheless most disturbed that he should remain invisible. For him to fall ill at their health spa was the ultimate disaster for the reputation of Biarritz, though the town authorities consoled themselves with reports that this was no local bacillus but something he had caught in that unhealthy capital far away to the north.

At last, on 21 March, King Edward emerged again for a motor drive, and when, the following day, he was seen to take an hour's walk with Soveral along the sandy cliffs of the Côte des Basques, Biarritz breathed again. So did England which, though not alarmed by Sir James Reid's bulletins, sensed that it must have been something more than a strong wind and 'a slight cold' that had kept King Edward a prisoner in his hotel for a whole week.

As the King wrote to Cassel (who had left his Biarritz villa empty but for the servants):

'Unfortunately, not long after my arrival here I developed a cold and bronchial attack and Sir J. Reid would not let me go out of my rooms for a week. It has greatly pulled me down, but I am now getting daily stronger and better. The Villa Eugénie is looking very bright and cheerful, but I need hardly say that we miss you and your sister very much.'

Then, in what reads like a reference to Sir Ernest's annual spring balance sheet of the King's private finances, the letter concludes:

'Many thanks for informing me that the matter you usually report to me at this time of the year is as satisfactory as the preceding ones.'[3]

The King stayed on in Biarritz for a whole month after writing that letter, despite the steadily mounting tension back in England over the future of the Upper House. It might be fanciful to suggest that he actually had a premonition that this would be the last time he would ever see either Biarritz or the Continent again. Yet one can sense him putting off his departure until the last possible moment, and cramming even more than usual into every day of his stay. Certainly, despite the continued vagaries of the weather (on 1 April, for example, the King awoke to find the grounds of the Hotel du Palais inches deep in snow, the first fall at that time of the year within living memory), his holiday programme had never been so restless and so varied. Apart from the usual picnics, the visit to the local aviation ground to see M. Blériot fly ('I wanted to see how you descend; it was very pretty,' he told the airman), another trip to the Basque mountain village of Sare to watch the pelota, and the usual afternoons at the Biarritz Golf Club and the racecourse at Anglet, the King also made his first three-day excursion into the interior.

This took him, on 20 April, to Pau, where he put up with Alice Keppel, Soveral and the rest of his party at the Hotel de France. The next day, delayed by periodic tyre-bursts, their convoy of cars drove up the lovely rocky gorge beyond Cauterets for lunch in the mountains, and then, in the afternoon, to Lourdes, where the King visited the holy grotto. On 22 April, they then returned to a slightly resentful Biarritz. A most unusual escort accompanied them on the homeward journey. This was a dirigible balloon called the 'Ville de Pau' which floated over the royal car all the way back to Bayonne. Had the King been reading any German newspapers, he would have noticed that, the same afternoon, dirigible balloons were also paying homage to his imperial nephew at Homburg. But these machines were not quite as peaceful. They were, in fact, three brand-new 'military air-ships' which had flown in single file from their base at Cologne all the way to Fried-richshof, in order to salute the Kaiser by circling over the castle grounds.

As April drew to a close, it was clear that the King could not linger abroad any longer. He had already been obliged to resist Queen Alexandra's pleas to leave 'that horrid Biarritz' (and, of course, Mrs Keppel) and join her for a Mediterranean cruise. From Biarritz he could at least reach London in twenty-four hours. From the middle of the Mediterranean, the journey home could take the best part of a week, which was far too long a delay once the smouldering constitutional crisis had erupted. Mr Asquith's famous Parliament Bill, aimed at reducing severely the remaining powers of the House of Lords, had been duly introduced on 14 April, and the Prime Minister had warned his absent monarch that he might have to be home any time after the 19th. The King stretched it a full week beyond that but, now that his own health seemed restored, he really had no business picnicking up and down the Pyrenees while his country was moving into the gravest political battle of the decade.

On 25 April, after a long day of walks and final calls, Biarritz staged for him a spectacular farewell. A miniature military tattoo was held under his balcony in the courtyard of the hotel. The soldiers of the 49th Infantry Regiment (which was moved each year to Biarritz while the King was there) had been reinforced by every uniformed Frenchman the mayor could find, including Basque sailors and the whole of the local fire brigade. To the strains of two military bands and by the light of torches, they paraded and cheered for nearly an hour below him, while fireworks shot up over the dark bay. There had never been such a farewell, and perhaps that too had a touch of presentiment about it. The King himself was certainly in a strangely sombre mood as the hour approached for him to leave the following day. When everything was packed, he went out on to his private balcony for a last look at the familiar view across the promenade to the sea. 'I shall be sorry to leave Biarritz,' he was heard to say, adding after a pause, 'perhaps for good.'[4] At 10.50 that night, he boarded his train for Paris and home.

To a sun-starved London, and especially to his exhausted Ministers, who had had no time for picnics for many a long week, the monarch must have looked the picture of health when he got back on 27 April. Indeed, for the first day or two, he seemed to be tackling both the back-log of work and his usual social round with renewed vigour. He was changed and at the Opera within two hours of entering Buckingham Palace; he paid his usual visit to the Royal Academy the following afternoon; and, on Friday, 29 April, he was at Covent Garden again,

FULL STOP

Below: Friday, 6th May, 1910.

Overleaf: Farewell to the King – the procession at Castle Hill, Windsor.
Eight kings attended the funeral.

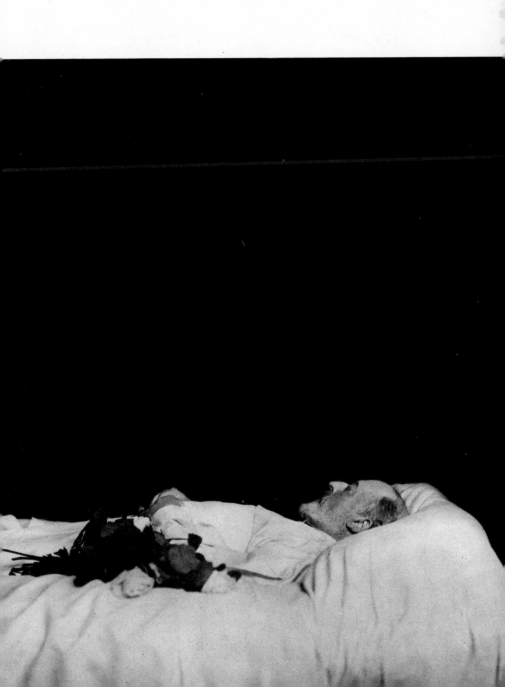

this time to hear *Siegfried,* which was just about the heaviest Wagnerian music that he could ever really enjoy. As to work, apart from the Lords versus Commons crisis, there was a deadlock over the next Viceroy of India to be tackled,* and the usual stream of Ministers, Governors-General and foreign envoys to be seen.

But the display of energy owed more to a sense of duty (probably sharpened by a slightly guilty conscience over that prolonged holiday in Biarritz) than it did to natural vigour. The bronchitis that had first knocked him out in public at the British Embassy in Berlin in February of 1909, and which had laid him low in Biarritz but six weeks before, was only dormant and waiting to strike again. It got that chance over the weekend, which the King spent at Sandringham. On the Sunday, despite the rain and cold winds, he spent several hours in the open, inspecting his gardens and farms. Nobody, it seems, had the nerve either to stop him going out or to persuade him to come back indoors in time. On Monday, 2 May, when he returned to London, his throat and chest were already inflamed and the severe cough had returned.

If love for his Norfolk estate had thus started the illness, the King's devotion to old friends now helped it to take a fatal grip. Instead of retiring to bed, he went out to dine alone with Agnes Keyser, an old flame of his from his Prince of Wales days, and still the only woman who could remotely rival Alice Keppel in his affections. Her house, 17 Grosvenor Crescent, which she ran as a private nursing-home for men,† was almost next door to the Palace, and the good Sister Agnes doubtless sent her King home early, as well as giving him something for his cough. But the damage was done, for he was not to leave the Palace alive again.

For the next three days, he struggled doggedly on, dressing each morning, spurning his bed, and trying to conduct state business from his private rooms in the north-west corner of the first floor. On 3 May, Mr Whitelaw Reid, the American Ambassador, called to discuss arrangements for the imminent visit to London of ex-President Theodore Roosevelt, the 'pen-friend' King Edward was so looking forward to meeting. Mr Reid found him coughing horribly and already yearning again for the bracing Atlantic air of Biarritz. More envoys, admirals, bishops and imperial pro-consuls trooped in and out the

---

* The King wanted to appoint General Kitchener, but the Secretary of State for India, Lord Morley, favoured Sir Charles Hardinge. Despite the fact that Hardinge was such a trusted adviser of his, the King opposed him as Viceroy, claiming that he was a diplomatist and not an imperial administrator.

† Thanks to generous endowments from Sir Ernest Cassel and several of the King's other wealthy friends, it duly became established as the King Edward Hospital for Officers.

next day, either to kiss hands or to present their compliments. When one of these last official visitors, appalled by what he saw, ventured to suggest that the King might rest, he got a characteristic reply: 'Of what use is it to be alive,' the dying monarch asked, 'if one cannot work?'[5]

Nobody outside the Palace except for that handful of visitors who had entered his rooms had any inkling that the King of England might be near to death. This was largely due to his own insistence that no alarm should be spread over an illness that he was determined to fight down. But by now all the royal family were gathering at the Palace and it was this which forced a bulletin out of the doctors. Queen Alexandra, alerted over the weekend, had hurried back from Corfu and had reached London on the afternoon of 5 May. Her husband was not at Victoria Station to meet her, an unheard-of event which sent a buzz of speculation round the capital and demanded an explanation. At 7.30 that evening, the nation learned that the King was ill with bronchitis and that 'his condition causes some anxiety'. From then on, he went swiftly downhill.

After a fairly quiet night, another bulletin, issued at 10.30 the following morning, warned that his condition was now 'grave', while a third report eight hours later spoke of it as 'critical'. This day was indeed to be his last. Yet his death, like his life, was one that most men would have envied. It was not a lingering end; the pain of the final phase was deadened by morphia; and he was lucid until his last breath. Moreover, he was at home, and comforted not only by his entire family but also by the friends who stood closest to his heart. Sir Ernest Cassel had called at midday to say goodbye and, doubtless, to give some reassurances about private financial arrangements to be made after the King's death. He found his monarch facing the end with the same jaunty self-assurance that had marked his whole life. Though he could barely speak distinctly any longer, he made an effort at cheerful conversation and even, as a superb act of defiance, lit up one of those huge cigars which had done so much to hamper his breathing over the years. It could have been that cigar which brought the collapse soon after luncheon.

As the heart now began to weaken, the doctors gave up all hope. Queen Alexandra issued instructions that any special friend who wanted to see him and whom he wanted to see was to be admitted to his rooms. In this way, both Alice Keppel and Luis Soveral came to bid farewell to the stricken figure, hunched in an armchair, with whom, less than a fortnight before, they had been happily exploring the mountain valleys of the Pyrenees.

It would be apt if one could say that the last news the impassioned royal diplomatist received on this earth was of some new pact or treaty. But it was not as the Uncle of Europe but as the King of the English Turf that he bowed out. Earlier that day, with some trepidation, they had allowed his promising two-year-old, 'Witch of the Air', to stand as a runner in the 4.15 Spring Plate at Kempton Park. At 4.18, with R. Marsh in the saddle, it had passed the winning-post first, beating the favourite by half a length after a thrilling finish. 'I'm very glad,' the owner whispered when he was told the result in the Palace half an hour later; and those were the last recorded words he spoke. King Edward died at fifteen minutes before midnight on 6 May, just as Big Ben was chiming out the threequarter-hour from the far end of Whitehall.

* * *

Pæans of praise usually ascend unto heaven alongside the spirits of departed kings. This is especially noticeable if they were popular rulers, in which case their likeability is often converted by the pane-gyrists into greatness. But the reaction which came back from all over Europe, once the sudden shock-wave of King Edward's death had been absorbed, contained at least three common themes which were neither conventional nor contrived. The first was that the light of a great personality had been snuffed out, a personality who, without any apparent striving, had so often dominated the European scene. The second was that, because King Edward had chosen to concentrate this magnetism on the field of foreign affairs, he had become the most influential statesman of his day. Finally, resulting from all this, there was agreement that, though he had ruled for less than ten years, compared with the sixty-three of his mother, his reign had also marked an historic era in that it had brought unheard-of prestige and power to the crown of England.

Such tributes were particularly convincing when they came from the rival camp, where there was more appraisal than praise. Here, for example, are the verdicts of three leading newspapers from different parts of Germany. In the west, the *Rheinisch Westfälischezeitung* wrote:

> 'To us Germans he was the great opponent, who inflicted on us immeasurable injury . . . We stand at his bier as that of a mighty and victorious antagonist.'

In Leipzig, the *Neuste Nachrichten* declared:

> 'For long years, King Edward wove, with masterly skill, the Nessus robe that was to destroy the German Hercules.'

And in Berlin itself (where the Kaiser had cancelled all plans to receive Theodore Roosevelt, ordered the English Red Ensign to be flown at half-mast from all German warships, and decreed twelve weeks of court mourning) the conservative *Reichsbote* made precisely the same point, but with rather more grace:

'He had the fortunate advantage that, in his political contest with other Heads of State, Ministers and diplomatists, there was really no antagonist of equal – let alone superior – talents to take the arena against him.'

If the Germans appeared to be dipping their swords in salute rather than baring their heads in mourning, the Austrians, more charitably, did both. In Vienna, they regretted the passing of 'the most influential man of the present day', a king who, in reality, 'had been his own Foreign Minister'. He had combined, said one commentator, 'the wisdom of the Coburgs with a typically British robustness, and with a light sceptical approach that one might almost call Parisian. He died at the end of a political era which he, more than any other, had helped to transform.'

In St Petersburg, the *Novoye Vremya* commented:

'According to common usage, the monarch of England . . . merely reigns without governing. But the late King not only reigned but also moulded the destinies of his realm . . . Bismarck created an overlordship for Germany in Europe. King Edward substituted for this the hegemony of England.'

In Paris, where the greatest shock and grief were felt, the politicians and newspapers of all shades of opinion joined in emotional tribute. Delcassé, his former collaborator, declared: 'He was a great character, and he played a great role in the world.' Delcassé's successor as Prime Minister, M. Ribot, said simply: 'He was one of the greatest Kings of England.'

But the French tribute that would have given King Edward the greatest satisfaction was not spoken by a politician nor written by a newspaper editor. On the Sunday after he died, the annual festival of Joan of Arc, that legendary martyr of the ancient fight against England, was held in the capital. But in this year of 1910 it was held not quite as usual. Following an appeal by the Archbishop of Paris to the Catholic population of the city, there were no special illuminations or decorations, as a mark of respect for the dead king and as a 'token of union with the English people'. The greatest of all the ambitions to which Edward VII had devoted his public life was to put out the flames of centuries of Anglo-French strife lit by that stake at which Joan of Arc was burned.

So much for the official and published tributes. Among the Soveral papers was found a pile of private and unpublished ones. It is made up of dozens of letters written to the Marquis that May from men and women who had all known the late king well and who had also known what he and Luis Soveral had meant to one another. It is remarkable how they unconsciously echo, not only each other, but also, in different language and from very different standpoints, the formal obituaries of the day.

'All the landmarks are gone . . . I am sure you feel as disorientated as I do,' writes a woman friend from the Rue de Grenelle in Paris. The same feeling and the same word crop up in a letter which Admiral Lord Fisher sent to Soveral from his Thetford home: 'I think we will find the landmarks of life greatly changed . . . I am still dazed by the suddenness of it all . . .'

From Germany, that old favourite of King Edward's, the English-born Princess Pless, wrote to Soveral, in much the same vein:

'It will be a terrible blank . . . Of course, in all loyalty I wish the present King a long and prosperous reign, but somehow the face of England has *absolutely changed* for me.' And then the former Daisy Cornwallis-West, sitting in her huge German castle, adds rather pathetically: 'I long to go to a nice English church to pray, but it's impossible here . . .'[6]

Was the common verdict that emerges from all these tributes, public and private, an exaggerated one? There was, perhaps inevitably, a reaction to it as the years passed, when a challenge to King Edward's political reputation arose from two main directions. First, after the First World War, when the great (and still insoluble) argument over 'war guilt' was raging, came the charge, levelled by German historians, that King Edward had shared in the responsibility for that war. He had not been 'Edward the Peacemaker', but 'Edward the Encircler', whose work in helping to create the Triple Entente had also helped towards creating the European catastrophe of August 1914.

The answer to this charge has already been indicated in these pages. Geographically, as Chancellor Bülow once tried to impress upon his Kaiser, the Germans had already been encircled for a thousand years before Edward VII came to the English throne: the mere fact of their position on the Continent, wedged between the Latin and the Slav peoples, had guaranteed that. Bülow might have added that even the *political* encirclement of Germany had been consummated, by the

Franco-Russian treaty of alliance, while Edward was still Prince of Wales, and with no initiative whatever from England. What he did do as King was to help strengthen that circle enormously: first, on its western and eastern arcs, by linking his country with both France and Russia; and second, on its southern arc, by increasing England's influence, and diminishing that of Germany, along the length and breadth of the Mediterranean.

Yet, even in becoming the 'Encircler', he still remained the 'Peacemaker'. For the purpose of all these moves was not to create an all-round base from which Germany could be attacked and crushed, but to set up a protective ring which would insulate England and the rest of the Continent from the explosion that Germany might one day produce. The Germans were absolutely correct when they noted that, at all points of the European compass, it was Edward VII and his government who were mainly responsible for frustrating their ambitions. But this weakening of Germany was not so much the aim of the King's policy as the result of it. From the time of the Prussian wars of the 1860s down to his dying day he was, however, genuinely afraid of the *Furor Teutonicus* – in the German people, the German Army and in the German Kaiser. What he sought to do was to sandbag the Continent against it.

A more formidable challenge which eventually arose to King Edward's stature as a statesman came from his own countrymen. There was the judgement, made in later life, for example, by one of his Foreign Secretaries, Lord Lansdowne, that no major decisions in foreign policy could be attributed personally to Edward VII.

It is true that his real power with his Cabinet at home could never match his enormous prestige abroad. If he was in any sense an 'arbiter', it was not because he could decide England's policy alone, but because he could influence and shape his government's decisions. The greatest of those decisions, and the most important shift in England's foreign policy for decades, was the move away from an alliance with Germany and towards an alliance with France and Russia instead. There can be no grander strategy than that, and though the government had to implement the moves, the King and his Ministers reached them in full accord and in parallel. Moreover, a generation before any of those Ministers took office, Edward as Prince of Wales had made an *entente* with France and Russia the chief aim of his life. And when he set out to fulfil that ambition, there was at least one most important occasion (the launching of his 1903 visit to Paris) when he raced out on his own, far ahead of his Ministers and far beyond the accepted bounds for any constitutional monarch.

But, as King Edward well knew, the business of diplomacy is only rarely conducted with such grand sweeps of the baton. It is, for the most part, an endless series of small, intricate and interlocking moves, designed only in their sum total to achieve any strategic aim. It was in this fine play that King Edward excelled, not only because he was the only Englishman who personally knew every European figure involved in the game, but because he himself was so good at the game. His cumulative influence here was considerable, whether it was nudging Italy a little farther away from Germany or binding Spain much more firmly to England; boosting the spirits of a France demoralized by the Tangier crisis or helping behind the scenes to forge the military links between London and Paris. And nearly always, the weapon of dynastic ties was gladly put at his country's disposal. The only exception, and it was admittedly a big one, was the King's total inability to communicate with the German Kaiser, and the constant postponement of that dreaded visit to his capital. But, on that, the uncle would doubtless be content to be judged by the record of his nephew's behaviour.

*   *   *

For the final word, we can go back again to the papers of King Edward's greatest friend. Among all the black-bordered letters that Soveral received in that sad month of May 1910 was a hastily pencilled note from Alice Keppel, who had moved out of her Portman Square house soon after the King died.* She wrote to Lady Knollys, wife of the dead monarch's Private Secretary, to assure her that, just because Soveral, Louise Sassoon and Captain Fortescue were coming to dine with her quietly the following evening, to talk about old times, that did *not* mean she was giving a 'dinner-party'. She ended:

> 'How people can do anything I do not know, for life with all its joys have [*sic*] come to a full stop, at least for me . . .'[7]

It was not only for Alice that a 'full stop' had come. It had come also for the British monarchy, seen as a direct influence on world affairs. King George V had all of his father's devotion to crown and country. But though he ruled firmly, and at times tyrannically, over the small, secure circles of his court and his family, he had neither the gifts of personality and character nor the desire to step out into the larger circles of Europe. And, in fact, after King Edward's death, the crown of England, which had not played such a continuous personal part in

---

* As much as to get peace and quiet as to 'escape her creditors' (as gossip had it at the time). The King had made generous financial provision, through Sir Ernest Cassel, to ensure that she should lack for nothing.

continental affairs for centuries past, was never even to seek such a role again.

*   *   *

Though Edward VII had not been crowned quite as he had wished, he would have found no fault with the way he was buried. His funeral, held on 20 May, was an international pageant of royalty as glittering and impressive as any he had witnessed in life. The prelude had been a three-day lying-in-state at Westminster Hall, when a quarter of a million of his subjects had filed past the catafalque. As the capital was honouring a monarch who had never stood upon ceremony in private (although he had adored it in public), it was fitting that the tokens of respect were such a mixture of the formal and the spontaneous.

It was on official orders that the guns boomed in London's parks (sixty-eight times, once for each year he had lived); that the church bells tolled, with the deep clang of St Paul's sounding through them all; that the flags were flown at half-mast, and the public buildings hung in black or purple. But thousands of ordinary citizens with no flags to lower and no purple to hang out marked the day by simply putting the shutters up in their shops, or drawing the blinds in daylight across their windows. And if the late King's courtiers and society friends had had their dress prescribed for them (the ladies, for example, were instructed by the Lord Chamberlain to wear 'black dresses trimmed with crêpe, black shoes and gloves, black fans, feathers and ornaments'), the driver of the London horse omnibus who was seen that day with just a snatch of black ribbon tied to his whip was paying his own tribute in his own way.

The last stage of this last journey was a short, familiar one. It ran from the little station at Windsor (where the body had been brought by special train from Paddington) up the steep road which winds under the grey flanks of the castle to St George's Chapel. It was here that the dead monarch had been christened; it was here that he had been married; and it was here that his vault now lay ready.

A blaze of uniforms flashed around the coffin as it was laid on the traditional gun-carriage, which was enveloped in the Royal Standard and the Union Jack, with the crown, orbs and sceptre placed on top. The black bearskins of British Guardsmen mingled with the red-plumed silver helmets of German officers and the grey astrakhan caps of the Cossacks. The splendour of medieval England, to which Windsor Castle itself bore massive witness, was there in force as the procession formed up – the heralds of Bluemantle, Norroy, Portcullis, Rouge Dragon, Somerset, Richmond and Ulster, each in his richly embroidered tabard. In fact, apart from Caesar, led on a leash by a footman near the head of the column (and fully aware, now as ever, of his special importance), there was only one homely touch to the scene. This was the squad of sailors from H.M.S. *Excellent* who drew and steadied the gun-carriage with long ropes. They were ordinary blue jackets, wearing plain straw hats which stood out among all this finery like a handful of pebbles in a cascade of gems.

But, next to the dead ruler in his casket, it was the monarchs walking behind him who held all eyes. Even Windsor had rarely, if ever, seen such a collection of crowned heads enter its walls. No fewer than nine sovereigns led the main body of the procession. Immediately behind the coffin marched the new King of England, George V, with, on his right, that imperial nephew who had brought the dead man so many personal and political problems, the German Kaiser. Behind them, after a line of aides and equerries, came King Edward's son-in-law, King Haakon of Norway, and two of his nephews by marriage, King Alfonso of Spain and King George of Greece. The King of Bulgaria, the King of Denmark and the boy-King Manoel of Portugal, who made up the next row, were all linked by blood or marriage to King Edward. So was the King of the Belgians, who marched behind them, flanked by the Hereditary Prince of the Ottoman Empire and the Archduke Franz Ferdinand of Austria. And so were most of the fifteen consecutive files of Imperial, Royal and Grand-Duchal and Serene Highnesses from Prussia, Saxony, Hesse, Teck, Saxe-Coburg, and the rest, who brought up the rear of this great monarchical phalanx.

This was the parade of the old (and, for the most part, doomed) European order that Edward VII had once hoped to assemble in England to launch him on his reign. Instead, it had gathered from all the courts of the Continent, almost for the very last time, to mark the end of that reign. The Uncle of Europe was thus buried by his own.

*　　*　　*

On the eve of the funeral, Halley's Comet had made one of its rare appearances, visible to the naked eye. All over the Western Hemisphere, watch-night parties had been held to observe the event and, in Paris, a Count de la Baume Pluvinel had even gone up in a balloon in order to see the spectacle more clearly from a height of nine thousand feet.

This juxtaposition of events, though bizarre, was also apposite. Edward VII himself had been almost an astrological phenomenon, streaking like a meteor across the political skies. Yet he had left more behind him than a trail of stardust and a fading blaze of light. In his brief nine and a quarter years on the throne, his impact had helped to shift the axis of that Europe he so dearly loved.

The Travels of Edward VII

Christiana (Oslo)
Stockholm
Reval (Tallinn)
Copenhagen
Kiel
London
Berlin
Potsdam
Cronberg
Paris
Homburg
Carlsbad (Karlovy Vary)
Marienbad (Marianska Lazne)
Bad Ischl
Vienna
Bairritz
San Sebastian
Lourdes
Lisbon
Rome
Gaeta
Naples
Majorca
Corfu
Algeciras
Tangier
Gibraltar
Cartagena
Athens
Malta

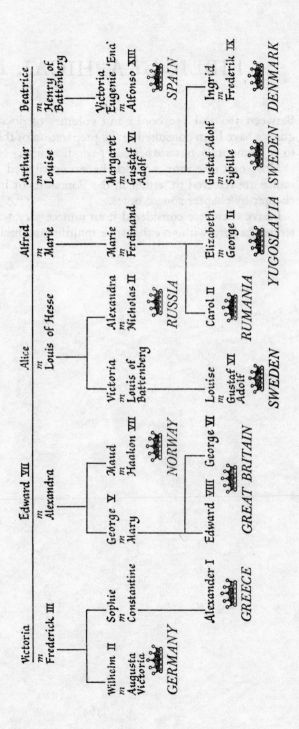

UNCLE OF EUROPE
A simplified family tree showing Edward's relationship to the crowns of Europe of his day

Victoria
m
Frederick III

Edward VII
m
Alexandra

Alice
m
Louis of Hesse

Alfred
m
Marie

Arthur
m
Louise

Beatrice
m
Henry of Battenberg

Wilhelm II
m
Augusta Victoria
GERMANY

Sophie
m
Constantine

George V
m
Mary

Maud
m
Haakon VII
NORWAY

Victoria
m
Louis of Battenberg

Alexandra
m
Nicholas II
RUSSIA

Marie
m
Ferdinand

Victoria Eugenie 'Ena'
m
Alfonso XIII
SPAIN

Margaret
m
Gustaf Adolf

Alexander I
GREECE

Edward VIII

George VI
GREAT BRITAIN

Louise
m
Gustaf VI Adolf
SWEDEN

Carol II
RUMANIA

Elizabeth
m
George II
YUGOSLAVIA

Gustaf Adolf
m
Sybille
SWEDEN

Ingrid
m
Frederik IX
DENMARK

BIBLIOGRAPHICAL NOTE

Between 300 and 350 books and volumes of documents in four languages have been consulted in the preparation of this work, in addition to contemporary newspaper and periodical files.

Most of those works which have contributed something of substance are referred to, either in the Foreword or in the footnotes and chapter-by-chapter source-notes.

I have therefore considered it an unnecessary waste of paper to fill ten pages here with an exhaustive multilingual bibliography.

G.B.-S.

SOURCE NOTES

From Pages 19 to 72

CHAPTER ONE

1. Letters of Queen Victoria, I, p. 457.
2. Quoted in *Queen Victoria*, by C. Woodham-Smith, I, p. 266.
3. Philippe Jullian, *Edward VII*, Paris, 1962.
4. Quoted in André Maurois, *King Edward and his Times*, London, 1933 (translation).
5. See Georgina Battiscombe, *Queen Alexandra*, London, 1969, who is excellent on this episode.

CHAPTER TWO

1. Sir Sidney Lee, *King Edward VII* I, p. 179.
2. Sir Philip Magnus, *King Edward the Seventh*, p. 228.
3. Given in Edward Legge, *More About King Edward*, pp. 80-91.
4. See *Taschenbuch der Freiherrlichen Haüser*, Gotha, 1880, p. 324.
5. Battiscombe, *Queen Alexandra*, pp. 122-3.
6. Battiscombe, p. 143.
7. The extracts from this, and all the other unpublished letters of King Edward VII to Mrs Langtry, are taken from the private collection of this correspondence in the hands of the Malcolm family.
8. Heinrich Graf von Lützow, in his Memoirs (p. 49) records the rebuke in its original French: 'Monseigneur, moquez-vous de ma tête tant qu'il vous plaira, mais, de grâce, laissez mon pays tranquille!'
9. This, and other quotations to the end of the chapter, from the private papers of the Soveral family.

CHAPTER THREE

1. Princess Marie Louise of Schleswig-Holstein, *My Memories of Six Reigns*, London, 1956, pp. 162-3.
2. *Les origins diplomatique de la guerre de* 1870-71, Vol. X, No. 738.
3. Quoted in Lee, op. cit., I, p. 451.
4. Lee I, p. 269.

5. Magnus, p. 248.
6. ibid., p. 249.
7. The fullest account of this trip and of all the Prince of Wales's visits to Hungary is given in a series of special articles by László Siklóssy in the *Hungarian Quarterly* (Summer 1938–Summer 1939).
8. Kaiser Franz Josef, *Briefe an Frau Katherina Schratt.*
9. From *Ich Sollte Kaiserin Werden*, by Princess Stephanie of Belgium, Leipzig, 1935, pp. 195–6. The Prince of Wales was uncle to Princess Stephanie, whose father was a Saxe-Coburg.
10. Kaiser William to Queen Victoria, 6 July 1888.
11. See *Grosse Politik,* Vol. VI. Footnote to No. 1351.
12. Quoted in Magnus, op. cit., who gives a comprehensive account of the incident in pp. 211–13.
13. Letters of Queen Victoria, Third Series, I, pp. 440–1.
14. H. von Eckhardstein, *Lebenserinnerungen*, Leipzig, 1919, Band, I, pp. 184–7.
15. Eckhardstein, op. cit., II, pp. 28–9.
16. Full text of memorandum in Prince von Bülow's *Memoirs*, Vol. I, pp. 309–11.
17. For full text, see Lee, I, pp. 754–5.
18. The relevant official Russian telegrams are quoted in Lee, op. cit., I, pp. 763–5.
19. Bülow, I, p. 356.

CHAPTER FOUR

1. *Documents Diplomatique Français*, Ser. 2, Vol. I, No. 100: Cambon to Delcassé, 23 February 1901.
2. D.D.F., Ser. 2, Vol. I, No. 54: Le Marquis de Noailles to Delcassé, 28 January 1901.
3. *Grosse Politik der Europaischen Kabinette 1870-1914* Vol. 17, No. 4999.
4. Frederick Ponsonby, *Memories of Three Reigns*, p. 108.
5. Prince von Bülow, *Memoirs*, 1897–1903, p. 510.
6. Bülow, op. cit., pp. 528–9. The Empress had already managed to spirit all her private letters back to England in two large boxes which she gave to Ponsonby at dead of night during the February 1901 visit to Friedrichshof. They were published in book form in London in 1928.
7. G.P., Vol. 17, No. 5302: Count Metternich to Berlin, 7 September 1901.

8. See on this *British Documents on Foreign Policy*, Vol. II, No. 92 (Lord Lansdowne's Memorandum).
9. G.P., Vol. 17, No. 5029.
10. Lee II, p. 143.
11. Emile Flourens, in *La France Conquise*, Paris, 1906.
12. Magnus, op. cit., p. 267.
13. *Public Records Office, Foreign Office* 371/461, No. 2669. Memorandum by Sir F. Villiers, 22 July 1902.
14. D.D.F., Ser. 2, Vol. II, No. 380.
15. Quoted in Lee, op. cit., II, p. 148.
16. D.D.F., Ser. 2, Vol. II, No. 450: Cambon to Delcassé, 11 November 1902.
17. G.P., Vol. 17, No. 5031: Emperor William to Count Bülow.
18. ibid.
19. Quoted in Lee, op. cit., II, p. 153.
20. Eckhardstein, *Ten Years at the Court of St James*, p. 245.

CHAPTER FIVE

1. Lee II, p. 284.
2. Bülow II, p. 285.
3. Private papers of Sir Ernest Cassel.
4. Ibid. 5. Ibid.
6. Lee II, p. 428.
7. D.D.F., Ser. 2, Vol. I, No. 282: Cambon to Delcassé, 12 June 1901.
8. Both versions given in full in Lee II, pp. 429–30.
9. Soveral Papers.
10. Hardinge Papers.
11. Soveral Papers.
12. This and subsequent extracts from the Mensdorff Diaries.
13. This, and all quotations to end of chapter, from the Soveral family papers.

CHAPTER SIX

1. Walter Bagehot, *The English Constitution*, 1867.
2. Lansdowne MSS. F.O. 800/125: Sir E. Monson to Lord Lansdowne, 7 March 1902.
3. D.D.F., Ser. 2, Vol. II, No. 135: Cambon to Delcassé, 13 March 1902.
4. Lansdowne MSS.: Monson to Lansdowne, 9 January 1903.

5. Soveral Papers.
6. ibid.
7. ibid.
8. Lansdowne MSS.
9. ibid.
10. ibid.
11. ibid.
12. Original of King Edward's draft in Lansdowne MSS.
13. Lansdowne MSS.
14. D.D.F., Ser. 2, Vol. III, No. 138: Cambon to Delcassé, 14 March 1903.
15. Lee, op. cit., Vol. II, p. 223.
16. *Old Diplomacy*, op. cit., p. 85.
17. All these exchanges from the Soveral Papers.

CHAPTER SEVEN

1. Soveral Papers.
2. Ponsonby, p. 86.
3. D.D.F., Ser. 2, Vol. III, No. 201: M. Prinet (Berlin) to Delcassé, 26 April 1903.
4. D.D.F., Ser. 2, Vol. III, No. 177: M. Rouvier to Delcassé, 12 April 1903.
5. Hardinge, *Old Diplomacy*, op. cit., p. 87.
6. R.A. (Edward VII to Prince of Wales).
7. Lansdowne MSS. (On 8 April Monson sent a copy of his letter to King Edward, with a covering note, to the Foreign Secretary.)
8. Soveral Papers.
9. Quoted in Lee, op. cit., II, p. 229.
10. Ponsonby, op. cit., p. 160.
11. Text in Lee, II, p. 230.
12. Ponsonby, p. 167.
13. On this, see Lee II, pp. 231–3; Magnus, pp. 309–11; and Hardinge, pp. 90–4.
14. Ponsonby, pp. 162–3. In his own account, Hardinge somewhat ungraciously omits all reference to Ponsonby's role, and assumes the entire credit for himself.

CHAPTER EIGHT

1. G.P., Vol. 14 (II), No. 3940: Münster to Chancellor Bülow, 13 March 1899.
2. Details of these postcards from Henri Daragon, *Voyage à Paris de S.M. Edouard VII*, Paris, 1903.
3. I am grateful to members of the staff of the Bibliothèque Nationale of Paris for producing the texts of all these 1903 songs.
4. In the description which follows, and for that of the whole visit, the familiar accounts given by Ponsonby and Hardinge have been supplemented by other private eye-witness material from the Soveral Papers; by reports in the diplomatic archives; and also by a cross-section of the day-to-day reporting of the events in both the British and the French press.
5. Printed in *Figaro*, 2 May 1903.
6. M. Meyer's account first appeared in *Le Gaulois* on 9 May 1922, when he was appealing to King George V to emulate, or at least imitate, his famous father, and visit a still devastated France. The next day *The Times* of London picked up the item which was in the form of an 'open letter'. From there it went straight into both official biographies of Edward VII and so into all subsequent literature about him.
7. The same M. Meyer provided in 1922 this version of the King's words. The fact that the King had recognized and greeted Mlle Granier was reported at the time – for example, on 3 May 1903 in *Le Figaro*, which described it as 'a charming act of gallantry by this most Parisian of Kings'.
8. Soveral Papers.
9. Quoted in Lee II, p. 241.
10. Memorandum of Sir E. Crowe, 1 January 1907 (B.D.F.P., Vol. III, F.O. 371/257).
11. Hardinge, p. 96.
12. Ponsonby, p. 173.
13. G.P., Vol. 18. Footnote to No. 5421 of 16 April 1903.
14. G.P., Vol. 18 (2), No. 5369.
15. For these reports and exchanges, see G.P., Vol. 18 (2), Nos. 5732–5735.

CHAPTER NINE

1. For this chapter, individual source notes have been abandoned. Some of the details have been taken from the files of the *Marienbader Tagblatt* from 1903–9, copies of which have survived in Vienna. Others come from contemporary accounts and memoirs, above all that humdrum yet indispensable book, *King Edward VII at Marienbad*, by Sigmund Munz, who dogged the King's footsteps there for six years. Ponsonby's *Memories of Three Reigns* has provided several anecdotes, and there are various political references in Volume 12 of Series 2 of the French Diplomatic Documents. The letters quoted of Sir H. Campbell-Bannerman are from *C.B.* by John Wilson.

For some hitherto unpublished details I am indebted to descendants of prominent Marienbad figures in the Edwardian era: Mr Victor Cavendish-Bentinck, for example, whose Aunt Venetia was, as Mrs Arthur James, a constant companion of the King's there; and to an old friend, Prince Ferdinand Liechtenstein, whose father was Provincial Governor of the region during King Edward's Marienbad 'reign'. Some extracts from King Edward's unpublished letters to Soveral and Cassel are also included.

CHAPTER TEN

1. D.D.F., Ser. 2, Vol. III, No. 317: M. Bihourd to Delcassé, 20 June 1903.
2. King Victor Emmanuel's proposed return visit had been put back until November, much to the Italian monarch's chagrin, to accommodate President Loubet. (See D.D.F., Ser. 2, Vol. III: M. Barbère to Delcassé, 29 May 1903.)
3. G.P., Vol. 20, No. 6374: Bülow's Minute of 9 April 1904.
4. ibid., No. 6378: Emperor William to Bülow, 19 April 1904.
5. Full text and details of negotiations in B.D., Vol. II, pp. 285–407.
6. D.D.F., Ser. 2, Vol. IV, No. 297: Cambon to Delcassé, 20 February 1904.
7. G.P., Vol. 19, No. 5959: Eckhardstein to Bülow, 11 February 1904.
8. Bülow memoirs, op. cit., Vol. II, pp. 102–15.
9. Bülow II, p. 104.
10. Maurice Paléologue, *Un grand Tournant*, p. 279.

11. Magnus, p. 339.
12. Soveral Papers: Sir Francis Knollys to Soveral, 8 April 1905.
13. Quoted in Lee, op. cit., II, p. 340.
14. Lansdowne MSS.: Bertie to Lansdowne, 4 April 1905.
15. Lansdowne MSS.: Bertie to Knollys, 4 April 1905.
16. King Edward VII to Lord Lansdowne, 14 April 1905.
17. Quoted in Paléologue, op. cit., p. 284.
18. See D.D.F., Ser. 2, Vol. VI: Delcassé to Bompard, 25 April 1905.
19. Most of the details which follow, both social and political, of the King's 1905 visit are drawn from Sir Francis Bertie's series of confidential letters to Lord Lansdowne (F.O. 800/127) in the Lansdowne MSS. See also Paléologue, op. cit., pp. 315 *et seq.*
20. See, for example, Bülow, II, p. 110.
21. Quoted in Magnus, p. 340.
22. Lansdowne MSS.: Bertie to Lansdowne, 5 May 1905.
23. Lansdowne MSS.: Lord Lansdowne to Mr Lister, 10 July 1905.
24. Quoted in Lee II, p. 344.
25. D.D.F., Ser. 2, Vol. VI, No. 200: Cambon to Delcassé, 28 March 1905.
26. D.D.F., Ser. 2, Vol. VI, No. 264: M. Geoffrey to Delcassé, 9 April 1905.
27. Cassel Papers: King Edward to Cassel, 17 August 1905.
28. D.D.F., Ser. 2, Vol. IX, No. 106: Cambon to Rouvier, 31 January 1906.
29. Quoted in Magnus, op. cit., p. 340.
30. For the details see, *inter alia*, D.D.F., Ser. 2, Vol. VI, No. 135, and Vol. VII, No. 155.

CHAPTER ELEVEN

1. G.P., Vol. 21 (2), No. 7180: Metternich to Bülow, 4 May 1906.
2. G.P., Vol. 21 (2), No. 417: Herr von Stumm to Bülow, 7 June 1906.
3. D.D.F., Ser. 2, Vol. X, No. 120: Cambon to M. Bourgeois, 26 June 1906.
4. For accounts of the 1906 Cronberg meeting, see especially: G.P., Vol. 21 (2), Nos. 7196–7198; B.D.F.P., Vol. III, Nos. 423–426; B.D.F.P., Vol. VIII, No. 163 and 164; D.D.F., Ser. 2, Vol. X, No. 187. Also Hardinge, pp. 127–8, and Ponsonby, pp. 181–3.
5. B.D.F.P., Vol. III, No. 425: Hardinge to Grey, 16 August 1906.
6. It seems to have been the British Military Attaché in Paris who first

tipped off the French Foreign Office. (See D.D.F., Ser. 2, Vol. X, No. 190, of 25 August 1906.)

7. D.D.F., Ser. 2, Vol. X, No. 191: Cambon to M. Bourgeois, 28 August 1906.
8. Quoted in Magnus, op. cit., p. 388.
9. See G.P., Vol. 21 (2), No. 7208: Prince Radolin to Berlin, 4 February 1907.
10. For a detailed account of the whole episode, see P.R.O., F.O. 800/103, No. 4367. Letter of Knollys to Hardinge, 6 October 1907, and Sir Edward Grey's letter of same date to Knollys.

CHAPTER TWELVE

1. G.P., Vol. 21, No. 7082: Stumm to Chancellor Bülow, 9 March 1906. (Emperor's footnotes.)
2. Paléologue, op. cit., p. 385.
3. D.D.F., Ser. 2, Vol. VIII, No. 246: M. Margerie to M. Rouvier, 16 November 1906.
4. As above.
5. See F.O. 800/127: Lansdowne to Bertie, 7 November 1905.
6. D.D.F., Ser. 2, Vol. VIII, No. 246: Rouvier to Cambon, 18 December 1905.
7. D.D.F., Ser. 2, Vol. VIII, No. 262: Cambon to Rouvier, 21 December 1905.
8. Lee II, pp. 535-8, gives the whole discussion in great detail.
9. D.D.F., Ser. 2, Vol. X, No. 166.
10. Hardinge, p. 134.
11. D.D.F., Ser. 2, Vol. XI, No. 2: Cambon to Rouvier, 17 May 1907.
12. Hardinge, p. 137.
13. Hardinge, p. 138.
14. D.D.F., Ser. 2, Vol. II, No. 3: Barrère to M. Pichon, 19 May 1907.
15. D.D.F., Ser. 2, Vol. XII, No. 192 (Footnote).
16. Hardinge MSS.
17. D.D.F., Ser. 2, Vol. XII, No. 192.
18. Paléologue, p. 47.
19. Ponsonby, p. 262.
20. Quoted in Lee, II, p. 517.
21. F.O. 800/103/4367, Nos. 249, 251 and 253 of 31 August and 1 September 1909.

CHAPTER THIRTEEN

1. Goluchowski described his talk with the King to the French Ambassador in Vienna, Count Reverseaux, who reported to Paris. (D.D.F., Ser. 2, Vol. III, No. 422, dated 10 September 1903.)
2. See Margutti, *The Emperor Francis Joseph and his Times*, pp. 259–61.
3. Papers of Sir Ernest Cassel.
4. Mensdorff Diaries.
5. Mensdorff Diaries. Entry for 21 August 1907.
6. Hardinge, op. cit., p. 145.
7. G.P., Vol. 25, p. 551.
8. Text of letter, in original English, in G.P., Vol. 24, No. 8181.
9. Text given in G.P., Vol. 24, No. 8183, of 22 February 1908.
10. Text given in G.P., Vol. 24, No. 8182: Lord Tweedmouth to the German Emperor, 20 February 1908.
11. Magnus, op. cit., p. 374.
12. Hardinge, op. cit., pp. 150–1.
13. See G.P., Vol. 24, Nos. 8204 and 8205; and B.D.F.P., Vol. VI, Nos. 95 and 96, for comment on the Fallières visit.
14. G.P., Vol. 24, No. 8212: Metternich to Bülow, 30 June 1908.
15. See Lee, op. cit., II, pp. 612–14, for the fullest account of this.
16. B.D.F.P., Vol. V, No. 111. On the preparations for Cronberg, see Lee, op. cit., II, pp. 614–17, and Magnus, pp. 410–11. Also, for the whole episode, Hardinge, op. cit., pp. 158–61.
17. Hardinge's account is in his Secret Memorandum on Cronberg to Sir Edward Grey, dated 16 August 1908 (F.O. 371/461/2669), which was first made public in November 1924 to 'correct' an account published by Admiral Tirpitz based on the former Kaiser's version of events. (See B.D., Vol. VI, No. 124.) On 11, 12 and 13 August 1908 the Kaiser had sent his running and detailed account of the Cronberg talks to Bülow (G.P., Vol. 24, Nos. 8224–8226).
18. G.P., Vol. 24, No. 8224 (Footnote).
19. Lee, op. cit., II, p. 619.
20. Mensdorff Diary, entry for 19 April when in Paris for Easter. The Hardinge MSS. show (Goschen to Hardinge, 17 April 1908) that, at the same time, the idea of another Bad Ischl 'summit' was being put forward in Vienna. The two carriers, bearing the same proposal, appeared to have crossed.
21. ibid., entry for 8 July 1908.

22. P.R.O., F.O. 371/461, No. 2669. Secret Memorandum of Hardinge to Sir Edward Grey, 16 August 1908.
23. Mensdorff Diary, entry for 15 August 1908.
24. See on this, F. R. Bridge's exhaustively detailed documentary study, *Great Britain and Austria-Hungary 1906–1914*, London, 1972.
25. Papers of Sir Ernest Cassel, Broadlands Archives.
26. D.D.F., Ser. 2, Vol. II, No. 448: Crozier to Pichon, 12 September 1908.
27. Mensdorff Diary, same entry as above. (In a letter to *The Times* on 10 November 1924, Hardinge strenuously denied that he had said, on leaving Ischl, that the Austrian Emperor had 'just missed one of the most favourable opportunities of his long life'.)
28. See, for the following episode, Steed, op. cit., pp. 283–4.
29. Lord Redesdale, Memoirs, quoted in Lee, op. cit., II, p. 633.
30. Mensdorff Diaries. Long retrospective entry made in London, 14 October 1908.
31. ibid. Magnus, p. 414, seems incorrect in claiming that the King 'vented his fury' on the Ambassador.
32. The exchange of letters, which was in French, is reproduced in that language in Lee II, pp. 632 and 636–7.
33. See on this, Bridges, op. cit., pp. 111–38. He rightly brings out the crucial role Germany played in getting a settlement and disposes of the impression given, for example, by Lee II, pp. 647–8, that the outcome was due to 'British firmness'.
34. G.P., Vol. 26. Footnote to Memorandum of Prince Bülow, dated 5 October 1908.
35. G.P., Vol. 26. Emperor William to the Emperor Franz Josef, 26 January 1909.

CHAPTER FOURTEEN

1. Mensdorff MSS.
2. Soveral Papers. Copy of telegram to Lisbon, 5 February 1908.
3. ibid., King Edward to Soveral, 23 February 1908.
4. Mensdorff Diary, entry for 8 February 1908.
5. See Lee II, p. 575.
6. Soveral Papers. File of telegrams for February 1908.
7. G.P., Vol. 19, pp. 458 *et seq.* These reports of the Kaiser to Bülow are the only first-hand accounts available, and the usual allowances should be made for exaggeration.
8. G.P., Vol. 19: 'Nicky' to 'Willy', 7 October 1905.

9. G.P., Vol. 19, p. 497: Emperor William to Bülow.
10. G.P., Vol. 19, pp. 513–14: 'Willy' to 'Nicky', 12 October 1905.
11. Quoted in Lee II, p. 565.
12. F.O. 800/103/4367: Sir E. Grey to Lord Knollys, 28 March 1906.
13. *Lord Carnock*, by Harold Nicolson, pp. 269–73.
14. Lord Fisher, *Memories*, p. 187.
15. See, for example, von Stumm's report to Berlin on a talk in London with Hardinge. G.P., Vol. 25 (II), No. 8798, of 20 May 1908.
16. B.D., Vol. 24, No. 8209, Footnote.
17. B.D., Vol. 25, No. 8803, of 9 June 1908.
18. G.P., Vol. 25 (II), No. 8824.

CHAPTER FIFTEEN

1. For example, the British Military Attaché at Berlin, Colonel Trench, reporting on 17 August 1908 on a tour of several weeks' duration in central and southern Germany, made 'to get in touch with very varied classes of people'. F.O. 371/461, No. 29260.
2. Report of Sir F. Cartwright to Sir E. Grey from Munich of 19 August 1908. F.O. 371/461, No. 29162.
3. Report on this in F.O. 371/463, No. 44354.
4. See G.P., Vol. 28, No. 10234: Metternich to Bülow, 27 November 1908.
5. See, on this episode, G.P., Vol. 28, Nos. 8249–8251; also Bülow's Memoirs, II, pp. 341–63; Hardinge, pp. 169–71; and B.D.F.P., Vol. VI, Nos. 125 and 134.
6. Magnus, op. cit., p. 400.
7. Reproduced in F.O. 371/461, No. 29672/08.
8. B.D.F.P., Vol. VI, No. 135: Sir E. Grey to Sir F. Bertie, 12 November 1908.
9. F.O. 371/463, No. 44852: Mr Findlay at Dresden to Sir Charles Hardinge, 8 December 1908.
10. Hardinge, op. cit., p. 171.
11. D.D.F., Ser. 2, Vol. XI, No. 558: Cambon to Pichon, 18 November 1908, with Huguet's report of 9 November enclosed as Annexe.
12. Ponsonby, op. cit., p. 255.
13. The description of the Berlin visit which follows is based on first-hand accounts such as Bülow II, pp. 407–11; Hardinge, pp. 173–5; Ponsonby, pp. 256–9; the Memoirs of Princess Daisy Pless, pp. 171–7; the Memoirs of Lord Grenfell; various pallid references in the English, French and German diplomatic archives; and the

highly coloured English and German press reports of the day which, however, miss a lot of the amusing happenings and play down the most serious ones. See also Lee II, pp. 673–7, and Magnus, p. 418.

14. Lee II, op. cit., p. 674.
15. Daisy Pless, Memoirs, pp. 176–7.
16. F.O. 800/103/4367: Knollys to Mr Tyrell, 11 February 1909.
17. Ponsonby, p. 257.
18. G.P., Vol. 28, No. 10255: Metternich to Bülow, 20 January 1909.
19. B.D., Vol. III, No. 143: Grey to Bertie, 7 January 1909.
20. Marginal comment of the Emperor William on Bülow's report to him on his general talks with Hardinge. G.P., Vol. 28, No. 10260.
21. B.D., Vol. III, No. 146: Goschen to Grey, 12 February 1909.
22. Hardinge, op. cit., p. 174.
23. Papers of Sir Ernest Cassel. Letter to Sir Ernest from the King, 19 March 1909.

CHAPTER SIXTEEN

1. Magnus, p. 450.
2. Soveral Papers.
3. Cassel Papers: King Edward to Cassel, 28 March 1910.
4. Lee II, p. 709.
5. *King Edward VII*, by Lord Redesdale, p. 33.
6. All the above letters from the Soveral Papers.
7. Soveral Papers.

INDEX

Index

Index

Index